W9-BAZ-501

DATE DUE

BLACK AND BLUE

THE LIFE AND LYRICS OF ANDY RAZAF

BLACK AND BLUE

THE LIFE AND LYRICS OF

ANDY RAZAF

BARRY SINGER

FOREWORD BY BOBBY SHORT

SCHIRMER BOOKS
An Imprint of Macmillan Publishing Company
NEW YORK

Maxwell Macmillan Canada
TORONTO

Maxwell Macmillan International
NEW YORK   OXFORD   SINGAPORE   SYDNEY

Schirmer Books
An Imprint of Macmillan Publishing Company
866 Third Avenue, New York, N. Y. 10022

Maxwell Macmillan Canada, Inc.
1200 Eglinton Avenue East, Suite 200
Don Mills, Ontario M3C 3N1

Macmillan Publishing Company is part of the Maxwell Communication Group of Companies.

Library of Congress Catalog Card Number: 92-11093

PRINTED IN THE UNITED STATES OF AMERICA

printing number
1   2   3   4   5   6   7   8   9   10

Library of Congress Cataloging-in-Publication Data
Singer, Barry, 1957-
    Black and blue: the life and lyrics of Andy Razaf/Barry Singer.
       p.   cm.
    Discography: p.
    Includes bibliographical references and index.
    ISBN 0-02-872395-3
    1. Razaf, Andy 1895-1973.   2. Lyricists—United States—
-Biography.   I. Title.
ML423.R28S56   1992
782.42165'092—dc20
    [B]   92-11093
                                                                  CIP
                                                                   MN

To Susanne Weil, for *all* the introductions

* * *

In memory of Eubie Blake

Contents

Illustrations

These illustrations follow page 220

Foreword

To realize the full impact of Andy Razaf's amazing success as a lyricist is for me simply a matter of remembering the 1930s. This rambunctious period in American social history seems to have produced more lasting popular music standards than any other. The great songsmiths Berlin, Gershwin, Porter, Kern, Youmans, Ellington, Schwartz, and Arlen were at their peaks, grinding out irresistible melodies for the Broadway musical stage and its California counterpart, the Hollywood movie. World War I was clearly behind, and although the Great Depression was heavily upon us, Prohibition had been eased out during the early part of the decade, leaving Americans everywhere the chance to dance the nights away, drink to their heart's content, and make whoopee as often as they dared. Jazz was riding high. Paul Whiteman, the soi-disant "King of Jazz," had by way of the air-waves politely taken it into the homes of the hoi polloi where it had been received with unbridled enthusiasm. This stamp of approval very likely paved the way for the emergence of the countless imaginative black musicians during this period when dance music was eagerly sought out by recording companies, music publishers, and, of course, the radio.

It was fashionable to recognize every popular song as it appeared, singing all the lyrics as often as possible. This exercise was often accompanied by mastering the latest dance steps. In our Negro community in the Midwest we hummed and sang "Honeysuckle

Rose," "Ain't Misbehavin'," and "Porter's Love Song," all of us blithely unaware of the fact that the lyricist was a black man. But ours was not an uncommon unawareness. It is only fair to acknowledge a general comparative ignorance of lyricists on the part of the layman public insofar as popular songs go. One spoke of a Kern song, a Gershwin song, an Arlen song, and so forth, never once mentioning (or seeming to care about) who might have created the words we so proudly crooned and belted. We truly admired the sentiments expressed but were simply not overly curious about who'd masterminded them. In my own case, the great lyricists like Ira Gershwin, E. Y. Harburg, Dorothy Fields, and Howard Dietz were unknown to me until I was well into my teens although I cannot recall a single day when I did not sing one of their songs.

Of his early collaborators, Andy Razaf stuck almost exclusively to the major black composers, instrumentalists, and arrangers of his time. And what a time it was! With Thomas "Fats" Waller's infectious and insinuating melodies, such hits as "Ain't Misbehavin'," "Honeysuckle Rose," and "Black and Blue" were born. Earlier on, the unjustly neglected J. C. Johnson supplied the blues-haunted melodies for "Lonesome Swallow" and "Guess Who's in Town," while the great Harlem stride pianist James P. Johnson contributed the irresistible melody for "Porter's Love Song." With Eubie Blake Razaf composed "Memories of You" and "You're Lucky to Me." Blake with Noble Sissle had made musical history with a tradition-shattering musical score for the long-running all-black musical revue *Shuffle Along*. Fletcher Henderson, the celebrated orchestra leader and arranger, supplied the music for "Christopher Columbus," popularized this marvelous song whose pioneering saxophone star "Chu" Berry (with Andy Razaf's lyric) as his theme. How well I remember being huddled close to the family radio in eager anticipation of those first notes of his live broadcasts from the Grand Terrace Cafe in Chicago.

It is plain to see that jazz music inspired much of Razaf's lyrical output during these years and this inspiration has paid off well. Today no jazz performer would feel well equipped without his own rendition of one these vintage efforts. Viewed today, some of the so-called salacious numbers reeled off by Razaf and Johnson in the early 1920s come across as merely highly entertaining and thoroughly delightful, with the exception certainly of "My Handy Man," for which Razaf supplied both words *and* music. Ethel Waters was a perfect interpreter for these gems. Rolling her eyes (and her Rs), her superb sense of drama and sublime diction turned them into trademarks for her, garnering more popularity for herself and, quite naturally, more success for the composers. Although this brand of suggestiveness began to melt away after a while, many perfectly innocent Razaf lyrics were to appear slightly risqué when performed by artists who would follow in Waters's tradition.

*

Long before Razaf's day African-Americans were a part of the popular music scene in this country. The late-nineteenth-century poet Paul Laurence Dunbar tried his hand but without notable success. In the early part of the twentieth century James Weldon Johnson enjoyed acclaim as lyricist for two widely diverse entries, "Under the Bamboo Tree," which he co-authored with Bob Cole, and "Lift Every Voice and Sing," often known as the Negro national anthem, written with his brother J. Rosamond Johnson.

Many of the "coon" songs used in the immensely popular minstrel productions at the time were the works of black composers and lyricists. And Bert Williams, the famous black vaudevillian, often wrote his own songs, frequently as philosophical as they were comical. For the 1940s Broadway musical version of Elmer Rice's *Street Scene*, poet Langston Hughes supplied lyrics for the musical score by Kurt Weill. Benny Benjamin wrote a string of Tin Pan Alley successes. Undoubtedly, there were many more. None of these, however, was prolific in the sense that Razaf was. His steady output, craftsmanship, and business acumen made his songs household words both at home and abroad, adding to the clinging mystery of how such a successful Negro in a relatively rarefied field of endeavor could be overlooked by the public at large.

*

Andy Razaf encouraged black artists of his era to perform his material and he was well rewarded. His collaborator "Fats" Waller, Ethel Waters, and Louis Armstrong featured Razaf songs throughout their long careers. Across the ocean in Europe Josephine Baker recorded "My Fate Is in Your Hands," and black American pianist and singer Nora Holt, in a letter to Langston Hughes, described a program in which she would include "Lonesome Swallow" as part of her repertoire on a world tour. But white artists like Rudy Vallee, Benny Goodman, and Mildred Bailey also regularly included Razaf's songs, often recording them, and much of this output became standard radio fare. His mournful "Black and Blue," composed for the 1929 revue *Hot Chocolates*, jumped the colorline altogether in time, almost totally obliterating its poignant message of a black woman whose skin was so dark that she found the going tough . . . within her own race. (In 1980, Edith Wilson, who had introduced it originally, recreated her show-stopping version in the New York retrospective production *Black Broadway*.) The popular radio show in New York hosted by Martin Block in the mid 1930s and calling itself *Make Believe Ballroom* employed a song of that title as its theme. It was written by Razaf and Paul Denniker, an Englishman who was said to be Razaf's favorite working partner . . . after Waller. Such an interracial collaboration, although it may have raised some eyebrows among a few, was most certainly not a rarity even in those days. Legitimately or not, the names of whites appeared with surprising frequency alongside those of the black authors whose works were published with that particular understanding. In Razaf's case, his open admiration for Denniker's talents overrode any consideration for the color of his skin. As a team they were eminently successful, both artistically and financially.

*

In the late 1940s I became acquainted with Andy. He approached me one morning as I was standing in front of my residence in Los Angeles. He was on his morning walk, living, as he did, around the corner. A rather slight but compactly built fellow, he had a twinkle in his eye as he introduced himself to me. We discussed show business and its current trends and he invited me to visit him at home. I went several times and was treated to "air-checks" of famous radio shows on which his songs had been featured. We talked about his old days in Harlem and he pressed several of his more obscure compositions into my hands. I must confess that I had no notion of the wide scope of his songs, nor was I aware of how many he had written during his lifetime until a few years ago when my old friend and mentor, Phil Moore, suggested that we record a group of them. It was a deliberate attempt on our parts to bring into focus once again the brilliance of a black composer all but overlooked in this present world of rock and rap. We called our collection *Guess Who's in Town* after one of his early works with the wonderful J. C. Johnson.

I saw Andy one more time in New York shortly before his death. He had, accompanied by his wife, made it to town for some sort of celebration. I visited him in his Central Park South apartment where he was bedridden, but the twinkle in his eye was still there. I thanked him for all the friendship he had offered me when I was young and for giving so much of himself during difficult times. I also thanked him for changing his last name.

Today we celebrate Andy Razaf for the highly gifted lyricist he was and for his vital contribution to the overall popular art of America whose spirit he captured so aptly, reflecting both the joys and the sorrows of being alive, being black, and being an artist to the very innards of his soul. In the end his art must be judged as infinitely American, but his African roots are as clearly etched as a Bill Traylor silhouette. From all indication, Andy was a very decent man whose only outstanding weakness was for a beautiful women. Now who can blame him for that?

Bobby Short
October 1, 1992

Prologue

There is a mystique attached to those names most associated with a certain sense of Harlem in the Nineteen Twenties. It is bred in the seductive sonorities and rhythms of early jazz music and the illusions that still haunt that music, bounded by the limiting stereotypes of race, and grounded in ignorance. It is founded upon extraordinary accomplishments only dimly understood and barely acknowledged.

There is a mystique particularly to an anonymous sense of Harlem in the Twenties—one that celebrates legendary occurrences long since detached from recollected, individual names.

All biographies, at bottom, are stories of detection. It is hard to conceive of a biography more in need of the detective's art than an account of Andrea Razafkeriefo, the prolific black lyric writer from Harlem in the Nineteen Twenties whose songs outlived his name. From the very outset of my investigation, over ten years ago, into the barest biographical details surrounding a doubtably pronounced name printed on a pile of favorite sheet music covers, I have been haunted by the purloined sense of Andy Razaf's life. Through the suggestive biographical fragments buried in obituaries, the tantalizingly incomplete evidence preserved in library archives, the misinformation codified in books and newspapers, the elusive, dreamlike recollections of aged surviving peers, and, at length, the letters, the lyric sheets, scrapbooks, news clippings, and diary notations that

Razaf himself left behind haphazardly boxed and waiting in the garage of his last home for someone curious enough to come looking, an unshakable detective story gradually has come to consume me, the sense of a crime committed in silence with fingerprints long since swept away.

"You can't never put it back together," one veteran Harlem musician had bluntly insisted to me, early on. "It's too jumbled, the history, too fragmented. Nobody never told it straight—even as it was happening, we was inventing it, And don't think that was no accident neither."

I don't. Yet the urge to reconstruct is uncontainable.

Barry Singer
NEW YORK CITY

BLACK AND BLUE

THE LIFE AND LYRICS OF
ANDY RAZAF

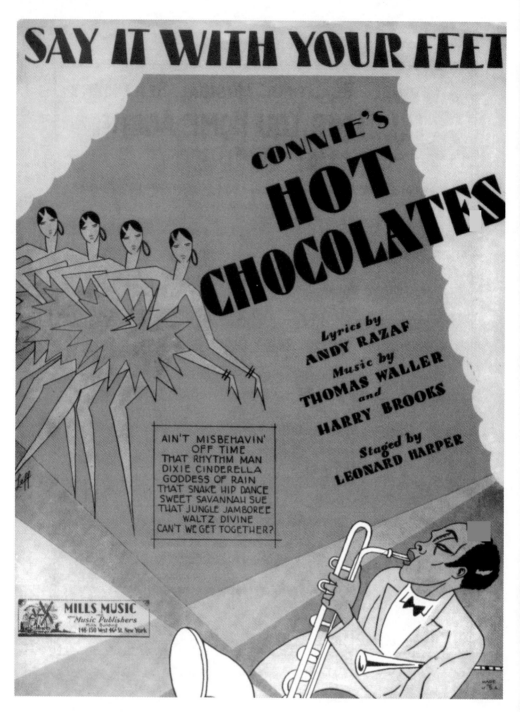

Courtesy Razaf Estate.

1

The Curtain Drawn Aside

If at the beginning, when we are warm with pride and hope, when our hearts, exultant, thrill with the realization of ambitions gained, when the object for which we have striven is within our grasp; if at this happy moment we could have the curtain drawn aside from the future to gaze for an instant at the cruel disappointments through which we are to pass before the end, how quickly would we lay it all aside, that which has seemed such a glorious possession but one short hour ago? And yet, would it be wise to lay it down? Would it be more judicious to discard it? I think not. It seems to me that if there is anything worth saving for us, after we have laid it all away and closed our eyes, it is that our conscientious endeavors will fill a conspicuous position and will be placed to our credit, whether crowned with success or failure. For to my mind, it is the effort that is meritorious rather than the result of it.

— Estelle A. MacNaughton, *Life's Phases or Biography of John Louis Waller (1913)*

You may call me "The Dreamer,"
I don't care if you do.

— *"The Dreamer"*
by Andy Razaf

T here was something gorgeously indiscriminate about the exuberant assembly of celebrities that crowded into Broadway's Hudson Theatre around midnight on the evening of July 23, 1929: producer George White; operetta diva Fritzi Scheff; torch singer Libby Holman; the entire companies from neighboring Broadway productions of *Street Scene* and *Journey's End*, along with a generous smattering from the *New Moon*, *Showgirl*, and *Follow Through* casts; Broadway entertainment entrepreneur and radio pioneer Nils T. Granlund; numerous Park Avenue socialites; vaudevillians Blanche Ring and Zolya Talma; stage sirens Fay Marbe and Valerie Valaire, even the Singer midgets—all mixed en masse in the Hudson Theatre lobby. It was hardly the group's collective quality that was so impressive. Impresario Florenz Ziegfeld, for one, frequently drew many more stylish patrons to the rooftop nightclub of his nearby New Amsterdam Theatre for the *Midnight Frolics* that followed performances of his *Follies* there. Rather, it was the presence of such a smart crowd specifically at the Hudson Theatre that was so incongruous.

Unfashionably situated east of Times Square, on the uptown side of West 44th Street, the aging, however physically distinguished, Hudson Theatre was not one of Broadway's more desirable show business destinations in 1929. Historically, it had long been something of a flophouse, its roster of theatrical tenants a parade of unremittingly second-rate comedies and melodramas extending back 25 years. Of the more than 100 productions mounted at the Hudson since its opening in 1903, only seven had lasted for even 200 performances, with the reigning champion, at 440, an entirely forgotten 1919 "comedy drama" entitled *Friendly Enemies*. Over the years, George M. Cohan had used the Hudson on occasion, most recently in February 1928 for "a farce" he called *Whispering Friends*. Just a year earlier Irish dramatist Sean O'Casey had presented his newest play, *The Plough and the Stars*, in its American premiere at the Hudson for a singularly undistinguished run of 32 performances. Beyond these rather insignificant high spots, though, the Hudson Theatre had managed to remain virtually untouched by the glamor of Broadway accomplishment.

The production that shattered the Hudson's theatrical torpor, drawing Broadway's entertainment elite to those unaccustomed precincts, after hours on the evening of July 23, 1929, was a raucous all-black Harlem-based musical revue called *Connie's Hot Choco-lates*. *Hot Chocolates* had so thrilled Broadway audiences since its speculative June transfer downtown from the celebrated Harlem nightspot Connie's Inn to the easily booked Hudson, that the revue's producers calculatingly had added this second, midnight performance almost solely for the benefit of the Great White Way's working showfolk, allowing headliners and chorines alike the opportunity to see firsthand what all the fuss was about. Factor in the hordes of fashionable followers who trailed after Broadway celebrities on any fashionable pretext, and it becomes obvious why the occasion quickly escalated into the hottest ticket in town.

All three members of the team creatively responsible for this phenomenon were, of course, in attendance that night. It is unlikely that many in the glittering crowd knew any of these tuxedo-clad black men on sight, however, or even necessarily knew their names. Leonard Harper, *Hot Chocolates'* 30-year-old stage director, was a former vaudeville hoofer—turned producer of black musical revues who had helped shape the Harlem nightclub floorshow in his own image throughout the 1920s, contributing enormously to the stylistic evolution of the genre at clubs like Connie's Inn, where he was the resident revue maker. Thomas "Fats" Waller, *Hot Chocolates'* composer, was a rotund, boundlessly talented 25-year-old Harlem pianist whose facility at the keyboard was matched by his exceptional melodic gifts as a composer.

The third member of the creative team was by far the most anonymous. Andy Razaf, *Hot Chocolates'* 33-year-old lyricist, was indisputably Harlem's preeminent lyric writer in 1929, the lyricist of choice for most of the uptown song men who regularly contributed tunes to Harlem's numerous nightclub floor shows. Razaf also was a favorite downtown in the tight, fraternal world of Tin Pan Alley, where he was appreciated both as a talented lyric craftsman and as an expert translator of uptown black experience for the general white song consumer. Yet the name Andy Razaf in 1929 was just about unknown beyond the two insular worlds in which he worked. From the perspective of Broadway's elite he was at best a curiosity.

Shortly after midnight, for the second time in less than five hours, the Hudson Theatre curtain rose on a Prologue scene set at Connie's

Inn, with the full *Hot Chocolates* company of 85 onstage in the roles of guests, waiters, orchestra members, and entertainers. Paul and Thelma Meeres set the evening in motion with an opening dance specialty to a lovely Razaf/Waller tune, "Waltz Divine," as the club's revue was reenacted in capsulized form by *Hot Chocolates'* nimble dance choruses—respectively, the 16 "Hot Chocolate Drops" (female) and the eight "Bon Bon Buddies" (male). Ever so quickly, the elegant Hudson Theatre audience was transported to Harlem. Seated in the theater's first row, legendary Harlem tap master Bill Robinson was suddenly recognized and applauded; he leaped to the stage and danced. The prima donna of Harlem divas, Ethel Waters, was then spotted in the second row, and was spotlighted. She sang from the aisle.

If one thing could be said to have characterized all great Harlem floor shows of the Twenties—beyond their music and their dancing (if not their racial coloration)—that quality was speed: a spectacularly frenzied pace. *Hot Chocolates* had glorious pace. By the fourth scene of the first act, the swank (and un-air conditioned) Hudson Theatre audience was in an uproar. With rapid-fire effect, they had been treated to a whirlwind Harlem nightclub excursion: a "song of the cotton field"—Razaf and Waller's evocative "Sweet Savannah Sue" as sung by Russell Wooding's marvelous gospel choir, the "Jubilee Singers;" and a broad burlesque-style comedy sketch, "The Unloaded Gun," followed by a riotous ensemble dance number led by Dolly McCormick, "Say It with Your Feet." They were no doubt ready for a more understated interlude when singers Margaret Simms and Paul Bass, elegant themselves in evening dress, sedately entered to a sweet vamp from the orchestra, and Simms began to croon the diffident opening lines that many in the audience already recognized as the verse to *Hot Chocolates'* emerging new song hit, lines that Andy Razaf had quickly written with his partner Waller during the final weeks of *Hot Chocolates'* pre-Broadway rehearsals. *"Though it's a fickle age,"* the lines of this knowingly turned verse began, *"with flirting all the rage, /Here is one bird with self-control, happy inside my cage./I know who I love the best, thumbs down on all the rest./My love is given heart and soul, so it can stand the test."* The cadences of the chorus that followed, even then, must have seemed to that audience transcendently familiar: *"No-one to talk with,/All by myself,/No-one to walk with,/But I'm happy on the shelf,/Ain't misbehavin',/I'm savin' my love for you."*

*

It is surely true that what little public recognition Andy Razaf receives today is attributable almost entirely to the enduring popularity of three songs, two that he wrote with Fats Waller in 1929, "Ain't Misbehavin'" and "Honeysuckle Rose," and the third, "Memories of You," written in 1930 with Eubie Blake. That these were composed within a year of one another—"Honeysuckle Rose" for a revue followup to *Hot Chocolates* at Connie's Inn in late 1929, and "Memories of You" for an original Broadway score commissioned by producer Lew Leslie the following year—suggests that Andy Razaf had grown astonishingly adept at his trade by the end of the Twenties. That he was, in later years, proud still to be even marginally remembered for having written these songs does not mitigate the fact that in the waning stages of a career that had spanned more than 50 years and well over 800 songs (many of them enormous hits of lasting quality), Andy Razaf was absolutely mystified at his continuing obscurity.

Of course, obscurity has always been the lot of lyricists and can be part of their charm—as with shy Ira Gershwin, drolly in the shadow of his expansive brother, George; or lost (and untraceable) Lorenz "Larry" Hart—ever dissolute, ever absent from his more famous, more stoic partner, Richard Rodgers. Andy Razaf's obscurity, though, held no charm.

How this black lyricist, peer to black songwriting giants, came to such utter anonymity has got to be the haunting refrain for any remembrance of Andy Razaf's life. To say that Razaf never was a household name, even at the height of an exceptional lyric-writing career, is tantamount to defining that career. Even along Tin Pan Alley during his most productive years, Razaf was regarded as something of a mystery. Among the industry's predominantly white song-publishing professionals, rumors abounded about both his background and his birth—no doubt in part because he was such an impressive black presence in this very white industry: a truly dignified man, honorable in his business dealings, strikingly handsome, an impeccable dresser, a real charmer in conversation. He was an African prince, born to African royal parents, certain Tin Pan Alley insiders would insist, no doubt influenced by the black lyricist's rather regal bearing and manner. He was an entirely self-educated man whose breadth of knowledge bordered on genius, others maintained, perhaps fabulistically endeavoring to account for the existence of a brilliant black man of words in an industry accustomed only to brilliant black men of music. He'd been a child prodigy, this retrospective line of rationalization ran, a writer of rhymes and lyrics since he was old enough to write.

Here was material for a really rich legend. Not ironically, there was some truth in all of it.

For many in attendance at the Hot Chocolates midnight performance of July 23, the most anticipated element of the whole unlikely occasion was a pending between-acts performance by the *Hot Chocolates* pit band. Throughout the show's opening week, unsuspecting Hudson Theatre audiences had been thoroughly beguiled by the unannounced intermission appearance of a band member, spotlit in the orchestra pit—a plump, ecstatically joyous character with gravel in his voice who, after the first-act curtain had come down, serenaded them in dazzling style with his trumpet, sang to them a reprise of the show's best number in irresistibly eccentric vocal fashion, and clowned with them mercilessly. Unbeknownst to these early audiences, this bandsman was Louis Armstrong, already the most admired "jazz" soloist of his generation, who had arrived in New York City shortly before *Hot Chocolates'* Broadway opening—jobless, for a variety of reasons—and had been persuaded at the last minute by the show's producers to join the company. Armstrong's intermission rendition of "Ain't Misbehavin'" so electrified opening-week theatergoers that the feature quickly acquired a "must-see" status on Broadway, and a new credit line in the *Hot Chocolates* program: *"Entre'Act trumpet solo by Louis Armstrong."*

Armstrong's appearance beneath the Hudson Theatre stage in a white tuxedo at about 1:30 on the morning of July 24 was greeted with a warm ovation by the knowledgeable show-business crowd, who clearly were expecting him. His ensuing solo recital would provide the trumpeter with new career cachet as a celebrity among celebrities, a new Broadway star impressing peers beyond the black music world. It also would help confirm the success of Andy Razaf and Fats Waller's "Ain't Misbehavin'," as a houseful of working entertainment professionals silently made note that night to add the delightful new number to their repertoires. How many among this group would recall the name of the delightful new song's *lyricist* the next morning remains a matter for conjecture.

*

Andy Razaf was born on the fifteenth of December, 1895, in Washington, DC, some 11 miles from the back door of the Capitol, at the "private sanitorium" of Dr. J. Francis, 2112 Pennsylvania Avenue. His father, Henry Razafkeriefo, was a native of Antananarivo, Madagascar—a nephew, in fact, of the island's hereditary queen, Ranavalona III. His mother, Jennie Maria, was the daughter of John Louis Waller (unrelated to Fats Waller), a freed slave from Missouri. The intersection of these two geographically disparate lives— Missourian and Madagascan—may be traced only through the exceptional history of Andy Razaf's grandfather Waller, whose rise from freed slave to hyperactive political careerist, U.S. diplomatic service, and, finally, to ignominious eclipse in the years preceding and just following his grandson's birth, constitutes as extraordinary and evocative a life story as Andy Razaf's own. Indeed, it is one that not only parallels the grandson's life, but inevitably illuminates it.

John Louis Waller was born a slave in Madrid County, Missouri, on January 12, 1850 (or perhaps 1851—conclusive birth records do not exist), the son of Maria and Anthony Waller, both the property of Marcus Sherwood, a wealthy local plantation owner. Maria and Anthony Waller were household servants to Sherwood, like their parents before them: Maria Waller probably was the Sherwood's cook, and Anthony Waller, the family's carriage driver. Historians of American slave life have long debated the significance of the house-slave "experience," differing on whether house slaves in fact possessed a generally stronger sense of their own self-worth that enabled them later to adjust more successfully than their field-slave counterparts to life as freedmen. John Waller's biographer, Randall Bennett Woods, does in fact suggest that Waller's preternatural ambition and subsequent achievements as an adult to some degree stemmed from the confidence that Waller gained while growing up as a house slave in a closely knit, loving family—one that was largely spared the most brutal vicissitudes of slavery.

John Waller's 11 brothers and sisters were not sold away; the Waller family did remain intact throughout slavery, and were, moreover, all able to escape the grueling hardship of field labor. While John Waller was apparently whipped at least twice as a child (at age 6 and again at 13), his experiences, as Woods observes, "did not produce personal disintegration, passivity, hopelessness. To the contrary, [Waller's] parents' confidence and relatively positive self-image were transferred to their son."

This is an intriguing supposition. Andy Razaf also possessed an impressive self-confidence that distinguished him from many of his talented but insecure black peers in the cutthroat and blatantly racist entertainment business of the Twenties and Thirties. Apparently the roots of this steely self-respect ran deep, nurtured by the Waller/Razaf family's distinctive historical circumstances.

It is clear, however, that though John Waller was spared a critical measure of slavery's worst pain and humiliation, his slave childhood very much marked him for life. From adolescence, Waller was driven by a fierce, even desperate need to transcend his slave beginnings and make an absolute success of himself both socially and economically—the two were inextricably linked in his mind—as a free American. Indeed, Waller seems to have masked whatever insecurity or uncertainty he may have harbored about his future with an ambition that bordered on the absolute, not simply yearning to be a success in white America, but fully expecting to be. Again the parallels between grandfather and grandson are almost chilling, for Andy Razaf also pursued a version of this dream—to achieve social and financial success in the popular-song business—with the same willful expectation as his grandfather that he would succeed, despite the miserable record for even modest professional or financial attainments among the black music men who had preceded him.

John Waller's post–Civil War path seems to have approximated the route taken by many motivated ex-slaves of the period, but with an added jolt of compulsive energy. The Waller family, like so many other slave families throughout the early months of the Civil War, fled their master, turning themselves over in mid-November 1862 with more than 100 fellow Madrid County blacks to a Union Army infantry troop garrisoned in the vicinity. The infantry troop commander, an Iowan, helped resettle his "contrabands" in Tama County, Iowa—where John Waller first learned to read and write, eventually entered the community high school, and quickly proved himself an exceptionally gifted student. Apprenticing as a barber to pay for his schooling, he entered Cornell College in Mount Vernon, Iowa, around 1871, only to be forced by illness in his family to set aside collegiate ambition and return home to manage his father's farm.

Three years later, with the farm afloat and family health restored, Waller moved to the largest city in the area, Cedar Rapids, where his high-school education and fiery intelligence seem to have made him something of a black community leader overnight. A dabbler in local politics, Waller often spoke publicly, and wrote on many issues, including civil rights. Late in 1874 he received an admiring offer from a prominent Cedar Rapids judge to join the man's law firm. Three years later, having apprenticed with the judge, John Waller passed his bar examination in an otherwise all-white class and was granted his certificate to practice law.

Waller moved his law practice from Iowa to Kansas in 1878—to Leavenworth first, then to Lawrence. Even before the Civil War had ended, slave-community rumor had been painting Kansas as something of a promised land for blacks, a unique state where a good climate, good soil, and, most important, a healthful racial atmosphere boded well for newly freed black families looking to establish themselves. Schools were integrated in Kansas at many levels, and the black vote was protected, though both advantages most assuredly were limited: blacks in Kansas after the Civil War still were widely discriminated against in public services, in the administration of justice, and in employment, with segregation remaining prevalent in hotels, restaurants, theaters, hospitals, churches, and many residential neighborhoods. Waller's arrival nonetheless marked the eve of one of this country's great nineteenth-century population movements, the "Great Exodus of 1879–1881"—a migration by tens of thousands of Southern blacks northward to Kansas.

Clearly expecting the new black numbers in Kansas to have a powerful political impact on the state, Waller determined to make his fortune there as a professional politician. He pledged his allegiance to the Republican party, the one most likely to offer newly liberated black men a voice in its affairs and to reward black loyalty with elective or appointed office. The ensuing years produced a modest résumé of political appointments for Waller, an aspiring public figure's upward-reaching resume: central committee chairman for the Kansas State Convention of Colored Men in 1880; Republican state central committeeman, also in 1880 (the first black man in Kansas history so honored); and founder and editor of two black newspapers, the *Western Recorder* (1881–1885), and the *American Citizen* (1888). Waller also married the widowed Susan Boyd Bray, a woman of striking intelligence and energy, as well as an outspoken suffragist, who aided him enormously in his political pursuits while bearing him three children.

Ultimately, the sum of Waller's political achievements during the

1880s in Kansas fell far short of the ambitious former slave's vast expectations. Again and again throughout the decade, white Republican party leaders in Kansas held out to Waller and his black constituents the promise of political reward in exchange for their votes—only to renege, citing their fear that black Republican candidates, even for such midlevel state public offices as lieutenant governor, would arouse the latent prejudice of white voters and lead to the defeat of entire Republican tickets. Unspoken, of course, was the Republican certainty that John Waller and all black former slaves had no choice, however they were treated, but to remain loyal to the Republican party. Their alternatives essentially ended with the Democrats—the party of the Ku Klux Klan.

Waller's political frustrations were analogous to the professional bind endured by his grandson Razaf, who lobbied inexhaustibly for black participation in the music business on equal professional and economic terms with whites. Neither John Waller nor Andy Razaf relinquished his dream of achievement within the system, though certainly both men sensed the implicit trap inherent in such thinking: that playing strictly by the rules meant empowering the racism that often underlay those rules. Outright rebellion nevertheless remained an unacceptable option for both—though Waller came far closer to it than his grandson ever did.

In 1888, Waller was designated by the Kansas Republican party as a delegate-at-large to the Republican National Convention. Admittedly, this was a gesture calculated to guarantee Kansas's black vote in the upcoming Presidential election, but it was also the result of his success as the party's most visible campaigner, the finest orator perhaps in the entire state. "He is surely one of the most eloquent men your correspondent ever heard address an audience," a disbelieving white Kansan had written early in Waller's career. "In fact his ability as an orator and public speaker is such that . . . no one could listen to him speak any length of time without being convinced that no mediocre mind is housed beneath his black skin." John Waller, like his lyricist grandson, possessed a devastating phrase-turning talent. He was also, like his grandson, a strikingly handsome man, six-feet-tall, barrelchested with dark skin accentuated by piercing eyes.

From August to October 1888, Waller delivered some 50 rivetingly theatrical speeches throughout Kansas on behalf of the party's Presidential nominee, Benjamin Harrison, brashly proclaiming from podium to podium: "My name is John Waller and I am continually Wallering the Democrats." When Harrison defeated the Democratic incumbent, Grover Cleveland, in November, carrying every Kansas county but one, it was Waller, as leader of his state's electoral effort, who proudly even if merely ceremonially delivered his state's electoral vote tally to Washington. To his chagrin, he received only the most paltry patronage rewards in return: stewardship at a state insane asylum; appointment as deputy county attorney for Shawnee County, Kansas; and finally, a transfer to the state school for the blind in Kansas City as superintendent of industrial arts—that is, overseer of the school's broom factory. His defeat, at the State Republican Convention of 1890 for a place on the Republican ticket as the party's candidate for state auditor, at last convinced Waller that racism had beaten him in Kansas politics. He immediately resolved to achieve outside the United States what was denied him in America, commencing in 1890, to lobby for a diplomatic appointment within what was then termed "America's New Empire": those countries in Asia, Latin America, and (of special interest to him) Africa, where the United States was beginning to expand its commercial and political interests.

Ironically Waller achieved far greater initial success pursuing overseas service than he ever had realized as a midwestern political aspirant. Several prominent white Republicans, concerned about the increasing desertion of their party at the polls by black Kansans in the wake of Waller's defeat at the State Republican Convention of 1890, hearkened to Waller's lobbying effort and pressed the Harrison administration for a Waller diplomatic appointment. "I want to say that Waller is a very prominent colored man," wrote Kansas Governor Lyman Humphrey to President Harrison. "If he were to be appointed and the fact announced very soon it would help us very much in our canvas in Kansas." "Waller has had reason to suppose for several months that he would be appointed," added Kansas Senator P. B. Plumb. "The suspense unsettles him and he ought to be relieved from it."

On February 5, 1891, President Harrison at last announced an appointment for Waller as United States Consul to Madagascar. The former slave's ambitious pursuit of his own American dream had reached a unique convergence of climax and beginning.

*

When the Hudson Theatre curtain was rung up on singer Edith Wilson in the tenth scene of *Hot Chocolates'* first act on the sweltering soon-to-be-morning of July 24, 1929, those attending the show's midnight performance certainly were as unprepared for what they were about to see and hear as any other *Hot Chocolates* audience before them. "Black and Blue" was by far the most surprising race number ever to be performed on a Broadway musical stage. Andy Razaf had fully intended the song as a stunner for white audiences, and "Black and Blue" played that way, thanks to Razaf's stinging lyrics and the surreptitious power those lyrics gained from Leonard Harper's strikingly theatrical staging of the song. In that staging, the jet black Edith Wilson was revealed to the audience on an all-white set in a white satin gown, lying amid white satin bedclothes on an enormous white bed.

Razaf's verse to "Black and Blue" allowed audiences the initial impression that the song they were about to hear was something of a tongue-in-cheek lament by a very dark-skinned Negress bemoaning the difficulties for women of a truly black pigment to attract a good black man, due to the fact that (as Razaf's lyric put it) *"Gentlemen prefer them light./Browns and yellers all have fellers."* This was the initial deceptive thrust, though, of a song whose lyric chorus quickly revealed itself to be far more pointed toward the universal plight of the black race within white society, abetted powerfully by composer Fats Waller's musical blending of torch song stylization with the soulfulness of a Negro spiritual. By the time "Black and Blue" had traversed its slow, tragic arc—from *"I'm white inside but that don't help my case. 'Cause I can't hide what is in my face"* to *"I'm so forlorn, life's just a thorn, my heart is torn, why was I born: All my life through, I been so black and blue"*—the midnight *Hot Chocolates* audience of predominantly professional theatergoers certainly must have appreciated the extraordinary coup de theatre to which they had just been treated. A few may even have appreciated that "Black and Blue" constituted the first racial protest song ever to have been sung on a Broadway stage.

*

John Waller's arrival in Madagascar on July 26, 1891, was the first step in what would prove to be a very poorly orchestrated State Department campaign for imposing America's growing interests on a hotly contested corner of the globe. A vast island off the southeastern coast of Africa, Madagascar was a largely underdeveloped site rich in such untapped natural resources as timber, rubber, ebony, and mahogany. Its two principal cities were Antananarivo, the country's thriving capital located at its center, and Tamatave, a bustling port on the eastern coast. Its native ruler was the Hova tribe, a ruddy-complected people who claimed Polynesian (rather than solely African) ancestry going back two thousand years. The intensely proud Hovas ruled Madagascar's 6 million multitribal inhabitants with an ironfisted absolute monarchy, titularly fronted by Queen Ranavalona III. True power resided with the Hova Prime Minister, Rainilairavony, who by tradition also served as the Queen's husband. The main threat to Hova hegemony in Madagascar came from France, whose government viewed the island covetously as a French protectorate. On the sideline, various European consular contingents bided their time, officially acknowledging Madagascar's monarchy while unofficially conceding the inevitability of French dominance of the island. The United States, however, was generally recognized as the only member of the international community willing to challenge French imperialism in Madagascar.

The prime motive behind this U.S. policy seems to have been economic: both President Harrison and his secretary of state, James Blaine, were convinced that one of the "highest duties" of their foreign policy was to expand the area of America's foreign trade. To this end, John Waller was instructed by the State Department to maintain cordial relations with Queen Ranavalona's government. He was specifically directed to make an initial symbolic gesture of good will involving the formality of *exequatur*—a sanctioning document, routinely provided to any foreign consul by his host country, granting the right to transact diplomatic business in that country.

The disposition of exequatur in Madagascar apparently had long since become a political phantom dance emblematic of the island's jurisdictional turmoil, with both the French and the Hovas claiming the sole right to issue it. Madagascar's foreign visitors meanwhile evaded the touchy question by applying to the French for the document even while admitting the Hovas' refusal to recognize any exequatur issued by the French. In a tacit bargain of expedience, consular business was thereby permitted to proceed without impediment by either side.

United States Consul John Waller's direct application to the Hovas for his exequatur detonated an instantaneous and rather dire confrontation with the French during his first week in office. The French were, in fact, so enraged by both Waller and his Hova application (the vociferously Negrophobic French seem to have viewed Waller's color and his action as a joint affront) that the French foreign minister, Alexandre Ribot, immediately issued an official protest to the State Department, intimating that Waller's action could be construed by France as a deliberately unfriendly act on the part of the United States. The State Department briefly considered pulling out of Madagascar as a result. Waller dissuaded them, encouraging his superiors to continue challenging France by pointing out that such a cowardly U.S. exit from Madagascar would be viewed by the Hovas as an unforgivable insult and by the French as an outright victory. Within days, though, a one-line communiqué arrived from Washington at Waller's consular headquarters in Tamatave: "Make application for your exequatur to the French Resident General," the dispatch redirected, "instead of the Madagascarian authorities."

For Waller, this was a humiliating betrayal. "I desire . . . to call the attention of the Department to the fact that a considerable faction of the French press charge me with having acted contrary to the instruction of my government," he wrote indignantly to Washington in the wake of his new orders. "I hope that the Department will relieve me from the charge since my instructions were 'to the government of Madagascar,' and not to the Resident General [of France]. I regret the charge as far too serious to be allowed to stand."

The charge, however, *was* allowed to stand. Waller's vulnerability to French bitterness and bigotry became the perfect target for deflecting criticism of America's erratic diplomatic posture in Madagascar away from Washington. In response to Waller's repeated pleas for support, the State Department maintained a stoic silence, coming to view their black consul in Madagascar as something of an embarrassment—the living embodiment of a policy gone awry.

Waller's response to his predicament seems, in retrospect, conflicted—even perverse. Certainly one might have expected the veteran politician to have submitted unquestioningly even to this most compromising official directive from his Republican superiors, pacifying, in this instance, both Washington and France, while perhaps still maintaining some semblance of cordiality with the Hovas. Alternately (however unlikely), Waller could have resigned his consulship in protest over his abandonment by the State Department and joined the Hovas, with whom the former slave felt a powerful kinship. At first he did none of these things. Refusing to be summarily humbled before the French, he also refused to play the rebel with his superiors. Rather, he continued to cultivate ever-closer ties with the Hovas, disdaining to make peace with the French as directed, yet stubbornly persisting in presenting himself to his superiors as the dutiful servant obediently discharging his other consular duties. Disingenuously he continued, however, to pester Washington for a formal U.S.–Hova alliance.

This was a futile if courageous position—at once childishly unrealistic and wildly stubborn. Because of it, Waller was forced to pass the balance of his consular term in virtual isolation from both his own State Department superiors and from a majority of Madagascar's European consular contingents—the latter led by the French, who ostracized the hated "coloured gentleman" at every opportunity. He had decided, however, that he could not afford to abandon the Hovas, for they were essential to his dream in Madagascar of entrepreneurial achievement.

On April 25, 1893, with his term drawing to a close, Waller moved to obtain official sanction from Washington for his ever more frequent visits to Ranavalona's court in Antananarivo. His influence in Washington, never strong in the Harrison administration, however, had been further weakened when a new Democratic administration led by the reelected former incumbent, Grover Cleveland reclaimed the capital from Waller's Republicans. Cleveland's secretary of state, Walter Gresham, pointedly rejected Waller's diplomatic initiative in Madagascar, concluding, in an interdepartmental memorandum, that "the eventual supremacy of the French in Madagascar is a foregone conclusion, which it is not incumbent upon us to avert or contest."

On October 10, 1893, in what would appear to have been a direct slap at the black consul, Edward Telfair Whetter, a southerner from Chatham County, Georgia, whose father had been a prominent slaveholder ruined by the Civil War and Radical Reconstruction, was sworn in as John Waller's consular successor. Waller departed from Tamatave on January 10 for a 60-day leave of absence in the hills of Antananarivo. Whetter arrived in Madagascar on January 20, 1894.

"It is unfortunate," he wrote in his first official dispatch to Washington, "that the Department failed to give me the special instructions I requested concerning such actions as I should take towards Mr. Waller, in case rumors concerning his mismanagement of the affairs of this Consulate were proven to be true."

Whetter quickly compiled a list of what he termed, "Ex-Consul Waller's Mal-Administrations," which he forwarded hastily to Washington. It consisted of six specific charges, four of them absurdly concerned with poor record-keeping on John Waller's part: "Failure to enter fees in National Fee Book"; "Negligent in keeping consulate records"; "No record of judicial proceedings kept in permanent shape"; and "poorly bound records." The remaining two charges addressed "unpaid witness fees and court costs" in a bank case over which Waller had presided as consul.

Whetter's State Department superiors could find little to pursue in their new consul's list of petty Waller crimes, and bluntly told him so. Within weeks of his initial "investigation," Whetter would in fact apologize to the Department for "some of his assessments in the Waller matter," withdrawing two items altogether from his list of accusations—one of them the most serious charge, relating to unpaid witness fees.

Waller, however, aggressively continued to pursue his own agenda in Madagascar, haranguing Queen Ranavalona and her prime minister during a series of audiences throughout January and February 1894 on the necessity of drawing American investment capital to the island. Waller's powers of oratorical persuasion, honed on the Kansas political stump, were irresistible. On the morning of March 19, 1894, Queen Ranavalona announced the dramatic bestowal upon Waller of a land grant totaling 225 square miles of Madagascar's most desirable territory, where the ex-consul now planned to establish a "colony for American Negroes."

Here at last was Waller's long-sought economic entrée. Fort Dauphin, the sight of his royal land concession, was the richest rubber district in Madagascar, and his agricultural rights there were exclusive. A swath of tremendously fertile ground on the island's southeastern coast, the district was rich also in ebony, mahogany, rosewood, and teak.

Both U.S. Consul Whetter and his French counterpart were outraged by the Queen's stunning gesture, which granted to Waller a degree of power and influence far beyond anything his political position might once have offered him on the island. The French strove furiously to undo the transaction, steadfastly denying the grant's legality. By May, though, advertisements were appearing throughout Madagascar and in the United States, offering "LAND RENT-FREE UNTIL MARCH 1896—TWENTY YEAR LEASES TWICE RE-NEWABLE AT TENANT'S OPTION," with John Waller concurrently announcing his intention to form townships on the land and to develop factories and steel mills, as well as to cultivate the rubber, the timber, and the crops of what was some of the most fertile land on the most temperate and fertile island in the world.

Before long, the announced union between the Hovas of Madagascar and the Wallers of Kansas was consumated with a crowning symbolic touch: 15-year-old Jennie Maria Waller, John Waller's eldest daughter, was married, with great fanfare, to Henri Razafkeriefo, a royal nephew of Queen Ranavalona. Though Jennie Waller, in later years, would insist that she and her young Madagascan husband had loved each other at first sight and had themselves initiated their union, the political implications of this marriage remain unmistakable. Her new husband, after all, was not merely a promising junior military officer in Madagascar, and a graduate of the French Royal Military Academy, but a potential successor to the throne.

To John Waller it must have seemed that Madagascar was yielding to him the foundations of a potential Waller empire. Initial offerings for "Wallerland" (as the ex-Consul formally referred to his colonistic endeavor) were being received back home with extraordinary fervor by many major African–American political leaders and the black national press. He now planned an imminent recruiting trip to the United States for his "colony of American Negroes," a back-to-Africa settlement that would certainly make his fortune in Madagascar. "Wallerland" could also, he hoped, tip the balance of power in Madagascar away from the French.

Increasingly, Waller's enemies grew desperate. The French press attacked him with vehemence, trumpeting their belief that his colony represented the first step toward an American invasion of Madagascar. Edward Whetter pursued him through litigation, convening his consular court on October 1, after months of Waller's procrastination in responding to Whetter's repeated summonses. Presiding as prosecutor and judge, with the accused ex-consul still conspicuously absent, Whetter quickly found Waller guilty on two counts: "gross mismanagement" of certain estate funds belonging to American nationals in Madagascar, and "abuse and negligence" of Waller's "fiduciary trust as an official and as a citizen." Denying all but one of eight expenditures that Waller had claimed against the estate, Whetter ordered Waller to pay back both the government and the estate within 45 days, and to pay the cost of his trial as well.

Early in November, on the first leg of his journey home to

America, Waller brazenly returned to the port city of Tamatave, disregarding both Whetter's court order and the increasingly militant French. France's confrontation with the Hovas had reached a critical juncture in Tamatave: four French men-of-war were now in the city's harbor, and their crews were assaulting and robbing locals and even, on occasion, foreign residents. Five thousand Hova soldiers were munitioned and within range of Tamatave's harbor. ("The Hovas," Whetter wrote, "continue to advocate patience and restraint, remaining a good deal more quiet than white men would be under the circumstances.") On the morning of December 12, at 7:30 A.M., the French Tamatave armada commenced shelling the city. Whetter's only official response to these hostilities was to detain John Waller formally, slowing his departing predecessor in the hope that the oncoming French might soon detain him permanently.

Waller was aware of Whetter's strategy. "Oh Sue," he had written to his wife at Antananarivo, late in November, "if you could only get friends to help me, I will teach Whetter a better lesson, if I could only get out of his hands and get hence. . . . You don't know how this man has wronged me." Finally, on January 23, still trapped in Tamatave, he wrote what would prove to be the final letter to reach his wife at Antananarivo. "We will demand $20,000 in damages of Whetter," he announced in closing, "for having compelled me to remain at Tamatave."

On March 11, 1895, Consul Whetter informed his State Department superiors in Washington of John Waller's arrest by the French: "I . . . immediately wrote demanding the reason . . . and expressing the hope that the evidence on hand was of such a character as to fully warrant such high-handed measures; later on letters came to hand from both the Navy and Land Commandants explaining Mr. Waller's arrest. . . . It is claimed that Waller wrote in a letter in January to one Tessier, enclosing another to Mrs. Waller, and that this letter or letters, now in the hands of the French authorities, prove that he was furthermore giving the Hovas advice and information. The French have been anxious to get at Waller for a long time and are, I feel sure, desirous of making the most of this opportunity. Whether they have a case made out or not I do not know."

John Waller's unjust arrest and subsequent ordeal in Madagascar —the John Waller Affair, as it would come to be known in this country—remains to this day a vivid piece of melodrama. The

"Affair" also stands as a landmark in the evolution of race relations in America. The unexpectedly fierce response that Waller's detention very quickly generated throughout the United States once details of his arrest were made public, was unprecedented—an American outcry for international justice on behalf of a former slave.

His trial in Madagascar before a French military tribunal had lasted a mere three hours and twenty-five minutes. Waller, defended by a French court clerk and denied any opportunity to speak in his own defense, had been found guilty by this tribunal and sentenced to 20 years in a French prison. He was denied the opportunity to appeal to a higher court. Manacled hand and foot, Waller was put aboard a French steamer, finally landing on April 21, 1895, in Marseilles, where he was immediately imprisoned.

Grover Cleveland's initial efforts on Waller's behalf appear to have been fundamentally sincere. From the first news of his arrest and quick conviction, Secretary of State James Gresham publicly emphasized the fact that Waller's situation should be viewed as that of an American citizen who had remained in Madagascar "with a view to establishing relations of trade between that country and the United States," and whose arrest, as a result, on charges of treason by the French, was unacceptable. The French, however, were determined to use the John Waller affair as a final means for ending American influence in Madagascar. Waller's release hinged on formal U.S. acknowledgment of France's Madagascar protectorate, including the abdication of Waller's land grant to France. Waller, moreover, was not well served in the early stages of his "affair" by the American minister to France, James B. Eustis, an avowedly southern gentleman, who viewed his role as a former-slave's advocate with extreme distaste. Thus, despite President Cleveland's stated intention to liberate Waller as soon as possible, one Washington newspaper soon felt justified in reporting that "Ex-Consul Waller is in great danger of being abandoned by this government. It is certain," the newspaper insisted, "that certain papers have been received 'showing conclusively' that Mr. Waller had connived with the natives of Madagascar to overthrow French authority, besides other things that took him far beyond the reach of the government of the U.S., and the result will doubtless be that Waller will have to work out his own salvation."

The editorial pages of several newspapers reflected deep frustration with Waller's continued incarceration: "We call upon the government of the United States in the names of the civil rights and personal liberties of all our fellow citizens to demand from the French Government that ex-Consul Waller shall be immediately released," one newspaper editorialized. Others were overtly accusatory: "In all sections and among all parties in the country, the conviction, too outstanding at first to be entertained, is penetrating the minds of men that this Administration is unwilling—not only to demand the release of Mr. Waller but even to demand the reasons for his incarceration," the *New York Herald* wrote on August 4. "Can Mr. Cleveland afford to let this impression go much farther? Is the Secretary of State willing to let himself open to the charges of race discrimination?"

Ultimately, the tragic proportion of John Waller's predicament overwhelmed even the most moderate public media voices. "The facts in this case of ex-Consul Waller are slow in coming," observed the *Cleveland Plain Dealer* on August 9, "but as they come in, they make it more evident that a great injustice has been done an American citizen and an affront put on the United States."

Another newspaper was even blunter: "Waller's color is a factor in this case, and it is why he has not received more attention from the Administration. . . . It remains to be seen whether or not this government, which the Negro fought to preserve and perpetuate, will protect a Negro when his privileges as an American citizen are assailed in foreign lands. The action of the French is undoubtedly founded on their observations that a government which permits lynching and burning alive of its Afro–American citizens at home would not exert itself to protect them so far away from home."

On the morning of October 17, 1895, Waller's wife and children arrived in the United States after a grueling sea journey that had carried them nearly halfway around the world. In France, John Waller was still incarcerated. In Madagascar, the brutal war of attrition between France and the Hovas was at an end, terminated by the unexpected surrender of Queen Ranavalona on September 30. In the wake of the Queen's capitulation (she was soon permitted to flee the island), bands of Malagasy marauders had taken to the countryside surrounding Antananarivo, harassing and on occasion slaughtering the French. They were led, according to published reports, by the son of one of Ranavalona's loyal princes. Neither father nor son was identified by name.

No record exists of Henri Razafkeriefo's activities in Madagascar after his pregnant wife escaped the island with her mother, brother, and sisters late in the summer of 1895. What seems certain is that by the time Jennie Waller gave birth to their child in Washington, DC, in December, Henri Razafkeriefo was dead, murdered by France's invading Madagascar force. References to Jennie Razafkeriefo's pregnancy turn up in numerous John Waller–related newspaper stories during this period, with subsequent Waller news stories later attributing Henri Razafkeriefo's death to military encounters with the French, though it is nowhere recorded precisely how or when Razafkeriefo died. Ultimately, all that can be said with assurance is that Jennie Razafkeriefo gave birth to Henri Razafkeriefo's son on December 15, 1895, eleven days before her own sixteenth birthday, naming the boy in the Madagascan fashion: Andreamen[en]tania Paul Razaf[in]keriefo.

Less than two months later, President Cleveland forwarded to Congress correspondence that he finally had procured from France detailing the French case against John Waller, together with a report from Secretary of State Gresham. The announced intention of both houses of Congress to investigate President Cleveland's handling of the John Waller Affair, combined with escalating pressure from the American public and the continuing refusal of Waller and his family to accept France's offer to release the former consul if all indemnification demands for the Waller land grant were dropped, impelled Cleveland and Gresham to end the Waller Affair with a sinister stratagem. Cleveland would accept Waller's release on France's stringent terms, including U.S. recognition of French rule in Madagascar and the abandonment of Waller's indemnification claim. However, to deflect further criticism for this blatant surrender of American rights, and to abort the ensuing congressional investigation of the White House's handling of the Waller case, Cleveland and Gresham worked to discredit Waller as a viable hero in the case. Gresham revealed a State Department investigation focused on Edward Whetter's long-since-dismissed charges relating to Waller's so-called "mishandling," as consul, of the aforementioned estate settlements on the island, his subsequent consular court trial presided over by Whetter, and—in direct contravention of the administration's stated position throughout the Waller affair maintaining John Waller's innocence regarding crimes against France—U.S. *assent* to the French charges that had led to Waller's conviction and imprisonment. The questionable summary of American Ambassador to France James Eustis's own Waller investigation provided the State Department report with its conclusion:

> It is proper to state that before examining the evidence I had been inclined to believe that Waller was perhaps convicted on insufficient evidence; that on account of the prejudice against him he might not have had a fair trial. After examining the original letters of Waller I have no doubts whatever of his guilt. It was not a case of inadvertent or imprudent writing, but was a deliberate attempt to give information to the enemy, to the prejudice of the military situation of France. The evidence fully sustains the charge. The whole tenor of the correspondence discloses his guilty intention and no court could have hesitated to condemn him.

In Congress, it was hurriedly announced by the State Department that an "understanding" had been reached by America with France and that John Waller would be immediately released. In exchange, the United States government agreed to make no claim on Waller's behalf against the French government based on Waller's arrest, conviction, or imprisonment. Additionally, Waller would be granted a full pardon by the French.

Although enraged Waller partisans protested that the prisoner had in no way consented to such an agreement, the John Waller affair was at an end—and on the evening of February 21, 1896, Waller was released from prison in Nîmes, France. Walking with the aid of a cane, his back according to witnesses "slightly humped" and his face "aged beyond recognition," he still walked "with [the] noticeable vigor . . . of a free man." Shortly thereafter John Waller came home to America, his beleaguered family, and his new grandson.

One week after *Hot Chocolates'* triumphant inaugural midnight performance at the Hudson Theatre, a financially straitened Andy Razaf sold his 1 percent interest in the show's box-office receipts for $2,000, also surrendering at that time his equity in any future *Hot Chocolates* editions. In August, he contracted with George and Connie Immerman, the owners of Connie's Inn, to write "lyrics and materials" for a new revue at their Harlem nightclub for $150 in advance and $25 a week for the run of the show.

In stark contrast, lyricist Ira Gershwin was at this time about to sign his first Hollywood screen contract with the Fox Film Corporation, a deal that would guarantee both Ira and his brother George, $100,000 for one motion picture's worth of music—$70,000 for George Gershwin, $30,000 for Ira. Lyricist Larry Hart also departed New York for Hollywood around this time, lured westward with his partner, Richard Rodgers, by a $50,000/two-movie offer from the First National Pictures division of Warner Brothers.

Lyricist Oscar Hammerstein also signed his first Hollywood contract during the 1929 Broadway season, a two-year/four-picture deal with Warner Brothers that not only guaranteed Hammerstein and his composer, Sigmund Romberg, $100,000 against royalties for each film score they wrote, but also granted Hammerstein and Romberg final approval on how their films would be cut. In the end, only two of these four movies would be made: *Viennese Nights* and *Children of Dreams*. To extricate itself from its excessive commitment in the face of a sudden screen-musical glut in Hollywood, Warner Brothers opted to pay Hammerstein and Romberg $100,000 apiece to stop writing movie musicals for the moment. "The most money I ever got for not making two pictures," Hammerstein would remark glibly after returning to New York from his brief Hollywood sojourn.

Courtesy Howard Wolverton.

2

Li'l Brown Baby

Now don' you cry li'l brown baby,
Don't mind what de white chillen say,
An' don' be shy li'l brown baby,
De Lord made yo' color dat way.
Honey dey's jus' jealous of you,
To see how much we love you,
An' dat de Lord above you
Has made you heart so gay.
So don' you cry li'l brown baby,
Don' min' what de white chillen say,
'Cause when you die li'l brown baby,
De angels won't turn you away.
　　— "Li'l Brown Baby"
　　　by Andy Razaf and Maceo Pinkard

The household of his grandfather in which Andrea Razafkeriefo would grow up was not the shadowed, unhappy home of a broken or defeated man. After his return to the United States in the spring of 1896, John Waller did not mourn what might have been. Though he comprehended the political practicalities that had led the Cleveland administration to (for all intents) frame him, he nevertheless recognized that his color had determined their policy. In fact, Waller immediately sought to turn his Madagascar ordeal to political and financial profit by seizing upon the racial dimension of the affair as a central issue. No sooner had he disembarked the U.S.S. *New York* at Manhattan on April 12, 1896—following a chilly Paris conclave (in the wake of his prison release) with American Ambassador Eustis, and a six-week sojourn in England, conferring with potential British investors—than Waller commenced pressuring the Cleveland administration for a claim to indemnification for his lost land grant.

Appearing before the 29th District Republican Club in New York City on April 13, Waller attacked the French government for abusing him, President Cleveland for neglecting him, and Edward Whetter specifically for betraying him. The group responded with a unanimous resolution affirming Waller's innocence and respectfully demanding that Congress exact compensation from France for the ex-consul's losses. An initial stirring of sympathy and support for Waller ensued nationwide, but Congress and the American public quickly wearied of this nettlesome black man and his hapless plight.

Waller soon reluctantly abandoned the reparation campaign, and turned his energies toward persuading France, through the State Department and his business acquaintances in Great Britain, to formally purchase the Wallerland territory from its ostensible owner. According to Waller biographer Randall Bennett Woods, the sale may have been consummated early in 1897 for a price of $10,000. Though evidence does exist to support this claim, details of the transaction appear to be unconfirmable. Members of the Waller/Razaf family themselves still consider the lost Madagascar land grant an unresolved economic issue.

Waller was also determined to reestablish himself as a force on the American political scene, and to this end arranged a whirlwind lecture tour, in order to finance his return to Kansas. From late in April through May 2, 1896, at which date he at last arrived in Topeka, Waller delivered speeches in Baltimore (where his wife, children, and grandchild had settled immediately following Andrea Razafkeriefo's birth), Philadelphia, Washington, Chicago, and St. Louis. Pausing in Topeka for a brief round of welcoming receptions and "socials," the Wallers then finally moved on to Kansas City and a small, comfortable house at 836 State Street.

Almost immediately upon his return, Waller was again pressed into Republican party service as a still-fearsome campaigner for the upcoming Presidential election. He gladly returned to the Republican fold, putting his Madagascar misadventures to work for himself and the party in dozens of impassioned speeches delivered throughout the summer and fall of 1896. "Mr. Waller is an impressive speaker," observed the *American Citizen* in a revealing account of one Republican rally at the Tenth Street Baptist Church in Kansas City. "When he told about how the French spat upon him and tried to kill him with abuse, all because he was an American Negro and a Protestant, the audience groaned in sympathy. . . . When he denounced the present administration for having allowed an American citizen to be trampled on by a foreign nation, the audience hissed. . . . When Mr. Waller said that James G. Blaine, the Negroes' friend, would have sent the whole American Navy to rescue him, the audience applauded."

Waller's political ambitions were still boundless. His efforts in 1896 on behalf of the Republican party were calculated, as he himself acknowledged, to bring about his appointment as recorder of deeds for the District of Columbia. This was the highest-paying and most powerful political office traditionally available to a black man, an office once held and made famous by such black political pioneers as Blanche K. Bruce and Frederick Douglass. Though Waller's candidate, William McKinley, captured the presidency in 1896, the fundamental racial realities of America's political culture were not altered. Waller could muster no support whatever from white Republicans for the recordership position. A white North Carolinian eventually was tendered the appointment by McKinley in April 1897.

Waller's continued lecture tours, and the law practice he opened in partnership with another black attorney, now provided most of the income for his family. His wife, Susan, supplemented this by taking in boarders and lecturing ladies' clubs on the charms of Madagascar. The Wallers were soon prosperous enough to send their children—John, Jr. and Minnie—to Emporia Normal School and the Chicago Conservatory of Music, respectively.

Frustrated, however, by his failure to achieve solid progress toward absolute equality in America, Waller could not find contentment in the segregated and incomplete nature of his achievements. Still consumed by the pursuit of his very recognizably American dream, yet still very much partial to the anticolonial activism of nonwhite cultures against European powers, he became an ardent supporter of the Cuban revolution against Spain, finally raising his own company of black volunteers—Company C, Kansas Voluntary Infantry—and leading them off to Cuba in August of 1898. Five months later, Waller brought his entire family, including Jennie Razafkeriefo and her infant son, down from Kansas to join him. The

Wallers and the Razafkeriefos would remain in Cuba for almost two years after the end of the Spanish–American War, an idyllic two years of expatriate tropical living for the younger Razafkeriefo, not unlike the life he might have led in Madagascar had his father survived.

Certainly John Waller perceived promising parallels between Cuba and Madagascar. With the conclusion of the war, he set out once again to create a new Wallerland colony, this time in Cuba: "The Afro–American Cuban Emigration Society"—a "refuge for the frustrated black entrepreneur in America." However, this Cuban plan shared much the same fate as his aborted Madagascar enterprise. The money, the property, and the popular interest simply were not present, and the American military government in Cuba gave him little cooperation. After desperately sinking his family's savings into speculative real-estate investments around the city of Santiago, Waller returned to the States almost penniless in September 1900. Pausing in Kansas City only long enough to sell the house on State Street, he soon joined his wife, daughters, and grandson in New York City, where he retired from public life, surrendering his ambitions for good.

Moving from Manhattan to Yonkers in 1905, Waller edited a newspaper, the *Yonkers Progressive American*, for a time. In the last year of his life he worked for the New York Customs House. On a Sunday afternoon in October, 1907, after calling at the Mamoroneck home of his foster daughter, he attempted to walk the several miles home in a cold rain, contracting pneumonia. Within the week, at age 56, he was dead.

It is likely that Andrea Razafkeriefo's first memories included the sight of his grandfather in uniform, the presence of his own mother always very close by, and perhaps the sound of his mother's step-sister Minnie singing. While it seems certain that John Waller influenced his grandson profoundly during these early formative years, both as a towering role model and as a chastening study in frustration, it is most tempting to speculate on Minnie Waller's musical influence on her nephew Andrea. A professional singer, Razaf's aunt wrote many songs over a long career, for her own performance repertoire, supplementing light classics, hymns, and spirituals with original compositions. In fact, each member of Razafkeriefo's immediate family seems to have harbored a versifying soul. John Waller wrote light verse frequently for his own amusement, and Susan Waller wrote too, privately, for pleasure. Jennie Razafkeriefo quite fancied herself a legitimate poetess. It is not at all surprising then that Andy Razaf exhibited poetic precocity. His ability at age 7 to beat perfect time is family legend. Razaf himself claimed that his first original verse was written at age 10.

Rhyming aptitude was matched early on by all-around scholastic ability: the young Razafkeriefo loved to read, and his teachers apparently were very encouraging about his prospects. In her son's promise, though, Jennie Razafkeriefo seems to have perceived two futures indivisibly joined, her adoring pride in her Andrea's potential an extension of her own self-absorbed hopes and dreams. Married at 15 and widowed before she was 16, the young mother's emotional development was severely affected by the premature demands of her politically charged union with Henri Razafkeriefo, and by the subsequent trauma of her own escape with her family from Madagascar, her father's imprisonment, and her young husband's tragic death. Now she passively settled herself with girlish willfulness on a life served to her by her son.

At some point during the years 1906 to 1910 Jennie married a man named Griffiths and settled with her teenaged child in Passaic, New Jersey, but the marriage did not last. By 1911, Jennie and Andrea were back in New York City, living together in a house at 220 East 25th Street. At first she supported herself and her son (although apparently unwillingly) as a stenographer. Within the year, though, despite the 16-year-old Andrea's unmistakable promise as a student, Jennie convinced him to drop out of high school for a job that could help support them both.

It is not at all clear why Andrea Razafkeriefo decided to become a professional songwriter. "I was not positive at first that I could write songs," he conceded years later, "but I knew that I wanted to compose." He later acknowledged to an interviewer that as a boy he had in fact "hoped to confine [himself] to poetry," but recognizing that he "had to earn a livelihood in a more material way," had decided "to versify for music."

Razaf's first song lyric was written as early as 1909, a lyric that the 13-year-old audaciously sent to the very successful popular composer Charles K. Harris, writer of the song standard "After the Ball." Harris soon returned the submission, deigning to enclose with it a personal reply: "Dear Andrea—Your lyrics show great merit but I would advise you to go into some other field." Harris's correspondent was, however, unyielding. "I did not take Mr. Harris's suggestion," Razaf explained simply, years later. "I had made up my mind to write songs and I was willing to do whatever was necessary to become a successful composer."

Angling his job search some few blocks across town from his home, toward Tin Pan Alley, the city's song-selling district situated along and around West 28th Street, Razaf soon secured work running an elevator in an Alley office building. "I liked it," he later insisted. "It gave me an opportunity to observe people. I studied my passengers as they came and went. I talked and made friends with them and soon they were telling me about themselves. They confided in me, their joys and sorrows, their ambitions, disappointments, happiness. . . . These are the things that songs are made of." At his leisure and on his lunch hour, he read: "I read everything I could get my hands on. I knew that I must learn words because words are the tools of a writer."

It seems reasonable to assume that Andrea Razafkeriefo would not have pursued songwriting as a career without his mother's consent. One way or another, Andrea Razafkeriefo was out of school, out where his mother wanted him: working. For one year, in fact, he labored contentedly in an elevator cab. The job offered him undisturbed reading time, while affording the young lyricist repeated opportunities to rub shoulders with songwriting professionals. Through the week, Tin Pan Alley roiled close by, a disembodied music beyond an elevator door.

The year was 1913. On Broadway 40 first-class theaters lit the Great White Way, housing an extravagant array of dramas, comedies, vaudevilles, and, of course, musicals—European-style operettas, mostly, with their decorous Teutonic scores, Cinderella plotlines, and old-world formalities.

The season's great hit was *The Sunshine Girl*, starring Vernon and Irene Castle, America's first nationally popular dance team, in their joint Broadway debut. Pointing the Broadway musical away from its stuffy Viennese antecedents, it heralded, with syncopated rhythm and the Castles' "modern" dancing, the dawning of a new esthetic in American musical comedy. At Florenz Ziegfeld's rooftop Jardin de Paris Theatre, the impresario was presenting the most opulent edition yet in his *Follies* series, a show so lavish it would force Ziegfeld finally to abandon Jardin the following year for more expansive premises on 42nd Street, in the New Amsterdam Theatre.

Initiated in 1907 as an American equivalent to the French Folies
Bergère, Ziegfeld's *Follies* had developed into the most glamorous
series of musical revues Broadway probably would (and perhaps
will) ever see, a series founded on beautiful girls and extravagance.
In 1911, Ziegfeld's fiercest competitors, the Shubert brothers, had
opened their own theater, the Winter Garden, itself dedicated to
"revue and extravaganza," on Broadway between 50th and 51st
Streets, reviving in it the following year Broadway's original revue
series (dating back to 1894), *The Passing Show.*

This new *Passing Show*'s second appearance at the Winter Garden
Theatre, in 1913, proved a choreographic tour de force for Ned
Wayburn, the revue's resident director and Broadway's slickest
dance stager, who slipped into his production bits of the tango, the
turkey trot, and any other popular dance steps he could appropriate
from what was already a dance-crazy year—even reviving the almost
forgotten cakewalk from the previous decade. The resulting spirited
revue was an audience favorite and a grudging critical success, with
the *New York Sun* describing it as "about the biggest and busiest
show of the season." The humor apparently ran heavily toward
blackface comedy, with George Le Maire and Frank Conroy, "the
blackface Weber and Fields," featured. Harold Atteridge received
credit for dialogue and lyrics, with Jean Schwartz composing most of
the forgettable music—excluding a handful of interpolated numbers
by Al W. Brown.

There were quite a number of further song additions, though, to
the *Passing Show* score of 1913. After opening in July, the production was reworked in September for a second *revised* edition, with
many new performers, several new sketches, and a quantity of new
songs. Among these late additions was one song entitled "Baltimo'."
Its composer: Andrea Razafkeriefo.

He was 17 years old. Somehow, riding his elevator cab daily,
piloting its music-business passengers to and from music-publishing
offices, the young, aspiring songwriter apparently had encountered
someone from the Shubert organization—most likely Oscar Radin,
The Passing Show's musical director. Razaf later recalled visiting
Radin at the Shubert theatrical offices, "one evening, after working
hours . . . and show[ing] a copy of 'Baltimo'" to the musical director." It had been Artie Mehlinger, though, the *Passing Show*'s
ranking tenor vocalist, who'd responded most enthusiastically to
"Baltimo'." Razaf remembered Mehlinger taking one look at the
music and having it played over again on the spot. As a result,

"Baltimo'" was acquired by the Shuberts as a feature for Mehlinger, to bolster the newly revised *Passing Show of 1913*.

Andrea Razaf, his last name truncated at the prudent suggestion of *Passing Show* music publisher James Kendis (whose sheet music cover mangled the young composer's name as "A. P. Razafkevifo"), was now in the song business, his first composition sold on Broadway —in the second smartest revue of the day. "Baltimo'," as it turned out, would not be a hit, but at least it had been a sale. For a black elevator boy, the accomplishment was enormous.

Hear that engine sneezin',
Now don't that sound teasin',
Soon I will be breezin'
Back to Baltimo'.
Now the whistle is smokin',
Listen to it chokin',
Nothin' but a token
That we're goin' to go—
I told you so,
I told you so,
Hear that whistle blow:

Toot, toot, toot, toot, toot,
The whistle is blowin', blowin',
Chute, chute, chute, chute, chute,
The train is goin', goin',
Soon I'll be with Flo',
Home in Baltimo',
Where the chickens have been known to crow:
Baltimo'.

When we pull in at that lovin'
Station, station,
On my knees, I'm goin' to bless
Creation, creation,
Listen, listen, engineer,
Go like the devil,'cause the track is clear,
For goodness sakes don't touch them brakes
Till we get to Baltimo'.

*

In 1914, a 15-year-old aspiring songwriter named George Gershwin went to work on Tin Pan Alley, in a song plugger's cubicle at the offices of Jerome H. Remick & Company, Music Publishers, where he played Remick-owned tunes eight to ten hours a day on a battered piano for anyone who would listen. The teenaged Gershwin's abilities as a piano player were extraordinary; within the year, he would come to be regarded as Remick's best. Gershwin, though, entertained only songwriting ambitions.

In 1916, George Gershwin sold his first song, "When You Want 'Em You Can't Get 'Em; When You've Got 'Em You Don't Want 'Em," to the Harry Von Tilzer Publishing Company. That same year, using his insider status at Remick's, Gershwin played another of his songs, "My Runaway Girl," for a representative of the Shubert brothers, hoping that the tune might be suitable for a Shubert production. The Shubert representative liked what he heard well enough to bring Gershwin to the attention of Sigmund Romberg, the kingpin of Broadway composers in 1917, who was then preparing a score for that season's upcoming *Passing Show*. Romberg suggested that Gershwin collaborate with him on a few numbers for the revue, and ultimately one song, "Making of a Girl," was used. Gershwin received program credit as Romberg's collaborator and gained his second publication the following January when Schirmer Music Publishers bought "Making of a Girl" and published it.

Within three years, George Gershwin was on Broadway with his first solo score for a production entitled *La La Lucille,* and on his way to theatrical immortality as a composer. His precocious appearance in *The Passing Show* at 17 was, of course, a mere harbinger of impending musical eminence.

Andrea Razaf was without question an exceptionally talented lyricist, as talented at 17 as almost any Tin Pan Alley peer. For him too, *The Passing Show* was a harbinger of future achievement, his admittance into the professional songwriting fraternity now promising a lifetime of song creation for popular consumption. Composing for Broadway as a career, however, was far beyond even Razaf's breathless aspiration. Blacks did not work *at all* on Broadway in 1913, and there was no reason to foresee any imminent change in that situation.

If the Broadway route that Gershwin (and so many lesser white composers) could pursue was closed to a black songwriter, however, one could travel the route of hack Tin Pan Alley with only token impediment. At 17, this path must have seemed not merely agreeable to Andy Razaf, but magnificently promising.

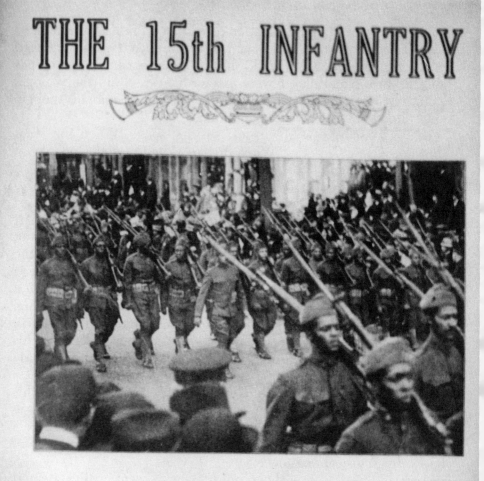

Courtesy Schomburg Center for Research in Black Culture.

3

Swanee Fashion Plate

King of styles, king of smiles,
I know of him you have heard,
All pressed up, all dressed up,
I mean that he's the last word—

He is their fate, this Swanee fashion plate,
See him come struttin' along.

> — *"Swanee Fashion Plate"*
> by Andy Razaf and Jimmy Johnson

When Andrea Razaf arrived on Tin Pan Alley in 1913, America's song business was in its prime. Along 28th Street, pianos sounded from the cramped cubicles of countless song demonstrators at work in the brownstone offices of innumerable music-publishing firms. Song pluggers crowded the sidewalks, vying for the attention of passersby—shouting, crooning, even whistling their musical offerings at the orchestra leaders, theatrical managers, and vaudevillians who scoured the area in search of new material. Sheet music was printed on basement presses for shipment in bundled tons across the country to a public hungry for the newest song lately heard at the local vaudeville house. The song industry was robust, chaotic, and, at times, disgracefully remunerative.

The name "Tin Pan Alley" itself apparently was first coined in 1903 by Monroe Rosenfeld, a part-time song and jingle writer and sometime newspaper reporter for the *New York Herald* who laid claim to the term's print debut and popularization with a series of articles titled "Tin Pan Alley." Legend, and Rosenfeld himself, recorded the reporter visiting the offices of music publisher–songwriter Harry Von Tilzer for an interview and hearing there a tinny piano tinkling in another room. The whole neighborhood, Rosenfeld purportedly remarked, was one "tin pan alley," a noisy stretch of low-rent publishing offices all rattling to the sound of tinny pianos in tiny rooms—though Von Tilzer, in later years, would insist quite vehemently that this offhand bit of phraseology had in fact been his. Tin Pan Alley's difficultly in ascribing credit fairly for its own creativity clearly was congenital, commencing at "the Alley's" very conception.

For more than two decades the industry had resided in and around Union Square, close to the city's premier theaters for operetta, grand opera, and musical variety—the Union Square Theatre, the Academy of Music, and Tony Pastor's Music Hall—as well as the sundry satellite burlesque and sporting houses, beer halls, restaurants, and penny arcades that dotted the district. Beginning in 1893, with Witmark & Son's pioneering move uptown to 49–51 West 28th Street, so many of the neighborhood's music publishing houses relocated to 28th Street between Fifth Avenue and Broadway, nearer the newer theaters opening in the Herald Square vicinity, that the 28th Street block, by the turn of the century, had come to be known as "The Street of Songs."

By 1913, fortunes were being made along Tin Pan Alley at 25 cents a copy (the going retail price for a piece of sheet music in the early 1900s), with 5-million-copy sales realized for each of several songs. A popular song hit sold between 600,000 and 1 million copies on average, earning its composer and lyricist anywhere from $9,000 to $50,000 in royalties, at a five-cent-per-copy royalty. Royalties, in fact, were being paid out far more regularly by 1913, with outright song sales for flat dollar amounts a thing of the past, at least officially. Tin Pan Alley was far more consumed with producing songs that capitalized on any new event or trend. Industry chronicler Isaac Goldberg would term this topical song fixation "musical journalism, emotional tabloids of the passing phase."

*

The Passing Show had closed in late October. Since, not surprisingly, no new Broadway offers had followed in its wake, 17-year-old Razaf returned warily to Tin Pan Alley's hustle—uncertain, despite his initial accomplishment, what was next for him. For a time, he clung to his elevator job, continuing to storm 28th Street with new songs. Ragtime was still very much Tin Pan Alley's commercial song currency in 1913, and so Razaf wrote and tried to sell ragtime songs. Ragtime, however, in 1913, bore scant resemblance to the elaborately syncopated music perfected during the previous decade by Scott Joplin and other black keyboard artists. Now stripped of its indigenous characteristics, ragtime was bowdlerized by Tin Pan Alley's white songwriting minions with callous infidelity.

A strong, however discomforting, argument can be made for Tin Pan Alley owing its fundamental existence to the distortion of black music. Though Irish-flavored sentimental ballads had dominated popular American musical taste from the very beginning of music publishing in this country (weepy melodic celebrations of home and hearth, constancy and virtue), it is nevertheless incontestable that, beyond these ballads, the essential source of most American popular music during this period was African–American music, specifically the musical inventions of African–American slaves.

The roots of this argument are not hard to trace. The first African slaves in America had voiced familiar chants from their tribal past, while sometimes rewording and resinging traditional English religious music that they learned largely from proselytizing Methodist and Baptist missionaries, transforming hymns into haunting spirituals, a fervent music laced with the tribal exuberance of their African ancestry. These spirituals, along with the rawer, rudely secular plantation melodies that slaves sang to entertain one another, grew to be so widely admired by white America that both song genres—particularly the plantation tunes, initially—were co-opted by white performers who took to performing them wearing burnt-cork "blackface" makeup in blatant, often brutal burlesque of their black originators.

White men in blackface had presented themselves as stage "Negroes" since well before the American Revolution. Prior to the War of 1812, though, these Negro characters had been depicted using dialect that was far more Anglo-Saxon than African–American in inflection. By the late-1820s, though, more and more blackface white performers could be found barnstorming the United States, performing alleged "Negro" songs and dances in circuses and between acts of plays. Though the melodies for most of their songs were of British origin, the lyrics now drew heavily on stereotypical American frontier lore of the Negro, and at least approximated African–American dialect while depicting blacks with comical and insidious exaggeration. "I ketch hold of Cuffee," went one such lyric line in the song "Coal Black Rose." "I take him by de wool,/I ketch hold of Cuffee, he try away to pull,/But I up wid a foot, and kick him on de shin,/Which put him breafless on de floor and make de nigger grin."

Throughout the nineteenth century, "minstrelsy" dominated American theatrical institutions with its blend of formulaic structure and racist messages. Unpretentious and immediate, devoid of plot, character development, structured musical score, or even set speeches, minstrel shows were utterly undemanding, tremendously accessible mass entertainments. They adhered to an absolutely rigid, nearly ritualistic three-part structure, which began with the "Fantasia," a standardized, formally patterned variety entertainment, full of jokes and music. This was followed by the "Olio," a straight variety section with no particular pattern or format, in which solo performers strutted their stuff individually. Finally there came the "Burlesque," a closing spectacular wherein highlights from the first two parts were reprised and broadly satirized. All minstrel shows also utilized an identical basic stage alignment, with the entire company configured onstage in a semicircle, seated around an "interlocutor," the show's more-or-less dignified master of ceremonies. The biggest stars, the "endmen" comedians "Brudder Tambo" and "Brudder Bones"—named for the rhythm instruments they played, the tambourine and animal bones, respectively—sat at the ends of the semicircle, made up in the most grotesque blackface and wearing the most garish tattered costumes. The whole business, peculiar as it may be to imagine today, projected a colorful familiarity that was endlessly diverting and, ultimately, for nineteenth-century audiences, enormously reassuring.

It was the vividly racist content of minstrelsy, though, that finally defined the genre's appeal. In the North, where minstrelsy enjoyed its greatest popularity, minstrel shows helped satisfy white northerners' curiosity about blacks (particularly black slaves), both before and after the Civil War. White minstrels emphased black exoticism, titillating their white audiences, who believed themselves to be observing Negroes, while simultaneously assuring them that these performances were "safe" white reenactments.

Minstrelsy remained almost exclusively a white institution until after the Civil War, when numerous black companies earnestly attempted to legitimate their participation in minstrelsy by characterizing themselves as "genuine," "real," and "bona fide" Negroes, more authoritative in their depiction of minstrelsy's craven stereotypes than whites. To promote their rather gruesome legitimacy even further, black minstrels emphasized the closeness of their links to the plantation, promoting their slave roots in the manner of Brooker and Clayton, who boasted that their "Simon Pure Negro" company was "composed of men who, during the war, were SLAVES IN MACON, GEORGIA." Capitalizing on the perception among some Americans that blacks were innately musical, black minstrels also encouraged their white audiences to view them not as skilled professional entertainers, but rather as authentic Negroes simply on display. Eventually, black minstrels were even forced by their white audiences to partake in the ultimate minstrel indignity: wearing the blackface "mask" that stood as white minstrelsy's pernicious emblem.

While Andrea Razaf's earliest black lyric-writing forebears were of course nameless (unattributed slave originators of spirituals and work songs whose anonymous folk compositions first came to the attention of Americans beyond the South as a result of the Civil War), there did evolve within minstrelsy the roots of a bona fide, attributably black lyric-writing tradition. The appearance of the Fisk Jubilee Singers—a group of black students from Fisk University, an all-black institution founded in 1865 by white Protestant missionaries in the city of Nashville, Tennessee—singing the religious music of the plantations some four years after the war's conclusion, ultimately proved a triggering mechanism for the introduction of genuine African–American music into minstrelsy. The Fisk group in fact toured widely throughout both the United States and Europe. Quickly, minstrel troupes responded to the Fisk popularity by hurriedly introducing some semblance of African–American religious music into their own synthetic minstrel repertoires.

This expropriation had an enormous impact on the lyric, as well as the melodic, content of minstrel songs, with the most apt and effective transpositions initially occurring among the all-black troupes. Many black minstrel performer–songwriters began to borrow freely from the melodies of black spirituals for their onstage "ditties" in the years following the Fisk Singers' debut. They also started to utilize the spirituals' colorful religious imagery for their own secular song purposes, an application not nearly so difficult to reconcile as one might imagine.

In accordance with African patterns of worship, black slaves had never divided their religious and secular worlds, as many European–Americans had. For the black slave in America the same "worldly" language always had sufficed to describe both spiritual and everyday experience, with songs of worship often sung interchangeably as work songs, social songs, and march songs, while biblical themes of morality and redemption were often expressed in earthly terms of plenty and celebration. Sumptuous quantities of food, fine clothing, fervent dancing, and unrestrained demonstrations of joy exemplified the pleasures of the world to come. Introduced into the minstrel pageant, black religious imagery brought minstrelsy closer to authentic African–American expression even as it seemingly confirmed for racist white audiences the stereotype of blacks as garishly buffoonish posturers.

For black audiences, though, the presence in minstrel shows of black religious music not only elevated the entire enterprise profoundly, but most important, allowed for previously unexpressible moments of protest within the minstrel song form. Heaven soon became a place, in minstrel songs, where "there is no overseer," where "de white folks must let de darkie be." More overt protest themes also began to creep into minstrel song lyrics, though the signals sent in these songs often were mixed—interpretable by white audiences as simply part of the show, decoded by black audiences as something infinitely more transcendent.

It was ragtime, with its peculiarly percussive, unmistakably African way with formal European music, that may well have been Afro–America's first truly original musical invention. This ragtime "beat" was inherent in the oldest Negro spirituals. It was latent in the plantation songs that minstrelsy imitated as "coon." The name "ragtime" itself suggested ragged rhythms, the sense of syncopation tearing a melody to rags. Early ragtime song lyrics were generally fashioned to fit the music's ragged, syncopated line with rough, crude, slang-filled imagery that blatantly employed the rawest racist minstrel stereotypes—black chicken thieves, black water-melon eaters, black razor toters.

Black songwriters like Al Johns, Shepard Edmonds, and Irving Jones had managed to wrestle a few dollars from Tin Pan Alley during ragtime's early period: Johns with "Go 'Way Back and Sit Down," the only song among many first-rate Al Johns compositions, including quite a few beautiful love ballads, to become a hit; Edmonds with "I'm Goin' to Live Anyhow until I Die"; and Irving Jones with both "Take Your Clothes and Go" and "I'm Livin' Easy," the latter a song American composer Charles Ives chose to transcribe in his *Memos* as a paradigmatic example of "black-faced comedians . . . ragging their songs." The great breakthrough for black Tin Pan Alley songwriters had come, however, with the innovations of Bob Cole and the Johnson brothers, whose songs of the early 1900s synthesized the contemporary slanginess of ragtime lyrics with the softening influence of the traditional Tin Pan Alley ballad to produce something distinctively fresh and eminently less objectionable.

Born in Athens, Georgia, on July 1, 1868, the son of former slaves, Bob Cole initially had moved to Chicago, working in Sam T. Jack's *Creole Show*, and publishing his first songs there ("Parthenia Took a Likin' to a Coon" and "In Shin Bone Alley"), with the Will Rossiter Publishing Company, before moving to New York, where he ran for a time a black stock company of 12 to 15 performers at Worth's Museum, on Sixth Avenue and Thirteenth Street. Contributing sketches and plays prolifically while appearing regularly as a per-former, Cole quickly revealed himself to be, at just 26, the "most versatile theatrical man" in the entirety of black entertainment, "a good singer . . . an excellent dancer, able to play several instru-ments," and capable of writing an entire dramatic or musical play (dialogue, lyrics, and music) staging it, and playing a role in it.

Lured away from the Worth Museum to write a show for Sissieretta Jones, known professionally as "The Black Patti"—one of the finest black operatic singers of her day—Cole created *Black Patti's Trouba-dours*, a highly proficient vehicle for the great diva, before finding himself in a nasty dispute over salary with the management. Forced to resign (and briefly imprisoned for breach of contract), Cole next decided to create a new production for himself and his performing partner, Billy Johnson. The result was *A Trip to Coontown*, the first black musical comedy to be written and produced by blacks, and the first to be written with a cast of characters, continuity, and a genuine plot that depicted its black characters not as shiftless, sunny savages but as human beings capable of thought and even emotion. In 1899, after three seasons playing *Coontown* in New York and on tour, Cole left his partner to work with J. Rosamond Johnson, a formally trained musician and singer with whom Cole proceeded to write, over the ensuing decade, some 150 songs for more than a dozen shows, many of them white Broadway productions. He often collaborated on lyrics in an unusual songwriting troika with Johnson's brilliant younger brother, James Weldon Johnson.

Both Johnsons were highly educated products of a prosperous Jacksonville, Florida, family. After traveling to New York with a largely completed comic opera in hand (*Tolosa*, never produced) and a letter of introduction to the editor of a music trade journal, the two brothers in a very short time had gained the attention of the city's top theatrical and musical figures (both black and white) with their undeniable talent. Their progress was swift, but James Weldon Johnson gradually grew disgusted with his life in musical theater and opted finally to leave the business (in 1905) for what soon became a multifaceted career in politics, journalism, and the arts, as a commentator, editor, poet, and novelist. His lyrics, while hardly as refreshing as Bob Cole's, were nevertheless enormously original in one potent sense: their implication that whites and blacks, in fact, experienced emotion in the same way.

It is clear that Bob Cole and James Weldon Johnson both were powerful lyric-writing influences in Andrea Razaf's early development. While Cole's 1890s songs were quite blatantly "coon," they nevertheless exhibited terrific cleverness, bristling with puns and pointedly disfigured language ("I'm driven to desperism/By her misconstrued behaviorism"). In their concern with mitigating the constraining song stereotypes of their race, Cole and Johnson pointed the way toward virtuoso lyric-writing dexterity on Tin Pan Alley by combining two fundamental popular-song formulas: coon song/ragtime, in which lyric lines were slangy and bent to fit a song's rhythm; and the sentimental ballad, which emphasized lyric storytelling, usually of a romantic and (if at all possible) heartbreaking nature.

Cole and Johnson were determined to write songs that avoided the brutishness of minstrelsy. To some degree they succeeded, particularly in tunes like Cole's great hit with J. Rosamond Johnson, "Under the Bamboo Tree," a song that, in its punning use of the slang form for the word "like" ("If you lak-a me,/Lak I lak-a you . . .") and its verbal sense of play—breaking up phrases oddly but rhythmically, splitting up words by musical pauses and rhythmic shifts—embodied a new style of lyric writing. By achieving a song's desired verbal effect not through straightforward storytelling but with witty lyric usage, they defused the racist content of many songs, placing the emphasis not on ugly stereotypical details but rather on the cleverness of the lyric writing.

By 1910, because of the lobbying efforts of such black artists and lyricists as Bob Cole and the Johnsons, Bert Williams and George Walker (the most successful black entertainment team of the age, who also occasionally composed their own material), and the marvelous conservatory trained composer/lyricist Will Marion Cook, the exaggerated stereotyping of blacks in popular-song lyrics reached a point where it was at least frowned upon by Tin Pan Alley. A new generation of lyricist–songwriters, led by R. C. (Cecil Mack) McPherson and Alex Rogers—the latter a Nashville-born former member of an early Fisk University quartet, who contributed the lyrics, and often the music, for many of Bert Williams's greatest song successes ("The Jonah Man," "I May Be Crazy but I Ain't Nobody's Fool," "Bon Bon Buddy, the Chocolate Drop," and "Nobody,")—now began to compose moderately understated, even sophisticated, popular-song lyrics, lyrics still grounded in race but far more subtly so.

What this new generation lacked, however, was the access to Broadway that their immediate predecessors had forcefully claimed for themselves. The tragically premature deaths of George Walker in 1908, Ernest Hogan (a minstrel veteran regarded as "the greatest of all colored showmen") in 1909, and Bob Cole in 1911, and Bert Williams's defection to Florenz Ziegfeld's *Follies* in 1910, combined with increasing nationwide racism to eliminate a black presence on Broadway during the years after 1910. Alex Rogers and Cecil Mack, in their connections with Bert Williams particularly, represented a surviving and, in many ways, transitional link to and from that pioneering generation of black lyric-writing theatrical professionals.

There were others, of course. Henry Creamer founded the Negro Players in Harlem with Alex Rogers in the spring of 1913. J. Leubrie Hill, an alumnus of Cole and Johnson's *Red Moon* Broadway company, inaugurated in the 1910s a series of black touring shows, *The Darktown Follies*, with such success that Florenz Ziegfeld himself purchased in its entirety one of Hill's songs and accompanying production numbers from the 1913 edition, restaging the piece verbatim the following season in his own Ziegfeld *Follies* downtown. Together with Alex Rogers and Cecil Mack, Creamer and Hill managed to keep alive, and even advance, the tradition and the lyric craft of black popular-song composition, preserving it for Andrea Razaf's generation to rediscover. They managed this with songs like Mack's "That Minor Strain" and Creamer's "After You've Gone" (music by Turner Layton), complementing the work of newcomers like James Burris ("Ballin' the Jack" and "It's a Pretty Thing," in collaboration with Chris Smith) and Shelton Brooks, whose "Some of These Days" in 1910 was perhaps the landmark song of this Tin Pan Alley epoch, whereby Brooks, with sophisticated lyric colloquialism and heartfelt passion, elevated the coon song into the realm of expressive emotion.

Razaf may have cherished one lyricist above all others as his role model and inspiration. This was the enigmatic and astonishingly talented young poet Paul Laurence Dunbar, whose premature death in 1906 from tuberculosis at 34 was a crushing blow to black theatrical aspirations. Born the son of slaves in Dayton, Ohio, in 1872, Dunbar had begun to write poetry while still in public school, before moving to Washington, DC and supporting himself for a time in ways that Andy Razaf clearly would later relate to: first as an elevator operator, then as an assistant in the Library of Congress. Dunbar's first book of poetry, *Oak and Ivy*, published at his own expense in 1893, had helped bring the 21-year-old poet to the attention of various editors and writers across the country, including the patriarch of American literature, William Dean Howells, who immediately recognized Dunbar's exceptional talent and began to write about it. With a glowing introduction from Howells, Dunbar's third book, *Lyrics of a Lowly Life*, published in 1896, garnered national recognition and an unofficial designation for Dunbar as the Negro poet laureate. Still, Dunbar bore an abiding affection for the stage, and in the summer of 1898, he set aside his burgeoning literary career to collaborate with Will Marion Cook on *Clorindy, or, The Origin of the Cakewalk*, a 45-minute operetta-like diversion that demonstrated for perhaps the first time the vast theatrical and formal possibilities of syncopated black music.

Dunbar the lyricist was first of all a poet, not a commercial lyric writer creating according to formula or trend. This distinction obviously impressed Andrea Razaf deeply, as did Dunbar's great affection for African–American culture and dialect, which evinced itself most powerfully in his poetry and novels.

From all these men Andy Razaf learned that the best black lyricists wrote with vivid colloquialism and brash vernacular color, and above all else trusted a melody's rhythm, shaping their lyrics not according to trite formulaic conceit but as a verbal complement to syncopated meter. Popular-song lyrics, he realized, could also be enormously uplifting (as exemplified by James Weldon Johnson's stirring "Lift Every Heart and Sing") and could even serve the cause of racial activism. But above all, Razaf discovered in the lives of the black songwriters who preceded him that no black lyricist had ever exclusively focused all his energy and talent on lyric writing. If he succeeded, Andrea Razaf would become the first black lyric writer.

*

Few black songwriters were afforded access to the ragtime feeding frenzy that consumed Tin Pan Alley following the 1911 arrival of Irving Berlin's "Alexander's Ragtime Band" (a song that, stylistically, was not a rag at all). Unable to follow his *Passing Show* success with any further song sales, Razaf finally abandoned full-time Tin Pan Alley pursuit in February 1914 to take a job as a telephone operator for one L. Schwank, at 604 West 146th Street. No doubt Jennie Razaf had much to do with her son's hasty exit from Tin Pan Alley in favor of a steady day job: Razaf still lived at home with his mother, who continued to work as a stenographer. Mother and son had moved again, to 104 Eighth Avenue, an unusually handsome block-long red brick–faced tenement building between 15th and 16th Streets on the east side of the avenue.

Razaf's new job, well away from home, brought the 18-year-old to the outermost frontier of a new black residential neighborhood just then taking shape within the confines of Manhattan's uptown "Harlem" district. The extension of the elevated rapid-transit lines into Harlem in 1880 had positioned it as a newly fashionable New York City neighborhood. Blocks were filled with aristocratic new apartment houses and smart brownstone rows. Fine horses soon appeared on the wide boulevards of Lenox and Eighth Avenues, and polo was played at the nearby Polo Grounds on 155th Street, with the crowning ornament of this late–nineteenth-century upturn in Harlem's evolution the construction and opening of the Harlem Opera House by impressario Oscar Hammerstein, at 209 West 125th Street, in 1889.

The first blacks in Harlem had arrived as beneficiaries of a deflated real-estate market in 1905. Newly built townhouses in the vicinity of 133rd and 134th Streets between Seventh and Eighth Avenues were not renting in 1905, victims of a mild but unshakable recession and Harlem's fundamental lack of suitable mass transit from midtown Manhattan for potential white middle-class tenants. These languishing townhouses eventually had drawn the attention of an enterprising black real estate agent named Philip Payton, who finally enlisted their owners in an unheard-of gamble. "Rent Colored," Philip Payton whispered persuasively to a host of desperate white landlords, and soon a pioneering few eager black blockbusters began making their way north to Harlem from the tenements of Greenwich Village and San Juan Hill.

Since then, with every passing year, Harlem's "Black Belt" had continued to receive infusions from black neighborhoods downtown in a migration that had intensified to the point where Negro Harlem by 1914 could legitimately be characterized as a budding black metropolis. Since 1911, almost all the major black churches and black political organizations, the black YMCAs, and YWCAs, and many local black doctors, lawyers, and businessmen had relocated, or very soon would relocate, to Harlem. A newer development was the increasing number of blacks mainly from the Deep South, but also from all other parts of the United States, along with blacks from the West Indies, Africa, and Latin America, who were now making their way to this new uptown black Manhattan neighborhood as a redemptive Promised Land.

Annabelle Miller was 24 when she first met Andrea Razaf in Harlem. A delicately built woman, five feet, three inches tall, with brown eyes, long auburn hair, classically chiseled high cheekbones, and the lightest freckled complexion, she had come to Harlem from Charleston, South Carolina, with her parents and five sisters, Florence, Hattie, Septima, Edith, and Lula. Both parents died soon after the move. Raised by her sisters, Annabelle, while still in her teens, had gone to work as a housemaid in the home of opera singer Eleanor Kent, reigning prima donna for the popularly priced Castle Square Opera Company. (The imposing Kent townhouse was located some 20 or so blocks below Harlem, at 134 West 95th Street, midblock between Columbus and Amsterdam Avenues.)

It is not known how Razaf and Miller first met. John Wain-right, sister Edith's husband, apparently "palled around" with the teenaged songwriter, and it is quite possible that Wainright intro-duced them. What seems very clear is the unlikeliness of their pairing. As anxiously confident, slick-speaking, and opinionated as Andrea Razaf was at this time (the consummate Tin Pan Alley sharpie), sweet-tempered, God-fearing Annabelle was at least equally retiring, reticent, even subservient in spirit, as mild and passive as her soon-to-be fiancé's mother was forceful and demand-ing. It is even likely that Annabelle Miller was initially unaware of her fiancé's songwriting ambitions, since her surviving family members still insist that Razaf, in Annabelle's presence, demon-strated neither an aptitude for nor any interest in songwriting as a career.

They were married in a small wedding at sister Edith's Jersey City home in April 1915. The bridegroom was 19, looking very much his age—a handsome, light-skinned Malagasy prince, physically some-what delicate, well under six feet and slender, with a royal counte-nance and a regal presence. His bride was 26. The top-floor apartment in a five-story walkup on 143rd Street between Seventh and Eighth Avenues was their first home, and Annabelle's sister Septima lived with them there for a time.

In August, Razaf changed jobs, leaving the office of L. Schwank for a return to the familiar confines of an elevator cab, this time in a building at 21 Fort Washington Avenue. His wife continued to earn good money in service to Eleanor Kent, and after a little more than a year (in January 1917) he apparently allowed her to procure a position for him at Madame Kent's, as a butler. The salary was acceptable—$50 per month, nearly twice what the elevator job had paid—but the duties demeaned the proud young Razaf painfully. He persevered, however, and spent most of the couple's joint wages on a new apartment at 30 West 136th Street, between bustling Lenox Avenue and more disreputable Fifth Avenue, across the street from the rather grand half-block-long Nurses' Residence of Harlem Hospital. Razaf endured the indignities of menial service until May 1918, when, ignoring his wife's more resigned wishes, he at last turned in his livery to become a "coater" in an "oriental cleaners" on Amsterdam Avenue. Again the pay was an improvement ($65 per month), but there hardly was any commensurate increase in the 22-year-old's sense of satisfaction with his career.

Tin Pan Alley was thriving in his absence, gorging itself on a diet of militaristic musical variations in the wake of America's recent entry into the "European War." Nothing in Tin Pan Alley's relatively brief, explosive history could compare with the boon that World War One was creating for the fortunes of America's music publishers in 1918. When the "Great War" in Europe had become America's war in April 1917, Tin Pan Alley had taken the conflict as its grandest inspiration to date. Moreover, with popular music suddenly deemed essential to the vast war effort, Tin Pan Alley publishers found themselves supplied, despite rationing, with all the paper they might need to print songs of martial spirit. Sheet-music sales had skyrocketed as each aspect of wartime experience, every campaign episode and individual battle, was ransacked tunefully by Tin Pan Alley songwriters: "My Boy He Just Can't Help Being a Soldier," "Goodbye Broadway, Hello France," "Keep the Home Fires Burning," "Over There."

To feed this jingoistic song market, a Negro touch was not required. War songs were not ragtime, they were not "coon"; war songs sang in any traditional music style. With the onset of war, whatever professional opportunity that might have existed for black songwriters on Tin Pan Alley was shut down practically overnight, smothering the established careers of such talented and productive black songwriters as Al Johns, Chris Smith, Will Marion Cook, Shepard Edmonds, and R. C. McPherson, along with the expectations of the ever-optimistic Razaf, who still scribbled down new lyrics on occasion. He even registered a set for copyright with the Library of Congress in January of 1918—a war song titled "Run, Run, Run, for I'm a Yankee" (lyrics and music by Andrea Razaf). The song failed to attract a publisher. Soon it seemed that the only active black American music men were in the military bands of black officer–bandleaders Lt. James Reese Europe (369th Infantry Band) and Lt. J. Tim Brymn (350th Field Artillery Band), who were touring the European war zone, to wild acclaim. Back home, Razaf took a job as a custodian in the U.S. Appraiser's Building, far downtown on Washington Street, in May 1918.

The Great War's conclusion in November 1918 brought a clamorous, triumphant renewal of black pride and hope, nurtured by the fact that those blacks who had been given the chance to fight in Europe had distinguished themselves beyond all expectation. This was particularly true of the 369th Infantry Regiment from New York City, Harlem's own troops, who, fighting under French command, had been awarded the Croix de Guerre, France's highest military honor, and were the only American unit so singled out. These black heroes returned home with a new sense of dignity. What they found was the racist society they had left behind. In the wake of the war's conclusion, vicious race riots broke out in Harlem, spawned by postwar economic hardship and spurred by racism. Hundreds of black citizens were shot and beaten, many of them soldiers recently returned from Europe. Across the country, similarly ghastly scenarios were played out, while in the South, the Ku Klux Klan began to make a vitriolic ascendance.

Many of Harlem's younger generation vigorously rejected the pleas of their elders for patience and restraint in the face of white violence, calling instead for more extreme action. At the corner of Lenox Avenue and 135th Street—at a sidewalk forum peopled by Harlem's political and race radicals lecturing from atop ladders and soap boxes—the "new Negro," as this younger generation already was beginning, collectively, to call itself, cried out for "socialism," "separatism," and a "new order." Andrea Razaf was among them. The political spirit of his grandfather, John Waller, had penetrated the grandson.

Like his grandfather, young Razaf nursed very specific ambitions for his future, even at the age of 23. The options available to a young black man of little formal education already had been made terribly clear to him: telephone operator, elevator operator, butler, coat cleaner, and custodian. The lone way out—show business, and (in his case) Tin Pan Alley—was still off limits to an aspiring black songwriter in 1918. Razaf, fed up and at heart a performer anyway, was reawakened to the activist sensibility bequeathed him by his grandfather. Taking to a soapbox (which he carried from his apartment, up 136th Street and across Lenox Avenue to the IRT subway station at the 135th Street corner), he delivered speeches that echoed the contributions he now was making regularly to several little magazines, founded during the war by radicals opposed to Negro military participation, magazines that were growing ever more belligerent in their editorial tone.

Among them were the *Messenger*, cited by the Justice Department as "by long odds the most dangerous of all the Negro publications"; the *Emancipator*, which came to "preach deliverance to the slaves";

the *New Negro*, for whom Razaf now worked as a sales agent at a sixty-cent monthly commission; and the *Crusader*, a handsomely produced magazine with a caustic editorial line that focused, in these postwar years, almost solely on the returning African–American soldier's right to "a piece of the PEACE." For these and other periodicals, Razaf wrote brief observations in rhyme, and lengthier verses brimming with bravado. Some of them were childishly vituperative; others were childlike in their literary technique. Many were searing and very much to the point.

"Beware! Race hater, how you play with fire," wrote Andrea P. Razafkeriefo (in print he always now signed his name as the unregenerate Madagascan). "For there are limits to your mad desire;/Too long we've stood your hanging and your burning,/But you are nearing where the road is turning!/We love the law but love of life is stronger,/We cannot play the 'gentle lambs' much longer;/ Soon comes the day when we must find out whether/Twelve million blacks shall live—or die together!"

The lines rarely were graceful. The rhymes often were elementary. But the poems communicated their purposes powerfully and, at times, eloquently.

> Throw off the yoke which long
>   has kept you down!
> Half men who've sold their race
>   to gain renown,
> The so-called leaders with their
>   spineless backs
> Who, when they face the white man,
>   Hide the facts.
> The "sissy" preachers with their
>   sugar tongues
> Who spit the germs of Judas
>   from their lungs,
> The "whitemen's niggers," who
>   deceive us for
> A filthy "mess of pottage"—
>   nothing more!

Andrea Razafkeriefo's poetic focus ranged across Harlem, embracing individuals and issues that were recognizable to any black Harlemite. "Elevator runners, send out your 'oral gunners,'" began one poem entitled simply "Attention!" "it is time to make a noise and get your rights!" Another, entitled "The Negro Voter on Election Day," posed some pertinent questions, plainly phrased:

> Say Mr. Candidate, where are you from?
> What of your family, from whence did they come?
> What do you think of "The Birth of a Nation,"
> Waco, St. Louis and race segregation?
> It's all right to say you'll do this and do that—
> But what have you done—let me know where I'm at?
> I'm the NEW NEGRO, of much sterner stuff,
> And not the "old darkey," so easy to bluff!

Razaf celebrated the small triumphs of his neighborhood minority community in odes "To the Lincoln Stock Company," Harlem's black theatrical troupe housed in the recently opened Lincoln Theatre on 135th Street, off Lenox Avenue: "No tongue can be too eloquent/In words of pride and praise;/Nor tire of voicing sentiment/For your uplifting plays./For you have proved that we should keep/Our face t'ward the sun;/That superstition oft' prevents/Great things from being done./You've shown that we can lay aside/The 'cork' and comic play:/That we should keep up with our stride,/And not with yesterday."

Acerbically, Razaf also caricatured, with an impressive sweep of colloquially comic, starkly depictive power, those among his own people who left him less than enthusiastic.

"Truth—Not Poetry"

> Sam Nut, of Lenox Avenue
>   Walks as one who owns the street,
> For he's the proud possessor
>   Of two educated-feet.
> His head is full of fancy steps,
>   As not a night can pass
> Without his quarter going
>   To some "bang-up" dancing class.

> "Sap-head" Jones draws twenty "bones"
>   Each week throughout the year,
> But still he's always borrowing
>   And pawning things, I hear.
> He has a wicked appetite,
>   A craze for booze and clothes,

So anyone can plainly see
    Just where his money goes.

Billie Shirk fell out with work,
    Yet fortune seems to court him,
For he has found a foolish maid
    To cherish and support him.
This worthless imp is now a pimp,
    And proudly, plainly shows it,
He is the lowest of the low
    And doesn't care who knows it.

Ben Buck, who haunts Fifth Avenue,
    Is of crap-shooting fame.
He'll "load the dice" or "cut you up"
    Before he'll lose a game.
He has no heart, his soul is dead,
    He'd knock a baby on the head.
His only aim's to make his bread,
    Regardless of all shame.

This poetical blossoming was a critical step in Razaf's evolution as a lyricist. Certainly the poems presented a marvelous opportunity for sharpening his rhyming skill. Perhaps even more important, though, was the range of voices that he now explored in the guise of political verse—a range that soon would serve him well as a songwriter for characters in the theater. Even the highly principled, morally disapproving voice of the scold that he often adopted in these writings was an essential aspect of the Razaf style that emerged at this time. The popularity that he came to enjoy in Harlem as a poet, moreover, encouraged him to return aggressively to songwriting.

Early in 1919 he hazarded one more new song, an unabashed yet hardly unreasonable attempt to marshal Tin Pan Alley's profitable military fixation behind a Negro theme. Titled simply "The Fifteenth Infantry," Razaf's first new song in nearly a year celebrated Harlem's war heroes, the all-black Harlem regiment of New York's National Guard.

The subject seemed to have at least regional commercial promise. Shipped to Europe in July of 1917, Harlem's Fifteenth Regiment, redesignated the 369th Infantry, had captured the grudging respect of their fellow soldiers with display after display of fighting mettle and outright heroism. The 369th had returned to Harlem on the morning of February 17, 1919, marching up Fifth Avenue before cheering crowds numbering in the hundreds of thousands. In Harlem, Razaf had their song ready—copyrighted on January 24 and published in February 1919 by Crusader Music, a vanity-music publishing offshoot of the *Crusader*. Doubtlessly aided by the frantic salesmanship of its composer, "The Fifteenth Infantry" enjoyed steady (if far from spectacular) sales uptown during the weeks following the regiment's return. The tenacious Razaf simply rented a pickup truck and took his song to the Harlem streets, personally performing it in a block-by-block song-plugging demonstration that would be remembered around Harlem for many years.

Razaf's social and political activism was not confined exclusively to speechifying, song-plugging, and poeticizing in Harlem. As a regular visitor to the city's vaudeville houses both uptown and downtown, where he studied new acts assiduously, Razaf was obliged to sit through frequent barrages of sterotypical racist epithets, grotesque racist caricature, and general racist shtick embedded in a frightening number of vaudeville turns. Characteristically, he often could not refrain from tendering his objections, after the curtain came down, directly to a theater's management.

In April 1919, Razaf addressed an angry letter to the NAACP about a white act he had witnessed at the Loew's Victoria Theatre using "material that was insulting to colored patrons."

"My dear Mr. R:" the NAACP's assistant director, William White, had written back, "Thank you very heartily for your letter of April 17. . . . It is a very vital thing that vaudeville performers, as well as all theatre folk, should refrain as far as possible from caricaturing colored people. . . . The method which you pursued of protesting direct is one very effective means of letting them know that colored people generally object to being held up to ridicule by this class of vaudeville performer.

"I am writing a letter today to the main office of the Loew Vaudeville Circuit, asking that not only in Loew's Victoria in New York City, but in all of their theatres, they take steps toward eliminating this evil which has existed too long."

White enclosed a copy of the letter he had written to Marcus Loew, chairman of the Loew Vaudeville Circuit: "Our attention has been called to the prevalence with which performers in the various vaudeville theatres operated by your concern, caricature and hold up to ridicule the colored people in attempting to be amusing to their audiences. One of the means of doing this is the frequent use of the most objectionable words 'nigger,' 'darkey' and 'coon.'

"I am sure that you do not realize how bitterly such epithets as these are resented by all self-respecting colored people. The American colored man wishes nothing in this country except to be allowed to be able to lead his life as any other man, without constantly being ridiculed in spite of all the steps that he may take to better his own condition and to advance his own right to be classed as a citizen of this Republic.

"Twelve millions of Americans of the colored race freely and unstintedly gave their lives, their sons, and their wealth to aid America in pursuing the war which has just closed. Does it not seem to you that after having served so selflessly, that to ask that they not be made the butt of cheap jokes is a simple enough recompense for the services which they rendered?

"If you, as head of the great theatrical syndicate bearing your name, should send out an order that this cheap, detestable practice of ridiculing colored people be stopped, it would be an innovation which would be greatly appreciated by all of the colored people, as well as by all broad-minded white people, and it could have a curative effect, not only in your own theatres, but would spread to the theatrical world in general. May we not ask that you take such a step as this?"

Though White's politely reasoned remarks to Marcus Loew certainly seem tame in comparison with Razaf's more fevered writings at this time, the channeling of Razaf's letter to Loew through White no doubt gave Razaf great satisfaction. Like his grandfather before him, Razaf respected—and throughout his life always continued to defer to—the conventions and formalities devolving from established institutions. Razaf loved to register a formal protest. For clearly as he saw the inequities of the society in which he lived, he also especially longed to correct them as a member, like any other citizen, in good standing.

Immediately following the Loew incident, Razaf tangled with yet another white theatrical institution in far less confrontational fashion, rising to the summit of Broadway chic as an elevator operator shuttling well-heeled passengers to the New Amsterdam Roof, Florenz Ziegfeld's sumptuous nightclub atop the New Amsterdam Theatre, home of his famous *Follies* on West 42nd Street. For four months, beginning in December 1919, Razaf angled to repeat his first songwriting success, hobnobbing with Ziegfeld patrons at every elevator-trapped opportunity. The scenario could not have been more glamorous—or more ludicrous. Since 1915, Ziegfeld had operated the intimate rooftop auditorium as New York's most elegant nightclub, stunningly appointed by the impresario's legendary designer, Joseph Urban, with a movable stage, a glass runway for Ziegfeld's showgirls, glass balconies, an open-air roof garden, and cross-lighting capable of creating extraordinary rainbow effects onstage. There was dancing at the New Amsterdam Roof, dining and drinking, of course, and even intertable telephones. Most important, there was superlative entertainment, Ziegfeld's "Midnight Frolic," most of its cast borrowed from the resident *Ziegfeld Follies* company downstairs.

In his elevator cab, Andrea Razaf must have yearned fiercely for all that the New Amsterdam Roof represented in 1919: theatrical attainment, social sophistication, wealth. The "Midnight Frolic" exuded such extravagant glamour that many audience members regarded the elevator ride from the terra cotta–ornamented New Amsterdam Theatre lobby (one of Broadway's most grandiose) to the sky-blue and gold lobby of the New Amsterdam Roof as a nearly euphoric social apogee—squeezed as they were in breathless anticipation among the most superbly tailored, superbly coiffed, superbly select elevator passengers the city could offer.

December 1919 was an especially auspicious moment for an elevator stint at the New Amsterdam. The 1919 edition of the *Follies*, then in its sixth month downstairs on the main stage, was quite likely Ziegfeld's greatest *Follies* achievement, with a cast that included Eddie Cantor, Marilyn Miller, and black comedic virtuoso Bert Williams himself, performing an Irving Berlin–dominated patchwork score that featured two quintessential *Follies* standards, "Mandy" and "A Pretty Girl Is Like a Melody." The "Midnight Frolic" that season—*Ziegfeld Girls of 1920*—meanwhile boasted the likes of Fannie Brice and W. C. Fields, along with Ted Lewis, in a completely distinct two-act revue.

Razaf's lobby elevator chores (there were, in fact, two side-by-side elevators) included ushering visitors during the day to the Ziegfeld offices in the New Amsterdam Building. Thus it seems likely that he sooner or later encountered all of these *Follies* luminaries. In later years, Razaf loved to recall one meeting with Irving Berlin when the 31-year-old white Tin Pan Alley legend offered the 25-year-old black elevator operator sincere encouragement on the subject of songwriting.

It is especially tantalizing to imagine Andrea Razaf catching moments of the *Follies* or the "Frolic" in progress from the back of either house. Florenz Ziegfeld employed the New York entertainment community's very finest theatrical artists, both onstage and behind the scenes, with the stagecraft practiced upstairs on the Roof quite as accomplished as anything displayed in the main theater. The stage opening of the Roof theater was, in fact, identical in size to the proscenium downstairs—*Follies* production numbers often were tried out on the Roof first, and popular *Follies* numbers often were moved upstairs after the main show had closed. The "Midnight Frolic" was similarly utilized by Ziegfeld as a laboratory and minor league for future *Follies* talent. Eddie Cantor was first introduced by Ziegfeld in a "Frolic," as was Norma Terris. Will Rogers was brought to the Roof directly from vaudeville, his lariat twirling and his sly, dry wit the perfect counterpoint to Ziegfeld's dazzling showgirls and brash, citified comedians. In a very short time he, too, graduated from the Roof to the *Follies*.

Razaf, no doubt, received the most intensive theatrical training of his early career at the New Amsterdam Theatre during the months from December 1919 through early May 1920, observing Ziegfeld's troupers at work. The experience would have been a rich one— dizzying, in fact. It may also have provided quite a devastating object lesson on the vast chasm that separated aspiring black theatrical professionals from the heights of white theatrical achievement embodied by the *Ziegfeld Follies* and the "Midnight Frolic." Razaf likely was offended by certain racist aspects of the *Follies* that year, including the usual blackface indignities inflicted upon Bert Williams, but perhaps especially by the corps backing Eddie Cantor's rendition of "Mandy" being identified in the program as "The Follies Pickaninnies." In later years pioneering black vocalist– lyricist Noble Sissle would often refer to the *Follies* as "glorified minstrelsy with girls." For Razaf, the experience must have been quite demoralizing.

Andrea Razaf copyrighted two new songs in the early months of 1920, "That Musical Tonical Dance," (words and music by Andrea *Razz*), and "The Farm Yard Jazz," written with one Ralph Rawson and arranged by Florenz Ziegfeld's hugely talented resident orchestrator, a black composer–arranger named Will Vodery, who no doubt made the young lyricist's acquaintance in the magnificent Art Nouveau precincts of a New Amsterdam Theatre elevator cab. Neither of these songs would ever be published, though Razaf clearly sold himself quite as hard as he could downtown over the first few months of 1920, hoping desperately to interest some theatrical manager (perhaps Ziegfeld himself) in his songwriting ability. By May 1920, he had had enough.

It was now seven years since his first song sale, seven years since his debut in the song business, and Andrea Razaf still sat in an elevator cab while his wife uncomplainingly helped support them both. Well away from Harlem an opportunity had recently presented itself whose frivolousness must at first have seemed entirely unsuitable, but the frustrated young lyricist now found himself reexamining even the most unlikely alternatives. For years he had indulged a modest talent as a baseball pitcher, pursuing a sideline semiprofessional ballplaying "career" around the city that had amused him enormously while paying him little. A new semipro Negro baseball league was now being formed in, of all places, Cleveland. For his leadership and intelligence, as much as for his arm, Razaf had been sought out by the league's organizers. The young poet–songwriter was known in Cleveland: his Aunt Minnie Waller-French's in-laws were prominent members of the Cleveland African–American community.

However absurd and useless Razaf initially thought his baseball invitation, he now came to perceive it as liberating, moving him far from the frustrations of Tin Pan Alley, Broadway, and songwriting. In May 1920, he abandoned Florenz Ziegfeld's New Amsterdam Theatre elevators and told both his wife and his mother to start packing.

Andrea Razafkeriefo, star baseball pitcher, in uniform, July 13, 1919; Alaska Field, Staten Island, New York. *Courtesy Razaf Estate.*

Boun' for a
One-Horse Town

I'm laughin' at sorrow,
He's knockin' in vain,
I welcome tomorrow,
And smile at the rain . . .
I'm so happy,
I'll soon be boun'
For a one-horse town,
Where I'll settle down;
All fed up with your Broadway lights
And your city sights,
Tired of sleepless nights . . .

> — *"Baby Mine"*
>   by Andy Razaf and Eubie Blake

On May 27, 1920, a scrawled postcard note from a New York friend who signed himself simply "Gib" found Andrea Razafkeriefo at his new home in Cleveland, Ohio. "To 'Our Andy'—" the note began:

Andy the poet, Andy our friend,
We miss your trusty arm, your logical pen,
The team has been weakened,

There's no one to lead.
Our papers are dull,
There's no wit to read.
Your absence has taught us your value true,
There's none can replace you, what shall we do?
The butcher, the grocer, why, even my wife
Has missed the sunbeam gone out of our life.
We treasured your friendship,
Cheered by your jokes,
Why, I've no one to go to
Now when I'm broke.
Best regards to your wifie, mother, and you,
And remember there's something you always can do.
That is to write and let us all know
That you are progressing and saving
"Some dough."

Razaf's "escape" to Cleveland in the spring of 1920 was a far more traumatic move than the young lyricist was willing to admit to anyone, particularly himself. Inherent in his decision to abandon the city for a summer of ballplaying in Cleveland and a chance to save some money away from New York was a terrifying sense of surrendering his songwriting career, which he altogether refused to acknowledge, maintaining simply that Cleveland would allow him to live frugally. The aspirations, the ambition, the friendships, the home left behind in New York were for the moment suspended, as was the frightening possibility that none of it might ever be fully recovered.

Along Lake Erie, at the mouth of the Cuyahoga River, Cleveland was in 1920 an earnest, energetic young metropolis, still maturing into an industrial, financial, and manufacturing hub. A burst of growth over the last half of the preceding century had transformed it into the nation's sixth most populous city. A substantial, initially well-integrated black constituency grew steadily more segregated within its diverse cosmopolitan mix of more than 600,000 residents, at least a third of whom were foreign born. Nine different brands of motorcar were manufactured in Cleveland, soon to be the country's leading producer of automotive parts. The city was also proud possessor of a major league baseball franchise, the Indians, along with a number of Negro professional and semiprofessional ballteams that barnstormed the country for a pittance, while playing nevertheless a caliber of baseball quite the comparative equal of that played on the formally segregated major league circuit.

The closest that Razaf would come to either major league or Negro League professional baseball in Cleveland was League Park (Dunn Field, as it was briefly renamed in 1920), the Indians' steel and concrete home at the intersection of East 66th Street and Lexington Avenue—just a short trolley ride, or long walk, from the Razafs' new home at 2345 East 43rd Street. The brand of baseball that Razaf had come to play in Cleveland was definitely semiprofessional, more of a diversion than any sort of big-league dream. If Razaf entertained any hopes at all of playing baseball professionally, he kept them to himself. He seems to have been a pretty fair country pitcher who loved the game and was glad to play it regularly.

Little is known about the *organizational* specifics of black baseball —professional or semiprofessional—as the segregated sport was played in America before the major leagues were integrated in 1947. The Cleveland Semi-Pro City League apparently came into being during the early months of 1920 after a series of organizational meetings at the city's Keystone Athletic Club on East 40th Street, where, according to the *Cleveland Call*, speeches were delivered, "several interesting debates between members of the special committees were settled . . . and laws to govern the new organization were promulgated." This creation of an all-black semiprofessional baseball league encompassing teams not just in Cleveland but as far away as New York was not at all unusual: black communities throughout the North and South alike fielded semiprofessional baseball teams by the score throughout the Twenties.

What seems decidedly unique about the Cleveland Semi-Pro City League was the degree of planning and organization that went into its formation. The Keystone Athletic Club elected a full complement of officers, chose umpires, and formed a "Class D amateur league to be governed by the semi-pro officials," while all "Class A, B, and C ball teams" were "kindly requested to take notice and get in touch with the sporting editor" of the *Call* about scheduling. Of course, Andrea Razafkeriefo (as the *Cleveland Call* identified him), still residing in New York during the early months of 1920, "was out of the city," as the newspaper put it, during these intensive organizational meetings. In absentia, he was nevertheless nominated and confirmed as league secretary.

One point about the whole business of semiprofessional black baseball in this country during the Twenties and Thirties remains abundantly clear: there was absolutely no money in it. LeRoy "Satchel" Paige, legendary Hall of Fame pitching ace for numerous Negro League teams, put the whole period into bold economic perspective with his blunt recollection: "In semi-pro ball . . . I'd get a buck a game when enough fans came out so we made some money after paying expenses. When there wasn't enough money, they gave me a keg of lemonade." Not surprisingly, while pitching for the Naco Giants throughout that summer of 1920 in the Cleveland Semi-Pro City League, Andrea Razaf also worked as a porter for the Hill Pty. (*sic*) Company, at a salary of $115 per month. No doubt Annabelle Razaf brought home a paycheck of her own that summer. Jennie Razaf may have worked, too. The family did manage to save some money.

In the end, though, it was almost farcical for the former lyricist to maintain that his presence in Cleveland with wife and mother was purely a financial matter, or even a matter of family finance leavened with recreational opportunity. Cleveland, for Razaf in 1920, was primarily an escape from the hardship of failure in the songwriting business back in New York. Between pitching assignments he still quietly monitored developments in the music industry as best he could, listening to the new songs that made their way west from Tin Pan Alley. Anxiously, impatiently, he bided his time.

The marginally successful distraction from songwriting ambition that baseball in Cleveland afforded Razaf ended in September 1920, when the Naco Giants won the Cleveland Semi-Pro City League's first championship. In October, Razaf was laid off by the Hill Pty. Company. In November, in New York a small, relatively new entrant in the recording business, OKeh Records, released an adventurous new recording by a black vaudeville singer from Cincinnati named Mamie Smith. In Cleveland, Razaf bought the disc and listened to it. The title song was called "Crazy Blues."

Months earlier, Mamie Smith had quietly made history recording for OKeh the first music record ever by a black female singing artist in America—"That Thing Called Love," backed with "You Can't Keep a Good Man Down," two songs composed by her nominal manager, Perry Bradford, who had lobbied OKeh tenaciously for this breakthrough session. Though Mamie Smith's OKeh sponsors initially proved unwilling to promote their new artist in terms of her race, choosing simply to credit her in their list of new releases as "Mamie Smith, contralto," the pioneering record had sold sufficiently among blacks and whites both to bring Smith back to the OKeh studios in August 1920. "As I remember it," her pianist on the date, Willie "the Lion" Smith, would later write, "the day . . . we went to make the sides there was only Mamie, Ralph Peer, myself, and the band in the studio. We waxed two tunes, 'Crazy Blues' and 'It's Right Here for You.'

"I taught the bandsmen their parts from the piano sheet music given to me by Mamie Smith. All stood in front of a large megaphone-like horn and Mamie really let loose with her fine contralto voice. As I recall, we got twenty-five dollars apiece for the two sides, and we had to wait two months for our money."

Andrea Razaf no doubt knew Mamie Smith's work. The "raven-haired, heavy-hipped, heavy-voiced, dark brown beauty" (as various contemporaries described her) already had made quite an impression on local audiences at Harlem's Lincoln Theatre, singing Perry Bradford's "Harlem Blues" (the tune Smith later would retitle "Crazy Blues," for recording purposes) in a 1918 summer revue called *Made in Harlem.* She had also become something of a regular on the uptown cabaret circuit, prior to the Razaf family's departure from New York City. In his pointed reconnoitering of musical trends, songwriting vogues, performance innovations, and new singers—black or white—on the local city scene throughout the years preceding his Cleveland exile, Andrea Razaf could not have missed Mamie Smith.

"Crazy Blues" represented the formal recording debut of an increasingly popular African-American song form that was destined to transform Razaf's songwriting career forever. The blues had not so much evolved as they had sprung up pretty nearly full-blown in the early 1900s among blacks in the rural south, a product of the same musical cross-breeding that had given birth to all prior African-American folk song types. Where plantation songs traditionaly had been performed by small groups of slave musicians, though, and spirituals were vehicles for black chorus singing generally, blues were songs for the lone voice: simple, artlessly straightforward vocal expressions of deep feeling, complete in a single verse. The earliest blues composer–singers usually had been outcasts within the southern black community—itinerant laborers, street corner guitar players, prostitutes, saloon pianists—whose blue melodies often were original, but certainly did not have to be; identical blues tunes frequently were sung throughout the South under different titles, set to vastly different words. The lyric and melodic architecture of these blues was, in fact, elementally uniform, commencing as a repeated single line interjection, followed by a third line that reflected the first two in a release of the tension built by their repetition. With each of these lines lasting for a duration of four bars, the traditional blues fell unconventionally into a twelve-bar form angularly at odds with the standard eight- or sixteen-bar forms common to most American popular music. Blues songs further differed from the standard popular song scales in their habitual use of the "flatted seventh note," and in their affinity for the key of the subdominant. The resulting morose "slurring" effect within the music— identifiably African in origin— the sense of these "blue notes" registered as not quite major or minor, would come to be regarded as one of the blues's most decisive characteristics.

While the blues clearly were a musical response to trouble, pain, and sorrow, they were not fundamentally melancholic in mood. There was an exuberance to the best blues tunes, a fatalistic defiance of sadness that often tipped over into humor. This sense of "laughing to keep from crying" led early on to a good deal of confusion about the nature of the blues. As Abbe Niles observed in his 1949 introduction to *Blues: An Anthology*, "White commercial songwriters were quicker to notice and imitate the spirit of the blues than their musical form." This shallow perception, noted Niles, bred a "basic distinction" between authentic African-American blues and their white facsimiles, a subtle yet enormously revealing variance, since "in the Negro blues" it was "the gaiety that is feigned, while in the white, it is the grief."

The blues might have remained an obscure southern folk music in America, little more than what Niles described as "a mold filled, emptied, and replenished, a mold so easy to fill that little trouble was taken filling it," were it not for the efforts of one man, a southern black musician named Handy, who singlehandedly lifted the blues out of backwater folk informality and rendered the form presentable and comprehensible to the world.

Andrea Razaf would come to know William Christopher Handy quite well in years to come, as well perhaps as anyone ever could know the incongruously genteel, monumentally reserved, so-called "Father of the Blues." Born in Florence, Alabama, on November 16, 1873, the son and grandson of Methodist ministers, Handy was from the beginning an especially unlikely spokesman for this disreputable outcast music. Handy's pious family heritage lacked any semblance of a musical tradition; music was, in fact, regarded by the elder

Handys as something of an abomination. From childhood the young Handy had been fascinated, though, by the work songs of the laborers on locks of the Muscle Shoals Canal near his grandfather's farm. He also wound up receiving, despite family disapproval, an unusually strong rudimentary public school musical education that impelled him toward a career in music. Handy, for more than ten years beginning in 1893, professionally had made music as best he could, organizing a quartet that roamed the South, singing in churches and town squares, even on railroad trains, leading bands in Indiana and Kentucky, teaching music for two years at Alabama's A & M College and, for almost seven years, performing in minstrel show bands. Throughout this period of peripatetic apprenticeship, Handy, with his extraordinary ear, embraced his passion for local black folk music, often committing scraps of song to memory after a single hearing, or notating them formally for his own personal record.

In 1909 Handy was in Memphis, leading his own band on what was then a bustling local music scene, when he was engaged to compose a campaign theme for E. H. Crump, one of three candidates for mayor in Memphis that year. Reverting to a blues strain that he had long since filed away, the young bandleader produced "Mister Crump," a robust three-part blues song—twelve bars each for the first and third choruses, sixteen bars for the second—that took Memphis by storm, sweeping Crump into office and elevating W. C. Handy to a position of local musical celebrity.

Handy would struggle aggressively to capitalize on this popular campaign song in the years following the election, to no avail. "Mister Crump" was turned down by countless New York publishing firms, many of whom pointed out, with rank ignorance, that the tune was short four bars—while in Memphis, local music publishers made it clear that they could not and would not handle the work—however popular—of a black man. Not until 1912 did Handy see his "Mister Crump" published, through the efforts of two white men—L. Z. Phillips, a local department store music counter employee in Memphis, and Theron C. Bennet, a Denver music publisher to whom Handy sold his "Mister Crump" copyright in desperation that year, royalty-free, for $50. Bennet mounted an aggressive sales effort on the song's behalf, retitling it "The Memphis Blues" and promoting it into a rousing nationwide hit. Handy responded to this, his first and last entry-level music business miscalculation, by piecing together an elaborate new tango-inflected blues song, which he called "The St. Louis Blues," this time realizing enormous financial benefit from the song's nearly instantaneous popularity. Handy soon ambitiously formed a music publishing firm of his own in partnership with a black Memphis businessman named Harry Pace, a pioneering endeavor that thrived from its inception on a seemingly endless supply of newly adapted W. C. Handy blues compositions. By 1918, Pace & Handy Music Company had relocated in New York City, reigning over a burgeoning blues song market from a five-room office in the Gaiety Theatre Building at 1547 Broadway, near 46th Street.

Andrea Razaf quite likely first heard W. C. Handy's "Memphis Blues" sung by a black female vaudeville team known as the Blanks Sisters (Osceola and Berliana) in a cabaret on 105th Street. According to Handy, himself, this accomplished duo "finally put the new song over in New York" with their rendition of "Memphis Blues" at the unidentified 105th Street cabaret. Young Razaf's initial opinion of these new Handy blues could not have been especially high. Like many self-pronounced "upright" New Yorkers, including not surprisingly, a majority of black Harlemites at that time, Razaf seems at first to have disdained the blues as rude, "in-the-gutter" music. While Perry Bradford's *Made in Harlem* Lincoln Theatre revue in June 1918 certainly helped begin breaking down Harlem's early blues antipathy, it did not persuade Razaf that his songwriting future resided with the blues. Like so many Harlem songwriters and musicians of his day, Razaf was a child of city streets, long since distanced from any trace of southern roots, and indoctrinated in the music of Tin Pan Alley and Broadway. For these men, the prospect of blues songwriting was unpleasantly regressive, a descent to an illiterate, unkempt country music comprising all the stereotypes attached to their race since slave days.

The slow-blossoming blues vogue hardly had been enough to keep Razaf in New York after 1920, when his patience with the music business ran out. Like many others, including numerous recording-company executives, he had dismissed the growing public appetite for blues songs as inconsequential. The November 1920 release of Mamie Smith's "Crazy Blues"—the first blues recording ever by a black singer backed by black musicians and, as such, the first authentic black blues performance many white record buyers would hear—therefore stunned Razaf when, in its first month of circulation, "Crazy Blues" sold more than 100,000 copies. Suddenly, irrefutably, the blues' unsuspected appeal among white record-buying novitiates, together with the previously unexercised purchasing power of newly blues-loving black record buyers across the country, was exposed for everyone to see. In Harlem record shops alone, well over 75,000 copies of "Crazy Blues" were reportedly sold within weeks of the record's release, at first prompting OKeh executives to undertake a disbelieving investigation into their "Crazy Blues" sales figures, followed shortly after confirmation by a frantic call for Mamie Smith to return at once to OKeh's record studios and resume recording blues. By December, "Crazy Blues" had sold in excess of 1.5 million records.

The self-exiled and unemployed Andrea Razaf hungered to hear of Mamie Smith's landmark release and the record-buying frenzy it had started. For Razaf, the "Crazy Blues" phenomenon was ripe with promise for his own stalled songwriting career. Unlike ragtime, which fundamentally was instrumental music, the blues were a vocal innovation. Blues tunes were sung; blues tunes demanded lyrics. Moreover, unlike ragtime songs (the craze Razaf had caught too late), everyone now perceived blues tunes as the exclusive domain of black music makers.

The explosive impact of these "Crazy Blues" sales figures demolished Razaf's resolve to remain in Cleveland. Where the blues, as black music for black audiences exclusively, had seemed shabby and second rate to many northern blacks like Razaf, the sudden overwhelming appreciation of the blues evinced by white record buyers very much transformed the music into something uniquely black, "something of our own" that one could be proud of. In any event, whatever demeaning qualties Razaf had perceived in the blues suddenly seemed beside the point. This music now represented access to the white marketplace. The price of accommodation, for the moment at least, was not so very high.

By January of 1921 the Razafs were home in Harlem. It is illuminating, and touchingly amusing, to note that upon his return to New York, Razaf still remained so uncertain about his songwriting future that he clung to his baseball diversion reflexively. "After having a successful season last year with the Naco Giants, Colored champions of Cleveland," the *New York News* reported in April 1921, "A. Razafkeriefo, Harlem's popular poet and ball player, known on the diamond as Andy Razaf, has returned to the city, and with the assistance of J. Pinkney and E. Brown has organized a strong semi-pro ball club which will be known as the New York Black

Sox. 'Razaf' claims he has the fastest bunch of youngsters in town, who are going to make the 'old timers' sit up and take notice. The team is fully uniformed and is being booked."

The Razafs' new home on West 141st Street was a four-room apartment furnished with Annabelle Razaf's "nice things"—her rosewood chairs and oriental rugs, her rosewood baby grand piano. It was a new home also supported, as before, by Annabelle Razaf in service. She had not doubted her husband's announcement that the time for black songwriters had come, like Jubilee. Meekly she'd repacked their life in Cleveland, boarded the train with her mother-in-law, stepped off where she was told, unpacked, and resumed her position in Madame Eleanor Kent's household, while her Andrea went off in search of the new blues revolution.

"To render a 'Blues Song' effectively," wrote pianist Porter Grainger and arranger Bob Ricketts in their primer *How to Play and Sing the Blues Like the Phonograph and Stage Artists*, one of many blues instructional booklets hurried into print during the early Twenties, "it is necessary to possess a fair knowledge of the spirit and circumstances under which this type of publication was created. If one can temporarily play the role of the oppressed or the depressed, injecting into his or her rendition a spirit of hopeful prayer, the effect will be more natural and successful." Granger and Ricketts went on to enumerate the best employment of chords to produce "'Blues' effects," the best instruments for optimal "wail-ings, moanings, and croonings" (saxophone, trombone, or violin), even a monumental list of breaks to be used in ending a blues performance convincingly: "The Harmony Break," "The Jazz Blues Break," "The Stop Blues Break," "The Levee Blues Break," "The Cabaret Blues Break," "The Gulf Blues Break," "The New Orleans Blues Break," "The Barrel House Blues Break," The Freight Train Blues Break," and "The Lullaby Blues Break."

What often was neglected in any of these early-Twenties blues crash courses was the essential role of the word in authentic blues expression. As one of Razaf's lyric-writing forebears now the elder statesman of black letters, James Weldon Johnson, would soon point out in an essay on the subject, "The original folk blues . . . interesting as they are musically, are still more interesting as verse." With origins rooted in the poetic voice of Scripture, the blues, lyrically, were folk poetry of a singular bipolarity—often religious in tone yet supremely secular in subject and spirit. Thus, to master the art of blues lyric writing was to master an often contradictory, endlessly variable art of terse simplicity, earthy wisdom, colorful, slangy phraseology, and implied, often suggestive double-edged meaning—all expressed with seeming effortlessness.

This mastery was quite a mouthful for any northern songwriter to tackle. For Andrea Razaf it did not come easily. With the proliferation of blues recordings throughout 1921, he was at least able to isolate the music and study the construction of blues songs closely. A more stimulating classroom, though, was the concentration of neighborhood Harlem cabarets in the blocks between Fifth and Seventh Avenues in and around 135th Street, where the house-piano players very recently had been supplemented by new blues singers in residence.

John W. Connor's Royal Cafe at 69 West 135th Street, between Lenox and Fifth Avenues, was one of the oldest "mixed" nightspots in the city, having carried its white trade with it after relocating to Harlem in 1914 from the downtown precincts of the teeming westside entertainment district known as the Tenderloin. Ed Smalls's Sugar Cane Club on Fifth Avenue was a particularly popular spot with local black patrons. William "Kid" Banks's place at 29 West 133rd Street, between Lenox and Fifth, was another long-term Tenderloin transplant, having moved from 37th Street near Seventh Avenue in 1917, along with Barron D. Wilkins's Astoria Cafe (2275 Seventh Avenue at 134th Street), perhaps the smartest of all black nightspots, with roots going back to Wilkins's Little Savoy Club on 35th Street near Eighth Avenue. Prior to his Harlem resettlement in 1915, Barron Wilkins had catered almost exclusively to a very high-toned white clientele, admitting only the lightest-skinned black patrons—a policy that he largely perpetuated uptown, unlike his older brother, Leroy Wilkins, whose cafe in a basement at 2202 Fifth Avenue on the northeast corner of 135th Street was home to black prize-fighters, black "sports," and "swells" from the black show world. Leroy's was the oldest cabaret in Harlem, opened in 1910 by its nonsmoking, nondrinking 250-pound proprietor, who insisted on formal dress in his establishment, loved good piano players, and opposed the mixing of races in nightclubs on the grounds that it was "tindery."

Beneath these stalwarts of the Harlem cabaret industry were any number of smaller, seedier establishments, popularly known as "buckets of blood," where the music was raunchier, the blues singing often far more authentic, and the surroundings eminently more intimidating—places like ex–prize-fighter Edmond Johnson's

Cellar Cafe on the Fifth Avenue corner of 132nd Street. Andrea Razaf frequented them all.

The blues sensibility that Razaf now encountered in his nightly circumnavigation of the Harlem cabaret scene was a vast change from the musical culture he had left behind just the year before. Black Harlem's musical taste immediately after the war still had been dominated by the "society orchestra" sounds of James Reese Europe's Clef Club, a musicians' union of sorts, organized by the enterprising and exceedingly talented black bandleader to stimulate (and ultimately to regulate) demand for legitimate syncopated black orchestras in the city's white restaurants and cabarets, and at white society functions. Europe's Clef Club musicians were without a doubt Manhattan's finest black players—including, at various times, pianist Eubie Blake; future orchestra leader–arrangers Ford Dabney, Tim Brymn, Will Marion Cook, and Will Vodery; composer James Rosamond Johnson; and even W. C. Handy. The music they played, while quite tame by the standards of black band music to come, nevertheless was strongly syncopated, elaborately scored for ensembles often numbering upward of 50 pieces, and enormously appealing to black and white audiences alike.

Europe's career had been given a boost in 1914 beyond the racial boundaries of Harlem with his introduction to the young white dance team of Vernon and Irene Castle, who soon engaged Europe as their musical director. Fronting his orchestra for the Castles' hugely popular dance demonstrations had brought James Europe international renown. That reputation was further burnished by his service during the war as General John J. Pershing's personal bandsman, leading his "Hellfighter" regimental military band in concerts all across the continent to thunderous acclaim. James Reese Europe's influence over black popular music surely would have extended into the 1920s had he not been tragically murdered back-stage by one of his musicians before a performance in Boston in May 1919. As it was, James Europe's presence in Harlem was so pervasive that throughout the year following his death, the year preceding Andrea Razaf's 1920 exit from New York City, a Clef Club–style orchestra, configured in typical Clef Club fashion for cornet, guitar, piano, two drummers, and seven mandolins, had remained in residence at J. W. Connor's Royal Cafe. By the time of Andrea Razaf's return to Harlem, though, the musical legacy of the James Europe sound was already a quaint and endangered species hurrying toward extinction behind the ascendant popularity of the blues.

Yet another musical fashion was gaining currency across Manhattan in 1921, just as the Razafs were returning to the city. Its pedigree was obscure and chaotic, its constitution, musically, was open to question and widely misconstrued. Yet its appeal, even at this embryonic stage, already was unmistakable.

The first so-called jazz bands to reach New York City had arrived before the war as vaudeville attractions. Vaudeville was the great indirect disseminator of this new music out of New Orleans; as jazz musicians from that city came and went with vaudeville troupes throughout the latter 1910s, individually in pit bands and collectively as featured onstage acts, audiences around the country slowly came to be introduced to "jazz," or "jass" music, as some called it. The first New Orleans jazz band to play a New York theater appears to have been a six-piece all-black ensemble led by the great New Orleans cornetist Freddie Keppard. Billed as "That Creole Band" in the Ned Wayburn–produced Broadway revue *Town Topics* at the Winter Garden Theatre in 1915, Keppard's musicians presented themselves strictly as vaudevillians, performing their oddly arhythmic, noisy new music largely for laughs. That is how jazz bands would be viewed by most audiences, at least outside New Orleans, throughout the infancy of jazz in America—as comic vaudeville curiosities almost exclusively.

It has never been possible to set down the history of jazz with anything approaching authoritative finality. The variegated steps of the music's evolution were so subtle, so brilliantly spontaneous, that they largely managed to evade even the microscope of history. That jazz was "invented" in New Orleans seems now the consensus among contemporary jazz historians; the turn-of-the-century transmutation of "pure" ragtime into jazz apparently did take place specifically in New Orleans—and not simultaneously in various locations throughout the country, as certain jazz scholars have argued.

What remains essential to any understanding of this ragtime-to-jazz transformation, though, is the singular factor of rhythm as it affected the birth of jazz. On the African continent, a shared appreciation of—even veneration for—the complexities of rhythm had always united otherwise vastly diverse tribal populations (specifically, the expressive musical tension imparted by different rhythms, different "beats," played simultaneously in patterns that at times locked them together and at other times allowed them to unlock and drift apart in complementary syncopation). The tribal musical memory that helped shape African–American music in slavery was fundamentally this transported African fascination with polyrhythm and syncopation: whatever native European music the African slave encountered in America—church hymns, secular dance music, military marches, even classical and operatic compositions—all were filtered through slavery's preserved African rhythmic sense, with the European melodic lines invariably set against a steady "ground beat" by the slave imitator and then sprung free to roam widely against that beat, according to the locking-and-unlocking rhythmic musical essence of tribal Africa. Ragtime, in its syncopated European classicism, was a more stylized byproduct of this interplay, as were, to a far less formal degree, slavery's plantation songs, field hollers, work songs, and spirituals.

Most ragtime music was composed at a march time, 2/4 beat. What seems to have occurred in New Orleans at some time during the height of the ragtime craze was the discovery that a 4/4 ground beat set against a 2/4 ragtime beat lent ragtime music a more propulsive, fluid rhythmic power. No pioneering single figure emerges as the originator of this revolution in "jazz time," though the New Orleans piano giant Jelly Roll Morton did lay claim hyperbolically to the invention of 4/4 jazz time and hence to jazz itself. No precise date can be attached to this development either, though the shift certainly seems to have occurred early in the new century.

All that remains is the turnabout—remarked upon by listeners—in the ragtime playing of New Orleans musicians during this period, and the inevitable question; "Why New Orleans?" The answer resides within multiple aspects of New Orleans's utterly distinctive metropolitan character: in the city's longstanding libertinism, for one thing, particularly in New Orleans's thriving, legalized red light district known as Storyville, where prostitution was permitted, though policed, and musicians black and white found ample opportunity for work in the district's bustling saloons, dance halls, and brothels. The vibrant musical street life of the city was another major factor in the New Orleans birth of jazz, the ubiquitous street parades that marked secular celebrations and religious holidays. Even funerals in New Orleans were frequently escorted by local brass bands: cornet-clarinet-trombone-led marching ensembles that handled ragtime's march rhythms with an incipiently revolutionary loose-limbed strut. Most significant, though, may have been the unparalleled mixture of races within New Orleans society, a consequence of the city's status as the ranking seaport of the American South, and

New Orleans' multicultural origins as a colonistic possession of both France and Spain.

The blending of races in New Orleans was more exotically pronounced than perhaps anywhere else in America—an intermingling of Africans, West Indians, French, Spanish, English, and native North Americans in a festival of miscegenation that produced a riot of racially intermingled splinter groups within the city's traditional minority communities. Of particular significance to the evolution of jazz in New Orleans were the black Creoles—the racial byproduct of repeated assignations that were nearly an institution throughout New Orleans history between upper-class white men and mulatto women of mixed French-Caribbean ancestry.

The black Creoles of New Orleans were an especially savory combination of Afro-Caribbean traditions and white aristocratic pretensions. By the late nineteenth century, many were often the illegitimate offspring of New Orleans' finest white families, and their orientation was decidedly upper-class European. The imposition of "black codes" in New Orleans in 1894, however, relegated the Creole population to a second-class status commensurate with the city's black laborer classes, from whom the Creoles had long striven to distinguish themselves. The intermingling of upper and lower, Creole and common, black classes in New Orleans by the early 1900s seems to have been quite pronounced, at least among the city's younger generation. In this downward mobility, Creole musicians were forced to embrace Storyville's music of choice—ragtime —in order to secure work within New Orleans's Storyville music axis, something they apparently managed with exceptional adaptability, bringing to Storyville's crude "rags" a new level of formal musicianship bred in the European school. Did these Creole musicians initiate the 4/4 jazz ground beat within ragtime's 2/4 meter? Possibly. Black Creole musicians did possess a familiarity with European dance styles that might have led them toward a fresh rhythmic approach to ragtime meter. They also were better musicians technically than their generally self-taught black peers and thus were perhaps more capable of experimenting with tempos. It seems also quite likely that in educating themselves from scratch regarding ragtime music these black Creole players may have filled out their limited knowledge of the form by improvising, advancing upon the rudimentary explorations into ragtime-based improvisation already essayed by New Orleans ragtime/jazz pioneers like the celebrated Buddy Bolden. However one accounts for it, the New

Orleans sound that locals soon would refer to as "jazzed up" certainly took a monumental evolutionary turn after the influx of young black Creole musicians during the early years of the twentieth century.

A critical turning point for this peculiar New Orleans music was reached in 1917, with the New York City debut of the Original Dixie Land Jass Band, a white New Orleans ensemble, at a small restaurant known as Reisenweber's on the southwest corner of 58th Street, off Columbus Circle. Their initial reception at this establishment (one of five in a New York chain of Reisenweber restaurants) was not much more than mild, at best. Broadway's amusement hub was some blocks to the south, and the group received scant advertising support early on. The Original Dixie Land Jass Band nevertheless did manage, with time, to attract a following at Reisenweber's and linger there for a while. The Columbia Phonograph Company was sufficiently impressed to bring the band into a recording studio in December 1917. With exclusive contracts still comparatively rare in these early years of recorded sound, the Victor Talking Machine Company followed Columbia's Original Dixieland Jass Band session with one of their own in February 1918, to be followed in turn by the Aeolian Company, who recorded the New Orleans group in July of that year. The first Original Dixieland Jass Band recording issued on Columbia —"Darktown Strutter's Ball," backed with "Indiana"—sold rather well, surprisingly. The second, issued on Victor—"Livery Stable Blues" backed with "Original Dixieland One-Step"—was a sensation. In the first year of release, over a million copies of the Original Dixieland Jass Band's "Livery Stable Blues" were sold, though the phenomenon largely was stoked by a philistine ignorance among record buyers who considered the song, with its instrumental breaks imitative of barnyard sounds, a hilarious novelty. The record nevertheless triggered a nationwide fascination with jazz, however ill informed, that soon would lead to a decade-long mania.

The music produced and promoted around the country as "jazz" in the wake of these recordings bore scant resemblance to the richly nuanced, ragtime-derived music that New Orleans had invented. Jazz, during these formative years across America, was played almost exclusively for whimsical effect by bands that reveled in a tediously forced, jazzy jocularity. New York City boasted its own laughing coterie of white Original Dixieland Jass Band imitators, groups like the Lopez-Hamilton Kings of Harmony, the Earl Fuller Band at Rector's Restaurant on Broadway and—at the Alamo Cafe on 125th

Street, in what was then still "white Harlem" Jimmy Durante's New Orleans Jazz Band, a group that did actually employ four imported New Orleans musicians—three whites and one light-skinned black passing for white—to back up the young Durante's shenanigans. Local black music men attempting to play jazz in New York City at this time were only moderately more earnest in their approach. Even capable black musicians like Wilbur Sweatman, New York City's closest thing to a resident black jazzman in 1920, still affected a certain hamfistedness rhythmically in their efforts to replicate that elusive New Orleans jazz creation.

It is likely that Andrea Razaf on occasion heard the touring black vaudeville jazzmen out of New Orleans in the years prior to his departure from the city. It is also possible that the generally conservative songwriter regarded their music negatively, perhaps sharing the opinion expressed by one local critic in his April 1917 review of That Creole Band in performance at Manhattan's Loew's Orpheum Theatre that jazz was "merely a noise that some persons called 'music.'" It is obvious that Razaf did at least listen to the hugely popular Original Dixieland Jass Band recording of "Livery Stable Blues" since he attempted his own knock-off of the tune's rustic barnyard theme with his "Andrea Razz" song "The Farmyard Jazz," copyrighted in February 1920.

New York City's accelerating (if generally misdirected) fondness for jazz hardly had proved any more sufficient, though, than the increasing popularity of the blues to keep Razaf around town in 1920. Desperate as he was to advance in the song business, he nevertheless had perceived jazz to be at best an exciting new instrumental music and at worst yet another white entertainment novelty expropriated at the expense of its black originators. Either way, Razaf had decided that neither the blues nor jazz could offer a young black lyricist very much in the way of new opportunity at that time. His return to New York from Cleveland in January, 1921 profoundly signified how swiftly events had changed that perception for him.

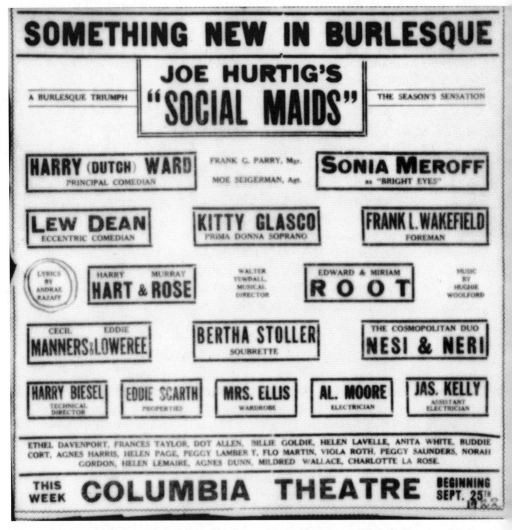

Handbill for *Joe Hurtig's "Social Maids"* with Razaf's name at the far left, midpage: "Lyrics by Andrae Razaff." *Courtesy Razaf Estate.*

5

Hotcha Razz–Ma–Tazz

Do not be among the late ones,
Change your dancin' ways,
Keep with the up-to-date ones,
Learn that brand new craze . . .
Hotcha Razz-Ma-Tazz!

— *"Hotcha Razz-Ma-Tazz"*
by Andy Razaf and Irving Mills

Andrea Razaf had not yet left New York City for Cleveland when the Volstead Act formally went into effect across America on the night of January 16, 1920. Enacted as legislative reinforcement for an eighteenth amendment to the United States Constitution, which on paper had already prohibited the manufacture, sale, and transportation of intoxicating beverages throughout the United States, but in practice had not managed to do so, the Volstead Act rendered illegal the selling or transporting of *any* liquid with an alcohol content of more than .5 percent. No one connected with the entertainment business in the city—least of all Andrea Razaf—could have known that night how this law would transform the essence of public entertainment in New York. It would do so dramatically not only for the duration of the Twenties but in various ways for decades to come.

There was of course dejection and chaos among the legal hostelries across Manhattan forced by the new activist legislation to shut down either their liquor trade or their businesses. Many did close, in the early months of 1920, with only about two dozen of the city's better-known nightspots remaining open at the time of Razaf's departure for Cleveland—the survivors including Shanley's on Broadway and Reisenweber's at Columbus Circle. Even in these long-time entertainment landmarks, however, business during the months of Razaf's Ohio exile soon fell off to desperate levels, as the initial shock of Prohibition drove New York nightlife regulars to their homes or private clubs.

As Razaf was returning to New York in January of 1921, Manhattan's beleaguered legitimate nightspots were finding themselves increasingly superseded by large numbers of illegal speakeasies, and by elegant but only marginally legal nightclubs. The speakeasies often featured small jazz-flavored combos as accompaniment to their liquor service, while the nightclubs—replete with hefty cover charges, intimate or elaborate floor shows, prancing chorus girls, and watered-down bootleg whiskey—also offered jazz as their entertainment focal point. Within a year of his return over 5,000 speakeasies were operating in Manhattan—over 1,000 in the area between Fifth and Ninth Avenues from 38th to 59th Streets alone. Nightclub income rapidly grew to such levels that at least one establishment would soon publicly acknowledge a stunning 1922 operating profit of $2,500 a week from the champagne that it bought at $80 a case and sold for $20 a quart; the Scotch whiskey, bought for $50 a case, that it dispensed at $20 a quart; the 12-cent bottles of mineral water served up at $1.50 a bottle; and the cocktails, poured for $1 apiece, at a cost of 11 cents each.

There was something about the liberated raucousness of jazz music, combined with the uninhibited lustiness of the blues, that made both seem deliciously appropriate background music for the sudden illegality of alcohol consumption. The source of this appeal was quite elemental: jazz and blues already were regarded by whites and blacks *both*—for better or worse—as raw expressions of the essential African–American soul. With so many Americans, particularly New Yorkers, embracing the imposition of Prohibition as an invitation to misbehave, African Americans quickly came to be perceived, along with their music, as paradigms of the new decade's glorified hedonism.

Andrea Razaf eagerly noted this attraction of jazz music to nightclubs across the city as sudden evidence of a potentially lucrative future for him. Perhaps even more promising, though, were the extraordinary rumors circulating throughout the Harlem theatrical and songwriting fraternities that drew both his attention and that of his peers toward Broadway. It had been nearly thirteen years since a musical production created and performed by black men and women had been presented on a Broadway stage. In fact, often just to visit a Broadway theater was an occasion burdened with humiliation and discomfort. Unspoken policies of de facto segregation ruled Broadway's box offices, and exclusive balcony seatings replete with ill-treatment at the hands of ill-tempered ushers kept black theater-goers, for the most part, uptown. But now, four black vaudevillians (pianist–composer Eubie Blake, and his lyricist, singer Noble Sissle, together with comedic song-and-dance men–libretticists Flournoy Miller and Aubrey Lyles) had "pooled their meager resources" and were striving to write, direct, manage, and star in their own Broadway-bound musical show. An open casting call already had drawn a dazzling array of hungry black theatrical talent: cabaret entertainers from San Francisco, New Orleans, and Memphis; terrific young performers off the vaudeville stages of Harlem's Lincoln and Lafayette Theatres; musical-comedy veterans from the former Pekin Stock Company, a Chicago-based all-black troupe that had specialized throughout the previous decade in musicals as well as saccharine comedies.

A partially completed Sissle/Blake musical score, auditioned for the once-notable theatrical producer John Cort, had impressed Cort sufficiently to extract a modest preliminary investment from the impresario together with some used costumes from two previous John Cort flops. Word had it that this new all-black production now teetered on the brink of bankruptcy while enduring a brutal Cort-sponsored out-of-town trial run—three weeks of one-nighters, touring rural Pennsylvania's more pathetic barns and small-time theaters. Word also had it that the show, despite its troubles, was exceptionally good. In May the company crawled back into New York on an $18,000 deficit, and took up residence at the 63rd Street Theatre, the only theater Cort could offer his ragtag troupe—a decrepit old lecture hall lacking any proper theatrical amenities.

Workmen were still trying to build a proper proscenium and hammer some marginal stage depth out of the old auditorium's cramped dimensions on the evening of May 22, a Sunday, when Broadway songwriters and performers attended a special invitational preview of the show. Their response, notwithstanding the rough conditions, was highly encouraging. The following night, Sissle and Blake and Miller and Lyles's *Shuffle Along* officially opened on Broadway. "It was really off-Broadway," Blake would later point out, "but we caused it to be Broadway. . . . It was the price of the ticket that mattered. Our tickets cost the same as any Broadway show. That made it Broadway!"

Early reviews were generally positive—approving if muted in their enthusiasm, respectful of the show for having pioneered something to do with jazz but confused in the main as to what that achievement was. The majority of first-string critics in fact passed up *Shuffle Along*'s opening night, and their follow-up coverage was agonizingly slow incoming. As the late reviews, many of them strongly favorable, began to appear, though, abetted by effusive praise from audiences attending the show, word began to spread that *Shuffle Along* was, in fact, unlike anything before seen on a Broadway stage. It was a show of irresistibly syncopated black music, torrid black dance, and flamboyant black style. "No musical show in town boasts such rousing and hilarious teamwork," insisted critic Heywood Broun in the *New York World*, while Alan Dale of the *New York American* lauded the production as "an infection of amusement impossible to resist." *Shuffle Along*, in short, was a hit.

From its frantic pace to its jazzy melodies, from its sassy chorus girls with their bobbed haircuts to its essence as an expression of contemporary black culture cleverly tailored for white Broadway consumption, what Alan Dale crudely described as "a semi-darky show that emulates the "white performance"—and goes it one better," *Shuffle Along* theatrically ushered in the Roaring Twenties on Broadway. Here was a show that, in its incorporation of black dance, black music, and black performance style, was destined to provide American musical theater with many of its most familiar twentieth-century conventions. More immediately, *Shuffle Along*'s unprecedented acceptance downtown by white audiences decisively certified the new decade's growing infatuation with the Negro. As Eubie Blake later remarked, "Society people felt that their guest tours were incomplete unless they brought their friends to *Shuffle Along*." A midnight matinee—an innovation adapted from the custom in segregated black southern theaters of performing a midnight show for whites only—was soon introduced on Wednesday nights to allow working Broadway show people their own opportunity to see *Shuffle Along*. White theatrical celebrities soon packed the 63rd Street Theatre. "Then Negroes came to see the celebrities," recalled Flournoy Miller. "[Mayor] LaGuardia came three nights one week," added Blake. "The traffic commissioner finally had to make 63rd a one-way street."

It was inevitable that someone would open a white nightclub in Harlem in the wake of *Shuffle Along*'s enormous downtown success. With the initial impact of Prohibition largely absorbed uptown on a small-time neighborhood level by countless storefront "hootch parlors" along Lenox Avenue, in neighborhood "liquor flats" along the side streets above and below 135th Street, and of course in the better-established local cabarets and saloons, the opening of the Shuffle Inn on Seventh Avenue between 131st and 132nd Streets, in the basement of the Lafayette Theatre building on the evening of November 19, 1921, immediately was interpreted by many black Harlem residents as a Prohibition-generated enterprise of a singularly intrusive nature. "Grand Opening: Harlem's Latest Amusement Resort—with a Girlie Revue Deluxe," the Shuffle Inn had advertised rather ominously in the *New York Age* during the weeks preceding its official uptown debut, alerting all of Harlem to the unmistakably boorish intentions of the Shuffle Inn's alien white owners from downtown. Within the year, the community's worst suspicions would be confirmed.

"Complaints are being heard concerning the operation of Shuffle Inn," the *Age* reported in October 1922:

> The place was closed down for some time following a raid by officers, but it is alleged that new proprietors have taken hold of the place and that it has become a nuisance. One report is to the effect that scores of young white girls from other sections of the city frequent the place and that it is the headquarters for gangs of white gunmen and hoodlums from downtown who are driven to seek new hangouts by reason of the restrictive measures put in force with regard to closing hours.
>
> Police orders have been issued to the effect that all cabarets must close their doors at one o'clock A.M. and officers are required to see that the orders are obeyed.
>
> Another cafe in the same section as Shuffle Inn, on Seventh

Avenue just below 131st Street, is alleged to cater to women, females being allowed to enter even by the front door. In regard to this place, the report is that when these women customers become too much under the influence of the hooch they are unceremoniously removed from the place, being thrown out a door opening into another hallway.

It is alleged that these conditions are so open and unbridled that it would be impossible for policemen not to be aware of them, and that it would be easy to suppress them if proper action was taken by officers.

In one sense, the Shuffle Inn's mere proximity to the cherished Lafayette Theatre was enough to incense Harlem's black community. The Inn's entrance stood very nearly opposite the Harlem theatrical community's touchstone "Tree of Hope," an aging elm off the uptown lane of Seventh Avenue that many Harlem showfolk treated as an unofficial labor-exchange site and rubbed nearly raw for luck as a sheltering talisman on their way to auditions, in the shadow of the looming Lafayette Theatre. (This "Tree of Hope's" talismanic presence is still invoked at the Apollo Theater today with a simulated tree stump set near the stage). Moreover, the Lafayette's often-tortured early history was in many ways regarded by black Harlemites as a mirror for their own historical evolution uptown, and the theater's presence in the community was closely monitored. The 1,500-seat auditorium had opened in November 1912, with a variety bill of white acts and a strictly segregated seating policy—whites in the orchestra, "colored" in the balcony. The Lafayette's white owners immediately had come under intense fire from the growing number of black residents uptown, many of whom proceeded to file discrimination suits within months of the opening. In time, the courts had ordered them to suspend their discriminatory seating arrangements, and the newly empowered black Lafayette audiences soon demanded black musicians for the Lafayette pit and black performers on the Lafayette stage. In 1913, an orchestra of African Americans led by William Tyler was installed as the Lafayette house band. With black entertainers soon regularly topping Lafayette bills, the theater's future was thereafter entwined inextricably with the life of Harlem's African–American community.

On a far deeper level, though, than Lafayette Theatre history, Harlem's native black community was confronting a monumental violation of its borders in the Seventh Avenue presence of the Shuffle Inn. The delicate proprieties of a community essentially conceived in turn-of-the-century sobriety were about to be inundated by an onslaught of the "modern," as the Twenties construed it, and Harlem's black community leaders at first seemed to apprehend that fact most concretely in terms of the Shuffle Inn. Already the sheer number of liquor purveyors in business along Harlem streets by the beginning of 1922 was disturbing, but even this, these leaders sensed, was not the sum of Harlem's Prohibition-generated difficulties. Sizable numbers of white *Shuffle Along* theatergoers, newly weaned from musical respectability by their first blues recordings and reeling from their recent introduction to bootleg whiskey, were exiting John Cort's 63rd Street Theatre altogether smitten with *Shuffle Along*'s jazzy, syncopated score and cavorting black chorus line, and heading right for Harlem in search of the high spirits and abandon that *Shuffle Along* seemed to promise them. These white "slummers" turning up after hours at back tables in Harlem cafes represented an even more complex problem.

"White people are taking a morbid interest in the nightlife of [Harlem]," the *New York Age* observed anxiously, as more and more uptown club bosses began encouraging their employees to show the visitors from downtown what they had come to see: grinning black waiters prancing with trays full of glasses; torrid black blues singers belting ever bawdier blues. Other clubowners, gamely trying to ignore the outsiders in their midst, helplessly watched their black regulars slip away to places as yet undiscovered by wide-eyed whites.

The looming danger for black Harlem in these nightly white uptown incursions, though as yet shadowed, was increasingly plain. The menacing forces behind Prohibitions's illicit new bootleg economy had begun to note the growing numbers of white visitors to Harlem and the increasing amounts of money that they were spending there. The opening of clubs like The Shuffle Inn was a harbinger signaling to some in Harlem the impending appropriation of their uptown neighborhood's very soul by white gangster speculators from downtown.

Andrea Razaf's reaction to all of this ominous late-night neighborhood activity was more akin to that of the average Harlem resident than to the dire warnings raised by the district's more alarmist forecasters. Certainly he was perceptive enough to sense what was happening in Harlem. Regarding the gangsters, however, as a force beyond his control, he preferred to view their looming presence practically reasoning that anything that brought white money uptown to Harlem was good for Harlem in the end, and anything that brought white audiences to Harlem for entertainment was especially good for him. He was 26 now, and eager to embrace at last his future as a songwriter.

"Andy would bring his songs down to the clubs," recalled Albertine "Silvertop" Glenn, a former uptown showgirl and alter ego to Ada "Bricktop" Smith (a transplanted former Harlem nightclub chorine) the celebrated mistress of Parisian nightclub society in the late Twenties. "All the songwriters brought their songs around uptown to get them played; he was no different. Sure he sold 'em; he had a beautiful voice and he sold his work with it. I never saw him with anybody when he came down—always alone. Didn't make no difference when he came down, though, whether it was ten or eleven or twelve or one o'clock—the musicians were always glad to see him."

Edna Brown Hunter, Annabelle Razaf's niece (daughter of Florence Miller, Annabelle's younger sister), was 18 when the Razafs returned to New York. She remembered the 141st Street apartment as "relaxed in atmosphere . . . a pleasant place, I don't think of it as loud, the music was not constant. It came in patches and then there'd be conversation, more playing again—very pleasant. Annabelle, when she was around, served them, cleaned up. Very quiet."

For Razaf, life soon became a renewed frenzy of songwriting activity. He revived his old demoralizing daytime routine of song salesmanship: first the late-morning subway downtown, alone or with other aspiring black songmen; then the door-to-door trek up and down Tin Pan Alley stairwells; interminable hours spent waiting in small outer offices; song demonstrations on scarred, lidless pianos —all of this leading to many rude rejections and, on occasion, an insultingly paltry offer.

Tin Pan Alley, in his absence, had continued its post war creep uptown from 28th Street, settling in and around Times Square during the early Twenties. New surroundings, of course, hardly altered Tin Pan Alley's fundamental business dynamic. White songwriters continued to be exploited, assembly-line style, by a cartel of music-publishing powers. Black songwriters continued to be similarly abused but with even less courtesy. For them, though, there was now the option of Pace & Handy Music, along with two other black-owned music-publishing enterprises—Bert Williams & William Vodery Publishers and Perry Bradford Music Publishing

Company—all three occupying offices in the Gaiety Theatre Building on Broadway near 46th Street. Razaf and his Harlem song peers now referred to the building as "Uncle Tom's Cabin."

Late afternoons, Razaf wrote at home. "He would lay a pillow beneath the piano pedals," remembered Edna Hunter. "He worried that they shouldn't disturb the neighbors. So many people took time at that piano. Andy would pace with a pad, scribbling—his 'little ditties,' he called them. Sometimes he'd stop and ask to hear something again—just like in the movies—I loved to watch. 'What was that again?' he'd ask, and they'd play it back. 'Yeah,' he'd say, 'try this,' and he'd sing something. Sometimes he'd reach right over the fellow's back and do the chords himself. 'How's that?' he'd say.

"If he so much as mentioned it," Edna Hunter insisted, "the money was in an envelope on his plate at breakfast the next morning. Annabelle gave him the money to go downtown, to pay publishing fees, to eat, to go out. She was too kind-hearted, she couldn't say no. She never went out with him to the clubs. She rarely went out at all, actually."

It was after dark that Andrea Razaf explored the heights and depths of his own potential transformation amidst the growing transformation of Harlem itself. Along brownstone-lined West 133rd Street between Fifth and Seventh Avenues, where there were now a number of new basement cafes, he plunged nightly into the strip that many already called Jungle Alley. Up and down Seventh Avenue, in the blocks north and south of the Lafayette Theatre and on Fifth and Lenox Avenues in the vicinity of 135th Street, he wandered and loitered—chatting, listening, sometimes singing but, rarely drinking (he did not hold his alcohol well, and knew it), seeking out potential collaborators—or seducing pretty women, and being seduced in turn.

"He was discovering wonderful, wicked Harlem," Edna Brown Hunter later remarked. "He was learning the morality of show people. It was a gradual transformation, first one night a week not returning home, then two. I would meet him on the street now with a strange young woman and he would run away from me with no greeting. With Annabelle, of course, there were no recriminations, no reproachments . . . she was not a person to speak her feelings. She kept everything inside. She was a religious woman, a devoted woman, and a simple, silent person. She had no place in what was coming to Harlem, no place in the life which he wanted there."

*

On the evening of October 17, 1921, *Shuffle Along* celebrated its impending 175th Broadway performance with a midnight appearance by the entire company at the Lafayette Theatre in a benefit for the NAACP. The result was pandemonium. "The Harlem house was packed inside and out," the *New York Age* reported, "every seat having been sold long before the hour for opening. . . . At midnight the theatre lobby was jammed with folks who were unavailingly seeking admittance, the crowd extending to the street and crowding the pavement from 131st to 132nd Streets. So great was the crush of would-be entrants that a glass in one of the lobby doors was smashed."

Consumed as Razaf was with exploiting Harlem's increasing nightclub bustle, he also intently pursued the intensifying black theatrical presence downtown. Some three months after *Shuffle Along*'s arrival on Broadway, a second all-black musical comedy, *Put and Take*, opened at the Town Hall theater, on 43rd Street just west of Sixth Avenue—much closer to the traditional Broadway theatrical zone than *Shuffle Along*'s 63rd Street home, though Town Hall hardly could be classified a first-tier Broadway house. In preparation for more than a year, *Put and Take* (produced by the owner of the Shuffle Inn, Jack Goldberg) was not in fact the hasty *Shuffle Along* spinoff that some observers considered it to be. With music by Perry Bradford, Tim Brymn, and Spencer Williams, and a book (such as it was) by Flournoy Miller's brother, Irvin C. Miller, *Put and Take* announced itself as an urbane, contemporary Broadway revue, discarding the southern plantation slant and general minstrel orientation of *Shuffle Along*. For this forward-thinking approach, *Put and Take* paid a steep price at the hands of narrow-minded New York drama critics.

"There is [in *Put and Take*] too much effort to be dressed up and dignified," *Variety* reviewer Jack Lait complained, for example. "Colored performers cannot vie with white ones, and colored producers cannot play within an apple's throw of Ziegfeld and try to compete with him. . . . And here the colored folks seemed to have set out to show the whites they're just as good as anybody. They may be as good, but they're different and, in their entertainment, at any rate, they should remain different, distinct, and indigenous. . . . A quartet hacked away in dress suits when it should have been in plantation jumpers. The girls' wardrobe ran to tawdry gowns when they should have been fancifully dressed as picks [pickaninnies], Zulus, cannibals, and cotton pickers."

Put and Take closed after a short run under highly questionable circumstances. Anonymous members of the committee charged with operating the Town Hall on behalf of the City of New York suddenly became concerned, in the wake of *Put and Take's* growing success, that presenting a musical comedy in Town Hall ran contrary to the Town Hall charter, which had been conceived with "civic purposes in mind." Even *Variety* acknowledged that the committee's objections quite likely were inspired by the mere presence of a "colored company" on the Town Hall stage. With no other Broadway theater available to it for a transfer, *Put and Take* closed down on September 23, 1921, and took to the road for an extended tour. From the box office point of view, even on its closing date *Put and Take* had been earning a profit.

In June 1922 another all-black *Shuffle Along* contender, *Strut Miss Lizzie,* slipped into town from Chicago, where the great black songwriting team of Henry Creamer and Turner Layton ("Dear Old Southland," "Way Down Yonder in New Orleans") originally had mounted it, opening at Minsky Brothers' National Winter Garden Theatre on Second Avenue near Houston Street—quite a distance downtown.

Despite *Shuffle Along's* clear-cut success, Broadway theater owners still refused to acknowledge in 1922 that there was much of an audience for "all-colored" musical comedy. Consequently, they opted only to book black productions into their houses out of season, after the onset of summer. Broadway's official theatrical season generally concluded in June, since it was generally believed that un-air-conditioned theaters could not sustain any new business during the city's sweltering summer months. *Strut Miss Lizzie* was invited uptown for just this reason, within weeks of opening downtown, by its white downtown theater owner, William Minsky, who offered Creamer and Layton's *Strut Miss Lizzie* company the vacant Times Square Theatre owned and managed by Minsky on West 42nd Street. "Had the show come in at any other time but the end of the season," *Variety* noted in reviewing the transferred production, "the chances are that it would not have secured a house in the theatrical zone. Uptown managers figure any profit at this period is gravy."

Strut Miss Lizzie's ultimate fate provided an even more brutally vivid illustration of the economic vagaries bred into the stifling second-class status accorded black-owned productions on Broadway. Conceived originally as a property of the black Creole Producing Company, a corporation created and funded by *Strut Miss Lizzie*'s lyricist, Henry Creamer, the show wound up in a very short time so bound in debt to its white theater owner, Minsky, its white music publisher, Jack Mills; and Arthur Lyons, a white vaudeville agent with ties to Minsky, that—despite a healthy opening-week gross of $8,000—*none* of the show's cast members were paid by Minsky and Lyons (who now owned 75 percent of the profits), while Creamer received a check from Minsky for $141, immediately attached by the IRS.

Desperate to extricate himself from the crushing grip of his white theatrical managers, Creamer, after a handful of Times Square Theatre performances, moved *Strut Miss Lizzie* to the newly built Earl Carroll Theatre on Seventh Avenue off 50th Street. Shortly thereafter, Arthur Lyons sued Earl Carroll for stealing his show. *Strut Miss Lizzie* finally collapsed in a sea of debt and litigation—a victim, in a sense, of *Shuffle Along*'s monumental success. No black musical comedy ever again would sneak into a Broadway theater beneath the notice of Broadway's producing establishment. Expectations had been raised. The margin for exploitation was now limitless.

"It's getting very dark on Old Broadway," sang Gilda Gray in the 1922 edition of Ziegfeld's *Follies*, dancing shamelessly across the stage of the New Amsterdam Theatre in a gown that alternately turned white and black with the light. "You see the change in ev'ry cabaret;/Just like an eclipse on the moon,/Ev'ry cafe now has the dancing coon./Pretty choc'late babies/Shake and shimmy ev'ry-where./Real dark-town entertainers hold the stage./You must black up to be the latest rage./Yes, the great white way is white no more,/It's just like a street on the Swanee shore./It's getting very dark on old Broadway."

Late in 1921, Lew Leslie, a former vaudeville song-and-patter specialist turned nightclub promoter, signed two replacement *Shuffle Along* cast members—singer–comedienne Florence Mills and her husband, dancer Ulysses S. "Slow Kid" Thompson—to perform nightly, after the *Shuffle Along* curtain came down, at the Folies Bergère restaurant atop the Winter Garden Theatre. The 17-year-old Mills, already an experienced vaudevillian as a child performer, had made something of a splash in *Shuffle Along* by taking over for the show's female lead, Gertrude Saunders. At the restaurant, Leslie had a floor show that he'd recently put together, featuring black vaudevillians. Now, with Mills and Thompson hired, Leslie closed the Folies Bergère in February 1922 in order to renovate it into "a plantation and levee scene," featuring "a special waffle counter" for the restaurant and a new "all-colored revue," which he would be directing.

Renamed The Plantation Cafe, Leslie's operation reopened on February 15, 1922, and immediately began to attract a devoted white patronage, largely due to the extraordinary talent of Florence Mills—though Leslie, as Jimmy Durante recalled in *Nightclubs* (his memoir of the New York night scene) knavishly orchestrated Mills's initial success at the Plantation to an extraordinary degree. "The smartest stunt Broadway ever saw pulled was executed by Lew Leslie," Durante wrote:

> He opened the Plantation in 1922 with a colored revue featuring Florence Mills. Florence had been a riot on Broadway. . . . Still Lew wanted to build her up even more. Lew is a practical psychologist. . . . He advertised the Plantation and Florence Mills; gave it a grand advance ballyhoo. On opening night customers started coming. They could hear a hot jazz band blazing away and Miss Mills singing and frantic applause. But they couldn't get in. Velvet curtains were drawn across the doorway. Two captains stood before them, bowing and explaining apologetically that the club was full. Reservations for tomorrow night? Ah, it was too bad but the reservation list was full for quite some time ahead.
>
> For more than a week the club was besieged by would-be patrons. Broadway was crazy to get in. Finally Leslie began to accept reservations. He was fairly flooded with them. The club became a mint.
>
> For the first two weeks the band played and Florence Mills did her stuff and the chorus went through their routine without a single customer in the place! That was the bait Lew had prepared. The club might have gone off to a weak start that would have ruined it. Broadway has time only for a winner, and the Plantation looked like a knock-out to the people outside before a dollar had been rung up on the register.

By July, Lew Leslie had already repackaged his hugely popular all-black Florence Mills–fronted nightclub floor show as *The Plantation Revue*, to reopen it, with Will Vodery leading the pit orchestra, on Broadway at the 48th Street Theatre. Leslie proved himself a brazen pioneer of sorts in his choice of composers for *Plantation Revue*: the show was the first "all-colored" production to be scored by white men—composer J. Russell Robinson and lyricist Roy Turk—despite the presence of the great black songwriter Shelton Brooks ("Some of These Days," "Darktown Strutters' Ball") in the cast and Will Vodery (contributor to the scores of numerous earlier black Broadway musicals) in the pit.

The final results were mixed, the *Revue* itself receiving scant critical praise for both its production values and its music, but high praise for the performance of the show's star. In the *Plantation Review* Florence Mills was anointed the first great black box-office attraction of the Twenties, transmuting Lew Leslie, in the process, into the dominant impresario of black musical theater on Broadway. Soon hyperbolically dubbed "the Black Ziegfeld," he would, in the course of mounting more than a half-dozen major black productions over the ensuing decade, eventually come to work with (and, in typically intemperate Lew Leslie fashion, torment) Andy Razaf— even while presenting Razaf with his first commission for a full Broadway score.

When it opened at the Columbia Theatre on Broadway near 47th Street in the week of September 25, 1922, *Joe Hurtig's Social Maids* bore no relation whatever to the ferment surrounding black musical theater on Broadway. This burlesque revue was presented by the impresario whose small chain of Hurtig and Seamon houses through- out the city included a theater on 125th Street near Eighth Avenue that was destined to be renamed the Apollo. Though *Social Maids* promoted itself as "Something New in Burlesque" (executives of the Columbia Burlesque circuit recently had begun a cleanup of their business, banning the "shimmy" from all Columbia burlesque stages and placing a taboo on "blue dialogue and indigo stage business"), the show was basically the same old grind. In a concession, perhaps, to the city's newfound fancy for black musical comedy, though, *Social Maids* did have a modest musical score by two black composers —the melodies by Hughie Woolford, a Clef Club alumnus and one of the living masters of ragtime piano; the lyrics, according to handbills for the show, by one "Andrae Razaf."

Touring through the fall of 1922 along the Columbia "wheel" of burlesque theaters, *Social Maids* managed to attract with this score the attention of someone at Jerome H. Remick, the Tin Pan Alley publishing power. Before the end of the year, Remick bought one of the Razaf/Woolford tunes "My Waltz Divine." They published it the following year, the first Andrea Razaf song to see print in almost four years.

While Razaf continued to study closely the new black musicals turning up on Broadway in 1922, his opinion of these entertainments was surprisingly low. Critical judgments passed by this twice-published 27-year-old songwriter (and part-time poet/athlete) clearly carried unusual weight, though, within the Harlem theatrical community. On November 29, 1922, Romeo Daugherty, entertainment editor for the *Amsterdam News,* turned one full column of his *Theatre* page over to Andrea Razaf. Under the title "An Appreciation," Razaf opened this column with a rhymed diatribe:

"Hats off to you, friend Daugherty!" he began. "For you have spoken truthfully/Of that present, most contagious craze;/These so-called musical comedy plays/Which some of our critics, with heads so flat, /Call the 'greatest' this and the 'greatest' that.

"Candidly speaking," continued Razaf, "there's only one show/ Today that has any right to go/Near Broadway, which is 'Shuffle Along';/And only a fool will say I'm wrong . . . /For if there isn't something done, to stop this most disgusting run;/Of copied, worn out, small-time stuff—Shows, one-tenth art and nine-tenths bluff;/ Some day, all Negro theatricaldom/Will wake up jobless, on the bum."

Razaf next enumerated a sarcastically pointed yet hardly facetious wish list illustrative of the sharp eye he had fixed upon the black entertainment industry in New York and the strict standard to which he held it, even in these giddy breakthrough years downtown. His title for this calculated exercise in punditry was "Dreams—Just Dreams."

Razaf began his manifesto by calling for a " 'get-together' movement . . . among our colored professionals with the object of checking the many jealousies and hatreds that exist within their group." Clearly Razaf was addressing himself to the horror stories already circulating throughout Harlem about black vaudevillians and songwriters, young and old, trampling one another in a mad dash to sign themselves over to white producers and music publishers—as well as to the growing backstage enmity within established black Broadway productions like *Shuffle Along,* whose quartet of creators soon would split up acrimoniously. Naturally, many in the business considered it a betrayal for any black professional to speak publicly about this rather ugly sidenote to black entertainment achievement in the Twenties, but Razaf had his own ideas. Throughout the decades to come he would never shy away from taking his own people to task for any foolishness, as he perceived it, in their behavior.

Razaf's next "Dream" decried an even more forbidden subject: "Colored shows [deciding] to take a few colored girls, for a change." Throughout the Twenties, just about every Broadway musical production (to say nothing of the white-trade, uptown nightclub revues) would hire only the lightest-skinned black women for their chorus lines—what Harlem referred to as "high yallers" ("high yellows"). The idea of a black man raising the alarm on this point, in print, in 1922, really was quite stunning.

"Silas Jones, who is to write the book for 'The Colored Ramblers,'" continued Razaf, inventing both an author and a production title to stand for all black book-writers and black Broadway musical revues, "[is] 'brushing up' in the knowledge of stagecraft by spending a few hours, daily, in the Public Library, and visiting the latest Broadway productions . . . in this way hoping to become a playwright." The criticism implicit in this gibe was clear, as were the criticisms expressed in Razaf's ensuing two "Dreams":

"A standing prize to each and every act that comes forth with at least one new situation or joke.

"[Admitting] the trouble with most of our blackface comedians is they let the cork do all the work."

Razaf's next-to-last "Dream" was a tart, moderately tongue-in-cheek summation of lofty, altogether unheard-of professional standards, offered by an equally unheard-of entertainment subspecies: a black lyricist—one who, moreover, despised songwriting clichés. "Our lyric writers . . . waking up" wrote Razaf hopefully, "[and] forming a league to encourage the study of English, geography, and current news and . . . discouraging the use of such overworked names and expressions as: 'Lida Jane,' 'Sister Birch,' 'Eagle Rock,' 'Baptist Church,' 'Deacon Brown,' 'Ball the Jack,' 'Do it slow,' 'Brother,' 'Low down,' etc."

Again and again throughout his career in music, Andrea Razaf would attempt to bring to fruition his dream of a black songwriter's union that could wield negotiating power with Tin Pan Alley. Fleetingly, over the years, he succeeded (at least organizationally) on a number of occasions. In each instance, though, the so-called unions—under a variety of formal names, such as the Tempo Club and the Crescendo Club—functioned for a time and failed again and again. Razaf's conclusion to his manifesto of "Dreams" in 1922, calling for "a Colored Song Writers Union . . . adopting 'One for all and all for one' as their motto, with no member henceforth selling a song outright for a ten-dollar bill and a pat on the back . . . ," was both consistent with his professional obsessions and sadly prescient.

On September 9, 1922, the *New York Age*, in a front-page story, lamented, "the wide-open conditions that are to be observed in Harlem and the failure of the proper authorities to correct them. The city administration seems to have given over this section of town for the exploitation of vicious practices in the way of open drinking, gambling, and other violations of the law without the slightest effort at restraint or concealment. The resorts which cater to the thirst for forbidden beverages and the desire for games of chance derive their main support from the colored men who frequent them. Most of the proprietors are white . . . the immunity which they enjoy is but another example of the exploitation of the darker race.

"Intoxicating beverages of all sorts are openly dispensed in cigar stores, delicatessen shops, drug stores, and other places. Almost every delicatessen store and many of the cigar stores on Lenox Avenue from 130th to 145th Streets are selling 'hootch' and all kinds of home-made intoxicating beverages . . . There is no need of a password, mysterious sign, or peculiar grip. [Twenty cents gets anyone a shot of] alleged corn liquor or gin said to rival the kick of a Georgia mule, forty cents, a four ounce vial; seventy-five cents . . . a half pint flask."

Some months later, in May 1923, a majority group of Harlem cabaret owners—"determined to remove all odium and blame from the cabaret business"—announced the formation of the Colored Cabaret Owners' Association, chartered by the State of New York, with the stated purpose of "regulating the conduct of their places with a view to eliminating all objectionable features."

The new association's president reported that, as of January 1923, there were about twenty "colored men" operating cabarets in Harlem and that it was a "fair conclusion" that fifty percent of these men were trying "with all their might" to "run decent places." "About thirty percent," the Association maintained, "wanted to do the same thing, but through lack of experience [and] being new to the business, they have an idea that it is necessary now and then to stretch a point and lean a little toward looseness of action in order to compete successfully with the other fellow." The remaining twenty percent were "'the black sheep . . .' running their places without regard to anything save desire to make money . . . in a manner that fits their idea of what they think some of the public desire." "The membership being of the opinion that . . . the business needed reforming in spots," the association president concluded, "it was better to reform from the inside than [have] reform forced from the outside."

One month later, the *New York Age* fired the first volley in a very public front-page showdown with the leading purveyors of "hootch" in Harlem. The battle proved to be a fierce, often frustrating investigative minuet in pursuit of the mysterious entrepreneurs behind the "host of cafes, delicatessens, and other places catering to the 'hootch' consuming clientele with wide open doors," especially a faceless fellow known as "Loui." "Particularly [on] Lenox Avenue," the *Age* observed, "the most conspicuous signs to be seen are those adorning the fronts of a series of delicatessens . . . blazoned in glowing red letters of considerable dimension the name 'LOUI.' . . . It was into one of 'Loui''s places that an unsophisticated lady walked one day and when she innocently asked for some pig's feet was handed a half-pint of gin. . . . 'Loui' has a number of delicatessen places, so called," the *Age* explained, "but in every one of them the main commodity is hootch.

"According to information," the *Age* added, "'Loui' is getting ambitious. He is not closing up his 'hootch' delicatessens but it is alleged that he is fixing his eyes upon the famous (infamous) Harlem pleasure resort known as the Shuffle Inn, located in the 131st Street corner basement of the Lafayette Building at Seventh Avenue, and that he is hoping to be permitted to reopen that place as a cabaret. The question agitating the 'hootch' crowd is: Will he serve Lenox Avenue booze (65 cents a half pint) to Seventh Avenue cabaret patrons at cabaret prices (75 cents a drink—$5 a half pint)?"

It is the seeming naïveté of the *New York Age* in breaking this story that is most revealing. Whether the *Age* was, in actuality, deeply shocked and a little bit dazed by what it was learning and reporting on the subject of bootleg whiskey, or whether it was simply trying to appeal to those among its readers who were, clearly Harlemites were now sharply divided between those who unquestioningly embraced the new outlaw machinery that was taking over the uptown Prohibition economy and those who were horrified to learn that this takeover was happening at all.

The reasons for embracing white gangster dominance in Harlem were several—among them, perceived employment opportunity and a perverse sense of prestige in Harlem's designation as a smart, "open," and dangerous new addition to the Manhattan entertainment map. It would seem that Andrea Razaf was among the former group of appeasers—one who believed that the gangsters invading Harlem would bring, in his case, employment opportunity for an aspiring songwriter. When in July, the *Age* revealed that it was not the mysterious Loui but "one Connie Immerman . . . a white man with past and present business connections to the delicatessen business" who was planning to reopen the Shuffle Inn, it could not have surprised Razaf. The 33-year-old Immerman, a regular for years at Barron Wilkins's cafe—lately renamed the Exclusive Club—was known to all the show people in Harlem, who'd long frequented the original, legitimate Immerman delicatessen, run by Connie Immerman in partnership with his brother, George. Was Connie Immerman, in fact, the dreaded Loui? Quite possibly—but if not Connie Immerman himself, then certainly one of his relations. The Immerman family had been avowed bootleggers since the start of Prohibition.

What Connie Immerman really wanted to infiltrate, though, was the nightclub business. He'd become friends with many of the regulars at Barron's, including "Bricktop"—Ada Smith—who was then working her first job in New York at Barron's as a soubrette. "He started telling me about his dreams," Smith later remembered. "When his dreams were still just dreams, he was already talking about a name for his place. One night I volunteered, 'How about Connie's Inn? That's your name, isn't it?'"

Despite the fact, as the *Age* reported, that Immerman, in an effort to "allay opposition and hostility, is advertising the fact that he has engaged a known colored Harlemite to take over the place when it reopens under the new name Connie's Inn and that he intends to employ nearly sixty colored people in his new cabaret," there was fierce disagreement in Harlem over his true intentions for his proposed nightclub. The poles of disagreement were sharply presented in the editorial lines of Harlem's two black newspapers, the *New York Age* and the *Amsterdam News*. The *News*, which had once run its own series of articles flaying the bootleg delicatessen business, suddenly was all for Connie Immerman and his new enterprise on the grounds that Immerman would bring "downtown" class and style, meaning white class and style, to Harlem with his new club, while employing in it sixty black workers. The *Age* was, of course, outraged by this sort of thinking and viewed the issue strictly on moral grounds.

"You mention that Mr. Immerman will employ nearly sixty colored people in this new place," wrote Lonnie Hicks, President of the Colored Cabaret Owners' Association, in an open letter in the *Age* to Alderman George Harris, editor of the *Amsterdam News*. "Grant that he will; for sake of argument make it a hundred. Does that fact overbalance the danger of a man coming into a business that is already dangling by a thread which is trying to be saved by men who have experience in the business, who have the interest of the weaker members of their race at heart, who have promised the police department, the minister, and congregations that they mean well and are sincere in their efforts to reform their business and also make Harlem a safe place to live in?

"As to Mr. Immerman personally, the organization has nothing against him, but we do claim that owing to his past and present business connections with the delicatessen business, which in Harlem seems to draw an unwelcome element of people, weak in mind, loose in morals, dangerous to the community, making life itself unsafe, is clearly unqualified to come into a business that, is as stated before, being uplifted by men who are absolutely sincere in their efforts to reform it and are willing and anxious to make sacrifices to further that end."

Connie's Inn opened nonetheless on the evening of July 21, 1923. The *Age* ignored the occasion entirely. "The color scheme of this elegant new cafe is a vision of beauty," the *Amsterdam News* reported two days later. "With its soft rose-tinted lights, its decorations in black and gold tapestry, its sunburst draperies over the raised dance floor . . . its calcium lights and general artistic arrangements, it is the equal in beauty of any other similar place in New York City. It is, in short, something that Harlem has never seen before."

There was seating for 500 and a cast of thirty-one onstage in a "novel" and "high-class" revue led by Osceola Blanks, dancing now with her husband, Leonard Harper, rather than her sister, Berliana. The orchestra belonged to Wilbur Sweatman, the foremost black jazz figure that Harlem could muster in 1923, leading his Acme Syncopators.

The former Shuffle Inn had been "renovated throughout—all the work having been done by colored workmen," with "colored artists" credited for the design of "exquisite decorations." "Seventy-one colored persons, including the actors," according to the *News*, "were employed nightly at the new cabaret. . . . Exhaust fans and numerous wall fans keep the temperature deliciously cool . . . and the food served was of the finest Chinese and American dishes. Broadway service at Harlem prices."

In the end, though, it was left to "the genial, good-hearted proprietor, Connie Immerman," as he was characterized by the *News*, to deliver the final word on the gala opening of Connie's Inn. "This place," insisted Immerman, "is for all decent, self-respecting citizens, regardless of who they may be."

The opening of Connie's Inn was a watershed in the histories of both Andy Razaf and the black Harlem community as a whole, though its importance would only gradually be revealed with time. Within five years, Connie's Inn would be Andy Razaf's professional home in Harlem, the entertainment institution with which Razaf most nearly would be associated, as resident lyric writer for the celebrated floorshows presented there seasonally. Connie Immerman's Seventh Avenue cabaret would, by that time, be recognized internationally as one of Harlem's gaudiest nightclub attractions. It also would be known throughout Harlem and New York City as a club that was fundamentally for "whites only," a club that rarely, if ever, admitted black patrons. In that respect, Connie's Inn, from its inception, revealed itself to be something of a pioneer.

"What has the appearance of a peculiar policy seems to be controlling the operation of Connie's Inn in the basement of the Lafayette Theatre building," the *New York Age* observed less than three months after the new nightclub's opening. "It has been rumored around for some time that the management of this cabaret is only desirous of having colored patrons on the off-nights . . . when the patronage is not heavy. Persons in position to know have hinted that on such occasions as Saturday and Sunday nights, when large numbers of the downtown whites are visitors, there are other places that extend a more cordial invitation to colored customers than Connie's Inn."

The *Age* proceeded to relate a recent incident at the Inn involving Charles Gilpin, the revered black thespian who, two years earlier, had been the focus of a widely publicized protest by many of Broadway's most distinguished theatrical personalities after being discriminated against by the Drama League as one of its designated 1921 dinner honorees for his performance in Eugene O'Neill's *The Emperor Jones*. Gilpin, the *Age* explained, had just visited Connie's

Inn on a Sunday evening with a party of four, including his wife. "To make sure of securing comfortable accommodations," the *Age* noted, Gilpin had taken "the precaution of making prior reservations for a table . . . with Harry 'Kid' Griffin"—the former house pianist at J. W. Connor's Cafe, installed by Connie Immerman as manager at the new club. "Feeling assured therefore that he would be able to offer his guests the facilities of the cabaret," continued the *Age*, "Mr. Gilpin piloted them to the place about midnight on Sunday. But as he reached the door and started in, Mr. Gilpin was stopped by a white man who stood at the door alongside of the colored man who ordinarily keeps the door. The white man asked in bruff and harsh tones, 'Where are you going?'

"'Into the Inn,' said Mr. Gilpin.

"'You can't come in here,' said the man, to which Mr. Gilpin countered by asking the reason, saying that he had made reservations for the party. The man at the door replied that it made no difference about the reservation, as the party would not be admitted. Mr. Gilpin then asked that Mr. Griffin be called, but was informed that Mr. Griffin could do him no good. The white man is quoted as saying . . . 'I say you can't come in . . . The place is crowded and there is no room for you.'

"And notwithstanding the strong and energetic protest made by Mr. Gilpin," concluded the *Age*, "the man usurping the place of the doorman would not permit the Charles Gilpin party to enter the sacred precincts of Connie's Inn.

"It is asserted on good authority," the *Age* added, "that following the barring of the Gilpin party, many others were freely admitted, but it was noteworthy that those admitted were all of the Caucasian race. In other words, it would seem that Negro guests are not welcome on nights when the cabaret is well-patronized by whites, and those who apply for admittance are sorted out and passed over . . . [while] the Connie's Inn management . . . exploits the Negro entertainers and musicians employed in that resort, holding them up to the slumming parties from the downtown white light districts as evidence of licensed debauchery and debasing revelry countenanced and engaged in by Harlemites."

It is perhaps difficult to fathom at a distance of seventy years how disbelieving the black citizenry of Harlem remained in the face of encroaching nightclub segregation during the early Twenties. Despite the lessons of history, no one, it seems, not even the acute Andrea Razaf, was prepared in 1923 for the degree to which discrimination was about to be visited upon Harlem, through its nightclub industry. Greatly encouraged by the evolution of their uptown neighborhood as a home to blacks from all over the world, Harlemites at first simply could not absorb the stinging racist rebuke to their aspirations that the nightclub policies of "whites-only" establishments were about to deal them.

Connie Immerman was not the cruelest white club owner in Harlem to practice racism on such a grand scale. He might, however, have been the first. Within months of opening Connie's Inn, Immerman was instructing the black producer of his floor show, Leonard Harper, to get rid of the few "dark-skinned girls" employed in the club's chorus line, for some "high yellows," who would be "more in harmony with the club's white guests when in close proximity." He also unofficially formalized the Inn's exclusionary policy toward blacks.

Immerman recognized that he was engaged in a very delicate image game with regard to his targeted white clientele. For Connie's Inn to succeed, it would be necessary to counterbalance the club's primary attraction as a forbidden piece of Harlem nightlife with an environment that would put Immerman's intrepid white patrons at ease uptown. Surrounding these patrons opulently with furnishings and food and drink of a familiar downtown caliber was one-half of the equation. Surrounding them comfortably with predominantly Caucasian faces was the other.

Ironically, Immerman has never gotten credit for these "innovations." A seer of hard-hearted foresight, while not necessarily a racist, he nevertheless wound up taking a back seat historically to the man and the institution that he, in a sense, inspired. The man was gangster Owney Madden. The institution, bankrolled and created by Madden with Connie's Inn as a model, was the Cotton Club.

The preliminary history behind this apotheosis of uptown glamor and racist exclusivity was a serpentine tale of Harlem nightclub birth and rebirth. In April 1923, Douglas Hall, a large auditorium space atop the Douglas movie theater on the northeast corner of Lenox Avenue at 142nd Street (644 Lenox Avenue), was reopened as the New Douglas Casino after extensive renovations only to be shut down, refurbished yet again, and renamed the DeLuxe Cabaret some months later. The nominal owner and fronting managerial presence at the new DeLuxe Cabaret was Jack Johnson, the controversial black former heavyweight champion, though the *New York Age*, in a brief news story on the new nightspot in January 1924, pointed out that the club's true "backers" were members of the "bootlegging gentry," identified by the *Age* only as "Hyman"—whose income from a chain of Harlem cigar store hootch fronts, according to the *Age*, "assumes plutocratic proportions"—and his partner, "Levy." These two had spent, the *Age* reported, "$27,000 refurnishing this resort in the hope of attracting a bunch of high-fliers from downtown, as Connie has done at the Inn." One month later, though, the *Age* announced that the "Club Deluxe" was for sale. "Notwithstanding that Hyman is alleged to have spent $27,000 in refurbishing and redecorating the place, it is [now] on the market for $2,000," the *Age* explained. "Failure of Hyman . . . to secure a license for the running of the place is said to have been the reason for its being . . . on the market."

Within a matter of months, the hapless Douglas Theater space would be retooled once again, this time under the auspices of Florenz Ziegfeld's brilliant set and costume designer, Joseph Urban. The result was a brazen riot of African jungle motifs, Southern stereotypology, and lurid eroticism—all packaged with great panache to yield a seven-hundred-seat horseshoe-shaped supper club for whites only to be called the Cotton Club.

The furtive, shadowy owner of this new club was the most powerful gangster in the Manhattan underworld, a quiet-spoken, murderously polite, British-born immigrant child of the Hell's Kitchen streets who'd risen as leader of the city's most brutal Irish street gang, the Gophers, to become one of the dominant forces of organized crime in America as the leading producer of illegal Prohibition beer in New York City.

Owney Madden was a wraith-like figure who always dressed stylishly while courting anonymity, avoiding cameras, and even paying columnist Walter Winchell to write him *out* of the news. Madden's shyness, though, belied a bloodthirsty ruthlessness and an entrepreneurial brilliance that enabled him to dominate the glamorous Manhattan night world as unspoken owner of the city's most elegant nocturnal establishments, including the Silver Slipper, the Stork Club, and a chain of downtown "joints" run in partnership with the nominal queen of New York speakeasies, Texas Guinan.

Madden's initial foray into the increasingly lucrative Harlem club world was plotted and executed with characteristic thoroughness. From the outset, standards were established: chorus girls had to be at least five foot six, uniformly "high yellow," able to carry a tune, and not over 21 years old, the behavior of the service staff had to be impeccable, and the floor show had to be multileveled, and extremely fast paced, with lavish production values on a Ziegfeld scale. A fundamental racial hierarchy also was firmly delineated for employees: whites only for backstage creative positions, blacks only in the kitchen, at the tables, and on the stage. Madden's discretion regarding his own role in the club's operation was meanwhile so acute that he listed himself on the Cotton Club corporate register as a minor official. Over the years, he was rarely seen on the premises.

Ultimately, the differences between Owney Madden's Cotton Club and Connie Immerman's Inn were qualitative rather than quantitative. Both clubs were enormously successful throughout the Twenties and early Thirties, though the Cotton Club garnered the greater publicity share, mostly due to its live radio broadcasts later on and a superior publicity link to the newspaper columnists of Broadway. Both clubs also remained steadfastly racist relaxing their restrictions against blacks but rarely as the years passed, and only for the occasional light-skinned black patron, as a rule.

Both clubs were not, however, qualitatively similar in their employment practices and general racial tenor, beyond the issue of admission. Where Owney Madden hired a white man, Lew Leslie, to stage his first Cotton Club revues, Connie Immerman tapped Leonard Harper, a black man. Where Owney Madden offered the composing job for the first Cotton Club revue scores to Jimmy McHugh, a white man—the professional manager at Jack Mills Publishing, a music house that was aggressively taking the lead in locking up black songwriting talent on Tin Pan Alley—and his young partner Dorothy Fields, a white woman, Connie Immerman soon offered the job of writing his scores to Fats Waller and Andy Razaf. Therein lay the definitive difference between Connie Immerman and Owney Madden, between Connie's Inn and the Cotton Club. Owney Madden was a businessman thug out to rape the new Harlem vogue through the ruthless orchestration of his Cotton Club machine. Connie Immerman was a Harlem native who'd realized his dream of owning a Harlem nightclub. Immerman's attitude toward Harlem's black population was, at the very least, familiar, and he privately acknowledged the contribution of blacks to his club's appeal, a contribution that Madden at the Cotton Club merely capitalized on. Certainly the relationship was a perverse one between Immerman and his black employees. The distinction may appear marginal in the generally virulent racist foundations of both establishments. It is the reason, though, that Andy Razaf eventually got his chance at Connie's Inn.

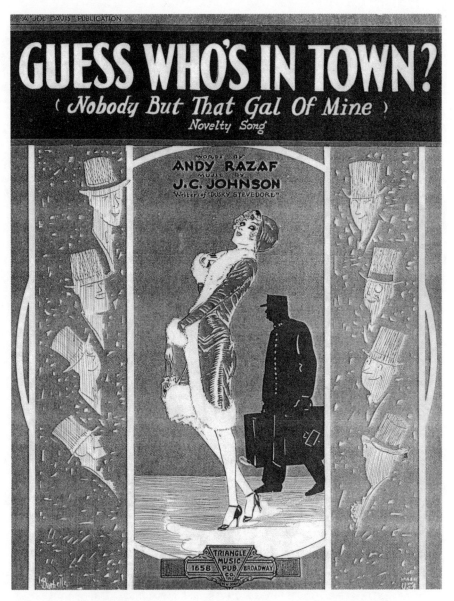

Courtesy Razaf Estate.

Courtesy Frank Driggs.

6

Who's to Blame

People used to call it "Ragtime,"
That was many years ago,
Then they spoke of "Syncopation,"
But that sounded much too slow,
Later all you heard was "Charleston,"
Finally "Blackbottom" came,
Each name meant the same,
I know who's to blame.

>   — *"How Jazz Was Born"*
>   by Andy Razaf and Thomas Waller

Andrea Razaf recognized that he needed a regular collaborator, some talented melodist with whom he could jointly begin to build a career. This search for a song partner increasingly became the focus of Razaf's solo excursions through the Harlem night world after his return from Cleveland in 1921.

Quite reasonably, Razaf quickly gravitated toward the club scene's preeminent music figures, the piano men, who could be found holding forth in the back rooms of Harlem's best cabarets. These exceedingly charismatic keyboard improvisers, after first coming to prominence during the ragtime age in the downtown black neighborhood cafes and the black saloons of New York's Tenderloin District, had migrated with the black population of the city to Harlem where they now were revered on the burgeoning uptown club circuit as a veritable pantheon of larger than life piano gods and demigods, renegade characters with vivid musical personalities, who in many ways emblemized the mystique of the Harlem club scene, circa 1923.

The pedigree of these piano men was traceable to the period immediately following Emancipation when an entire generation of black musicians had taken to the road, addressing a lack of steady work down south by touring the red light or tenderloin districts of black neighborhoods across the country, playing for the entertainment of local carousers. Many were pianists—piano playing precluding the necessity of carrying an instrument along on one's back—with a subculture soon taking root of itinerant, ruthlessly competitive black piano "ticklers," many of them flashily dressed, garishly colorful vagabonds who supplemented their sporadic earnings as musicians through pool hustling, card sharping, and pimping.

In the Twenties hierarchy of Harlem musicians, few could compare in talent, in technical skill, or in breadth of fundamental musical acumen with these piano "professors." In the clubs, they generally were the focal point: ceaselessly soloing, accompanying singers, directing whatever band was on hand, policing the tip box, routing the drunks—hosting the party as all-around showmen. Most were exceptionally capable composers as well; some had numerous formally copyrighted compositions to their credit, many simply carried around a wealth of unpublished original specialty numbers created solely for purposes of reputation on the furiously competitive circuit.

William Henry Joseph Bonaparte Bertholoff-Smith, Willie "the Lion" Smith, was one of Harlem's finest and certainly its most loquaciously entertaining piano "pounders." Razaf may have first encountered Smith at Leroy Wilkins's establishment, at 135th Street and Fifth Avenue, during Smith's initial stint as the "take-charge guy" at Leroy's—playing the piano there accompanied occasionally by instrumentalists—late in 1919. Or Razaf may have run across Smith during the several occasions early in 1920 that the pianist took leave from Leroy's to help gambler Jerry Preston open and establish his new club, the Orient, on the second floor of a building further down 135th Street.

Alternatively, Andrea Razaf and Willie "the Lion" Smith could have been introduced in 1921 at "Jop's Place," the 131st Street boardinghouse (number 163 West) run by composer Scott Joplin's widow, Lottie, where pianists like Eubie Blake and Willie Smith often could be found lounging around Lottie Joplin's parlor at six in the morning, talking or tickling the piano, unwinding from gigs just concluded perhaps blocks away. Or the initial encounter could have occurred as late as 1923 at the Garden of Joy, an open-air, tented cabaret constructed atop a great rock shelf in a vacant lot on Seventh Avenue between 138th and 139th Streets; Willie Smith, after returning from a lengthy piano stint in Chicago and nearly a year touring in black vaudeville, spent many summer afternoons at "the Rock" with other local pianists in 1923. He also worked the Garden of Joy nightly for several months in tandem with a clarinetist.

At the very latest, Andrea Razaf and Willie "the Lion" Smith perhaps made their initial acquaintance toward the end of 1923 at the Capitol Palace, a large and fancy nightclub between 139th and 140th Streets on Lenox Avenue, where Smith held the piano job during what for him was a fairly extended term. Twenty-four-year-old Duke Ellington, recently arrived in Harlem from his home in Washington, DC, first encountered "the Lion" at the Capitol Palace. His description of this run-in conjures vividly the experience of discovering Willie "the Lion" Smith for the first time in Harlem during the early Nineteen Twenties.

"My first impression of the Lion, even before I saw him—was the thing I felt as I walked down those steps," Ellington recalled. "A strange thing. A square-type fellow might say, 'This joint is jumping,' but to those who had become acclimatized—the tempo was the lope—actually everything and everybody seemed to be doing whatever they were doing in the tempo the Lion's group was laying down. The walls and furniture seemed to lean understandingly— one of the strangest and greatest sensations I ever had. The waiters served in that tempo; everybody who had to walk in, out, or around the place walked with a beat."

Born November 25, 1897, in the Hudson Valley town of Goshen, New York, William Bertholoff-Smith had been raised in Newark, New Jersey, by his mother and a stepfather, his natural father—a "light-skinned playboy," according to Smith, who "liked his liquor, girls and gambling"—having died when Smith was 4. A stammerer as a child, something of an athlete as a boy, and a bit of a brawler as a young teen, Smith grew up cocky, contentious, incisively quick witted, and, after conquering his stammer, fiercely charming in endlessly expressing that incisiveness—an incessant talker. Initially self-taught at the piano, he received early musical encouragement from his family, particularly from his mother and his grandmother, a banjo-playing veteran of the Primrose and West minstrel troupes of the 1890s. Gravitating at age 14 to the Newark district known as "the Coast," he'd gained his basic piano training there playing by ear in saloons and brothels.

Smith apparently crossed the Hudson River to New York in 1914. Immediately he'd begun familiarizing himself with the many legendary local piano regulars around town—Willie "Egg Head" Sewell, "One Leg" Willie Joseph, "Jack the Bear," and Richard "Abba-Labba" McLean, as well as listening to inumerable itinerant piano men passing through the city from Memphis, St. Louis, New Orleans, Atlanta, Charleston, and Baltimore. "Many of the transients had gotten run out of their home towns because their stable of women had been caught pulling a fast one and the local cops were after them," he later wrote, recalling this period of profound education. "Many of these got as far as Newark or Jersey City, where the railroads coming up from the South ended in those days. When they crossed on the ferry to New York they wouldn't stay long because the local players resented the intrusion on their territory."

After enlisting in 1916 and fighting quite valorously in France with the all-black 153rd Brigade of the 350th Field Infantry, Battery A, Smith had returned in 1919 to the city's piano wars with a new leonine nickname, bestowed, he would claim, for his prowess handling a 75-millimeter French cannon. A strapping, swaggering six-footer, with piercing eyes and a wide, expressive mouth invariably clenched around a cigar, he was an intimidating presence on the Harlem music scene, all coiled intensity, fast talk, and even faster hands. The young "Lion" was, however, a deceptively reflective swaggerer as well, and that unpredictable blend of boastful bravura and moody sensitivity was most vividly expressed in his playing. Smith was fully capable of pounding a piano with the best of them, but his most dominating characteristics at the keyboard nevertheless proved to be a delicacy of touch and a taste for impressionistically diaphanous compositions inspired by the French "modernists," Ravel and Debussy, characteristics more in tune with the deeply thoughtful, enormously romantic side of his tempestuous nature. Possessing the piano pounder's requisite powerhouse left hand, Willie "the Lion" Smith nevertheless preferred to swing a cabaret room into submission with buoyant, refined subtlety.

Opinionated as he was endlessly inquisitive, conversant in several languages, enamored of astrology and the more mystical side of philosophy, it is easy to understand how attractive the hyperactive

Smith must have seemed to Razaf as a potential collaborator. It is also easy to imagine the disputatious Smith jawing late into the night with the nearly as talkative Razaf, two years his senior and some inches and pounds his junior, the two of them together strolling through the Harlem night or perched on a Harlem brownstone stoop, cigar butts glowing in the dark, animatedly discussing in voices similarly volatile and high-pitched the mysteries of music, the loveliness of women, the vagaries of the local Harlem scene, or simply the stars.

While Smith knew every piano performer in town, his closest friend was a 29-year-old player named James P. Johnson, who, in Harlem circles, generally was acknowledged to be the finest black piano player alive. "All the licks you hear now, as then, originated with musicians like James P. Johnson," Ethel Waters, one of the seminal figures of black music in the Twenties, later insisted. "And I mean *all the hot licks* that ever came out of . . . the rest of the hot piano boys. They are just faithful followers and protégés of that great man Jimmy Johnson."

A large, lumbering, somewhat diffident man as shy and self-effacing as "the Lion" was sociable and self-promoting, Johnson originally met Smith at a Newark "Coast" saloon known as Randolph's in the fall of 1914. Smith was Randolph's house pianist. Johnson, traveling with the woman who soon would become his wife, singer Lillie Mae Wright, was looking for a job. Smith sized up the pair instantly.

"She had been around the business for several years," he later wrote, ". . . a singer–entertainer from the South. Her . . . husband [was] Fred Tunstall, a New York City piano-playing pimp called 'the Tonsil' . . . Tunstall wasn't what you'd call a good husband for Lillie, so she left him [for] James, a guy she could boss around."

Though the two young pianists were entirely opposite in temperament, they soon became intimate friends, "like twins," Smith later observed. "I did a lot of his fighting for him, as he never seemed to want to bother. That is, I helped him out in the brawls around the saloons. . . . He was always a sincere guy, easily hurt, and I used to sort of watch after him."

Born in New Brunswick, New Jersey, on February 1, 1894, the youngest of five children in a stable lower-middle-class family, Johnson got his first exposure to the piano via his Virginia-born mother, who bought an instrument for her home and shared her love of both church hymns and popular songs with her young son while playing it. Johnson's parents often also entertained friends around their piano at parlor socials. Johnson's most vital childhood memories later would revolve around his parents and their guests down in the Johnson living room singing and dancing the old Southern "ring shout"—a shuffling, circling slave dance derived from African religious ritual as refracted through Christian Baptist observance, and secularly extrapolated for social occasions as emotionally intense, almost narcotically rhythmic square dance or cotillion variations. The musical essence of these "shouts" would prove central to James P. Johnson's originality as a composer.

In 1902, the Johnson family moved from New Brunswick to Jersey City, New Jersey, where their youngest son soon was exposed to his first authentic piano "ticklers." "They were popular fellows, real celebrities," Johnson later reflected. "They had lots of girlfriends, led a sporting life, and were invited everywhere there was a piano. I thought it was a fine way to live."

For the next six years, the aspiring young "tickler" applied himself to mastering the instrument of his chosen avocation. In 1908, he was granted an opportunity to study up close the finest New York piano practitioners when his family again moved, this time to the San Juan Hill section of New York City, the area known as "the Jungles." "This was the Negro section of Hell's Kitchen and ran from 60th to 63rd Street, west of Ninth Avenue," Johnson later recalled. "It was the toughest part of New York. There were two to three killings a night. Fights broke out over love affairs, gambling, or arguments in general. There were race fights with the white gangs on 66th and 67th Streets."

In the Jungles and down on the Tenderloin, Johnson stalked the same local piano heroes that his soon-to-be friend Willie Smith was then listening to. Like Smith, he studied the technique of these players closely, incorporating their best effects into his own playing, forging an individual piano style for himself out of admiration and imitation. Unlike Smith, though, who was consumed with playing in the clubs, Johnson already was intrigued by composition—both for the legitimacy he believed it could bestow and the opportunity it afforded him to escape the disrespect implicit in rowdy barrooms. By the time Smith met him in 1914, Johnson already had arranged certain "homemade blues" tunes of his own for possible publication, and had begun as well to familiarize himself with the music of Bach and Beethoven. These blues remained the extent of the young pianist's compositional efforts until a musician named William Farrell at last taught Johnson how to notate his music, sometime in

1915. After jointly selling two or three original songs that year, Johnson and Farrell opened their own theatrical office and began pursuing contacts in the entertainment business. It was Johnson's fondest ambition now to compose for the musical theater.

His focus on songwriting did not, however, cause Johnson to neglect his piano playing career. From 1914 to 1916, the highly regarded young keyboardist regularly worked piano jobs at downtown clubs like Allan's, Lee's, and the Jungles Casino—"a beat-up small dance hall . . . in a damp cellar," according to Willie "the Lion" Smith, where the dancers, "many of them just off the boats docked in the West Sixties . . . really went for our style of playing," —while occasionally appearing uptown at Barron Wilkins's establishment, at Leroy's, and at a saloon called Wood's, then under the management of Edmond "Bucket of Blood" Johnson. "I went around copping piano prize contests," James P. Johnson would later remark matter-of-factly about this period, "and I was considered one of the best in New York—if not the best. I was slim and dapper, and they called me 'Jimmy' then."

Johnson's growing keyboard reputation in 1916 also led to his first contract as a recorder of rolls for player pianos, the highest commercial compliment, in many respects, that a popular pianist of the day could be accorded. All told, the sleepy-eyed, reserved, seemingly unmotivated piano giant would produce twenty piano rolls for the Aeolian Company through February 1918—seventeen of them original James P. Johnson ragtime-based compositions, including the landmark piano improvisation with which Johnson's name thereafter would be linked, "The Carolina Shout": an homage to the "shouts" Johnson had witnessed at his parents' home as a child and an attempt to capture in music the frenzied dance spirit of the Jungles Casino. Johnson at this time also began to play regularly with Clef Club ensembles, though the rigidity of the Clef Club's musical repertoire soon grew too stifling for him.

The declaration of war did not, in fact, interrupt James P. Johnson's piano career unduly; the pacific young pianist, in a characteristic and successful effort to avoid active duty, took a job in a Quartermaster Corps warehouse for the duration of hostilities. With the war's conclusion, Johnson embarked with his wife on an extended vaudeville tour before returning to the city in 1919. His reputation ascended rapidly, in the wake of Prohibition and the growing public fancy for African Americans and their music, as Johnson cut numerous piano rolls, began to record phonograph records as both accompanist and soloist, traveled to Europe in 1922 with an all-black revue called *Plantation Days* (unrelated to Lew Leslie's *Plantation Revue*), returned sporadically to occupy piano chairs in various Harlem cabarets, and at some point, amidst all this activity, received his introduction to an ambitious young lyricist named Andrea Razaf.

Though Razaf became closely acquainted with both Willie "the Lion" Smith and James P. Johnson, under the general auspices of the gregarious Smith, he nevertheless did not yet begin to write songs with either man. The reasons were various. Smith, of course, was a dynamo of late-night piano activity with little time or patience for formal songwriting sessions. He also was not disposed as a writer to compose music that was tightly formatted and structured along popular song lines. Smith preferred more impressionistic prelude- or etudelike piano compositions, pieces more suited to improvisational expression than to the application of lyrics, pieces that could not, for the most part, be sung at all.

James P. Johnson's unavailability to Razaf, on the other hand, was more purely a professional scheduling matter. Johnson's involvement as musical director with the *Plantation Days* company occupied the pianist throughout the latter months of 1922. Then, in the spring of 1923, Johnson was approached by the young Broadway showman George White to compose the score for a new all-black Broadway-bound revue. Best known for his Ziegfeld Follies–inspired revue series known as the *Scandals*, White already had under contract *Shuffle Along*'s libretticists, Flournoy Miller and Aubrey Lyles, along with a number of former *Shuffle Along* company members. Plans to title the show *Shuffle Along of 1923* had, however, been blocked by a lawsuit filed against White by the original *Shuffle Along* producers. *George White's Black Scandals* and *Miller & Lyle's Cakewalkers* were further titles tried and disgarded before White finally settled on a suitable name for his new black entertainment: *Runnin' Wild*.

Johnson's lyric partner on *Runnin' Wild* was another black enter-tainment industry veteran, 40-year-old Richard (R. C.) McPherson, a songwriter who had also founded one of the first music publishing firms devoted to the songs of African–American composers— Gotham-Attucks Music Company, home to every black songwriter of significance during the century's early decades, from James Rosamond Johnson and Bob Cole to Will Marion Cook and James Reese Europe. Writing under the name Cecil Mack, McPherson had written special material for the vaudeville team of Bert Williams and

George Walker while working most frequently as a collaborator with the talented black composer/entertainer Chris Smith.

Johnson and Mack contributed an exceptionally strong score to *Runnin' Wild*. "Old Fashioned Love" was deemed a certain hit by critics and audiences alike during the show's exceedingly well received tryout stops in Washington, DC and Boston, with songs like "Open Your Heart" and "Gingerbrown" also singled out for praise. Strangely overlooked by out-of-town critics, if not audiences, was a torrid dance number composed by Johnson for *Runnin' Wild*, again in deference to the uninhibited dancers he'd played for years earlier at the Jungles Casino.

"The people who came to the Jungles Casino were mostly from around Charleston, South Carolina, and other places in the South," Johnson later explained. "Most of them worked for the Ward Line as longshoremen or on ships that called on Southern ports. . . . They picked their partners with care to show off their best steps and put sets, cotillions, and cakewalks that would give them a chance to get off.

"The Charleston . . . was just a regulation cotillion step without a name. It had many variations—all danced to the rhythm that everyone knows now. One regular at the Casino named Dan White was the best dancer in the crowd and he introduced the step as we know it. But there were dozens of other steps used, too.

"It was while playing for these southern dancers that I composed a number of Charlestons—eight in all—all with the damn rhythm. One of those later became my famous 'Charleston' when it hit Broadway."

Runnin' Wild was not, in fact, the first Broadway musical to present something called a "Charleston." *Liza*, the first black production to open on Broadway during the "legitimate" (nonsummer) theatrical season—on November 27, 1922—had featured in its finale, comprising several specialty dance numbers, a tune entitled "Charleston Dancy" by *Liza* composer Maceo Pinkard. *How Come?*, a failed April 1923 follow-up to the long-running *Liza* (169 performances), had contained two Charleston-based bits: "Charleston Cut-Out" and "Charleston Finale."

Despite these Charleston precursors, James P. Johnson's version of the dance debuted in *Runnin' Wild* with the impact of a firestorm after the show's Broadway opening at the Colonial Theatre, Broadway and 62nd Street, on October 29, 1923. In part, this could perhaps be accounted for by the electrifying manner in which the song was staged by dance director Lida Webb, whose *Runnin' Wild* chorus amplified upon the wailing Will Marion Cook–led pit band with hand-clapping and "foot-patting," beating out the irresistible Charleston rhythm in a veritable Charleston seminar for white Broadway audiences. Though the song and the dance thereafter only gradually, if inexorably, evolved into the signature sound and step of the Twenties, *Runnin' Wild*'s reception on Broadway was immediate and resounding, with business kicking off three times stronger than *Shuffle Along*'s during the show's first three weeks. The production remained on Broadway for 213 performances, surviving into the spring of 1924, before embarking on a successful road tour. It also perpetuated the breakthrough in Broadway theater attendance for blacks begun by *Shuffle Along*, which, with its success, effectively had helped undermine the industry's insidiously segregated seating practices. Despite producer George White's claims that *Runnin' Wild* was patronized largely by "opera singers, actors . . . socially prominent people," the show was, in fact, strongly supported by blacks, "some of the dusky theatergoers attending as often as three times," according to a report in the *New York Herald*, "and knowing just the right place to keel over in a paroxysm of joy."

Clearly James P. Johnson had little time for Andrea Razaf after *Runnin' Wild* established itself downtown on Broadway in the fall of 1923. The "dean of Harlem piano players" quite naturally found himself deluged with offers: to write new all-black revues for the Lafayette Theatre in tandem with his new partner Cecil Mack; to consider another show downtown on Broadway; to produce new songs for Tin Pan Alley. Johnson, however, had a protégé, a plump 19-year-old piano player whom he essentially had taken in off the Harlem streets some two years earlier and was still tutoring. "He brought him down one Sunday afternoon to Leroy's," Willie "the Lion" Smith later remembered. "We were all dressed in full-dress suits and tuxedos, the place was crowded, everything was jumpin', and in comes this guy with a greasy suit on. Walks right down the aisle ahead of everybody, wasn't even introduced, walks right up to the bandstand and says, 'Hello there, Lion, what do you say?' 'You don't know me that well, man,' I said. 'Sit that guy down . . . get that guy down,' I said, 'he looks filthy. Get them pants pressed, there's no excuse for it.'

"So he sat down until I got finished and when I got finished he was insistent, very persistent. 'I come in to cut you, Lion,' he says. 'You'll get your cutting, son,' I said, 'I'll give it to you in a minute.'

"He insisted he wanted to play Jimmy's 'Carolina Shout.' 'He's learned it very well, Lion,' Jimmy said. 'You brought him to the wrong place, man,' I said, 'cause I'm gonna cut him to a gravy.

"When I got through he sat down and played 'The Shout.' He made Jimmy like it and he made me like it. From then on it was Thomas 'Fats' Waller."

If Harlem in the Twenties—"hot," "forbidden" late-night Harlem *and* daylight, family-centered God-fearing Harlem—could be said to have produced one figure who embodied the neighborhood's extravagantly conflicted two-sided nature, this figure was Thomas Waller. Waller's Harlem lineage was not merely typical, it was definitive. His parents, Edward and Adeline Waller, after migrating from Virginia in 1888, had been among the first blacks to move to Harlem, following sojourns on Waverly Place in Greenwich Village (their initial home in the city) and along 63rd Street in the San Juan Hill "Jungles." Born May 21, 1904, in a brownstone apartment at 107 West 134th Street between Lenox and Seventh Avenues, Waller had grown up with the new black Harlem neighborhood—the seventh of eleven children, only five of whom survived childhood, doted on by a pious, lovingly overprotective mother who seems to have consoled herself for the six children she'd lost by smothering her surviving three sons and two daughters with claustrophobic affection. Not until Adeline Waller's health began to fail during the last years of her life were the youngest Waller children allowed outside the family apartment for any extended time beyond their hours attending school (P. S. 89—conveniently situated next door), church (Abyssinian Baptist), and the occasional family outing—a cloistering that seems only to have left the children, particularly young Thomas Waller, with a ravenous social appetite.

Though Waller's interest in the piano apparently announced itself as early as age 6 with surreptitious visits to a piano owned by an upstairs neighbor, the boy's basic introduction to music would come through his church-going parents. Waller's mother, a leading soloist in the choir of the Abyssinian Baptist Church, apparently delighted her children with her joyous singing at home. Waller's father, an overtly solemn and dignified, even stern, man, and a hard-working provider for his family as the owner of a small but modestly successful trucking company, was Chairman of the Board of Deacons at Abyssinian before rebaptizing himself, his spouse, and his children in the Pentecostal faith and leading them all in regular morning street services near their home, accompanied by young Thomas

Waller on a portable harmonium. Waller's early enthusiasm for church music already had led his family to buy a piano, with lessons ensuing for a brief time before Waller's extraordinarily quick ear and brief attention span put an end to his patience with any further formal training.

Spoiled shamelessly by his adoring mother, continually at odds with his unremittingly righteous father, Thomas Waller had grown up a mischievous charmer who escaped punishment from both parents for his frequent scrapes and pranks by interrupting impending preaching lectures and the occasional licking to ask, "Don't you think we ought to pray?" while ascribing responsibility for much of his childhood misbehaving to "the devil."

Increasingly, music offered Waller escape from his sheltered home life. After dabbling with violin and string bass lessons, he concentrated his attention fully on the piano and improved his reading skills to the point where he was invited to play at morning school assemblies, engagements that Waller apparently milked for all the attention he could draw—clowning, rolling his eyes, making faces over his shoulder while he played, delighting his P. S. 89 schoolmates with rollicking musical asides and a thumping beat never before heard in a public school assembly hall.

Soon the cherubic child pianist was a minor neighborhood celebrity—inevitably dubbed "Fats" by the schoolkids who shuffled down the aisles to his daily piano accompaniment. Adeline Waller was mortified by her son's new nickname and lobbied forcefully against it among Waller's many new friends, but of course the name stuck. Surprisingly, Edward Waller seems, for a time, to have been quite proud of his son's piano accomplishment, at one point even attempting to steer his boy along the correct musical path by escorting him to hear Paderewski at a Carnegie Hall recital. Waller was, in fact, deeply impressed by the Paderewski performance and would speak of it often in later years. His own taste in piano music, however, already tended toward ragtime—"the devil's music," heard now throughout the Waller's Harlem neighborhood—an abomination, in the eyes of his parents, to which they would never be reconciled.

The physical strain of repeated childbearing coupled with the emotional strain of six premature fatalities among her children would take a toll on Adeline Waller's health. As her youngest son entered his teens Mrs. Waller was forced increasingly to her bed for extended periods, allowing Thomas Waller more and more hours at liberty on the Harlem streets. For a time he worked as a home delivery boy for Eckert's Delicatessen and for two cousins who, respectively, owned a grocery and a pigfoot stand. Moving through Harlem's predominantly white neighborhoods, Waller made personal contact for the first time with a white world beyond the "black belt" he'd inhabited since birth. On one occasion, while making an Eckert's delivery, he was attacked by a gang of white youths and stabbed, though not seriously injured.

He would leave school for good in the spring of 1918, taking a summer job between semesters at DeWitt Clinton High School with his older sister in a lower-Manhattan jewelbox factory blocks away from Trinity Church, where Waller befriended the sexton and played the church piano on lunch breaks. Less than one year later, he would accept another delivery job for a Harlem delicatessen owned by the Immerman brothers, his delivery duties this time including frequent "hootch runs" carrying bottles of bootleg liquor concealed in the baggy clothing that draped his oversized frame.

Always a colossal eater, Waller now weighed more than 200 pounds. He was becoming quite a familiar sight on the Harlem streets and was, in turn, coming to know those streets intimately. Of particular interest to him were the cellar clubs and cafes in and around 135th Street and the seductive music pouring out of them day and night. After working briefly as a keyboard accompanist to silent film serials on Saturdays at the Crescent motion picture house on 135th Street (number 69 West), between Fifth and Lenox Avenues, Waller managed to persuade Mazie Mullins, resident pianist at the Lincoln Theatre—the Crescent's neighbor at number 58 West 135th Street, a former nickelodeon turned–silent-film house—to let him sit in at the Lincoln's new $10,000 Wurlitzer pipe organ on her breaks. Within weeks, after drawing a foot-stomping crowd of his former classmates to the theater on a regular basis to hear him pound out his own versions of raunchy tunes like "Monkey Rag" and "All Night Long" (to which the kids shouted out their own suggestive, parodying lyrics in accompaniment) Waller was offered the regular organist's job at the Lincoln.

He soon was a fixture there, known to many in Harlem for his abilities on the Lincoln organ and his antics in the Lincoln orchestra pit. His playing improved appreciably with regular work, and Waller began to think of himself for the first time as a professional musician. Meeting other professional Harlem musicians also opened up for Waller a vastly attractive new world of fluent sight reading, orchestral arrangements, jazz and blues music, chorus girls, and backstage alcoholic intermissions. With the Lincoln Theatre also frequented for its between-film stage shows by white theatrical and Tin Pan Alley professionals, Waller sent many of these emissaries from the downtown theatrical establishment home with at least an amused awareness of the singularly talented and popular young organist at the Lincoln Theater.

The death of Adeline Waller from a massive, diabetes-related stroke on November 10, 1920, brought to a premature end Thomas Waller's rather idyllic Harlem boyhood. His relations with his father, who vehemently disapproved of his son's working as a musician in a motion picture house, had never been the best. Left alone with his older sister and the grieving man in a house that had once been the sum of his existence, the 16-year-old Waller did what he would often do in years to come when confronted by trying circumstances: he ran. On a summer night, months after Adeline Waller's death, a former classmate of Waller's, Wilson Brooks, found him waiting on the stoop of the Brooks's 131st Street residence. Waller informed Brooks that he'd left home for good.

With the permission of the Brooks family (and his own father's consent), Waller moved into the Brooks household. One immediate dividend was access to the player piano in the Brooks's parlor. Waller began to spend entire days at the instrument, fitting his fingers to the depressed keys as it played, trying to follow in the chordings of the popular piano roll makers of the day: Eubie Blake, Charles "Luckey" Roberts, and James P. Johnson.

It was Wilson Brooks's older brother, Russell, an admired Harlem pianist himself, who introduced Waller to Johnson. "I asked James P. if he knew Fats Waller," Russell Brooks later recalled, "the kid who played organ at the Lincoln. James P. said he knew who Fats was but didn't know him personally. I told James that Fats wanted to meet him real bad and that he wanted to play just like him. I asked him to listen to Fats and maybe help him a little. I kept telling James P. how much Fats wanted to play like him and eventually he agreed to see him."

Hulking, reticent, absorbed solely by music, the 28-year-old Johnson was a highly unlikely candidate for willing mentor to a 17-year-old kid piano player. Yet Johnson took the teenager brought before him by Russell Brooks and adopted the boy musically.

"I took Fats home," Johnson remembered. "I was living with my sister at 267 West 140th Street. She had a piano and I brought mine there, too . . . I'd get on one piano, he'd get on the other, and we'd work together. This went on for a couple of years, steady. He picked up all the stomps and rags I knew and that walkin' bass, too . . . I taught him how to groove, how to make it sweet. . . . He stuck pretty well to my pattern, developed a lovely swinging tone, a large melodic expression and, being the son of a preacher, he had fervor."

"Right after James P. heard Fats Waller playing the pipe organ, he came home and told me, 'I can teach that boy,'" Lillie Mae Johnson would add to her husband's recollection. "Well, from then on it was one big headache for me. Fats was seventeen, and we lived on 140th Street, and Fats would bang on our piano till all hours of the night—sometime two, three, four o'clock in the morning. I would say to him, 'Now go on home—or haven't you got a home?'

"But he'd come every day and my husband would teach. Of course, you know the organ doesn't give you a left hand, and that's what James P. had to teach him."

Johnson disciplined the youngster's technique with scale exercises. He impressed upon him the unsurpassable value of melody in the improvisational scheme, instructing Waller in the history of ragtime-based improvisation. Most thrillingly, Johnson inducted his protégé into the Harlem piano fraternity.

By the Twenties, that fraternity covered a colorful variety of venues, an ever-widening map of cabarets, cafes, saloons, nightclubs, and dance halls where pianists played, plus that supreme performance forum for any Harlem piano man, the "rent party."

"Even before the Depression," related Willie "the Lion" Smith, "Harlem citizens having a hard time meeting their high rents latched onto the gimmick of having a party and charging anywhere from twenty-five cents to a dollar for admission. Piano players called these affairs 'jumps' or 'shouts'. . . . On occasion these sessions would start early in the afternoon and keep going until far into the next day. . . . But you had to stay by the keyboard to hold your own reputation for being a fast pianist. . . . Some of the greatest stride piano ever heard in New York City was played at rent parties."

Stride piano was a keyboard style indigenous to New York City, and it would be impossible to appreciate the music made by its foremost innovator, James P. Johnson, and his disciple, Fats Waller —the music that Andy Razaf soon would set lyrics to—without understanding, at least superficially, the stride piano technique.

Predominantly, it was a two-handed style. While the right hand "tickled" the melody in a counter-rhythmic arabesque of chords and arpeggios, the left hand pounded bass lines, alternating mid-keyboard chords and octave-distant single notes: rapid-fire strides. The left hands of the very best stride pianists ruled the lower keyboard regions with machinelike efficiency, producing a pulsing, full-bodied piano sound, one that approached pianistically the richness of a full orchestra's. Stride piano was party music— exhilarating, room-filling. Stride pianists were party virtuosos, in many ways the first virtuosos of jazz.

"Every move we made was studied, practiced, and developed just like it was a complicated piano piece," remembered James P. Johnson, whose seeming shyness belied the theatrical savvy of a prima donna.

> When you came into a place you had a three-way play. You never took your overcoat or hat off until you were at the piano. First you laid your cane on the music rack. Then you took off your overcoat, folded it, and put it on the piano with the lining showing.
>
> You then took off your hat before the audience. Each tickler had his own gesture for removing his hat with a little flourish; that was part of his attitude, too. You took out your little silk handkerchief, shook it out, and dusted off the piano stool.
>
> Every tickler had his special trademark chord, like a signal— players would start off by sitting down, wait for the audience to quiet down, and then strike their chord, holding it with the pedal to make it ring.
>
> Then they'd do a run up and down the piano—a scale of arpeggios—or if they were real good, they might play a set of modulations, very offhand, as if there was nothing to it. They'd look around idly to see if they knew any chicks near the piano. If they saw somebody they'd start a light conversation about the theater, the races, or social doings—light chat. At this time, they'd drift into a rag, any kind of pretty stuff, but without tempo. Some ticklers would cross their legs and go on chatting with friends nearby. It took a lot of practice to play this way, while talking and with your head and body turned.
>
> Then, without stopping the smart talk or turning back to the piano, he'd attack without any warning, smashing right into the regular beat of the piece. That would knock them dead.
>
> After your opening piece to astound the audience, it would depend on the gal you were playing for or the mood of the place

for what you would play next. It might be sentimental, moody, stompy, or funky. The good player had to know just what the mood of the audience was.

At the end of his set, he'd always finish up with a hot rag and then stand up quickly, so that everybody in the place would be able to see who knocked it.

When James P. Johnson was satisfied that Thomas Waller's tender stride technique was up to it, he turned Waller loose on the uptown rent strut circuit. He introduced the young pianist to, "Lippy" Boyette, a sometime player who booked talent for the "shouts," to "Corky" Williams, "Beetle" Henderson, "the Lion," of course, and the other professional party pianists, the veritable handful who had created for themselves near mythic Harlem piano reputations with fleet musical imagination, boundless physical stamina, and herculean left hands.

Thomas Waller's first Harlem rent party performance occurred at the Lenox Avenue Apartments on 141st Street sometime in 1921, performing at the behest of James P. Johnson, who arranged for the date with the unofficial rent strut booker uptown, "Lippy" Boyette. Johnson and Willie "the Lion" Smith were the two pianists most in demand on the Boyette circuit—"the Big Two," as Smith put it. Johnson, in fact, was committed elsewhere the night of Waller's rent party debut (the young novice would perform with "Corky" Williams and the man who had introduced him to James P. Johnson, Russell Brooks). Waller's mentor had however, prepared him well for this unveiling: Waller dazzled his co-performers, as well as the strut's assembled revelers. For the previous year or so, Thomas Waller had been accompanying Johnson and Smith to these affairs as their "shadow," in Smith's words. Now he would join them as an associate, even a competitor, at the keyboard. "The Big Two" had become "the Big Three."

The 17-year-old Waller's development at this time was nothing short of mercurial, both personally and professionally. Early in 1921, he had attempted to assuage the loneliness that had enveloped him since his mother's passing by marrying Edith Hatchett, a devout and quite unworldly young woman—very well brought up and very much the girl Adeline Waller would have wanted her son to marry—after meeting the teenaged Hatchett on a small band date near her home on Brook Avenue in the Bronx. With little money in his pocket, Waller had moved in with his young bride and her parents, placing himself in debt to the Hatchetts, who repeatedly made it clear to their new son-in-law that they, like his father, deeply disapproved of careers in music.

After briefly taking leave from his Lincoln Theatre post to appear out of town for the first time as an accompanist to a vaudeville act—"Liza and Her Shufflin' Six"—in a tour that Waller stuck with through New England and down so far as Washington, DC, he returned to the city to take over the prized piano chair at Leroy's, recently and unceremoniously vacated by temperamental Willie "the Lion" Smith. Rescued from a terminal case of pre-opening stagefright by James P. and Lil Johnson, who drilled him incessantly on the art of accompanying chorus dancers, Fats Waller in his Harlem nightclub debut proved another unqualified success.

In the spring of 1921, Waller's first child, Thomas, Jr., was born. Within weeks of the birth, in a quite wrongheaded attempt to pacify his increasingly disenchanted wife and her disapproving family by somehow earning more money, he embarked on an eastern circuit burlesque tour. His return brought Waller face to face with the fundamental disintegration of his marital life, as his wife, loudly threatening divorce, essentially drove him from her parents' home. It was the beginning of an endlessly woeful battle with Edith Waller over his duties as a husband and father that would come to consume the greater part of his life.

The story of Andy Razaf and Thomas Waller's first encounter long ago descended into the doubtable realm of legend and a firm date remains speculative. Harlem's Roosevelt Theatre on 145th Street and an amateur piano contest constitute the setting, with Waller, the youngest contestant entered playing James P. Johnson's "Carolina Shout." Certain chroniclers and survivors of that time in Harlem have generally recorded the year as 1923. One or two other, fairly reliable sources, though, have placed the contest in 1921. The notion of Waller entering an amateur competition rings far truer in 1921 than in 1923, by which time the young pianist had been playing professionally among Harlem's piano elite for at least two years. It also seems highly improbable that Andy Razaf, in his endless circumnavigating of the Harlem music scene, would not have had the chance to meet Waller before 1923—at Leroy's, at the Lincoln, or at any number of rent parties. Razaf himself acknowledged this in a 1955 interview, while refusing to contradict the Roosevelt piano contest legend, conceding that, "I used to listen to [Waller at the Lincoln Theatre] often. . . . Eventually, because everyone knew him and everyone was his friend, I somehow came to meet him, too."

It is certain that Waller won the Roosevelt Theatre contest. On the sidewalk outside the theatre at the corner of 145th Street and Lenox Avenue, the story goes, audience member Razaf chased down the victorious young pianist, congratulated him on his success, introduced himself as a poet and lyricist, and invited Waller to stop with him for a cup of coffee in Razaf's apartment, which proved to be just on the other side of the block from Waller's own residence.

The mismatched pairing, in retrospect, seems almost preordained. Waller was an extroverted, wildly carefree spirit just then discovering the fullness of his performing personality, as well as the great bacchanalian thirst that would stoke it. Razaf was an intense craftsman, equally charming and hardly shy but utterly temperate. Razaf's talent was no less effusive than Waller's; it was the finer element of discipline that would divide them. They were opposites who counterbalanced beautifully, their contemporaries later insisted, odd partners in a perfect if unlikely marriage. "During their years together," Waller's son Maurice later observed, "Andy's methodic planning and discipline served as a necessary balance for his partner's instability."

The equation was hardly so elementary. In attitude, even in physical dimension, no two more dissimilar types could have existed, the rotund Waller a jovial, childish, towering misbehaver; the slender, slight Razaf a droll, princely mannerist. Beneath the surface, though, the two men were surprisingly similar. As impractical, for instance, as Waller undeniably could be, he also would prove far more worldly than his more business-wise but often artless partner. As levelheaded as Razaf was, the lyricist's sense of what was right and just could move him to behavior as volatile and sometimes self-destructive as that which would make his new partner so justly famous. Both were mama's boys, dutifully bound in love to mother, and by marital devotion to exceedingly maternal spouses. This devotion did not, however, include for either man anything remotely resembling marital fidelity and neither perceived the slightest inconsistency in his respective conjugal juggling act. Lastly, both wrote quickly and hardly ever rewrote. For Fats Waller and for Andy Razaf, songwriting would be an act of spontaneous creation.

In joining with Andy Razaf, what was young Fats Waller getting? A Broadway songwriter—once; a published songwriter—three times; a struggling Harlem songwriter favored by local Harlem musicians; a promising professional who knew his way around a lead sheet and also knew his way downtown.

Ultimately Waller responded to the elder Razaf as he responded to all the older musicians who took an interest in his career. He let them take care of him in any way that suited them. If Razaf wanted to write lyrics to Fats Waller's as yet unwritten music and sell the resulting songs downtown, that was fine with him. Give him time and he would try and write some.

Of course, Waller's rank among Harlem piano men was already acknowledged by the time he met Andy Razaf, whether in 1921 or 1923. Opportunities were materializing for him beyond 135th Street, and many friends, old and new, were trying to get the boy's attention. New friends like Bud Allen, the owner of a small music shop on 135th Street near Lenox Avenue, who idolized Waller, urging him to write his music down, to notate and copyright and perhaps even get lyrics set to his tunes, and then to try selling them downtown. Friends like James P. Johnson introduced Waller to the QRS (Quality Reigns Supreme) Piano Roll Corporation, where Johnson himself recorded; Waller cut his first piano roll for QRS in March 1923. More and more, though, questionable friends now began to enter Waller's life, like the rascally, if marginally benign, Clarence Williams.

A composer himself, New Orleans born, with a number of popular song hits to his credit, including "Baby, Won't You Please Come Home?" (written with Charles Warfield) and the jazz standard "Royal Garden Blues" (with Spencer Williams), as well as a former Clef Club pianist who played, according to Willie "the Lion" Smith, "as if he was wearing mittens," the somewhat owlish, roly-poly Williams had left New Orleans in 1917 at the age of 19, after achieving some early publishing success there initially selling songs on street corners. Arriving in New York, following a stint as a music publisher in Chicago, Williams really had hit his stride pushing his own songs to the city's growing minions of female blues singers, even marrying, in 1922, one of these potential customers himself, a talented *Shuffle Along* chorine named Eva Taylor whom he would successfully promote throughout the Twenties.

Recognizing perhaps faster than most the surpassing value of phonograph recordings in the new blues boom, Williams also had ingratiated himself with the white men who ran the recording industry's new "race labels"—Fred Hager at OKeh and particularly Frank Walker at Columbia, who took to using Clarence Williams as his race record "scout." It was in this capacity that Williams gained credit for discovering the greatest of all blues singers, Bessie Smith, and bringing her to Frank Walker, though it has since become clear that Williams did not actually discover Bessie Smith but merely collected the already popular blues singer from South Philadelphia, where she was appearing in the musical comedy revue *"How Come?"* and delivered her to Walker in New York at Walker's request. One way or another, Williams did manage to place himself as Bessie Smith's accompanist for her first Columbia recording sessions, an arrangement that lasted perhaps two months. As Smith's "manager," it appears, Williams took to pocketing half of the singer's $175-per-selection recording fee. The "Empress of the Blues" did not stand for this sort of thing. Contentiously, she cornered her manager/accompanist in his office and, so the story goes, pummeled him, the beating ending only after Williams consented to Miss Smith's contractual release.

Clarence Williams, with characteristic assiduity, befriended the young and easy Thomas Waller very early on, after duly noticing Waller at the Lincoln Theatre. In one month, Williams secured at least three gigs for a very disinterested Waller in the downtown recording studios, persuading Fred Hager to hire the young Harlem pianist as an accompanist to blues singer Sara Martin for a first session early in October 1922. Waller, almost predictably, failed to show for that date. Undaunted, Williams again prevailed upon Hager to book Fats Waller for Sara Martin's next session. Once again Waller was a no-show. Williams, though, was tenacious and finally managed to lure the footloose young pianist to an Okeh recording studio for his own Fats Waller solo session still later in October of 1922, at which time Waller recorded solo piano renditions of an anonymous something called "Muscle Shoals Blues" and also "Birmingham Blues," his own original composition. Before the year was out, Waller would appear on six more sides for OKeh as Sara Martin's accompanist, and under Clarence Williams' stewardship, his recording career was launched.

Clarence Williams looked out for himself. That also meant looking out for his dependents—the musicians for whom he found record dates, the singers for whom he found songs. A far more talented entrepreneur than piano player or composer, Williams recognized the opportunity inherent in the growing audience for new black music both uptown and downtown. Not content simply to compose or record music for this new market, Williams, in 1922, formed his own publishing company. Clarence Williams Music Publishing proved no benign sponsor of black songwriters, however. Setting up shop downtown in the Gaiety Theatre Building, near the new Times Square heart of Tin Pan Alley, and taking his cue from the song publishing racketeers who were now his neighbors, Williams perpetuated many of the Alley's seamiest practices, reneging on advances, abstaining from royalty agreements, conducting himself with a general unscrupulousness that black songwriters narrowly had believed was the exclusive domain of white publishers.

Having at last captured young Waller's attention with the breakout series of OKeh recording sessions that he'd engineered for him, Williams now began to press the pianist for new, publishable songs. At first Waller merely responded to William's entreaties with casual visits to the Clarence Williams Music Publishing offices, noodling at Williams's in-house piano, amusing himself simply by being downtown. But Williams persisted. "Do you want to stay in Harlem all your life?" he is reported to have asked Waller at one point. Finally the young pianist, genuinely impressed with the money and acclaim accruing to his mentor James P. Johnson from the success of *Runnin' Wild*, submitted a pair of original tunes to Williams for consideration.

Unsurprisingly, both displayed a strong James P. Johnson influence, Waller having borrowed liberally for both songs from his favorite Johnson composition, a tune called "Fascination." "Wild Cat Blues," in many ways an early draft for one of Waller's more celebrated later piano pieces, "Handful of Keys," impressed Williams mildly. He bought the song, would record it himself with a small group in July 1923, but never, in fact, chose to publish it.

The second song, also derived thematically from "Fascination," proved to be a tune with a rather grubby history that soon would grow even murkier. One of the bawdiest and most frequently performed naughty blues numbers on the rent-party circuit was a vivid bit of vulgarity entitled "The Boy in the Boat." Every musician in Harlem knew the tune, including Clarence Williams, of course. What Waller had done for his second song effort (and the young pianist readily admitted this) was take the unmistakable limerick-like cadence of "The Boy in the Boat"'s obscene lyric and compose his own tune for it, which, Waller informed Williams, he called "The Boston Blues."

Clever song connoisseur that he was, Clarence Williams recognized that musically there was much merit to Waller's peculiar creation. Toying with the tune's blue melody, he first rendered "The Boston Blues" into popular song form by having Waller inflate it from twelve to sixteen bars. Williams then composed his own lyric for "The Boston Blues," a lyric that parodied (for reasons known only to Clarence Williams) the popular Victor Herbert waltz "Kiss Me Again," from Herbert's 1906 operetta *Mlle. Modiste.*

At this point, specifics about the song's final stages of gestation grow even more undecipherable. Somehow—it is not at all clear how—Victor Herbert's music publishers for "Kiss Me Again," M. Witmark and Sons, apparently learned what Clarence Williams had done with Herbert's lyric and threatened Williams with court proceedings if he published his song parody. Williams had no choice but to shelve the tune, which he did—publishing it instead some two years later, retitled and with new lyrics again credited to Clarence Williams. This new song, now called "Squeeze Me," turned out to be a charmingly understated, wryly lascivious gem that would endure over the years as one of Thomas Waller's most appealing efforts. The song's terrifically sexy and supple lyric, however, always would trouble many knowledgeable listeners with its utter lack of stylistic resemblance to anything Clarence Williams ever had or ever would write, a conundrum that was either resolved or exacerbated by Andy Razaf, toward the end of his life. Suspending a categoric, career-long refusal to address the issue of authorship for any songs that might somehow have appeared over the years with other names than his own on them, Razaf did quietly acknowledge to a journalist in 1960 that the clever and in many ways exceedingly characteristic lyric for "Squeeze Me" had, in fact, been his.

Whether the "Squeeze Me" lyric was supplied by Razaf as early as 1923 or as late as 1925, this example of music publishing pilferage by Clarence Williams stands as a perfect symbol for the song partnership of Andy Razaf and Thomas "Fats" Waller. Of all the songwriters to emerge from Harlem in the Twenties, Razaf and Waller were destined, as a team, to become the most prolific, the most indigenously representative of Harlem and its music during this decade, and, in that respect, the most important. That they also wound up, in many ways, the most victimized professionally by the dubious business practices of Tin Pan Alley only confirms how symbolic their partnership was to the decade. The many object lessons that Razaf and Waller came to embody for the world of

American music ultimately are transcended, though, by the songs that they soon produced as one of the greatest songwriting partnerships in history. "Squeeze Me," then, which may or may not have been Razaf and Waller's debut song composition, certainly remains clouded enough in its history and exceptional enough in overall quality to qualify as having been the first.

Courtesy Razaf Estate.

PROGRAM

The "Creole Follies"

Presented Nightly
—— at the ——
CLUB ALABAM'
Formerly THE LITTLE CLUB

44th ST. THEATRE BUILDING
NEW YORK

Courtesy Razaf Estate.

7

Ain't-Cha' Glad?

Ain't-cha' glad,
We were mated for each other?
Ain't-cha' glad
That we waited for each other?
We agree—
Constantly.
Life is just a symphony
Of perfect harmony.

> — *"Ain't-Cha' Glad?"*
> by Andy Razaf and Thomas Waller

Nothing about Andrea Razaf's association with Thomas Waller was ever tidy or even remotely businesslike. After discovering each other in the early Twenties, the two songwriters hardly embarked on anything resembling a regular work schedule. Essentially, the bulk of Razaf's creative energy from the outset of his collaborative life with Waller was expended in tracking his partner down around Harlem and inducing him, by stealth, sagacity, and cunning, to stop at a piano for an hour or so and write. Waller, therefore, never could be the sum of Razaf's collaborative universe; alternates and stand-ins always had to be employed. While beginning to work, more or less, with Waller in 1923, for example, Razaf also sold four songs to Tin Pan Alley in collaboration with other songmen: "Waltz Divine," with Hughie Woolford; a tune entitled "There Never Was a Girl Like

You, Wonderful Girl of Mine," music by Babe Thompson and S. Walter Williams, published by Maison-Blanche Music in December 1923; and two songs composed with pianist Edgar Dowell, a first-rate ragtime player out of Baltimore, remembered particularly by Eubie Blake for his playing in an organ duel at a Baltimore party thrown by a girlfriend of Blake's, when Blake was 15 years old. "He cut me so bad," the veteran keyboardist later recalled. "He played more notes in his left hand than I did. He had this great left hand, wiped me right off the place. Then he took my girl. She had her arms around him . . . Dowell killed me . . . I didn't play the organ for two years after that."

Razaf may have met Edgar Dowell through Hughie Woolford, a Baltimore native himself, who had grown up with both Dowell and Blake. A skilled, ragtime-inflected songwriter, Dowell's greatest success had come the previous season, in 1922, with his rather eccentric "That Da Da Strain," a roiling novelty number written with Mamie Medina that many early jazz musicians took to as a favorite improvisational theme. Dowell's work with Razaf in 1923 was not quite so memorable. Their two songs together, "No One Can Toddle Like My Cousin Sue" and "He Wasn't Born in Araby (But He's a Sheikin' Fool)," ultimately were purchased in October 1923 by Rainbow Music (a new firm recently established by Irving Berlin as a "Race" subsidiary to his own Irving Berlin Music publishing company at 1607 Broadway, under the direction of black songwriters Bob Ricketts and Porter Grainger) after "He Wasn't Born in Araby" was featured in the 1923 edition of Lew Leslie's *Plantation Revue*, upstairs over the Winter Garden Theatre.

Despite their frivolous titles, both tunes had merit, particularly "No One Can Toddle Like My Cousin Sue"—a light spoof on "I Wish I Could Shimmy Like My Sister Kate," a song hit the previous season by New Orleans clarinetist Armond Piron—with a delightfully dry, offhand Razaf lyric that told the modestly salacious tale of "that cousin of mine" who "toddled from the time that she was nine months old." "No-one can toddle like my cousin Sue," Razaf wrote, "It is the bestest thing that she can do,/Everytime she puts it on she makes a hit,/She has a tantalizin' way of doin' it"—quite effectively laying the word "tantalizin'" atop the rolling, toddling cadence of Dowell's insinuating melody. "They like her toddle," Razaf then added, "and she's got good sense,/It floored the landlord—he cut the rent"—a sly bit of Harlem-directed social commentary expressed with an effortless "floored-landlord" interior rhyme—

before concluding, "We've got to thank our stars, the work she's done,/She toddled for the coal man—he left her some,/We'll have her do it for the tax possessor too,/No one can toddle like my cousin Sue."

Published in February 1924, these new songs quickly received recording coverage: "He Wasn't Born In Araby" by vocalist Lena Wilson, accompanied by Porter Grainger on piano for the Ajax label in March 1924, and "No One Can Toddle" by Lillian Goodal and her Jazzin' Trio for Ajax as well, in December 1923. The two records appear to have constituted Razaf's debut as a songwriter on disc.

The association with Rainbow Music on these songs was, in itself, quite significant, though. During the initial years of the black blues vogue, Tin Pan Alley's dominant white music publishing houses categorically had ignored blues music as something beneath their consideration, ceding the field to the industry's new black music publishers W. C. Handy, Clarence Williams, and Perry Bradford. This abdication did not last long. In July 1923, the Jack Mills Publishing Company, in a lengthy *Amsterdam News* feature story, confirmed that, in addition to having recently acquired the publishing rights for at least 60 "blues" numbers, it also had now signed to exclusive contracts a very impressive stable of black songwriters, including Will Vodery, Henry Creamer, Tim Brymn, Spencer Williams, Chris Smith, Shelton Brooks, James P. Johnson, and Edgar Dowell, among others. "The permanency of the purpose to corral the Negro musical talent is best expressed by the fact that in their advertising they are especially interested in encouraging the younger and newer composers to submit their offerings," the *News* story observed. "Add to this the picture presented by a view of the [Mills] home office with its big percentage of Negro visitors, the race members of the staff in open evidence, and the ease with which members of our group obtain an interview with the executives, and one begins to believe that . . . one liberal-minded concern [has] opened wide the gateway for Negroes into a field that very properly belongs to us, yet under whose fence we have heretofore been obliged to crawl, if we would enter."

Mills' activism impelled other white publishers to join the black blues fray. E. B. Marks Music Company announced their *"African Opera Series of Blues."* Shapiro, Bernstein & Company set up a "race" subsidiary of their own, Skidmore Music Company. In September 1923, former song plugger and long-time publishing industry merchandiser of black music Joe Davis announced his

Triangle Music Publishing Company's "serious entry into the 'blues' business," with the signing of four new "blues" singers: Josie Miles, Ludie Wells, Gladys Jordan, and Ruth Coleman.

After testing this marketplace with Edgar Dowell, Razaf began to explore in earnest the new publishing climate on Tin Pan Alley in 1924 together with his new song partner, Thomas Waller. Though still largely unproven as song professionals, they enjoyed a mutual popularity downtown—Waller for his unpredictability and boundless talent, Razaf for his ebullient charm and dignity—that made them an irresistible team. Waller also introduced Razaf to the new world of thoroughly unmanaged late-night drinking, eating, and womanizing after hours in Harlem with James P. Johnson and Willie "the Lion" Smith, weekend orgies of food and liquor at Clarence Williams's handsome new house out in Jamaica, Queens, and regular late-afternoon meetings of the "Joy Club," an alcoholically convivial gathering of black songwriters in Perry Bradford's offices at the Gaiety Building that officially concluded the song-selling day downtown preparatory to the long nights ahead uptown. The Joy Club's motto: "Whenever business mess up with pleasure, then cut out the business and let the pleasure roll on."

Clarence Williams now monopolized Waller as a songwriter; Williams would acquire some seventy Fats Waller tunes over the next five years, only a handful of which he ever published. Razaf, in turn, sold Clarence Williams thirteen songs in 1924, eleven of them in collaboration with Waller, the other two with words *and* music by Andrea Razaf. Of these many songs, only one proved worthy of publication, so far as Clarence Williams was concerned—"I'd Rather Be Blue Than Green," which Williams released on August 4, 1924, credited by committee to Clarence Williams, Spencer Williams, Andrea Razaf, and Thomas Waller.

Williams also was instrumental in Razaf's radio debut in 1924 over station WGCP, the "Grand Central Palace" frequency, at which time the young lyricist performed as "Crooning Andy Razaf," accompanying himself on ukelele. Ever the enterprising visionary, Clarence Williams already was something of a radio veteran in 1924, though wireless radio broadcasts had been a fact of life in the United States for only four years, and network radio still was a renegade affair, comprising exclusively small local radio stations across the country randomly sending out experimental programs over the airwaves. Appreciating the potential value of wireless broadcasting as free promotion for himself and his various musical enterprises, Williams, in the summer of 1922, had dragged his "Blue Five" jazz ensemble over to a tiny, sweltering radio studio on Tenth Avenue to broadcast in their shirtsleeves for whoever might be listening. Since then, Williams had made frequent use of radio, bringing Waller out to Newark for his first broadcast, over a local Newark station, in 1923, live from the stage of the Fox Terminal Theatre in concert with Clarence Williams' "Blue Five" and Williams' wife, vocalist Eva Taylor. For Razaf, Williams's debut radio bookings were the beginning of a marginally rewarding but quite active secondary career over the airwaves. They also marked his professional debut as a singer.

In the basement of the 44th Street Theatre Building at 216 West 44th Street, between Seventh and Eighth Avenues, just opposite the downtown end of Shubert Alley, there was, in 1923, a cabaret called the Little Club. Partly owned by Broadway's Shubert Brothers, whose offices overlooked the Little Club from the upper floors of the Sam S. Shubert Theatre across 44th Street, and managed by Paul Salvin with his son Sam, who together also ran the Plantation Cafe on 50th Street and several other downtown nightspots, the Little Club, in its three Prohibition years of operation, had been raided only once, before Federal agents moved in on it in March of 1923 and closed it for good. Within a matter of months the Little Club space was reopened, again under Shubert auspices, as Club Balagan, "a quiet cabaret with Russian entertainment," according to *Variety*, boasting a chorus of 16 and a Russian orchestra, "which plays jazz and classic music with equal skill." When, in turn, Club Balagan closed, rather quickly and quite unceremoniously, a new ownership team took over the basement Little Club space with the more timely intention of turning it into a new downtown supper club showcase for black talent to be called the Club Alabam.

The Club Alabam opened in January 1924 with dinner, dancing, and black entertainment—"The Creole Follies," starring Edith Wilson, Maude Mills, Arthur Bryson, and a company of twenty entertainers—along with the Club Alabam Orchestra, led by Fletcher Henderson, a slender, light-skinned young bandleader with a strikingly cultivated, elegantly impassive demeanor. As one of the few "colored" floor shows below 125th Street, the Club Alabam "Creole Follies" was greeted warmly by those among Broadway's after-theater night crawlers who preferred to pay for their Negro entertainment, if possible, without the inconvenience of a journey uptown.

In March, a second edition of "The Creole Follies" was introduced. Added to the bill, alongside Edith Wilson and the Club Alabam Orchestra, was a veteran vaudeville comedic dancer named "Doc" Straine, who later teamed up quite successfully with Edith Wilson in a vaudeville act of their own. Straine's partner at the Club Alabam, however, was a man: "Anthony," according to surviving club programs; Straine often billed himself as "Strange" when working with a partner—these programs identified his "Creole Follies" act as "Strange and Anthony."

Few beyond the insular Harlem song and entertainment world were aware that Strange's "Anthony" in this instance was a 28-year-old lyricist named Andrea Razaf. Believing that "it should be part of a songwriter's education" to learn the "inside workings" of all aspects of the show business, "in order to be able to write all types of songs," Razaf had said yes when Harry Goldberg, the Club Alabam's "promoter in residence," invited him to work the Club Alabam revue in 1924 as Straine's partner, under the name "Anthony." Razaf believed the new experience onstage would be highly educational. He also, secretly, found it quite gratifying.

Perhaps the greatest dividend that this engagement paid Razaf, though, was the lifelong friendship that it kindled between the novice performer–lyricist and the Club Alabam's enigmatic orchestra leader, Fletcher Henderson. Born December 18, 1897, in Cuthbert, Georgia, the son of an upper-middle-class Cuthbert schoolmaster and his wife, a pianist and music teacher, Henderson was a proud, chronically reticent musician who had received sound fundamental piano instruction from both parents and a series of classical piano teachers, yet seems never to have warmed wholeheartedly to music as a career. Initially Henderson had come to New York with a bachelor of arts degree from Atlanta University in the summer of 1920, intending to enroll at Columbia University for graduate work in chemistry, an intention he never fulfilled. Securing summer employment quite casually at the Pace & Handy Music Publishing offices as a song demonstrator, transposer, and song plugger, Henderson soon found his plans for graduate school overwhelmed by the glamor of Tin Pan Alley, combined with increasingly regular night work as a musician. When Handy's partner, Harry Pace, left their publishing business to form the first all-black phonograph record company, Black Swan records, up in Harlem in January 1921, the 23-year-old Henderson had gone along with Pace as his musical director or "recording manager," charged with selecting and rehearsing the musicians for Pace's record sessions. It was as a piano-playing participant on many of these early Black Swan sessions, backing the likes of Ethel Waters and other young black vocalists on the hot new song material provoked by Mamie Smith's recent recordings, that Henderson, essentially a classically trained pianist, gained his introductory blues education, as well as a few early pointers on the subject of jazz.

After working incessantly throughout the years 1921 to 1923—in the recording studios for Black Swan, on tour with the Black Swan Troubadours, an aggregation of Black Swan artists sent out on a series of promotional junkets throughout the Northeast and Deep South in 1922, and increasingly as the accompanist of choice for numerous blues record dates, backing just about every female blues singer of note—Henderson in late 1923 had hauled a band of his regular studio session mates, including at least two budding jazz titans— Don Redman on alto saxophone and Coleman Hawkins on tenor— over to an audition at the old Little Club space on West 44th Street and won the incipient Club Alabam's orchestra job. A moderately ambitious young man with an acute musical mind, decent piano skills, and a potent facility for spotting young musical talent, but very little appetite for taking charge and running things, the 26-year-old Henderson was ill suited to the responsibilities of band management, yet extraordinarily well suited to the band duties of musical direction, as it turned out. At the Club Alabam, for better or worse, he found himself, almost overnight, a big-time Broadway bandleader.

Henderson and his orchestra concluded their very successful Club Alabam debut at the end of six months and prepared to move seven blocks up Broadway to perform for the summer season before dancers at the whites-only Roseland Ballroom at 1658 Broadway, near 51st Street. It was during this Roseland residency, a stint that extended by popular demand well beyond the summer of 1924 to the very end of the decade, in fact, that Henderson and his superb orchestra evolved into the finest jazz ensemble yet seen or heard in New York City. Pioneers of a highly sophisticated, "arranged," "big band" approach to jazz improvisation, rooted in the grandiose New York City band style of James Reese Europe's Clef Club, Henderson and a host of superb musical arrangers captured an essence of jazz expression that the Henderson band eventually came to embody: swing.

It is easy to imagine Andy Razaf and Fletcher Henderson striking up their friendship at the Club Alabam: two educated and profoundly dignified, even aristocratic young black men in the frequently coarse backstage surroundings of a Prohibition-era, whites-only nightclub where the black talent could not have been treated with particular gentility. In April, at an Emerson recording session for blues singer Ethel Finnie led by one of Henderson's favorite trumpeters, Joe Smith, Fletcher Henderson teamed up with various Henderson sidemen for one more recording of the Razaf-Dowell composition "He Wasn't Born in Araby (But He's a Sheikin' Fool)." Eight weeks later, Henderson departed the Club Alabam, while Razaf stayed on for perhaps a month more.

Henderson's replacement at the Club Alabam was the highly regarded Harlem bandleader Sam Wooding, fresh from an opening engagement at the new Nest Club on West 133rd Street. "The Creole Follies" was again revised on the occasion of Wooding's arrival and, though "Doc" Straine appears to have departed at this point along with Edith Wilson, he left behind his partner "Anthony," who now persuaded Harry Goldberg to give him his own number in the revue. Razaf also gained Goldberg's permission to write the tune for this spotlight turn himself, words and music. The whole business was staged by the Club Alabam dance director, Elida Webb, for full chorus and an "eye-pleasing bevy of showgirls," billed as "The Honeysuckle Rosebuds." The title of Razaf's tune was, in fact, "Honeysuckle Rose"—an early version that Razaf later would recall with dismissive affection, though he did admittedly junk this original lyric and melody without hesitation immediately following his "Creole Follies" run at the Club Alabam. Only the title seems to have struck Razaf as worthy of further consideration. He would save it.

Every Saturday afternoon throughout the winter months of 1924, at the Anderson Art Galleries, 59th Street and Park Avenue, newly anointed white jazz "experts" like Professor Edward B. Hill, a "scholar" of the music's history, or popular arts pundit Gilbert Seldes, who favored jazz theses geared to esthetics, now delivered lecture–demonstrations on the newly fashionable subject of jazz. In magazines like *Harper's, American Mercury,* and the *New Republic,* dance critic Carl Van Vechten, composer and music critic Virgil Thompson, music copyright lawyer-turned-blues archivist Abbe Niles, and dilettante jazz devotee Henry O. Osgood each addressed the swiftly spreading national passion for "hot" jazz music from various lofty and cerebral vantage points. The thrust of all this well-intentioned pedagoguery was quite simply the "legitimacy," the substantive value of jazz music, in the context of classical European culture. As white America wrestled with an almost unquenchable national appetite for jazz in 1924, thoughtful white adherents of the music stepped in to assure America that jazz and the troubling feelings of liberation that it invoked were, in fact, legitimate.

Ironically, jazz was not the music that Andrea Razaf was writing lyrics to, for the most part, in 1924. Black musicians in New York City still had not entirely apprehended the mysteries of this raw yet hardly uncomplicated music out of New Orleans, though more and more were endeavoring to do so. Chicago was where New Orleans jazz musicians had been settling since the onset of World War One at least, for a variety of reasons, and Chicago was the only major American city beyond New Orleans where authentic jazz really was being played in 1924. What most Americans, including New Yorkers, were listening to and sinfully loving as jazz in 1924, was, in fact, a pasteurized derivative of the original New Orleans invention; not raw jazz at all but rather "symphonic" jazz, according to its adherents, music that was smoother, less uninhibited, more "under control." In short, to read between the implied, if unexpressed, racial lines of distinction drawn by both jazz defenders and defamers, this was music that had been rescued from its essential blackness.

The ostensible father of "symphonic" jazz was a plump, moon-faced violin-playing bandleader from Denver, Colorado, named Paul Whiteman, who'd begun his career as a classical musician in a number of symphony orchestras out West. An extraordinarily ambitious and surprisingly astute observer of the American music scene in the years immediately following World War I, Whiteman had abandoned the symphonic world to embark on a premeditated, jazz-centered program for success in the popular music marketplace. After first attracting attention with his new jazz orchestra at San Francisco's Fairmont Hotel in 1919, Whiteman had moved quickly, from the Alexandria Hotel in Los Angeles to the Ambassador Hotel in Atlantic City before reaching New York City and opening at a large Times Square supper club, the Palais Royal, on 48th Street between Broadway and Seventh Avenue, in October 1920. Playing the milkiest jazz-flavored semiclassical arrangements over a strong and square dance beat, Whiteman soon became an enormous attraction at the Palais Royal. A recording contract with the Victor Phonograph Company already was bringing his "symphonic" jazz to listeners beyond New York City in ever-more-astonishing numbers. By the beginning of 1921, Paul Whiteman was a phenomenon.

With his token jazz band instrumentation—sporadic trumpet growls, a politely wailing saxophone section—suffused in a sea of strings, a musical esthetic that either missed or dismissed completely the music's most significant revolutionary characteristic (its passionate improvisational nature), Whiteman made jazz seem safe and respectable, even classy, deflecting the criticism pointedly directed against it that it was "crude," "vulgar," and "debasing." In short order Whiteman's successful jazz seduction of the American public ironically led to a wider interest in authentic New Orleans–based African-American jazz expression as listeners across the country began to investigate the roots of Whiteman's music. Whiteman meanwhile crowned his own reign over the jazz realm of the early Twenties with a concert of so-called serious jazz on the evening of February 12, 1924 at Aeolian Hall, an "Experiment in Modern Music" that presented a melange of rather trivial compositions nearly bereft of jazz significance. A fiasco from its opening moments, the evening was saved by the performance of an original piano rhapsody, ostensibly on a jazz theme, by a 25-year-old Tin Pan Alley prodigy named George Gershwin, whose "Rhapsody in Blue" electrified Whiteman's mostly invited audience of extremely distinguished musical personalities. Though the piece really was not a jazz expression at all but a marvelous maiden excursion into formal composition by a legitimate musical genius whose passion for black music imbued his rhapsody with an invigorating jazz sensibility, it nevertheless furnished Whiteman with the promotional ammunition that he needed to term his poorly conceived American Jazz Concert a success, helping immeasurably to justify the countenance of "art" that Whiteman now claimed for his rather vapid brand of jazz music.

As sincere in his adoration of African–American music as Whiteman largely was not, Gershwin was in fact a fascinating product of the complex influence that the Harlem music scene already was exerting over local white musicians in New York City. Having grown up partly in Harlem, Gershwin was on exceedingly familiar terms with African–American music, his earliest exposure coming in 1905. He was 7, Gershwin later remembered, roller skating past Barron Wilkins's newly resettled Astoria Cafe on Seventh Avenue at 134th Street when he heard James Reese Europe's band performing inside. By 1924, Gershwin was so intimately involved with Harlem musically that many of his piano-playing friends on the rent strut circuit, including James P. Johnson and Willie "the Lion" Smith, recalled the young pianist at this time often sitting cross-legged on the floor at rent struts, joyfully drinking in the music, agape at the goings-on in various Harlem apartments. He was not alone. Many white composers like Gershwin were penetrating Harlem nightlife at this time, to the innermost low-down dives, in their passion for black music. And lyricists like Dorothy Fields, Ted Koehler, even the young Lorenz Hart and Ira Gershwin, though at a greater physical distance, studied closely the slangy, impudent lyric argot of black music. This attention was enormously flattering to Harlem's black songwriters. James P. Johnson, Willie "the Lion" Smith, and young Thomas "Fats" Waller would all be terrifically proud, for example, when Gershwin invited them to the party following his "Rhapsody in Blue" premiere at a very fashionable Park Avenue hotel. Yet inherent in this studious attention were the seeds of usurpation. Black songwriters were never encouraged by Tin Pan Alley nor even permitted to attempt songs in supposed "white" style. Thus, when in time Gershwin, Arlen, McHugh, Koehler, and Fields at last mastered music and lyric writing in the black style, they inevitably, however unintentionally, begat the disenfranchisement of the very black music makers whom they venerated. Calculatingly or not, Harlem's white musician admirers were all party to this ruthless cycle. That is why, with Gershwin's delightful "Rhapsody in Blue" as a misinterpreted beacon, the marketing value of the word "jazz," from a strictly commercial songwriting perspective, continued to be pried away from black musicians by Tin Pan Alley in the name of Whiteman and Gershwin in 1924.

There was nothing remotely calculating about Andrea Razaf and Fats Waller's songwriting method in 1924. Quite simply, the method was mood of the moment. If Razaf or Waller was tired or hungry or broke, they simply composed a tired, hungry, or broke song, as in

"Broke but Happy," a tune that, appropriately enough, appears never to have been sold.

> *I'm not complaining,*
> *Yes, I am broke—but happy,*
> *All optimistic,*
> *Nothing but skies of blue,*
> *Let it keep raining,*
> *Yes, I am broke—but happy,*
> *Seems ev'ry clock-tick*
> *Brings a new joy in view;*
> *I've something which is greater than riches,*
> *A gift from above,*
> *Someone to give for, someone to live for,*
> *What's better than Love?*
> *Now nothing grieves me,*
> *Ev'rything leaves me happy,*
> *I'm broke — but happy,*
> *'Cause I have you.*

Razaf usually suggested the title or perhaps just a theme—light subjects, simple emotions. Waller's melodic capacity was so encompassing, so miraculous and unquenchable, combined with an attention span so breathtakingly brief, that Razaf often bombarded his partner with potential song concepts and titles simply to keep Waller alert and productive. The results, nevertheless, were frequently astonishing to Razaf. The boy's raw talent was inspiring.

Yet Waller, at first, quite disbelieved his own talent and doubted the value of his songs, even as they began to sell. Tin Pan Alley had to convince Thomas Waller that his music in fact possessed substantial dollar value downtown. When it did, the 20-year-old pianist was, of course, ready to part with every melodic note that he could conceive, for whatever money he could get—immediately. Waller simply could not or would not try to comprehend the potential long-term value of his music. To him every musical scrap was grist for the moment, nothing more, while his partner always looked resolutely beyond the moment and counseled his impetuous collaborator to look with him to their professional future.

Wildly unsuited to a wife who'd finally divorced her unreliable musician–husband in late 1923, and still sorely missing his late mother, young Waller reveled in the camaraderie of musicians, loving to jam with them, loving to drink with them. The orchestra rows surrounding his organ post at the Lincoln Theatre often were filled with musician friends drinking in Waller's astonishing keyboard talent, passing the bottle, laughing with him as he often provided outrageous musical accompaniment to the action on-screen. Willie "the Lion" Smith would later suggest that Waller's unsuspected, painful shyness was the cause of his early alcoholism. Everyone, including young Waller, loved the person he became boozed up. The drinking escalated rapidly.

In March 1925 Marie Downes, owner of the Lincoln Theatre, informed her organist that she had decided to sell the old film house to Frank Schiffman and his partner Leo Brecher—two white men, operators of the Odeon Theatre on 145th Street and both the Harlem Opera House and Loew's Seventh Avenue burlesque theater on 124th Street, who were about to attempt an ambitious consolidation of black vaudeville entertainment in Harlem.

The news stung Waller, who viewed the Lincoln in much the same light as he did the revered memory of his late mother. Schiffman and Brecher, however, cordially brought the young keyboardist up to their offices, where they openly informed him of their plans to turn the Lincoln into a straight movie house while transferring the old theater's successful vaudeville programming to the larger Lafayette, which, after undergoing continual policy reconfigurations over the previous few years, was for the moment a straight movie house presenting only sporadic stage shows. The two men then offered Waller the Lafayette organist's job for $50 a week (double his Lincoln Theatre salary), crowning the news with the information that if he accepted, Waller could expect to play a Robert Marston–model organ at the Lafayette, the first grand organ to be found in Harlem.

Waller proved to be an instant hit at the Lafayette and was utterly at home in the grand old theater and its surrounding Seventh Avenue precincts. After closing out his work day there, Waller often floated over to Connie's Inn, just down Seventh Avenue, closer to 131st Street. The Immermans always welcomed him—their former delivery boy. Though he couldn't sit at a table, the bar was open to him, as was the piano, if he wished to play it. That year, Waller often provided intermission music at the Inn, clowning through countless requests. He also enjoyed rehearsing new acts, especially in the company of chorus girls, and even supplied Inn revues with incidental music on occasion, all for cash, on the side.

Among the many white patrons who encountered Waller at

Connie's Inn in 1925 was George H. "Captain" Maines, an influential downtown press agent. Waller fascinated Maines. The powerful PR man returned to the Inn repeatedly with his wife that year, insatiable in his appetite for the 20-year-old pianist's effusive personality and raw piano-playing skill. In time, Maines introduced himself to Waller and began to take Waller and "some of the boys," including Andrea Razaf, "on tour" with him to many of the better downtown nightspots that Maines brokered publicity for. Finally, one night, Maines invited Waller to his 107th Street apartment—an apartment that Waller and Razaf later would use on occasion as a writing studio. From there, Maines and his wife led Waller down West End Avenue to a friend's apartment equipped with both piano and organ, where Waller entertained for hours, his display that evening certifying for Maines the young pianist's enormous potential as an entertainer.

One of the downtown spots that Maines represented was in the basement of a building on West 49th Street, between Broadway and Seventh Avenue, around the corner from Whiteman's Palais Royal. Since September of 1923—first as the "Hollywood Cafe," now, in 1925, as the "Club Kentucky" — this low-ceilinged, dank den of a nightclub had offered a black revue modeled after the Plantation Cafe's, staged by Leonard Harper and accompanied by a seven-piece dance orchestra billed as the Washingtonians, whose piano player and leader was a youngster named Duke Ellington, 24 years old, and fresh from his parent's home in Washington, DC.

With Maines acting as his advocate, Waller soon was added to the Club Kentucky's nightly entertainment roster, which included a female blues vocalist, chorus girls, an "oriental" dancer, emcee Bert Lewis, and Ellington with his orchestra, already described in *Variety* as "one of the best 'hot' colored combinations in town." Waller's duties at the Kentucky Club included accompanying Lewis during Ellington's breaks, both on piano and as a bantering foil for the wisecracking emcee, and Waller's own solo piano set, with the corpulent young pianist billed as "Ali Baba, the Egyptian Wonder," bedecked in Eastern finery and a jeweled turban.

According to one of Ellington's later trumpet stars, Rex Stewart, Waller also instructed Ellington on matters of orchestration and arranging. Ellington, Stewart later insisted, "absorbed Fats' teachings and proceeded to utilize them until he brought his own inventive mind to jazz." Though Waller always claimed to hear his piano solos on an orchestral plane—a saxophone phrase here, a trumpet phrase there, percussion, bass—it seems unlikely that the 20-year-old pianist at this point would have had very much to offer the equally inexperienced Ellington on the subject of orchestration and arranging. What he did no doubt do was help Ellington with his piano playing and his overall improvisational method. Waller also may have tempted Ellington with stories of quick Tin Pan Alley money, for at this time Ellington apparently did sell some original tunes to Alley publishers on typical Waller terms—outright, for cash, without royalty or copyright protection.

The Kentucky Club was one of the last Times Square district cabarets to wind down on a given night, and many neighborhood musicians frequented the place after their own club work was done, including, on occasion, Paul Whiteman himself, rumbling in from his Palais Royal bandstand around the corner. As a result of this residual musician traffic, Fats Waller came to the attention of many downtown white entertainment professionals in 1925 through his presence at the Kentucky Club. Word quickly got around, fanned out with the influential assistance of Maines, who even managed a one-night booking for the entire Kentucky Club company at Ziegfeld's New Amsterdam Theatre on the Ziegfeld Follies' dark night. According to certain accounts, the show actually carried on at the New Amsterdam one night a week for over two months.

George Maines also made it his business to introduce Waller and his song partner Razaf to white Tin Pan Alley luminaries. He presented them to Irving Berlin in Berlin's offices at 1607 Broadway, though Razaf reminded Berlin that they, in fact, had met before. He also brought "the boys" around to see Harry Link, a publisher's representative who would become one of Razaf and Waller's strongest music industry allies.

Andrea Razaf made one other significant publishing acquaintance on his own at this time, in many ways, the most enduring and emotionally fraught business contact of his career. Joe Davis, in 1925, was an energetic Tin Pan Alley adherent of black music. In that capacity, he was almost by definition among the most suspect, if not altogether unscrupulous, music publishers in the business. Yet Davis was an enormously endearing man and in many ways a decent one. His endlessly convoluted relationship with Razaf alternately intimate and infuriating would haunt the lives of both men.

Born in New York City on October 6, 1896, the youngest of eleven children, Joseph Morton Davis had resisted the inducements of his Germanic father's family soda water business on 121st Street and

Pleasant Avenue to pursue instead a career as a singer and (frustrated, unsuccessful) lyricist before effecting his first song sale, "Down Where the Old Road Turns," in 1914, at the age of 17. Davis's father later would loan his son $50 to buy back the rights to this song, decisively establishing a principle that ruled Joe Davis's career as a song publisher thereafter: "Never sell a copyright."

After working as a song plugger in the ten-cent stores of the McRory chain, Davis in 1916 again borrowed $50 from his father to rent, in his own words "desk space" on West 45th Street, wherein he launched, in characteristic Joe Davis fashion, two publishing operations, Cathedral Music Company, and Triangle Music Publishing Company, the latter in partnership with trombonist George F. Briegel. Following brief duty in the Navy during World War One, a stint that produced at least one Joe Davis song, "If You Can't Enlist, Buy a Victory Bond," composed with J. Fred Coots, Davis returned to song publishing excited by the jazz-inflected music of black instrumentalist Wilbur Sweatman, whom he'd encountered during naval service. Triangle Music published Sweatman's "That's Got 'Em"in 1919—co-written, according to the song's credit, by Joe Davis—and also helped to arrange in February for Sweatman's recording of the song on Columbia.

That year Davis also bought out his partner in Triangle Music, George Briegel, and began to publish ersatz blues of his own composition, songs like "Lovesick Blues" and "Why Don't You Drive My Blues Away," while continuing to indulge a personal preference for love ballads that would characterize the Davis publishing taste throughout his long career. Davis actually sold some of his own blues to Pace & Handy Music Company in 1920, with one of the tunes, "Lovin' Blues," published that year by Handy. By 1921, though, Joe Davis was himself moving aggressively into the realm of black music. Triangle Music published an original Mamie Smith tune, "Weepin'," in 1921. It also released, among many others, "Louisville Blues," by black pianists Bob Ricketts and Mike Jackson, and "You'll Want My Love But Honey It Will Be Gone," by Spencer Williams and one of the *Shuffle Along* company's featured vocalists, Lucille Hegamin, as well as songs by comical "jazz" pianist Jimmy Durante—"I'm On My Way to New Orleans," "Mean Daddy Blues," and "Let's Agree to Not Disagree," all co-written with black composer Chris Smith— and a tune by two Original Dixieland Jazz Bandsmen, cornetist-leader Nick La Rocca and clarinetist Larry Shields, "Ramblin' Blues," with lyrics by Al Bernard.

In that same year, Davis also signed his first black blues artist, Daisy Martin, to a recording contract through Triangle Music. With rather astonishing speed, he then quickly established himself at all the major record companies as something of a black blues resource, placing another of his contracted blues singers, Josie Miles, exclusively with Gennett, in a series of recordings that Davis himself produced, squeezing a number of sessions featuring Triangle songs and artists out of the Edison organization, and placing Rosa Henderson with the Brunswick Record Corporation just as Brunswick was beginning to issue black music on their Vocalion label in 1923, also securing Henderson's husband, Slim Henderson, a spot in Columbia's new "race" series that year. Davis even began handling "race" talent for the Canadian Ajax label at this time, producing an astonishing number of sides over a period of about seven months in an acoustic recording studio at 240 West 55th Street, including the two initial recordings of Andrea Razaf's "No One Can Toddle . . ." and "He Wasn't Born in Araby. . . . " By 1924, Davis was also, perhaps inevitably, running a booking agency for black blues talent, featuring, among his many clients, Lizzie Miles, Rosa Henderson, and "exclusive" Columbia recording artist Maggie Jones.

In or around 1924, Andrea Razaf entered Joe Davis's music publishing premises in the Broadway Central Building near 51st Street at 1658 Broadway, upstairs over the Roseland Ballroom and some five blocks up from the Gaiety Building. There he met an unmistakably lean, hungry-looking, pint-sized, slightly balding music publisher with a reputation among songmen—black and white, but especially black—as a fast-talking operator who would readily buy almost any song outright, if he could. Yet Joe Davis also seems to have been, unlike many of his Tin Pan Alley contemporaries, entirely free of prejudice. Davis genuinely enjoyed the company of the black musicians and songwriters who were helping to make his fortune. He may not have dealt with them fairly from a business angle, but he did treat them squarely, if not as equals, then at least as human beings—a comparatively forward thinking approach on Tin Pan Alley in 1924.

Shortly after meeting Andrea Razaf, Joe Davis did two extraordinary things. He handed Razaf his first publishing advance check against future royalties. And, quite casually, he turned a desk at Triangle Publishing over to the black lyricist for in-house songwriting purposes. Alley publishers had long been willing to provide white songwriters with workspace in their back offices, but rarely

was a black songwriter offered space to write in. Davis, moreover—
again without much thought, it seemed—left Razaf alone in the
Triangle offices that evening to close up, while he hurried off to his
next recording date or song plugging rendezvous. Razaf was hugely
moved by this gesture, endowing it with a powerful symbolism.

"Dear Joe," he wrote in a letter scrawled that night on Triangle
letterhead,

> I am compelled to let you know how much I appreciate the *faith*
> you have in me by leaving me in your office last evening. Words
> cannot express my feelings and I do trust that I shall always
> justify that faith and trust you have in me. A thousand thanks for
> that check, it saves me from a very uncomfortable situation. As
> ever
>
> Your friend
> Andy

Fletcher Henderson's increasing popularity at the Roseland Ballroom during the summer months of 1924 was an enormous boon to
black musicians and songwriters throughout the city. The unprecedented acceptance and popularity of a black dance orchestra in a
white dance emporium had not been seen downtown since the days
of James Reese Europe, and the music industry took Henderson's
achievement as a sign to begin aggressively pursuing a new black
bandleaders and black songwriters for their white audiences.

Henderson responded to this growing popularity downtown with a
surprising aggressiveness of his own. Finding himself in direct and
rather unexpected competition with white jazz orchestras like the
ubiquitous Whiteman's, Henderson could have homogenized his
sound in deference to the very successful Whiteman style. Instead
he opted to further distinguish his band from Whiteman's by
emphasizing the band's fundamental strength, its black improvisational roots, hiring superior "hot" improvisers as a contrast to
Whiteman's accomplished "sweet" musicians, who read arrangements beautifully but offered listeners little in improvisational or
emotional terms. To accomplish this, the clever black bandleader
turned quite naturally to Chicago and the city's wealth of resident
New Orleans jazz talent.

Henderson, while on tour with the Black Swan Troubadours in
1922, had heard an impressive young cornetist late one night in a

New Orleans cabaret and had tried then without success to persuade the man to join his band. Four months later, Joe "King" Oliver, the foremost horn-playing exponent of New Orleans style in the jazz world, and a mentor to the young cornetist, had wired his young acolyte an invitation from Chicago to come join Oliver and his "Creole Jazz Band" in a local black dance hall on Chicago's South Side, the Lincoln Gardens, where they were gigging. The cornetist had instantly accepted and soon Fletcher Henderson and just about every other black musician with an interest in jazz nationwide began hearing extravagant things about this young player and his extraordinary evolution on the bandstand beside his hero, the man he called "Papa Joe," into an unparalleled jazz soloist.

With these reports still ringing out from Chicago in 1924 and in the wake of his band's grand Roseland summer, Fletcher Henderson decided to try again. He wired the cornetist an offer to join the Henderson orchestra at the Roseland Ballroom in New York for the forthcoming fall season at what would amount to a pay cut of $20 a week from the $75 a week that Oliver had been paying. To Henderson's surprise, the young cornet player—eager to escape his mentor's shadow and intrigued by what *he* was hearing about this new Henderson aggregation—accepted. Late that September, or about the first of October, Louis Armstrong arrived in New York City to join Fletcher Henderson's band.

With his singular, stunningly new conception of the jazz solo, his virtuoso brilliance both as an improviser and as a technician on his instrument, and his pioneering improvisational sensibility as a vocalist—an improvisational singing style that truly began to flower that fall in front of the Henderson band—Armstrong effectively reinvented jazz in his own image after his arrival in New York in 1924, restoring it to its rightful black musical heirs by consolidating, refining, and clarifying for the New York music world the thrust of New Orleans's incomparable creation. His fellow musicians, black and white, recognized this: they flocked to the Roseland in droves and stood in worshipful attention around the dance floor (black musicians were forbidden from actually crossing the Roseland dance floor). Roseland's dance public also recognized this; soon they were crying out for "Louis" to solo and, perhaps, even sing a song. Black Harlem certainly recognized this: Armstrong was introduced to Harlem in an electrifying midnight appearance with the Henderson band at the Lafayette Theatre sometime in early 1925 and performed thereafter with the band on a number of occasions at various unsegregated Harlem venues for black audiences, who quickly came to adore him.

Andrea Razaf may have met Louis Armstrong for the first time at an NAACP fundraising benefit at Happy Rhone's Orchestra Club, 654 Lenox Avenue, between 143rd and 144th Streets, on the evening of November 10, 1924; Razaf appeared that night on a bill that included Sissle and Blake, vocalist Alberta Hunter and Fletcher Henderson's Roseland Orchestra. One month later, Armstrong went into a Columbia recording studio with Henderson to accompany blues artist Maggie Jones on three numbers—"Poor House Blues" and "Thunderstorm Blues" by Spencer Williams, and a raunchy new tune composed by Andy Razaf with Fats Waller, "Anybody Here Want to Try My Cabbage?" Ironically, when Armstrong at last left Henderson to return to Chicago in late November or December of 1925, he invited Waller, whom he'd inevitably encountered and instantly befriended during the course of his Harlem sojourn, to come visit him sometime in Chicago. Waller promptly had jumped onto Armstrong's train and joined him. He remained in Chicago for some months.

Louis Armstrong's presence in New York affected Andrea Razaf as profoundly as it affected anyone. For the first time, Razaf's mind was opened to the vast musical possibilities that legitimate jazz presented for a songwriter and even a lyricist—the liberating sense of rhythm that jazz projected, the fabulous, witty sense of play in Armstrong's music that demanded an equivalent, loosely liberated lyric expression, the intensity and depth of feeling in Armstrong's artistry that seemed to sum up African–American history in its entirety. Razaf realized that this depth and intensity of feeling particularly deserved something more, lyrically, than anything Tin Pan Alley had yet devised.

Razaf had sold twenty-two songs to music publishers in 1924, a thrilling increase of eighteen over his total the previous year. Eight had been composed with Waller (none of them initially published), one with Waller and Spencer Williams (also initially unpublished), one with Waller and Clarence Williams (unpublished), one with Waller and both Williamses (published), one with Maceo Pinkard, composer of "Mammy" and "Sweet Georgia Brown," among other song hits, as well the score for the recent stage success *Liza* (unpublished), one with Phil Worde, a copyist in the Handy Publishing offices, and a Gaiety Building music publisher named Allie

Moore (published), one with Moore alone (unpublished), one with banjoist Maceo Jefferson and pianist/songwriter Jack Palmer (unpublished), four by Razaf alone, including one registered inexplicably under the pseudonym James Cook, and three other published tunes composed with a cast of truly anonymous collaborators. None of these sold in any significant quantity, but a good half dozen were recorded that year by various female blues artists. In a sense, they represented Razaf's farewell to a suddenly obsolete era of black song style.

On the record, Andrea Razaf sold but six songs to music publishers in 1925. Of these six, only two were composed with Thomas Waller. This very small number, while certainly the result of Waller's frantic schedule in 1925 at the Lincoln and Lafayette Theaters during the day and at the Kentucky Club after dark, may very well have been a function as well of the type of song-selling opportunities that Razaf and Waller were limited to, individually and as a team, on Tin Pan Alley in 1925. It will forever be impossible to account for those songs that the two men sold outright to various music publishers and to many unidentifiable songwriting peers that season. "Let me tell you how that worked," bandleader Sam Wooding later explained. "They didn't want blacks down there on Tin Pan Alley in the beginning. Sometimes the [white] songs were good but there was something lacking. Then they had to say, well, we gotta go and get one of those spades to come in here and straighten this out. That's what happened. 'Cause a lot of those white composers, they were fresh off the boat, they didn't know what America was. They were on the right track, they almost had the idea but it wasn't there yet, so they called in Andy Razaf to straighten out the lyrics and Luckey Roberts or Shelton Brooks to straighten out the music, and they were paid maybe fifty dollars for the whole thing and it got the Negro some beef stew and he was satisfied with that."

In years to come, Andy Razaf would open a small window onto his and Waller's underground song-selling practices during these early Tin Pan Alley days with one brief remark, delivered in the context of black Harlem's explosive postwar population growth and the great number of West Indians who helped to fuel it in the Twenties. James P. Johnson, in particular, had found the deeply accented speech of these West Indians hugely entertaining and he soon had devised his own pidgin version of their dialect, a privately encoded gibberish vocabulary that instantly became the toast of the rent strut circuit and inevitably was co-opted and embellished upon by all the members of Johnson's circle, including both Waller and Razaf. When the taste for this sort of talk trickled down from Harlem to the publishing offices of Tin Pan Alley as yet another potentially lucrative Negro musical curiosity, Razaf and Waller, of course, latched onto the trend themselves. Only one West Indian–derived song title, however, appears in their shared roster of song copyrights for the years 1923 to 1925: "My Jamaica Love," purchased by Clarence Williams Music in July 1924. Twenty years later, Razaf provided this simple explanation for the seeming discrepancy. "Soon as we got broke," he admitted in a 1944 interview, "all we had to do was grind out two or three West Indian numbers, take them up to Mills, or some Broadway office, and get a nice sum for them. . . . Around that time there was [also] a heavy demand for cabaret-type songs with blue lyrics. We did hundreds of those."

Razaf sold one additional tune officially in 1925, with Edgar Dowell ("Too Bad Jim," three times recorded that year); another with Theodore Fenderson Nixon, "Honey Man Blues," that Bessie Smith would record in 1926; and even one more solo Razaf composition (unpublished). His final 1925 song sale, though, marked the formal beginning of a richly rewarding songwriting partnership for Razaf with a white pianist of British descent named Paul Denniker.

Denniker to this day remains something of a mystery. Born May 30, 1897, in London, he'd studied with Britain's most notable black composer, Samuel Coleridge-Taylor, and had served in the British Army before emigrating to the United States in 1919, where he'd led bands in vaudeville and was directing the orchestra at Shanley's Restaurant on Broadway when he encountered Andrea Razaf in 1924. Denniker also apparently worked for Joe Davis in some capacity as a house arranger or staff pianist, and it was perhaps at the Triangle Music offices that he and Razaf met.

They made an interesting couple—Razaf the regal African, Denniker the slight, towheaded Englishman whose elfin Saxon features and surprising comprehension of black music were an incongruous blend. The pair sold their first song together, "A Bobbed-Haired Bandit," sometime in 1924, and their second on November 17, 1925, to Elliot-Chilton Music, which published the tune early the following year—"Falling for You," also recorded by Razaf in his debut as "Crooning Andy and his Ukulele" on Harmony Records, no doubt under Joe Davis's auspices. Razaf was quite active now as a vocalist, broadcasting regularly on radio stations WGCP and WOR, often with Phil Worde as a piano accompanist, and even appearing occasionally for hire at fraternity smokers with his "uke."

Clearly Denniker shared with his new lyricist a certain confrontational attitude toward Tin Pan Alley that Razaf must have appreciated. On December 17, 1925, Denniker announced his plans for a new publishing venture, in partnership with Razaf and Elliot-Chilton founder Phil Elliot, in response to Denniker's complaint that music publishers would not give him a hearing when he had "a manuscript to submit, on the ground that they have their own staffs." Between the lines, it is possible to read this action as Razaf and Denniker's aggressive response to the assured unwillingness of most Tin Pan Alley publishers to grant this biracial song team any sort of in-house hearing. The Denniker/Razaf/Elliot publishing gambit does not appear, however, ever to have really gotten off the ground.

Razaf and Waller meanwhile both stepped up their on-the-books professional activity in 1926 to a significant degree. They did so, however, largely away from one another. It is quite possible that Razaf decided to push off independently of Waller and his retrogressive song-selling habits. While Waller was still out "visiting" Louis Armstrong in Chicago (supporting himself by performing solo at the Hotel Sherman), Razaf opened the year working with Dan Wilson, the husband of Club Alabam vocalist Edith Wilson and brother of another talented black female vocalist, Lena Wilson. A conservatory-trained pianist from Charleston, South Carolina, Wilson was a black entertainment veteran, his wide experience ranging from the military bands of World War I through the founding days of S. H. Dudley's Theatre Owners' Booking Association black vaudeville circuit (known in the industry as the TOBA) during the early Twenties. With Razaf, late in 1925 or early in 1926, he composed two rather standard blues, "How Could I Be Blue?" purchased and published by Clarence Williams in January 1926, and "Mama Stayed Out the Whole Night Long," sold two weeks later to Williams.

Both songs were extensively recorded throughout the ensuing months, with the vaudeville team of Butterbeans and Susie kicking things off on March 5, 1926, cutting "Mama Stayed Out the Whole Night Long" for Paramount, accompanied on piano by Eddie Heywood. Clarence Williams then recorded "How Could I Be Blue?" himself on March 25 for OKeh, supporting blues singer Sara Martin with an unusual ensemble comprising a select group of Fletcher Henderson and Duke Ellington sidemen. This was followed, in turn, by a Caroline Johnson recording of "Mama Stayed Out" on April 26 for Paramount, quite possibly accompanied by Fats Waller on piano; Maggie Jones in a terrific rendition of the same song, backed by Clarence Williams, for Columbia on July 22; Bessie Brown singing "How Could I Be Blue?" with Williams on piano, in July, for Banner Records; and finally, Elvira Johnson's recording of "How Could I Be Blue?" for Gennett in October.

"Mama Stayed Out the Whole Night Long" remains lyrically an interesting tune in its expression, for perhaps the first time, of a key Razaf lyric-writing characteristic, namely the sense of *demurring*— of *not* performing as anticipated within standard black songwriting cliché. "Mama Stayed Out the Whole Night Long" could have been just another slightly bawdy blues tune about the wife of "Pastor White," who "it seems . . . was out all night." Rather than regale his listeners with a naughty litany of all the things that Mama did, however, Razaf instead toyed with convention by suggestively allowing Mama to steadfastly maintain that she "didn't do nothing wrong," conceding that, yes, she'd "Stayed out all night/Till broad daylight,/But I kept my conscience strong. I lost my doorkey, left it on the table,/Couldn't get in, so I slept in the stable . . . Mama stayed out the whole night long/But Mama didn't do no wrong/I didn't cheat you/Mama didn't do no wrong."

Back in May of 1925, Thomas Waller had been featured on a bill at the Lafayette Theatre in his first solo vaudeville turn. The Lafayette had a long tradition of presenting "varieties" or "tabloid"— commonly known as "tab"—shows: small-scale, Broadway-style musical comedy productions, appointed fully with sets, costumes, a flimsy book, fluid choreography and often sizable casts. With his recent purchase of the theater, Lafayette owner Frank Schiffman had preserved many Lafayette production traditions, including the tab show. James P. Johnson had filled the initial role of composer-designate, following the full scores that he'd provided at the Lafayette for *Raisin' Cain* in 1923 and *Sunshine Sammy* in 1924 (lyrics by Cecil Mack), with *Moochin' Along* for Schiffman in 1925. In 1926, though, with Johnson no doubt occupied elsewhere, Schiffman decided to offer the composing chores for the Lafayette's next tab show to his organist, Fats Waller. The opportunity was a significant one, and Waller might have brought Andrea Razaf in as his lyricist on the project, but Schiffman chose to hire Spencer Williams for the job instead. Waller knew Williams well as another hard liver in the James P. Johnson–Perry Bradford–Joy Club axis, and liked him very much. Their score for the new Lafayette production *Tan Town Topics* would produce Waller's first significant song hit, a sweet tune with a Spanish tinge, "Señorita Mine."

Lafayette tab shows enjoyed stage lives of a very brief duration: three to four weeks at the theater itself, then a couple of weeks more generally touring the Eastern TOBA circuit. After his own maiden tab show closed down at the Lafayette, Waller returned to perform for the week of July 17–23 at the Lincoln Theatre, between films, in an act billed as "Signor Fats Waller's Lincolnians." He was then brought back by Schiffman to compose a second Lafayette tab score, ostensibly with Spencer Williams again, though Williams in fact merely left his lyric notes for the project with Waller before sailing to Europe at the behest of Josephine Baker, the former *Shuffle Along* chorus girl who'd recently found rapturous success in Paris, crooning, shimmying, and nakedly posturing through *La Révue Nègre* at the Champs Élysées Théâtre. Williams would remain in Europe on and off for the next twenty years, writing for Baker throughout her reign over the Follies Bergère. His absentee score with Waller, however, for their latter Lafayette tab show, brazenly titled *Junior Blackbirds* after the latest Florence Mills/Lew Leslie downtown revue smash *Blackbirds*, left no mark on the popular-song marketplace in 1926.

From February 12 to March 23, 1926, Razaf sold five songs with Paul Denniker to Phil Elliot at Elliot-Chilton Music. During the same period, he sold two more songs written with Maceo Pinkard— one to Chilton, "Why Did I Go Wrong?," the other to Shapiro Bernstein, "Li'l Brown Baby," a haunting children's lullaby filled with particularly forthright race-driven sentiment: "Don' you sigh, Li'l brown baby/Don' mind what de white chillen say,/An' don' be shy, Li'l brown baby,/De Lord made yo' color dat way . . . 'Cause when you die, Li'l brown baby,/De angels won't turn you away." "Li'l Brown Baby" was introduced publicly by Paul Robeson but went nowhere, in the end, commercially. "Why Did I Go Wrong?" on the other hand, while not an especially memorable song, did play a small role in Razaf's Tin Pan Alley career as catalyst for an amusing burst of pure Tin Pan Alley nonsense that nicely illustrates Razaf's hard-earned acceptance downtown as an Alley insider in 1926.

Publisher Phil Elliot apparently believed he had a hit with Razaf and Pinkard's "Why Did I Go Wrong?" The song was a "weeper" dedicated to a "Public Enemy" named Gerald Chapman who'd recently gone to the gallows with the question "Why did I go wrong?" on his lips. Though Tin Pan Alley's flamboyant song-plugging imagination pretty much had exhausted itself by the Twenties—no more bouncing-ball lantern slides projected in music halls, no more singalongs spontaneously ignited on street corners, in taverns, and in theaters by effusive Alley song pluggers—stirrings of the old aggressive routine did still rear up on occasion. In this tradition, and with Razaf's assistance, Elliot devised a scheme for acquainting the public with "Why Did I Go Wrong?" in a really big way.

"'Why Did I Go Wrong?' came to Broadway with a bang on Friday, April 30th," reported the entertainment industry journal *Orchestra World* in an eyewitness account the morning after, describing how Razaf and Elliot had "packed Broadway at 48th Street through the medium of an 'unusual publicity stunt.'" A man "strolling out on a perilously narrow window ledge" had initiated the drama by directing attention with a pointer to signs in the third-story window of the Elliot-Chilton offices at 1595 Broadway. A burst of melody megaphoned through two huge horns set above the building's second story then had captured the other passersby, to the point that two "blue-coated minions of the law" soon were on the scene, officiously "trying to keep the listening and upgazing people from stepping in front of streetcars or automobiles." "New York's Main Stem," observed *Orchestra World*, "was indeed a busy place."

The plan for acquainting Broadway pedestrians with 'Why Did I Go Wrong?' had been hatched "under the expert direction" of Phil Elliot, in concert with Razaf, whose contacts at radio stations WOR and WOKO had wired the microphones, radio broadcasting apparatus, and outdoor loudspeakers. With the technology in place, and a ledge-walking emcee guaranteeing an attentive audience, Razaf had simply "lifted up his voice . . . to ask the mike, 'Why Did I Go Wrong?'" "As the words reached down into the street," remarked *Orchestra World*, "a few passersby paused, wondering whence came the melody. Eyes were immediately upraised to the windows of the publishing house. More people stopped to listen and then more. Andy at the microphone, later assisted by other singers, kept the crowd entertained for over an hour with the music of the song that seems destined to prove successful.

"It was something new," *Orchestra World* concluded, "and if there's anything Broadway likes, it is a novelty."

*

Despite the enormous popularity downtown of dance palaces like the Roseland, Arcadia, and Cinderella ballrooms, there were no dance halls to speak of in Harlem in 1925 beyond a few often illegal cramped, cellar like establishments and ancient monoliths like the shabby, red-brick Manhattan Casino—or Rockland Palace, as it was now called—near Harlem's outermost extremity, on 155th Street and Eighth Avenue. It was with this fact of neighborhood Harlem life very much in mind that a real estate consortium consisting of I. Jay Fagan, the man more or less responsible for the Roseland and Acadia ballrooms downtown, Larry Spier, two Galewski brothers, Charles and Murray (backed by their father), and a young Harlem realtor named Charles Buchanan had scouted out potential uptown sites for a deluxe new dance hall in 1925, finally settling on an entire blockfront along Lenox Avenue, between 140th and 141st Streets. Committing more than $200,000 to the project, the group then produced a truly sumptuous, legitimate dance palace on a monumental scale, from the dazzling, capacious lobby dominated by a towering cut-glass chandelier and marble staircase to the hall itself—dance capacity, 3,500—appointed in orange and blue, heavily carpeted, laced with tables and settees, a soda fountain, and a 250-by-50-foot, sleekly varnished wood dance floor, laid out before two bandstands and a "disappearing" stage. Dubbed "the Savoy," a name the owners believed "exemplified all the elegant splendor of fabled old-world palaces," the ballroom proved, in many ways, and however unintendedly, a gift to black Harlem, savored by black Harlemites from the Savoy's first moments for the simple reason that *anyone* could dance there.

Fletcher Henderson and his band could not escape their Roseland bandstand until 1:00 A.M. or so on the morning of the Savoy's gala grand opening "Inaugural Ball," March 12, 1926. When they at last arrived uptown and took the Savoy stage for the first time, the response was something akin to pandemonium. They returned almost immediately to the Savoy on April 27 and again on May 8. At one of these performances, it was suggested to Fletcher Henderson that 22-year-old Thomas Waller, in attendance that night, be allowed to sit in with the band. Henderson in fact knew and admired Waller's Lincoln and Lafayette Theatre organ work. To the mild surprise of many, he turned his piano chair over to Waller for the rest of the evening.

Waller and the great trombonist Jack Teagarden may have been the only outsiders ever allowed to sit in with the Fletcher Henderson

Orchestra during the Twenties. Waller appeared frequently with the band throughout 1926, and Henderson also helped the young pianist with his alimony payments that year, frequently buying original tunes from Waller for the Henderson band book, which Don Redman then arranged. On one occasion, as Redman was dining in Jesse Wynn's Hamburger King, next to the Rhythm Club on 132nd Street and Seventh Avenue, up the block from Connie's Inn, Waller, discovering him there and desperate for cash as usual, offered to sell Redman eight new Fats Waller tunes for $10 apiece. Redman demurred, instructing Waller instead to take the songs to Henderson, to sell them to Henderson if he needed money but, above all else, not to sell them cheap. Waller did so, more or less. By the end of the year, Fletcher Henderson and his band would record several of these Waller compositions, some with Waller's name on them, some not. Waller's first recorded performance with the Henderson band on the 3rd of November, 1926, featured, in fact, a Henderson-credited tune, "Henderson Stomp," that rumor—if nothing else—has since ascribed to Thomas "Fats" Waller.

"Dear Andy," Annabelle Razaf wrote in a hastily scrawled note dated "Wednesday, May 22/9/30 P.M.,"

> I want to see you concerning some very important matter and trust you will find time to come up to the house at an early date. You will find me at home between the hours of eight and nine any evening. Brabant and I are quite well, trust you are the same.
>
> Why didn't you answer my previous letter?
>
> As ever your wife
119 West 141st Street, apt. 69
>
> I put the address in case you have forgotten it

Brabant was the name of Annabelle Razaf's dog. Though Andrea Razaf and Thomas Waller lived diametrically opposite lives in many respects, the irresponsible, high-flying private party that constituted their day-to-day existence in 1926 was fundamentally shared by the two song partners. For Waller, the concept of marital fidelity inevitably crossed with some lapsed sense of the term responsibility —Waller, of course, had none—unlike his mentor, James P. Johnson, who quite simply was a conflicted soul, truly shy yet driven by his piano talent to perform, dismissive of popular attention yet desperately hungry for critical acclaim, happily married and a true family man yet drawn to carouse endlessly on a scale that was, in the end, self-destructive. Razaf, however, at least publicly embraced responsibility as the touchstone of his existence, resulting in a dichotomy between personal and professional commitment that was pronounced so far as his wife Annabelle was concerned. And though Waller particularly, along with Johnson and the rest, clearly liberated Andy Razaf, or at least exposed him to the wonder of liberation as Harlem's entertainment world lived it in the Twenties, there can be no doubt that Razaf knew all along precisely what he was abandoning with this liberation and no doubt persuaded himself in the process that he was somehow justified in doing so.

When he married Annabelle Miller, Razaf was not much older than Waller had been at his marriage to Edith Hatchett. Both, in a sense sought out maternal surrogates. It is interesting that Razaf, while endeavoring to escape his domineering mother's home, found his surrogate in a passive woman seven years his senior, while Waller, in mourning his dominating, if not quite domineering, mother's passing, attached himself to a rather strong-willed child bride. Both choices were disastrous in the end, and when both men stopped coming home to their respective wives, each woman reacted differently but no less futilely. Razaf's Annabelle martyred herself in silence. Waller's Edith harassed him tenaciously.

The stories are part of the Waller legend. From the moment that Edith Waller's divorce settlement was established at $35 per week for child support and alimony, Waller apparently never once paid out the sum fully or promptly. He moreover seems to have decided in childish retaliation that if there never again was money in his pocket to collect, then Edith Waller, after a fashion, could be thwarted. From that point on he worked as erratically as he could to survive on the brink of insolvency.

Process servers soon became fixtures in Waller's daily routine. They turned up frequently at the Lafayette Theater, where Waller repeatedly dodged them, on one occasion evacuating his keyboard post in mid-chord and not reappearing at the Lafayette for days thereafter. Courtroom hearings became a regular function of his existence. Jail terms were served—at least six, it appears—and anecdotes spun off from these periods of incarceration that today embellish the Waller legend outrageously. Spencer Williams, Perry Bradford, Andy Razaf, and Ken Macomber—an arranger on the

Fletcher Henderson band payroll in 1926—recounted a visit to Brooklyn's Raymond Street jail, for example, when Waller was being held there on $500 bail. A flurry of desperate activity by Waller's friends had raised the necessary funds and the four men arrived, cash in hand, to find their wayward pianist ensconced in absolutely astonishing penal luxury, supplied with liquor, dining on steaks, smoking cigars in a cell plushly outfitted with, among other things, a piano—all of it supplied by Waller's cellmate, a divorced millionaire (some sources suggest that he was in fact an ex-city commissioner) determined to thwart his former wife in *her* alimony demands and quite content to buy off his time lingering in prison with Fats Waller as an entertaining companion. Waller, of course, told his friends to go away.

The Daisy Chain was a Harlem brothel operated throughout the Twenties and Thirties at various locations around and about West 141st Street by Hazel Valentine, as attractive and sociable a madam as one might expect to find running Harlem's favorite good-time house during the Twenties, according to the recollections of many former clients. No one was more welcome at Valentine's Daisy Chain apparently than Waller and his circle, including Andy Razaf and James P. Johnson. The parlor had a piano, of course, a first-quality grand piano, in fact, and Waller often found inspiration there surrounded by Valentine "cuties," frequently with Razaf at his elbow. "If Fats Waller could be locked up at the Daisy Chain with a piano, a bottle, and several beautiful chicks, he would certainly come up with some of the most beautiful music this side of heaven," W. C. Handy (of all people) is said to have observed at one time, though Eubie Blake later confessed to seeing it all just a bit differently. "That Fats was from a very fine family," Blake insisted. "His father was a minister. As soon as they got about a hundred dollars between 'em, though—well, the kind of women that they went around with, I wouldn't let in this door. I don't know where they found 'em. These were tough women." Blake grabbed his lip and yanked it out emphatically: "Snuff! They carried snuff here— these were snuff-tasting women! I'm not lyin'!

"Now, Andy couldn't drink. Take a glass of beer and he starts gigglin'. But the loudest damn women. When they got a couple of hundred dollars together between em'—how they could jelly to-gether!"

Incredibly, amid all this continued debauchery, Waller remarried in 1926, taking another child bride, 16-year-old Anita Rutherford, granddaughter of the proprietress of Mother Shepherd's, a combination lunchroom, barbershop, poolroom, and rooming house that Waller frequented at 107 West 133rd Street. Waller, in fact, lived with his bride at Mother Shepherd's for a time (just around the corner from the house in which he'd been born and raised at 107 W. 134th Street) immediately following the nuptials. Anita Rutherford-Waller apparently cultivated a much more sympathetic relationship with her unpredictable, frequently uncontrollable new husband and is said in many ways to have gradually transformed Waller over the ensuing years. Whether or not this was so, Waller certainly loved his second wife in his way, and there was a sense among his friends at this time of the young pianist beginning to gain a measure of maturity from his marriage. He even is said to have initiated, purportedly on George Gershwin's recommendation, lessons in counterpoint and advanced harmony with the esteemed classical concert pianist Leopold Godowsky, after Godowsky began to turn up regularly as a spectator on the uptown rent strut circuit.

While both Razaf and Waller were making money in 1926, both still lived a hand-to-mouth existence. Razaf's office at this time was the Greyhound bus station on 50th Street between Broadway and Eighth Avenue; his mailing address, Room 602 at the Gaiety Theatre Building. Breakfast and lunch usually were measured out at the Turf Club restaurant on the ground floor of the Brill Building at 49th and Broadway, surrounded by hosts of hungry "Alley boys." Dinner was scraped together late at night in transit from nightspot to nightspot. Where Razaf slept during this period is a point beyond conjecture. While both Razaf and Waller, at the ages of 31 and 22 respectively, clearly were chronically immature, incapable of living up to any sort of emotional commitment with members of the opposite sex, their ragged personal lives, along with those of their peers, also reflected a sensibility imposed upon them, as black songwriters, by Tin Pan Alley—the sense of always being outlaws, always the fly-by-night outsiders paid off on the sly, always the repositors of the low-down and the forbidden. After a while, perhaps only in furious surrender, many of these men simply came to live out the illusion, and even to like it. Not even Razaf seems to have been entirely impervious to the perverse allure of this stereotype, though his partner certainly was more taken with the outlaw life than Razaf, who desperately yearned for a better—if decidedly unmarried—life.

"Dear Andy," wrote Annabelle Razaf again on December 25, 1926,

> It's about five years since *we* have had a home of our own, and have spent an Xmas together in it. Tho there is little spirit of love in our home, let us at least *pretend* to each other and make it as bright as possible this Xmas day at home. For we know not how long we may be together. God or we ourselves may cause a change. I trust neither will come about so soon, but we do not know the future. So let us make the home happy at least for today. A Merry Xmas to you and a long and prosperous life.

It does not appear that Andy Razaf ever returned to his home or his wife for another Christmas, though Razaf did continue to visit Annabelle Miller infrequently and send money fairly regularly. She was the wife of another time, the wife of a man who'd been a laborer and who was now indisputably a lyricist. It does not appear that Razaf ever formally divorced himself from Annabelle Miller, either. Rather, henceforth, he simply denied her existence.

Andrea Razaf saw 1926 out at the palatial Harlem home of vocalist Lucille Hegamin, celebrating at a "Too Bad" birthday party for Hegamin, the release of Hegamin's latest hit Columbia recordings: "Señorita Mine," by Thomas Waller, and "Nobody But My Baby," by Razaf and Clarence Williams. The party was a lavish affair, attended by a host of Harlem theatrical celebrities; Hegamin's star was ascending at Columbia and money was plentiful. For Razaf, the evening was a gala coda to a torrid year of songwriting achievement: twenty-seven songs sold, including a half-dozen composed with his companion that night at Hegamin's, a Chicago-born pianist and songwriter named James C. Johnson, with whom he was now collaborating regularly. Johnson, known as J. C. (to distinguish him from James P.), was, in many ways, Razaf's true alter-ego. A boisterous, salty character with an irrepressible disposition and a pungent, slangy conversational flair that translated into a distinctive lyric writing personality, he had come to New York from Chicago in 1915, intent on making his way in the New York entertainment world as a piano player. Exposure to the brilliance of Harlem piano men quickly had convinced Johnson to abandon his piano ambitions for songwriting, both as lyricist and composer. He'd apparently run across Fats Waller and, in passing, had collaborated with him as early as 1923. Johnson no doubt met Razaf through Waller, and late in

1926 they started writing together, while also beginning to perform as a team on radio station WHN, plugging their own songs.

Razaf's collaboratorative life now was quite rich. He had Paul Denniker, he had Johnson, and he had Waller, all on a fairly exclusive basis. There was the occasional work with Maceo Pinkard, Clarence Williams, Jack Palmer, and Phil Worde. New melodists also were beginning to cue up for the wit and the light-handed grace that Razaf clearly had demonstrated in the coarse medium of "race music," talents that were endearing him not solely to black songwriters around town but to innumerable, unknowable white ones as well, all of whom purchased Razaf's lyric talent anonymously.

Already, by consensus, Razaf was the most promising young lyricist on the black music scene in 1926. The segregated foundation of his career was at last in place. The time had come for Andrea Razaf to greet the white world.

Courtesy Razaf Estate.

8

Harlem Hotcha

It's a dance that never seems to slow down,
Done by every uptown high and low brown,
It's like a shotcha,
That Harlem hotcha; . . .
Takes all you can bring.

— *"Harlem Hotcha"*
by Andy Razaf and James P. Johnson

To travel to Harlem from Times Square by taxi in 1927 cost a minimum of $2.15, excluding tip, and as much as $2.85, depending on the class of conveyance—taxis, by class, varying widely in length, seating capacity, and relative interior luxury. Exiting the New Amsterdam Theatre in January 1927 following a performance of Florenz Ziegfeld's poorly received new musical comedy, *Betsy,* or the Eltinge Theatre, four doors down, after three acts of *The Love Thief,* one angled across 42nd Street in the westward direction of Times Square, dodging streetcars and the crowds of theatergoers pouring out into traffic from beneath the lit marquees of ten 42nd Street theaters, rounding the corner onto Seventh Avenue and possibly glancing upward to the Paramount Building clock pointing past eleven. It was still early—Harlem nights did not come to life before twelve.

A car might already have been hired—a Packard from Packard

Motor Car Renting on 47th Street or even a Pierce Arrow, the speciality of Pennsylvania Terminal Auto Rental on West 30th Street—at a $3 hourly rate. The illicit matter of alcohol was, however, a priority before one headed uptown, and midtown side streets were honeycombed with liquor dispensaries. You plunged through the rarefied bustle of Times Square, then, into the gaudy white luminescent glow, beyond the clattering of motor car engines, the blare of horns, the Sixth Avenue El's distant roar, to a basement door beneath a darkened stairwell: the bell, the spy-hole, moving shutter, peering eyes, padlock, chain, password. Inside, the walls were often plain, the tables workmanlike, the straight-backed chairs thin-legged and uncomfortable. Throughout the small room, men and women convivially stooped to drink.

A bottle of High & Dry Gin could be purchased for two dollars—a bottle of Bacardi for three, with both bottles stowed away in evening clothes. "Even the smallest flask rather disfigures a tuxedo," a visiting British journalist would observe in 1927 during a nightlife tour of Times Square. "It seems appalling for rich and elegant males to dance with bottles in their pockets. Ladies of course have to risk leaving their bottles on the tables, but it was sad to see . . . [a] beautiful wom[a]n exquisitely dressed yet pressing a big bottle of whiskey to her bosom under her shawl of Persian silk."

With liquor secured, a car boarded, or a cab hailed—"Twentieth-century Brown-and-White," standard Yellow Cab, or something from the fleet belonging to gambler, nightclub operator, and penny-ante racketeer Larry Fay, with its distinctive swastika logo—you edged into Broadway's northbound traffic lane. Passing the Gaiety Theatre marquee on 46th Street, where British drawing room dramatist Frederic Lonsdale's imported comedy *On Approval* was proclaimed in blazing lights beneath the darkened windows of black music publishing offices, you motored up Broadway beyond the Turf restaurant at 49th Street, the Roseland Ballroom near 51st, and onto "Automobile Row"—block after block of grand, glass-fronted automobile showrooms throughout the upper Fifties. Rolling past Reisenweber's boldly lit on the far corner of Eighth Avenue at 58th Street, and into Columbus Circle, you entered at last the inky darkness, the hush of Central Park at the 59th Street gate, off Central Park South.

As one cruised uptown in the sharp January chill, the car's leather top would be up and the temperature inside not especially warm. A bottle might be opened and flasks filled before the automobile had circumnavigated the Green, then the Lake, around the Reservoir, swinging east to the North Meadow, back again around the Harlem Meer, to emerge at last from the Park at 110th Street, crossing Cathedral Parkway and entering Harlem officially in the uptown lane of broad, dimly lit Lenox Avenue.

At 116th Street, an invasive glare—brightening toward 125th Street as you passed the Theresa Hotel and the Harlem Opera House on the left. Ahead, the glow of an even brighter light at 133rd Street. The car would flash through this light, race beyond it—past 134th Street, 137th Street, 140th Street. In the backseat, flasks might now be sealed, necktie knots straightened, lip rouge reapplied, as the marquee of the Douglas Theatre motion picture house loomed, brilliantly lit, at the corner of 142nd Street and Lenox—a corner now teeming with vehicular traffic. The taxi would pull to the curb alongside a host of private automobiles and idling taxicabs, cruising to a halt just past the Douglas marquee and the darkened bakeshop squeezed beside it, midblock between 142nd and 143rd. There, the long dark awning of the Cotton Club ran from a lighted, log cabin–faced entranceway practically into the street.

If Harlem, by 1927, had come of age as an "entertainment center" for slumming downtown white entertainment seekers—and many, though not all, downtown arbiters of fashion and taste in 1927 believed that it had—the epicenter of this evolution was the Cotton Club, Owney Madden's "Aristocrat of Harlem" upstairs over the Douglas Theatre at 644 Lenox Avenue. With emphatic Broadway style, superb taste, and efficient gangland muscle, the Cotton Club had now firmly established itself as the quintessence of late-night Harlem glamor, frequented by Broadway newspapermen like Walter Winchell and Louis Sobel, among others, who sang the club's praises in their columns and brought the elite of Broadway showfolk with them almost nightly at the behest of press agent Lee Posner. It was Posner who, in the words of one observer, had put "Broadway north of 125th Street . . . on New York's amusement map, [bringing] big names uptown and send[ing] entertainers with bigger names downtown . . . so thoroughly . . . publiciz[ing] what was once mere colored territory that it has become one of the first places to which welcoming committees, official and otherwise, rush assorted visitors to this fair burg."

After a brief three-month padlocking in June 1925 for Volstead Act violations, along with eight other Harlem establishments, the Cotton Club had reemerged in 1926, strengthened in its graft-secured coexistence with the local powers of Prohibition in New York City.

Operationally it was more powerful, too, with a new front man, Harry Block; a savvy new manager, former machine gunner Herman Stark; and a new producer for its elaborate floor show, Dan Healy, a relatively young, though veteran, song-and-dance man, designated by Stark as Lew Leslie's replacement. It was the "quick-witted, irrepressible" Healy who was devising a signature style for the Cotton Club revue, a silken combination of supper-club plush, lavish Ziegfeld production values, and electrifying performance pace, all wedded to an exotic "jungle" sensibility centered around a company of tall, stunning, light-skinned black showgirls and a multitude of exceptionally talented black performers. "The chief ingredient was pace, pace, pace!" Healy later insisted. "The show was generally built around types: the band, an eccentric dancer, a comedian— whoever we had who was also a star. The show ran an hour and a half, sometimes two hours; we'd break it up with a good voice. . . . And we'd have a special singer who gave the customers the expected adult song."

White patrons who could afford the Cotton Club loved it. The floor show was familiar to them in its replication of the slicker black Broadway theatrical revues that had first introduced black music and black dancing downtown. The setting was impeccably high toned, the service, by smartly trained black waiters, polished and decorous, but with a flourish that seemed distinctive to the Cotton Club. Additionally, for many, there was the reassuring absence of black patrons, an absence ensured by "brutes at the doors," according to Carl Van Vechten, "to enforce the Cotton Club's policy, which was opposed to mixed parties." As Jimmy Durante rather disingenuously pointed out, "Racial lines are drawn there to prevent possible trouble. Nobody wants razors, blackjacks, or fists flying—and the chances of a war are less if there's no mixing."

For some, though, an evening of choreographed, predigested Cotton Club entertainment lacked the authenticity, spontaneity, and brazen excitement that sensational literary depictions of black Harlem life—like Carl Van Vechten's recently published bestselling novel *Nigger Heaven* and recently staged, tawdry Broadway melodramas like *Lulu Belle*, by Edward Sheldon and Charles MacArthur— now were conjuring for white America. So, after the requisite upstairs stopover on 142nd Street, a slug, for a buck, of Owney Madden's "No. 1 Beer," and a $2.25 order of Moo Goo Gai Pan to nibble during Healy's snappy floor show, with its score by Mills Music professional manager Jimmy McHugh, you paid the $3 cover charge, took in quickly the celebrities down front (often including New York City Mayor Jimmy Walker), tossed some change at the performers onstage, winked at the hatcheck girl, and moved on.

Some two blocks down Lenox Avenue, at number 575, the Saratoga Club was a practical newcomer to the Harlem nightclub trade, recently opened by the inventor of the Harlem "numbers game," Caspar Holstein, a West Indian whose gambling racket income was now so enormous that he could blithely ignore the prospect of profitability at his club, outfitting the premises gorgeously, with one of Harlem's largest nightclub dance floors, while allowing the sizzling house band led by pianist Luis Russell to play whatever and however long they pleased. The temptation to linger at the Saratoga Club was powerful and many did pass the night away listening to the Saratoga waiters sing as they served and dancing to Russell's furious music. There was, however, still infinitely more to Harlem at night in 1927. You could move on.

Tabb's, on 140th Street, was not a hideaway or a nightclub but a restaurant, where the Southern fried chicken and candied yams were outstanding. Locals enjoyed looking in at Tabb's to watch visiting Park Avenue socialites tackle Tabb's edibles in their formalwear with fingers and bare hands. It was, in many ways, a dizzying tableau, knots of neighborhood black faces at the window of this familiar Harlem eatery staring in at the white visitors who had come uptown to stare, in turn, at them.

In 1927, there were perhaps 300,000 African Americans living in the vicinity of Fifth and Seventh Avenues, roughly from 130th to 155th Streets. They lived, according to census and Urban League studies of the period, in housing designed for 16,000. At least 48% spent twice as much of their income on rent compared with white New Yorkers, and many lived in tenements so "unspeakable" and "incredible," in the words of a 1927 city housing commission report, "the state would not allow cows to live in some of these apartments."

Certainly the prosperity of the Twenties had touched select Harlemites. On Sugar Hill, in the northwest corner of Harlem, high along the cliffs of Edgecombe Avenue, sloping north from 145th to 155th Streets, newly affluent young blacks like entertainer Ethel Waters had begun to move into the handsome apartments still dominated by upper-middle-class German, Jewish, and Irish families. In a very short time, the whites would flee these buildings, transforming Sugar Hill into one of Harlem's elite black neighbor-hoods. Another was "Strivers' Row," a stunning stretch of town-houses designed by architect Stanford White in 1891 on the tree-lined blocks of 138th and 139th Streets between Seventh and Eighth Avenues. Gradually abandoned after 1918 by their well-to-do white owners in flight from the black "invasion," the townhouses had been held off the market for almost a year by their nominal owner, the Equitable Life Insurance Company, as far too good for black occupancy, before the company finally relented in 1919. By 1927, Strivers' Row was firmly rooted in Harlem as a bastion of the black bourgeoisie, who "strove," almost desperately, in the eyes of poorer Harlemites, to emulate the upper-middle-class life-style embodied by these brownstone rows.

Sunk between Sugar Hill and Strivers' Row, however symbolically, if not quite topographically, was "the Valley," Harlem's essential black residential district, where working-class hordes crammed into tenements designed for no more than half their number. Barbers, laundresses, laborers, household menials, cooks, shoeshiners, and shop clerks watched with a mixture of pride, bemusement, embar-rassment, and increasing anger the callous nocturnal parade of white "slummers" through neighborhoods that by day actually were turning slowly into slums. Certainly these Harlemites did not unanimously disapprove of the heated nightclub industry that had rapidly sprung up in their midst, nor did they in any way perceive themselves to be poverty-stricken residents of a slum-ridden ghetto. Increasingly, though, among many, there was a foreboding sense of an unhealthy if not irrevocably diseased and corrupt future, embod-ied in the feverish climate of Harlem's late-night world.

Those blacks who could afford it generally spent their hootch-fueled Harlem nights on Jungle Alley, between Fifth and Seventh Avenues along 133rd Street. According to Willie "the Lion" Smith, there were at least fourteen different cafes on Jungle Alley by the late Twenties, though clubs here, as everywhere throughout Harlem, came and went with unchartable frequency, victims of the local police, Federal Prohibition agents, and gangster competitors. Turn-ing in off Lenox, one could begin at Harry Hansberry's Clam House (Number 146), one of the district's dizzier spots, where Gladys Bentley dressed in men's clothing and sang truly raunchy songs accompanied by her pianist, "Shrimp," while Hansberry served up splendid bacon and eggs, often to local floor show performers who stopped by the Clam House at four in the morning for breakfast.

White people were admitted here, but reluctantly, though that hardly stopped them from coming. As one guide from downtown put it, "you'll see some queeriosities without half-looking."

Tillie's Inn (number 148), also known as the Chicken Shack, offered the best fried chicken, sweet potato pie, and bacon and eggs in all New York, according to its regulars. This, along with the midnight, piano-accompanied torch singing of Elmira, admired for her unexpurgated renditions of "Stop It Joe," "Frankie and Johnnie," and "St. James Infirmary," brought both whites and blacks in great numbers to Tillie's, where, it was pointed out, a party of four could eat what would be nine dollars' worth of food downtown for around two dollars and ten cents.

The entrance to the Catagonia Club (Number 166) was fronted, like the Cotton Club, with a log cabin facade. Inside, there were about twenty-five tables with red-and-white checkered tablecloths, dim lighting, a small bar down at one end of the room, and an old upright piano with chipped, yellowed keys that often was the provenance of Willie "the Lion" Smith, who ruled over the Catagonia Club for approximately two years in the late Twenties.

Charles Holingsworth, nicknamed "Pod," a jovial, sweet-natured man, who liked to call people "Pod-ner," and Jeremiah Preston, a gambler known downtown as "West Indian Jerry," were the owners of the Catagonia Club and the place, as a result, was known to everyone as "Pod's & Jerry's," or simply "P & J's." "Everyone" included a preponderance of black locals as well as Broadway worthies like George Abbot, Helen Morgan, Joan Crawford, Belle Baker, Beatrice Lillie, and Tallulah Bankhead; songmen Hoagy Carmichael, Arthur Schwartz, and Howard Deitz; heavyweight titlists Jack Dempsey and Gene Tunney; Mayor Walker, of course; and a gang of white musicians—Eddie Condon, Jack Teagarden, Benny Goodman, and the legendary cornetist Bix Beiderbecke, among many others.

Everything at Pod's & Jerry's cost a dollar. For that dollar you could get a bottle of Madden's No. 1, of course, or a "top-and-bottom" — an indigenous Harlem mixture of gin and wine; an order of fried, boiled, or roasted chicken, hog maws and red beans; or just plain ham and eggs. Smith usually accompanied three entertainers: one "high-class" female singer, often Mary Stafford or Mattie Hite; a bawdier, second female vocalist/dancer; and "Little Jazzbo" Hilliard, a dark, hunchbacked fellow, four feet tall, whose baritone voice, according to Smith, carried a block away. "The waffles and bacon are grand," summed up one visitor, after an evening at Pod's & Jerry's, "the clientele colorful, and the repartee that is bantered back and forth is absolutely priceless. . . ." There was also, according to this visitor, "a grand piano soloist . . . one Bill Smith, Harlem's only genuine colored Jew, who cheerfully speaks a fluent Yiddish on no provocation whatever."

Across the street from Pod's & Jerry's was The Nest (Number 169), another "black and tan" establishment that cultivated white trade, "with no one caring much with whom he mingles, or why or how," according to one regular. The Nest was owned by Mal Frazier and Johnny Carey, who had themselves put up the building housing the club in a vacant lot back in 1923, opening The Nest in the basement with a Leonard Harper revue and Sam Wooding's band on October 18, 1923. At The Nest, the bandstand was on the west wall, the tables all around along the east, with a dance floor running between the two. Soft drinks were available at a small mixing bar toward the back. Nest customers generally brought their own alcoholic refreshments, though owners Frazier and Carey might serve those they knew well—including regulars like Phil Harris, Otto Kahn, Paul Whiteman, and Carey's frequent companion, Mae West—some "Chicken Cock," a prepared bootleg concoction packaged with a tin cover over the bottle that was very popular around Harlem. Frazier and Carey were local boys, uptown natives, who handled their neighborhood police force generously. The Nest was rarely raided.

The Nest revue's first show went on about 11 or 11:30, with the second show ending around 3 A.M. By 4 A.M. the Nest bandstand usually was packed with jamming musicians who overflowed nearby tables, anxiously awaiting their chance to blow. Jazz in New York City was still an educational experience in 1927, even uptown, among its most professional practitioners. Harlem was teeming with young players still learning their instruments, still learning about jazz, still digesting Louis Armstrong's lessons, all of them wildly eager to play. The Nest, at this time, was particularly cordial in receiving them.

"Between the hours of midnight and 5 A.M.," wrote the *Amsterdam News* during the mid-Twenties, "Seventh Avenue from 130th to 145th Street is as fully alive as Main Street in some little town on a Saturday night. Taxicabs dart from side streets with honking horns. . . . In the very heart of the colored residential district, night is made hideous by cabarets run by white men."

In the aftershock of Owney Madden's arrival in Harlem, the downtown gangster hammerlock on Harlem's nightclub industry had grown exponentially with every passing year to the point where mob rule now reigned preeminent among Harlem's elite late-night establishments, particularly along Seventh Avenue. "The best of Harlem's black cabarets have changed their names and turned white," wrote Rudolph Fisher, one of Harlem's resident literary lights, in the *American Mercury* in 1927, for an article titled "The Caucasian Storms Harlem." Shortly after the arrival of Madden's Cotton Club in Harlem, Barron Wilkins had been stabbed to death one early morning in May 1924 outside his Exclusive Club near the corner of 134th Street and Seventh Avenue, apparently at the hand of a tubercular local drug dealer known as "Yellow Charleston." Many in Harlem believed that Wilkins's murder had been a hit, engineered by Owney Madden, ostensibly in response to Wilkins's complaints about a recent beer order that had come in short. In fact, Wilkins would seem to have been eliminated by Madden as the foremost pillar of African–American ownership among the Harlem nightclub fraternity. In August of 1925, the bullet-riddled body of John Ciaccio, Wilkins's successor at the Exclusive Club, was fished out of the Harlem River by a barge captain. One month later, on September 3, 1925, "Yellow Charleston," *a.k.a.* Julius Miller, was granted a reprieve by New York Governor Franklin Roosevelt, at the request of the Manhattan district attorney's office, six hours before he was due to go to the electric chair. According to the D.A., an affidavit had been received, signed by one Jimmie Denby, in which Denby claimed he had been an eyewitness to Wilkins's murder and could attest to "Yellow Charleston"'s innocence. The affidavit, the D.A.'s office added, had been obtained through Broadway showman Earl Carrol, who "confessed to having an interest in the condemned man."

Andrea Razaf frequented Harlem's torrid nightclub world on a rotating basis in 1927, breezing in and out of numerous establishments throughout a given evening, from the Saratoga Club and Happy Rhone's on Lenox Avenue to the north, down to the Spider Web at the southernmost active tip of Seventh Avenue near 126th Street, a "black and tan" where the maître d' and nominal front man was Florence Mills's husband, U. S. "Slow Kid" Thompson. Razaf's primary nightspot destinations in 1927, were, however, Connie's Inn, near 131st and Seventh, where he was surreptitiously admitted into the club's cavelike, segregated basement precincts on partner Waller's say-so, and Smalls' Paradise, a relatively new venue opened by the fiesty black owner of the Sugar Cane Club over on Fifth Avenue, Ed Smalls—a South Carolina-born descendant to black Civil War hero Captain Robert Smalls, and, like Razaf, a former elevator operator. Smalls, after transfering his Sugar Cane operation to 2294 1/2 Seventh Avenue, between 134th and 135th Streets, in late October, 1925, had nurtured the Paradise into one of Harlem's most successful nightclub ventures. A large room, with capacity for nearly 1,500, a superb dance band—perhaps Harlem's finest in a genuine jazz sense, led by pianist Charlie Johnson—a relatively offhand "black and tan" admittance policy with prices that generally "kept out the riffraff," and a floor show second only to those at Connie's Inn and the Cotton Club in quality, were a combination that rendered Smalls' Paradise perhaps Harlem's hottest nightclub entrant in 1927, successful particularly in its casually orchestrated juggling of low-down, neighborhood informality with Cotton Club esthetic pretense. While the waiters at Small's danced the Charleston as they served, spinning traysful of drinks expertly, they still waitered with courtly precision. Moreover, as one visitor observed with some relief in 1927, "This is the nicest of the places sometimes referred to as 'black and tans,' chiefly because the clientele is mixed,"—meaning, there were far more whites in attendance but just enough blacks to avoid the bleached unreality of thoroughly segregated clubs like Connie's Inn and the Cotton Club. "There's no cutting in, though," the visitor added, reassuring potential Smalls patrons about the possibility of being forced to dance with a black partner, "so nobody need feel squeamish about that."

There was another layer to Harlem's glamorous late-night veneer that only a small percentage of white visitors ever penetrated. "There are those who are sickened by the sight of a naked woman and those who cannot tolerate the public knowledge that men are a mammalian species," wrote one rather overstimulated white European explorer into this darker side in 1927. "America, because of her primitive origins, has had to be highly perfumed. Hence, among other things, the draped statues, elaborate bathing costumes, and the infrequency of comfort-stations. But one can be as free in mind as the French and yet be nauseated by Harlem."

The visitor went on to describe the goings-on in one of Harlem's grittier after-hours establishments.

The lights are so few that it is almost dark and yet one sees enough. The dancing square is crowded. The music is harsh staccato punctuated by vociferous horns. All rhythms are blurred. There is no smooth dancing, no gliding, scarcely any forward movement. The dancers hold body to body, they keep on their toes, they sway, they seek contact, they interpret the savage rhythm in sex sensation. Cold partners do not dance there with pleasure. Those who can take pleasure from intimate contact are not content till they have a physical entente, and then they let the music do the rest. The dance lasts a long time . . .

One of the hostesses in black pajamas mingled constantly with the crowd; other hostesses in elegant kimonos sat at tables with guests. In the dim light a marvelous Ethiopian girl with silvered eyelids sang and danced. A naked contortionist tickled her own chin with tenuous fingers of arms which were locked behind her. A stove-black boy with white enamelled lips sang in a voice like three megaphones. A cat-like dwarf girl, the colour of a cocoa-nut, did the splits on the floor and pulsated with her little stomach and thighs to the heavy music . . . The waiters, wearing low shoes, white gaiters, and white smoking caps scooted, dancing, across the floor, bearing above their heads ginger-ale bottles and pots of ice. They stamped, they did step-dances, they surrounded revue singers, they crouched, they jumped, they flew.

The gin-bottle reposed on the floor under the table. A tall policeman was strutting among the bedizened dancers and guests, swinging his nightstick suggestively, as if he longed to crack a skull. But his function was the protection of law-breakers . . . The club was disobeying the curfew, for it was after three o'clock and also there was much open drinking. It was he . . . who gave the 'up bottles' signal. Waiters with electric torches came searching among the legs of the guests under the tables and made every one pick up his liquor and put it into his pocket. The cop had advised a safety measure.

Harlem, of course, had many after-hours spots. There was the Rhythm Club, a "hanging-out place for musicians" in the basement of the building next door to the Lafayette Theatre on Seventh Avenue at 132nd Street, where the house band worked from 3:30 until 7:30 in the morning. Basement Brownie's on 133rd Street was operated by "two ex-vaudevillian opium smokers," according to Willie "the Lion" Smith, the 300 pound Brown and his pal "Gulfport,"—you had to knock three times and blow your nose to get in there, while Mexico's—"the hottest gin mill on 133rd Street," according to Duke Ellington—was run by a fellow named Gomez, who was from one of the Carolinas, according to Willie Smith, and had never actually seen Mexico. Then there was the Madhouse, upstairs over the Nest, where the door was alternately padlocked and unpadlocked and one was best advised to "phone first—or ask anybody you meet," and Johnny Jackson's on 135th and Seventh, where locals wound up when there was "absolutely no other place left for them to wind up." Beyond even these after-hours establishments, however, were the squalid marijuana parlors, the "sex circuses" hosted on 140th Street by Waller and Razaf's favorite madam, Hazel Valentine, the roisterously secretive basement nooks with drag parade floorshows, the blocks between 132nd and 138th Streets along Fifth Avenue known as "Coke Village," and Dad Brooks's good-time house upstairs above Leroy's cabaret at 135th Street and Fifth Avenue, where, for a modest admission, the musical ambience of a rent parlor social was recreated with a good piano, the frequent presence of Harlem's best piano men, and the added inducement of numerous willing "queens" in the back room.

Andrea Razaf absorbed all of this, the high and the low, the illegal and the illicit, studying it all like a visiting professor, savoring much of it as a fellow night crawler. Razaf was, as well, very much aware in 1927 of Harlem's burgeoning, eminently more respectable cultural renaissance, an uptown effusion of African–American creativity in literature and the visual arts that since 1923 had been offering black Americans a radically elevated cultural role model, the "New Negro." Many today apply the "Harlem Renaissance" label indiscriminately to all that was Harlem culturally in the Twenties: to the literature and the jazz music, the nightclub revues and the ambitious poetry and painting. Razaf, though, very much distinguished his accomplishments, if not his general aspirations, from those of Jean Toomer, Countee Cullen, Zora Neale Hurston, Claude McKay, Rudolph Fisher, and Langston Hughes, the literati of the Harlem Renaissance. Razaf, in fact, at this time befriended most of these writers, growing closest to Hughes. As a black Harlemite, though, Razaf also understood that this Harlem Renaissance was hardly a spontaneous event, that the movement largely was being orchestrated by local black leaders like sociologist Charles Johnson as a social revolution mounted on a cultural premise: that black America's best chance at gaining approval and, ultimately, acceptance from white America was through artistic creativity that commanded respect. For this Renaissance dream to succeed, Johnson and others believed, its substance would have to be unimpeachable—esthetically and racially neuter, as far removed as possible from that which Johnson considered to be the clichéd, the stereotypical, the low-down artistic contributions of the African in America to date.

Heading Johnson's roster of unsuitables were minstrelsy, ragtime, "coon tunes," and the blues, the coarse, vulgar, bottomless blues, including everything that these various expressions of black culture currently meant to black theatrical and musical creativity in Harlem. This surely left Andrea Razaf and his peers well outside the Harlem Renaissance mainstream, a position Razaf may not have appreciated but one he did accept, perhaps taking some satisfaction from the fact that this Renaissance was at least partly descended from the loud preaching of Harlem's angry, young postwar poets like "Razafkeriefo." Ultimately, Razaf did find peace at this time both in what he was and what he was not. He was not conventionally educated. He was not an artist, not a poet in any literary sense. He was a lover of rhyme and simple emotions, a manipulator of fundamental song forms and uncomplicated sentiment. Andy Razaf was unapologetically a songwriter.

"Andy had a sensitive, kind of active personality," recalled newspaperman Ed Morrow, a scholarship student at Yale during these Renaissance years, who came down to Harlem from New Haven as frequently as he could (as he said), "to drink it all in." "Andy was a truly cultivated person, without affectation, a person who really loved things of the mind. I remember he would walk along—my late wife was one of his girlfriends at the time—and Andy would get an idea for a song or a lyric and he'd just start chanting and reciting, walking down the street, getting carried away by the thing. My wife Ruby Williams—Ruby Downes Williams, she later danced in the original *Showboat* in 1929—she and Andy were sweethearts and she said Andy was always full of his notes and his books. He had a sort of lyrical ebullience and fire."

Late in November 1926, Razaf had taken to the road as advance man for the new all-black revue *Desires of 1927*, produced by Irvin C. Miller, one of the last old-time black impresarios still functioning in this white-dominated, Harlem-infatuated theatrical age. A brother to *Shuffle Along* librettist and costar Flournoy Miller, Irvin C. Miller had gradually progressed from the blackface burlesque musical comedy revues that he still produced regularly under the title *Brown Skin Models* to moderate success on Broadway as a librettist himself with *Put and Take* in 1921 and *Liza* in 1922.

Running approximately an hour and fifteen minutes, Miller's *Desires of 1927* appears to have been more of a touring revue, à la *Brown Skin Models,* than a full-blown Broadway-bound production, and details about the show are few. The only certainties seem to be that Irvin Miller produced *Desires* and that Andrea Razaf, in concert with J. C. Johnson, contributed "special music" to the score for a company that included black musical veteran J. Homer Tutt, young black vocalist sensation Adelaide Hall, and Razaf himself, performing as "Crooning Andy."

Desires appears to have toured from October 1926 roughly through the early months of 1927. *Opportunity: The Colored Weekly,* in its review of the 1927 black theatrical season, cited *Desires* as "the outstanding musical revue . . . out of a total of 43 shows . . . A real show in its entirety . . . [it] tops the list." Ultimately, *Desires* seems to have achieved just about everything that a "colored revue" could hope to achieve in 1927, filling black theaters across the vast TOBA wilderness of the northeastern United States throughout the winter of 1926–1927—everything, that is, but a production on Broadway.

Razaf's songwriting efforts in 1927 essentially centered around J. C. Johnson, with whom he was now rooming in a boardinghouse near 125th Street. After they'd concluded 1926 with a number of song sales to various Tin Pan Alley publishers (including a pair to Irving Berlin), Razaf and Johnson had carried their success forward into 1927, composing four more songs to open the year. Of these, three were published immediately in February and March of 1927: "I Once Was Yours, I'm Somebody Else's Now," "What Have You Done to Make Me Feel This Way?," and "Havana Nights." The fourth, "Louisiana," soon would become a hit and even something of a standard, recorded at least seven times throughout 1928, both in the United States and in Great Britain, by artists ranging from Paul Whiteman, Duke Ellington, and Bix Beiderbecke to Allan Selby and his Picadilly Dance Band.

"Louisiana" presents itself today as something of an enigma from an authorial perspective. Two songs that Razaf and Johnson sold to Irving Berlin Music Publishing in December 1926—"Desire" and

"Wondering When"—languished throughout 1927 in Berlin's un-published file of properties. A third, "When," which the team copyrighted themselves on November 26, 1926, finally was pur-chased and published by Berlin in February 1928. The song gained an additional collaborator, though, in the interim, with lyric credit ultimately ascribed both to Andy Razaf and one Bob Schafer, a 30-year-old, New York–born singer, songwriter, and music publish-ing house manager. Similarly, when "Louisiana" first received its copyright on March 3, 1927, the credit line read, "Words by Andy Razaf, melody by J. C. Johnson." One year later, after selling the song to Irving Berlin's former Lower East Side songwriting rival and occasional collaborator, Al Piantadosi, who published "Louisiana" on March 6, 1928, Razaf and Johnson's credit line on the song had somehow come to read: "Words by Andy Razaf and Bob Schafer, music by J. C. Johnson."

The mystery deepens still. Razaf and Johnson, on September 22, 1926, copyrighted a song entitled "My Special Friend." Ten months later, on July 27, 1927, the song was published by Broadway Music Company as "My Special Friend (Is Back in Town)," with composi-tional credit ascribed to Andy Razaf, Bob Schafer, and J. C. Johnson.

Was Bob Schafer an integral third contributor to these three most successful Razaf–Johnson songs from the initial year of their collab-oration? Each of the tunes would achieve substantial success on records, with "When" a big hit for Paul Whiteman in 1928, and "Louisiana" a hit for both Whiteman and his star soloist Bix Beiderbecke, respectively, in 1928. "My Special Friend" already was a great hit for Ethel Waters at the time of that song's release, via a recording waxed by Waters for Columbia on September 18, 1926, six months *before* "My Special Friend"'s official publication.

Thus there is strong reason to believe that Bob Schafer may have been the price Razaf and Johnson paid to secure a publisher for these songs. The mysterious arbiter of that price? Razaf, toward the end of his life, expressed himself tersely and without elaboration on the subject of "Louisiana" only: "the unethical work of Joe Davis," Razaf remarked, "who God has already punished."

Ethel Waters's way with a blues tune was a refined variation on the standard, belting blues-mama approach of the mid-Twenties. Blessed with bell-like vocal timbre that was complemented by a vaudeville-derived conscientiousness about enunciation, Waters, un-like the rawer, more rural belters, delivered the blues with urbane elegance and a lilting melodicism, an ideal delivery for putting across the niceties of a blues lyric by Andrea Razaf. Still active as a singer on both white and black vaudeville circuits, while making more frequent appearances in downtown black nightclub revues, Waters recently had signed to record with Columbia, an arrangement that was bringing her to the attention of a wider and whiter audience in late 1926. Apparently J. C. Johnson made the initial overture to Waters on behalf of the newborn Razaf–Johnson team, persuading Waters to take on "My Special Friend." Backed by her highly capable accompanist Pearl Wright, Waters offered up a raucous, effervescent reading of the song, one that captured perfectly Razaf's quite revolutionary transformation of the traditional, smirking, contemporary blues lyric into something much more sophisticated and amusing, even droll. The record would be Razaf's first significant hit.

> *It can rain, it can snow, it can sleet, it can blow,*
> *Doggone it, I don't give a hang.*
> *You can read in my face something soon will take place,*
> *I'm saying goodby . . . to the gang.*
> *I'm acting like a nut,*
> *No, I'm not crazy, but*
> *My special friend is back in town.*
> *I've not been treated right*
> *But I'll make up tonight,*
> *My special friend is back in town.*
> *Now don't stand in my hall*
> *Or I'll call you down,*
> *From today keep away*
> *'Cause I'm true when he's around.*
> *Take care, don't talk too much*
> *Or we'll both get in dutch,*
> *My special friend is back in town.*
> *Don't phone me at the store,*
> *No, you can't write me anymore,*
> *My special friend is back in town.*
> *Of course, when we meet on the street,*
> *Merely stop to say,*
> *Howdy do. How are you?*
> *After that you be on your way.*
> *Go on and tell what you know,*
> *I'll swear it isn't so,*

My special friend is back in town.
No parties from tonight,
My poker games are tight,
My special friend is back in town.
Take back your jewelry,
It can't be seen on me,
My special friend is back in town.
Take back this, take back that—
After all, they're yours—
Take your dog, take your cat,
Or he'll think you're Santa Claus.
Excuse me while I laugh
But I just hid your photograph,
My special friend is back in town . . .
First we'll go to a show,
Later on we'll dine,
After that, to my flat,
Can't you guess what's on my mind?
If you don't see no lights,
Don't you ring my bell tonight,
My special friend is back in town.

Razaf continued to record during 1927, concluding his relationship with the Gennett label as "Razaf (The Melody Man)," to begin recording for both Harmony and Columbia under the name "Crooning Andy Razaf." He also continued to perform on a multitude of radio stations—WHN, WOR, WJZ, WEAF, and WGCP—frequently in tandem with J. C. Johnson. Razaf and Johnson, by December 1926, had evolved what can only be termed an Amos-'n-Andy–style, minstrel-based comedy act, with Razaf playing the drawling, slow-witted comedic butt, and Johnson the interlocutor and straight man. Billed as "the Two Watermelon Seeds," the pair performed these routines on radio and even recorded excerpts for Cameo Records. Their comic patter today strikes a listener as rather demeaning.

Johnson: What did you do with that bag of chicken seed I gave ya?
Razaf: I planted them.
Johnson: What was the thought behind that?
Razaf: I wanted to raise some mo' chickens.

Both Razaf and Johnson, even as their fortunes began to climb toward the end of 1926, clearly were in rather straitened financial circumstances at the time they developed these routines. "Do you remember the December we recorded 'Two Watermelon Seeds' on Cameo?" J. C. Johnson wrote to Razaf in August 1961. "Can you really recall how bad things were at the time? But everything worked out O.K. when I threw my six bits worth of charm on the cat and he came through with our checks before two hearts stopped still."

It is interesting to contrast these painful "Watermelon Seed" routines with some of the very militant writing that Razaf still contributed to newspapers in 1927. Juxtapostion of the two seems to highlight a basic inconsistency in Razaf's character, an ability to ignore, or at least deny, those abdications of personal standards he allowed himself in his own single-minded drive to achieve entertainment industry success, in contrast to the rigorous, unblinking scrutiny he still objectively focused upon that entertainment scene, often with brutal candor.

Throughout 1927, for example, Razaf contributed a column irregularly to the *Amsterdam News,* "At Home Abroad; Being Comments on Our Entertainers in All Parts of the World." "There's a dreadful disease known in the theatrical world as 'the big head,'" he wrote boldly in a September 1927 submission. "Like pyorrhea, four out of every five performers have it.

"Take an ignoramus out of a cotton field with a few dance steps and no brains and he is a perfect subject for this disease," wrote Razaf, with a stinging frankness that no one else inside the Harlem entertainment community seems to have hazarded publicly during the Twenties. "Sneak him on the bill some Plantation Night and let him get 'a hand,' and the next day you can't give him a letter from home. The minute he signs his first contract, providing he can write, he'll demand the best dressing room and his name out in lights.

"After becoming 'a star,'" continued Razaf, "will he spend some of his money and spare time polishing up mentally? Will he go to some capable instructor and improve his dance routine? We should say not! He feels 'too big' to take instruction from anyone; in fact, what he doesn't know isn't worth knowing. With his patent leather head and dressed like a fashion plate he may impress you—until he opens his mouth.

"Many a girl with a Rolls Royce figure, a Pierce Arrow face, and a flivver brain has allowed 'the big head'" to ruin her career.

"A prima donna with a voice as thin as a veil will tell you she 'never associates with the chorus.'

"Even a wardrobe mistress will stop speaking to 'ordinary people' and will tell her friends that she is 'on the stage.'

"When a performer with talent and intelligence gets the 'big head,'" Razaf concluded, "nature seems to throw in the reverse clutch and leaves him skidding backwards. He is often worse than his mental inferiors.

"If it's your ambition to become a truly great artist like Florence Mills or Bill Robinson, pray every night never to get the "'big head.'"

"The Producer: A Sketch Featuring Ham & Sam, by Andy Razaf," also ran in The *Amsterdam News* that year.

Place: Harlem
Time: Constantly

Sam: Whadder yer say? What you doin' these days?
Ham: I'm producin' a revue. Got sick of runnin' elevators.
Sam: What you producin' a revue for?
Ham: Everybody else is—ain't they?
Sam: Got any material to work with?
Ham: Don't need any.
Sam: What, are you crazy?
Ham: No—the public is.
Sam: Don't you know that it takes ability, experience and money to produce a show?
Ham: Feller, you're all wrong.
Sam: Then what does it take?
Ham: Few rehearsals and lots of nerve.
Sam: Where you gonna get your scenery and costumes?
Ham: How should I know? I'm no fortune teller.
Sam: Ain't you got no money?
Ham: Ask me another.
Sam: Who gave you the idea that you could produce a show?
Ham: My janitor! He hit the numbers and produced twelve of them before his money ran out.
Sam: Did he realize anything out of it?
Ham: Sure. He realized that he was a better janitor.
Sam: But wasn't one of his shows a success?
Ham: Yes. The last one.
Sam: And how was that?

Ham: Theatre burned down before it opened.
Sam: Where do you think your show will open?
Ham: In some theatre, I hope.
Sam: How are the scenes laid out?
Ham: The whole thing is done in "one."
Sam: How's that?
Ham: We'll open and close in one week.
Sam: Where are you headin' for now?
Ham: I'm lookin' for some girls.
Sam: Say, I know some up-to-date brown-skinned girls, pretty, clever and all that. Shall I send them to see you?
Ham: Sure—but they can't be too dark.
Sam: What difference does that make? Ain't you gonna have a colored show?
Ham: Yes, but I can only use a Creole chorus.
Sam: Creole? I bet you don't even know what a Creole is.
Ham: Who said I do?
Sam: Then how will you know Creole when you see one?
Ham: Shucks. See that pretty high yeller over there? Now that's a Creole. She's from home, too. Born right next door to me.
Sam: In New Orleans?
Ham: No—Alabama.
Sam: Well, I'll be seeing you later. Where can I find you?
Ham: You can find me all day and all night either at one of these gin mills or at the sidewalk N.V.A.
Sam: Where is the sidewalk N.V.A.?
Ham: Man, wake up. Outside the Lafayette, you dumbbell.

For so many of Razaf's desperately ambitious black entertainment peers, so long shut out of the entertainment mainstream in America, the "Black Vogue" of the Twenties on Broadway and up in Harlem very quickly had become something of a wide-open feeding frenzy. Access to the trough of popular success had been granted, with restrictions, so suddenly. Hungry black performers, composers, and entertainment producers now were grasping at whatever morsels of achievement they could reach, at almost any price.

Andy Razaf strongly believed that to make it this way was tragically debasing. Earning it, working for it, and maintaining a standard of excellence while making it concerned Razaf far more, at least intellectually, if not altogether personally. His *Producer* "sketch" dramatized this quite forcefully. In fact, Razaf seems almost to acknowledge in the sketch that the truth of the matter in black entertainment did largely reside with "Ham" in 1927, that really one didn't necessarily need ability, experience, or even money to produce a show, that all it did take was a "few rehearsals and lots of nerve." The lyricist nevertheless makes it amply clear, through tart, understated sarcasm, that, for him, this state of affairs was not merely ludicrous but self-annihilating, leading to "colored shows" that were more concerned with some dimly perceived white sense of light, "Creole" skin pigment than formal theatrical esthetics. Such ignorance, Razaf concluded, could lead in the end only to professional obliteration, which he obliquely conjures as the "sidewalk N.V.A." (a facetious reference to the formal guild for vaudeville entertainers nationwide, National Variety Artists) ". . . outside the Lafayette Theatre." For years now, the image of nattily dressed Harlem entertainers clustered around the "Tree of Hope" out in front of the Lafayette Theatre on Seventh Avenue had been presented as one of the most evocative glories of the Harlem entertainment world of the Twenties. Razaf here debunked this romantic illusion by reminding his readers that many of these picturesque loiterers were at bottom shiftless, confirmed minions of the unemployed.

Razaf recorded with a group of Fletcher Henderson bandsmen, led by Henderson's new young trumpet star, 20-year-old Rex Stewart, under the name "Rex Stewart's Serenaders" on April 4, 1927, for Vocalion, vocalizing on something called the "Ten O'Clock Blues," along with a song entitled "Oh Malinda," the product of Razaf's first documented songwriting activity with James P. Johnson. For reasons known only to Vocalion, however, all takes of this session were rejected. Then, throughout August and early September, Razaf sold six of his own blues tunes to various publishers, with five of these six songs enjoying wide recording coverage over the ensuing months by a host of notable female vocalists—Lizzie Miles, Martha Copeland, Gertrude Saunders, Rosa Henderson, and Alma Henderson. Razaf, with J. C. Johnson, also composed a lovely requiem to the memory of Florence Mills on the occasion of Mills's tragic and untimely death at the age of 32 on November 1, 1927, apparently from the general effects of a professional hyperactivity that exhausted Mills's notoriously fragile constitution. Razaf recorded the tune himself on November 4, 1927, for Columbia: "All the World Is

Lonely (For a Little Blackbird)," accompanied by J. C. Johnson on piano and Eddie King on organ. Razaf also recorded on November 26 with the full Fletcher Henderson aggregation for Regal Records, vocalizing on three tunes, none of them his own—"Dear, On a Night Like This," by Irving Caesar and Con Conrad, "There's a Rickety Rackety Shack," by Charles Tobias and Roy Turk, and "Sorry," by Raymond Klages and Howard Quicksell. The results this time were deemed worthy of release.

Thomas Waller had spent 1927 vigorously involved in various musical and nonmusical adventures. Twice during the first months of 1927 he had recorded a series of genuinely scintillating organ solos for Ralph Peer at Victor Records, a total of eleven in all. Then, in March, Waller had accepted an invitation to join Erskine Tate's superb orchestra in the pit of the Vendome motion picture theater in Chicago, performing on both piano and organ beside Tate's trumpet star, Louis Armstrong, who again hosted Waller's Chicago stay, putting up both Thomas and the now-pregnant Anita Waller at his home on East 44th Street, near the lake on Chicago's South Side. For at least three months, Waller again enjoyed himself enormously in Chicago, attracting an adoring following at the Vendome on State Street, while sitting in nights with an exceptional small jazz group that featured Armstrong at the Sunset Cafe, three blocks away from the Vendome, on 35th Street and Calumet Avenue.

At some point, though, during this Chicago stint, Waller was served with an arrest summons, again on charges of alimony nonpayment to Edith Hatchet. Stranding his pregnant 17-year-old wife, he was returned to New York, where a sympathetic judge shocked the young pianist by letting him off with a stern lecture. In time, Anita Waller's family retrieved the abandoned young mother from Chicago and Waller was reunited with her. He soon resumed his spot in the Victor recording studio rotation, and was restored as well to his organ post at the Lafayette Theatre. On September 10, Waller's second son was born. Shortly thereafter, Waller celebrated his wife's return from the maternity ward one afternoon, while working at the Lafayette, by inviting Anita Waller to join him on the organ bench. According to an ensuing report in the *New York Age* on October 1: "The management objected. Words. Fats quit there and then."

The balance of the year, for Waller, was filled out with an ever-increasing number of recording sessions for Victor—as an organ-playing accompanist to vocalists Juanita Stinette Chappelle and Bert Howell on a Florence Mills memorial program, as a pipe organ soloist, and in a small group setting with cornetist Tom Morris.

Con Conrad was one of Tin Pan Alley's quintessential songwriting hacks in 1928, a former film theater and vaudeville pianist whose novelty hit "Barney Google" in 1923 represented the commercial summit of Conrad's songwriting achievements, outselling all other previous and subsequent Conrad song compositions, including "Margie," "California," and "Singin' the Blues." A New York native originally, named Conrad K. Dober, Con Conrad at the age of 36 was a mixer along Tin Pan Alley, chummy with all factions in the theatrical and songwriting game, from the black music publishers toasting their Joy Club in the Gaiety Building, to the bootlegging gangsters who'd become Broadway's most reliable sources for production capital in the Twenties.

Late in 1927, Conrad patched together his own unlikely alliance between these two diverse entertainment poles on the Broadway scene. The alliance began with Miller and Lyles, celebrated cocreators of *Shuffle Along*, whose most recent Broadway endeavor, *Rang Tang*, had enjoyed a rather successful run at the Royale Theatre on 45th Street after opening in July to substantial critical approbation. Surviving into the winter of 1927, *Rang Tang* apparently had only one failing, and that had been managerial—the show's producers continually failed to make good on their salary obligations, and by the time *Rang Tang* closed in November after 119 performances, salaries to all company members, including Miller and Lyles, were well in arrears.

With the unfortunate financial failure of their otherwise highly successful show as a taunting inspiration, Miller and Lyles were eager to return to Broadway and recoup some of their losses. Apparently Con Conrad was aware of their eagerness. With consumate nerve, he approached the man whom columnist Damon Runyon called "the Brain"—bootlegger, gambler, loan shark, businessman, entrepreneur, and presumed fixer of the 1919 World Series Arnold Rothstein, who had been laundering money via the Broadway theater for years—about possibly backing a new "colored" musical. With predictable crap-shooting venturesomeness, Rothstein said yes.

Conrad next turned to an old ally in the Gaiety Building, blustering blues booster–songwriter Perry Bradford. Bradford later claimed that Conrad in fact invited Bradford to compose the score for Conrad's newly financed Broadway production himself, in collaboration with Henry Creamer. If so, it seems odd that Bradford, as he also later claimed, demurred in favor of James P. Johnson. What seems more likely is that Conrad, recalling Johnson's extraordinary work in *Runnin' Wild*, solicited Bradford's help both in persuading Johnson to take on the assignment and convincing Miller and Lyles to accept him; the three *Runnin' Wild* collaborators' previous association had ended acrimoniously during that show's post-Broadway tour, with a royalty accounting in Pittsburgh filed against Miller and Lyles by Johnson and his lyricist partner Cecil McPherson.

In time, Bradford succeeded in selling Johnson on the new undertaking. He also persuaded Miller to embrace Johnson's participation. Lyles, a late holdout, finally gave in with a terse and simple statement: "I don't like to put bread in that guy's mouth—and I ain't gonna take none out. So tell Con it's O.K., and also tell him that I'm hoping that the same bee don't sting me twice."

Conrad now wanted Johnson to assume the new production's musical directing chores as well as commit himself to playing piano in the pit. Johnson, who was working on many fronts at this time, including the beginnings of a formally composed original rhapsody, suggested the possibility of sharing the burden of all this work with a young pianist he knew named Waller. It was agreed that Waller and Johnson together would audition for Conrad *and* Rothstein in Rothstein's office, which apparently was equipped with a piano. In the end, the audition so delighted Rothstein that he called for a case of his pre–war liquor to toast Thomas Waller's hiring.

Presumably it was Waller who chose to share all this sudden good fortune with Andrea Razaf by tapping Razaf as his lyricist on the new project. With astonishing speed, in the waning weeks of 1927, the song team of Razaf and Waller was reunited in a rush to compose half a score for their first Broadway musical. Fortunately for all concerned, the frenzied circumstances suited both men completely.

Predictably, Waller and Rothstein also became fast friends. Razaf, ever practical, remained wary. Waller discovered that Rothstein, who kept his Prohibition fortune invested in numerous legitimate businesses, including a New York real estate trust, the city's largest insurance company, and a bail-bond business, was one of Broadway's softest touches, when well disposed to the solicitee. "How 'bout some trash for a cab?" Waller asked Rothstein one day, in Razaf's presence. "Sure," replied Rothstein. "Will five hundred do?"

"The goose who laid the golden eggs," Waller called his "silent" producer.

In *Rang Tang*, Miller and Lyles had suffered a wicked financial embarrassment. *Keep Shufflin'*, as the new show was titled in deference to Miller and Lyles's greatest success, consequently became something of an obsession for the two veteran troupers, and their book soon evolved into something more ambitiously elaborate than the standard musical comedy scripts of the day. Certain critics would, in fact, hail *Keep Shufflin'* as "smart satire slanted towards the impracticality of communism." Razaf and Waller simply concentrated on keeping their songs memorable.

The characters Steve Jenkins and Sam Peck—theatrical alter-egos for Miller and Lyles throughout many of their Broadway stage appearances—are against work. That was the premise behind *Keep Shufflin'*. The two friends organize a society devoted to the getting of money without work—"The League of Equal Got"—and enlist a group of workmen in a scheme to dynamite and rob a bank. A bad dream, suffered by Jenkins after he is accidently knocked unconscious, eventually forces him to recognize the folly of his and Peck's undertaking, as he is presented with a catastrophic view of their world—"Jimtown"—following the successful redistribution of the bank's wealth; a world in which no one has to work. Wakening, he saves Peck from their law-breaking scheme.

As one critic later wrote, "It doesn't sound so amusing in the re-telling, but you'll find in visiting the theater that it plays damn well."

Unwilling to rest on the success of their satirical book, Miller and Lyles nervously fidgeted with the production throughout rehearsals, injecting it continuously with further doses of "pep"—pep in the dance ensembles choreographed by Clarence Robinson and in the orchestrations devised by Will Vodery, pep in the wisecracks and the music and the dancing. By the time *Keep Shufflin'* reached its Philadelphia run-through at Gibson's Theatre on February 13, 1928, as one local critic observed, "instead of the verb 'shufflin' to indicate the speed at which one must keep going, the management of *Keep Shufflin'* is hereby respectfully notified that 'speedin' is the word they are searching for."

Dizzy as it was, though, the show apparently was a delight.

"*Keep Shufflin'* is a long way the best of the colored shows seen here this year," the *Philadelphia Record* insisted in its opening night review. "It has the kind of marvelous abandon which can be found only in a Negro entertainment, and then only now and again. There is no adagio dancing in *Keep Shufflin'*. There is no adagio any-thing. . . . Everything the most exacting audience wants is there: Singing, Dancing, Personality. The house . . . went wild over num-ber after number.

"The main ingredient . . . is the shufflin'. . . . Vitality? Probably so much vitality was never expended in an equal length of time on a Philadelphia platform before. . . . They dance till your head whirls."

"A rather bald man seated ten rows back was mildly surprised," recounted the *Philadelphia Inquirer*, "when a rose-hued slipper suddenly left the foot of one of the dancers and described a neat parabola into his lap. This one incident is fairly indicative of the brutal speed attained by this jet-propelled musical comedy. On another occasion a headdress also went wild and, leaving the raven tresses of its owner, did a couple of turns into the audience. The only wonder was that anything was able to stay in place amid the speed-limit prancing and general turn-everything-loose that makes this one of the fastest shows of its kind ever seen in this city."

Keep Shufflin' returned to New York and opened on the evening of February 27, 1928, at Daly's 63rd Street Theatre, the original home of Miller and Lyles's *Shuffle Along*. The songs were credited to Jimmie Johnson, Fats Waller, and Clarence Todd, the lyrics to Henry Creamer and Andy Razaf. The show boasted a company of sixty, with Waller and Johnson featured in the orchestra pit (Waller "On the White Keys," Johnson "On the Black Keys"), alongside cornet star Jabbo Smith ("Behind the Bugle"). The New York critics, by and large, were impressed. "Red hot tunes, lightning dance steps, a batallion of frenzied song and dance purveyors, and Miller and Lyles—that's *Keep Shufflin'*, the latest and one of the best colored shows to hit Daly's Theatre since the memorable *Shuffle Along*," summed up *Daily Mirror* critic Robert Coleman.

For Razaf, *Shuffle Along* represented the culmination of a dream. Out of twenty-one numbers, including an interpolated handful by Will Vodery and Con Conrad, he had contributed lyrics to seven. The songs today reveal many things about the state of Razaf's songwriting craft in 1928. They also prove especially revelatory with regard to the racial constraints imposed upon a "colored" Broadway musical comedy in 1928, while also illuminating Razaf's gutsy, subtle balking at those sad constraints lyrically in this, his long-awaited return to Broadway.

"Choc'late Bar" was *Keep Shufflin'*'s first Razaf/Waller number—appearing immediately after the show's opening chorus by Creamer and Vodery. As an example of the Razaf lyric writing style, "Choc'late Bar" stands, in retrospect, as an accomplished trial run for "Honeysuckle Rose": "Your kiss surpasses; sweeter than 'lasses/ My little choc'late bar/They drive me daffy; better than taffy/My little choc'late bar." The song's most striking characteristic remains the grotesque "Jim Crow" perspective that Razaf was forced to adopt in it:

> *When it comes to sweetness hon' you sho' am sweet,*
> *Honeysuckles droop their heads in shame . . .*
> *Sweeter than a watermelon right off the vine,*
> *Sweeter than the sweetest 'tater, and you're all mine.*

After nearly fifteen years serving a protracted apprenticeship uptown in Harlem and down on Tin Pan Alley, Razaf was finally back on Broadway. The privilege afforded him the opportunity to write lines such as these in the tune "Happy in Jimtown":

> *Ev'rybody's happy down in Jimtown tonight,*
> *Ev'rybody's lucky, not a care is in sight,*
> *No-one is a stranger here; we wish you could see*
> *How we show you good old Southern hospitality,*
> *Come on down to Jimtown and you'll find livin' sweet,*
> *Where the sun is shinin' on both sides of the street,*
> *Faces dusky but hearts are light,*
> *We're happy in Jimtown tonight.*

Razaf was able to work some cleverness into the stale, often offensive formulaic clichés of the *Keep Shufflin'* score. "How Jazz Was Born," for example, provided him with an opportunity to deliver his own tart, encapsulated history of the music:

> *People used to call it "Ragtime,"*
> *That was many years ago,*
> *Then they spoke of "Syncopation,"*
> *But that sounded much too slow,*
> *Later, all you heard was "Charleston,"*
> *Finally "Blackbottom" came,*

> *Each name meant the same,*
> *I know who's to blame—*

Razaf also worked his own stoic brand of lyric defiance into the *Keep Shufflin'* score. The gesture was modestly camouflaged, and few, if any, among *Keep Shufflin's* predominantly white attendees in 1928 probably even absorbed a sense of Razaf's subversive implication. The song "Willow Tree" was initially held back as an encore number. Its popularity with *Keep Shufflin'* audiences quickly drew the song into the production's standard running order, though, and, in time, "Willow Tree" became the show's biggest hit.

"I saw a darkey in the woodland, bowed down with sorrow all his own," began Razaf in "Willow Tree," invoking a reassuring minstrel presence for openers. "He went to nature with his trouble," continued Razaf, just a bit more disturbingly now, "with tearful eyes I heard him moan:

> *Oh lordy, Willow Tree,*
> *Hear my plea,*
> *When you weep, think of me,*
> *'Cause I'm so weary*
> *With misery.*
> *Happy breeze, pity please,*
> *Sigh for me thru the trees—*
> *My life's so dreary with misery.*
>
> *For me, it rains and rains,*
> *Each day brings aches and pains,*
> *Feel like a stranger everywhere,*
> *Nobody seems to care,*
> *The burden's more than I can bear.*
>
> *Willow tree hear my plea,*
> *When you weep, think of me,*
> *'Cause I'm so weary*
> *With misery.*

Composed and sung in the show as a ballad, "Willow Tree"'s melody had the true majesty of a genuine blues. Subtitled by Razaf "Musical Misery," it stands, in retrospect, as a clear precursor to Razaf's most adamant protesting lyric of racial shame, "Black and Blue." In that sense, "Willow Tree" does now seem quite a courageous effort. As consumed as Razaf was with achieving success in the white world of Broadway, he nevertheless opted to flout his long-sought return to Broadway by brazenly composing a lyric that was racially problematic. The song was also eloquent in its lyric conciseness. Never before had Razaf achieved so much by writing so little. It was, in many ways, a revelation for him then and remains so today, for those who may know it.

On April 23, Con Conrad moved his successful *Keep Shufflin'* production from the outskirts of the "Great White Way"—Daly's 63rd Street Theatre—to the heart of 42nd Street, the Eltinge Theatre, three doors down from the New Amsterdam Theatre. One can only imagine Razaf's joy at this proximity. The enormous audience reaction that Waller and Johnson were generating in the *Keep Shufflin'* orchestra pit also had recently prompted Conrad to suggest that the two pianists perform their own intermission set of piano duets. Between acts, Waller and Johnson were now firing salvos of pianistic fireworks at one another, delighting themselves and *Keep Shufflin'* audiences with duels reminiscent of uptown nights on the rent strut circuit. Particularly exhilarating were the variations that they ran on one of Johnson's contributions to the *Keep Shufflin'* score, "Sippi," a song that was rapidly becoming a hit beyond the Eltinge Theatre.

Some Monday nights it became necessary to send out in search of Johnson and Waller, though, after the two had been in Harlem *"recreating"* since Saturday night and, as one former member of the *Keep Shufflin'* pit band later observed, "they'd be ossified." Even while on the premises, Waller and Johnson provoked one another alcoholically. Years later, Flournoy Miller recalled how he often had to push the two pianists out into the orchestra pit after they'd raced back to their dressing room at the first-act curtain for some liquid refreshment.

In March, Johnson and Waller had recorded two numbers from the *Keep Shufflin'* score, "Willow Tree" and "Sippi," in a session for Victor that featured cornetist Jabbo Smith and reedman Garvin Bushell from the *Keep Shufflin'* pit band. Predictably, neither song was alloted a vocal—Waller still refused to sing publicly at this time, insisting that his voice was professionally unacceptable. In June, Waller left the *Keep Shufflin'* company for a job as organist at the Royal Grand Theatre in Philadelphia, while the production, still led by Johnson, took to the road after a summer respite, traveling to Michigan, Ohio, and as far west as St. Louis. On November 4, Arnold

Rothstein was shot on the third floor of New York's Park Central Hotel. Two days later he died at Polyclinic Hospital. For months Rothstein had been falling behind on his payroll to *Keep Shufflin's* performers and creators. Rumor had it that "the Brain," in financing a substantial new drug operation, had overextended himself but nothing along these lines, of course, was ever confirmed. His death did, however, bring the *Keep Shufflin'* road tour to a sudden end in Chicago.

Razaf, meanwhile, had composed a new score with J. C. Johnson for another edition of Irvin C. Miller's *Brown Skin Models* revue series and was touring with the show in Washington, DC, as a replacement for one of Miller's leads, George Randol. In this role, Razaf served as comedic straight man, "raving . . . over a lady in a turkish towel doing the usual wiggling dance," while also crooning, among other tunes, an interpolated number by James P. Johnson and Henry Creamer that would in time reach the top of the popular song charts throughout the country, securing Johnson membership in the American Society of Composers, Authors and Publishers (ASCAP); perhaps Johnson's single greatest original song composition, the lyrical "If I Could Be with You (One Hour Tonight)." "Razaf impressed us as being more fitted for the role," wrote one reviewer. "His crooning style, accompanying himself with a 'uke,' was very entertaining. Especially noticeable was the distinct way in which he pronounced his words."

By any measure, 1928 had been an astonishing year for Razaf. Thirty new songs had been composed with five different collaborators; sixteen of these had been sold, fourteen had been published, and, extraordinarily, forty-seven different recordings of Andy Razaf songs had been cut by year's end. One Ethel Waters session for Columbia on August 21 had featured Razaf songs exclusively: "Do What You Did Last Night," "Guess Who's in Town?", and "Lonesome Swallow," composed with J. C. Johnson, and Razaf's own "My Handy Man," a bawdy blues of such transcendant craft and consummate comic timing that it nearly overwhelmed all memory of its inumerable predecessors, becoming, on the instant, the genre's quintessential representative and remaining so till today.

> *Whoever said a good man was hard to find,*
> *Positively, absolutely, sure was blind,*
> *I've found the best that ever was,*
> *Here's just some of the things he does:*

He shakes my ashes,
Greases my griddle,
Churns my butter,
Strokes my fiddle;
My man, is such a handy man.
He threads my needle,
Creams my wheat,
Heats my heater,
Chops my meat;
My man, is such a handy man.

Don't care if you believe or not,
He sure is good to have around,
Why, when my burners get too hot,
He's there to turn my damper down.
For everything he's got a scheme,
You oughta see the sodder he uses on my machine;
My man, is such a handy man.
He flaps my flapjacks,
Cleans off the table,
Feeds the horses in my stable;
My man, is such a handy man.
Sometimes he's up long before dawn,
Trimming the rough edges off my lawn,
My man, is such a handy man.

Never has a single thing to say
While he's working hard,
I wish that you could see the way
He handles my front yard—
My ice don't get a chance to melt away,
He sees that I get a nice, fresh piece every day.
My man, is such a handy man.

On Broadway, despite his often less than respectable lyric themes, Andy Razaf was at last a respected figure in 1928, an accredited Broadway lyricist. On Tin Pan Alley, he was an increasingly marketable commodity. In Harlem, he was, quite simply, revered. There were even stirrings of a promotional legend in the making, mythologizing this steadfastly principled and opinionated talent, via the Razaf family's opaquely exotic personal history.

"*Duke Andre Still Warbling at WCGU,*" read a 1928 headline in the *Brooklyn Daily Times,* "*Crooning Grand-Nephew of Madagascar Queen Possesses Exciting Historical Background.*

"Because Duke Andre Paul Razafkerie [*sic*], grand-nephew of Ranavalona III, late Queen of Madagascar, has chosen song plugging as his career, his mother, the Duchess Christian, has refused to have anything to do with him," this story began, with brazen obfuscation. "It is not generally known that 'Crooning Andy,' singing over WCGU every evening, is none other than the Duke himself."

The article went on to present a highly biased, comically unstable account of Razaf's colorful ancestral roots. "The fall of a kingdom, the fleeing of a royal family, or the capturing thereof, which is ofttimes described in dramatic fashion upon our silver screens, all make up the real life of Andy," explained the *Brooklyn Daily Times.* "During the war of 1890 between the former Malagasy Kingdom and France, the Duchess Christian, who is a daughter of the late John L. Waller, America's Consul to Madasgascar during the Harrison Administration, returned to her native America, where Duke Paul Andre Razafkerio, who now prefers to be called just 'Andy,' was born. News of Andy's father's being severely hurt in battle with the French troops brought the Duchess and Andy back to Madagascar," the newspaper maintained, rather guilelessly and quite falsely. "Just at this time the French had broken through the lines and seized the country of Madagascar. Consul Waller tried to harbor the Duchess and Andy," the newspaper insisted, fabricating its own Razafian twist to the tale. "It was because of this mainly that the French Government arrested Consul Waller, charging him with harboring prisoners of war and conspiring against the French. Then life's future looked pretty dark for Andy, although he was too young to realize what it was all about.

"The move of Waller immediately attracted the world's attention, and it became known as the "Waller Case. . . . At this time the United States Government intervened by effecting a settlement in the form of releasing Consul Waller, who was really an American subject. Queen Ranavalona and other members of the royal family were exiled to Algeria. Andy's father died of wounds received in the war.

"Andy recently wrote a song, 'Dusky Stevedore,' "added the news story, shifting gears hilariously, "and highly elated over his new number, he purchased a radio set for the Duchess, and asked her to tune in on the Amberol Hour at WCGU. Afterward he confessed that it was he that was doing all the crooning.

"The Duchess thinks that his present profession is so very undignified and unbecoming to a Duke, that she will not have anything to do with him, but Andy says that he will continue because titles don't mean anything and this pays him pretty good money."

For Razaf, certification of his ascendancy as a songwriter came in strikingly concrete domestic fashion during the latter months of 1928. Sometime that winter, for the first time since he'd decamped from the apartment on West 141st Street, Razaf was able to afford a new apartment, number 5B at 55 West 129th Street. Perhaps even more significantly, Razaf also was able to treat himself at this time to the first home telephone of his adult life. The number: HArlem-0641.

Courtesy Razaf Estate.

A Low Down Treat

Tan Town has a low down treat,
Red hot dance that can't be beat,
When you see it you will feel elastic.
Got a special name for it,
Funny but it seems to fit,
Watch the way we do this new fantastic.

— *"Zonky"*
by Andy Razaf and Thomas Waller

The most productive and successful songwriting year in Andrea Razaf's life did not begin auspiciously for his irresponsible song partner Thomas Waller, who was again in prison for nonpayment of alimony following his arrest in August 1928. Hauled before Judge Albert Cohen at the Bronx County Courthouse sometime in mid-September, a "wistful and repentant" Waller (according to a report in *Variety*), who already had served thirty-one days in prison while awaiting this hearing, had pleaded with the judge for leniency, insisting that he'd "learned his lesson." Cohen had, however, been unmoved, sentencing Waller to serve an additional six months to three years in the New York County Jail on Welfare Island, a term that was proving the darkest in the young pianist's life to date. Though his wife, Anita, who was pregnant again, his mother-in-law, and his friends scrambled frantically to raise the four-figure sum for which Waller was in arrears, the money proved beyond their reach. Humiliated and despondent, Waller languished in prison into the New Year. During this period of incarceration, his father also died, the victim of a heart attack. A grieving, thoroughly chastened Waller declined an offer from prison officials to attend the funeral, claiming that he was too ashamed.

Razaf continued to work with other collaborators during his partner's enforced absence, composing at least eleven songs with J. C. Johnson during this period, including "Empty House Blues," a solid, straightforward bit of blues craftsmanship that Clara Smith recorded in January 1929, and the effusively urgent "If You Really Love Your Baby," recorded by Viola McCoy in November 1928. Interestingly, at least seven of these songs, including the latter two, were purchased and/or published by Joe Davis. Though Davis had been a strong supporter of Razaf's work since 1925, Razaf's Broadway success seems to have fanned in the opportunistic publisher a feverish proprietary sense of the lyricist's worth. This would reach unprecedented levels of manipulative fervor during the coming years in ways that would finally victimize Razaf severely.

Waller's unofficial employers, Connie and George Immerman, were similarly affected by the downtown success of their former delivery boy and his favorite song partner. Furiously competing with the Cotton Club and a host of imitators for white entertainment dollars in Harlem in 1928, the Immermans were eager to gain any possible edge. The promising Broadway debut of Fats Waller and Andy Razaf clearly seems to have struck the Immerman brothers as a marvelous opportunity.

It is likely that Connie and George Immerman approached Waller and Razaf sometime in 1928, during or immediately after the run of *Keep Shufflin'*, regarding a new revue score for Connie's Inn. Waller, in fact, may have been returning from his Philadelphia organ job at the Grand Theatre in August to begin work along these lines. His imprisonment had, however, put the whole matter into suspension for the foreseeable future. The year 1929 dawned at Connie's Inn with little prospect for Waller's imminent release.

Yeoman efforts by Waller's many devoted friends paid off surprisingly, though, shortly after the new year. A particularly helpful contribution was made by the popular white vocalist and entertainer Gene Austin, then at the peak of his career, following the multimillion-copy 1927 success of Austin's recording of "My Blue Heaven." A frequenter of the Kentucky Club during Waller's term there, a regular drinking buddy, professed admirer, and, quite possibly, surreptitious song purchasing customer of Waller's, Austin appears to have stepped forward early in 1929 to provide Thomas Waller with a portion of the money required to clear his alimony debts and his name. At a hearing preliminary to Waller's potential release in January or February 1929, Austin also is purported to have helped sway the presiding judge by testifying that Waller was needed for an upcoming Austin recording session, insisting that without Waller the session could not take place; consequently, by not releasing him, the judge would be putting other musicians out of work. Whether or not this plea influenced the court—and whether or not this session ever occurred or even was slated to occur—Waller was apparently paroled sometime in early February 1929.

Razaf immediately celebrated his old partner's freedom by completing a song with Waller and Clarence Williams, a song published by Joe Davis on February 18, 1929, "Why Am I Alone with No-One To Love?" On the instant, faced with an absolutely withering two-week deadline, Razaf also began work with Waller on their first revue score for Connie's Inn.

The team did most of their preliminary composing at Waller's 133rd Street apartment, running titles, lyric ideas, and melodic fragments back and forth freely. They then quickly brought the results down to their producer Leonard Harper at Connie's Inn, where Waller was most comfortable improvising at an upright piano with Razaf curled in a corner scribbling furiously, while Harper pieced together the material at hand. This operational method gave birth to a host of songs bursting with Waller's singular brand of spontaneity along with fabulistic recollections of Waller, in rehearsal, "overflowing the piano stool" at Connie's Inn, hat off, collar open, a bottle of gin nearby, improvising songs on the spot for Leonard Harper's delectation. Of course, much of the music for any Harlem nightclub revue was of an incidental nature as dance or comedy routine accompaniment, the sort of catchy, melodic musical wallpaper that Waller could in fact turn out endlessly, almost without thought. Although Waller's best work with Razaf was often written quickly, the compositions intended *as songs* were crafted carefully. Razaf later pointed out that Waller "took great pains . . . [to] set a melody . . . getting the exact mood and phrasing. . . . He took great pride in doing an accurate, perfect job, with every note in the right place, so much so that even if he finished a whole piano copy in half an hour, it could be sent right down to the printers without any changes."

From time to time Razaf jammed his pen into the lapel pocket of his suit jacket, relit his cold cigar, and strolled across the scuffed wood dance floor at Connie's Inn with his lyric sheets to sing a number through with Waller at the piano. Certain witnesses to these rehearsal performances remarked then that the two should have appeared in the revue themselves, as a team. Waller still was quite diffident, though, about singing in public.

Leonard Harper, according to one of these witnesses, was a "formidable producer of revues . . . a black producer who, if by some miracle he'd had the chance, could have made most of the Hollywood dance numbers of later days seem stupid and lightweight . . . He ran through [a] rehearsal with the dancers on the floor, showing them the routines, guiding each number." Born April 19, 1899, in Birmingham, Alabama, Harper received his formative theatrical training as a child dancer, partnering black producer George Freeman in touring medicine shows throughout the South. After meeting Osceola Blanks of the Blanks Sisters vaudeville team in Chicago during the early Twenties, Harper had formed a very popular song-and-dance team with Blanks (whom he married in 1923), and they successfully toured the country's major vaudeville circuits as Harper and Blanks for several seasons. In 1923, Harper also became a pioneer in a new form of musical comedy production, the intimate nightclub revue, when he produced *Plantation Days* at the exclusive Green Mills Gardens on Chicago's chic Gold Coast. Following the close of this engagement, *Plantation Days* had climaxed a record-breaking tour of larger Eastern and Midwestern cities with a long run at the Empire Theatre in London. When Harper finally returned to the states he immediately was hired to stage the debut floorshow entertainment for George and Connie Immerman's new Harlem nightclub, Connie's Inn. Since that day, Harper's name had come to be synonymous with the success of Connie's Inn, and with the popularity of nightclub revues in general throughout the Twenties in New York City, as he continued to stage with impeccable taste and superb, jet-propelled theatricality floorshow productions for such famous nightspots as the Cotton Club uptown and the Club Lido, the Club Richman, the Hollywood, and the Plantation Cafe downtown.

Despite his matchless, almost monopolistic dominance as a creator of black floor shows for nearly every "colored" nightclub in New York City, uptown and downtown, throughout the Twenties and

Thirties, as well as his frequent cameo work choreographing set pieces for white Broadway revues like the *Passing Show*, his coaching work with numerous white performers, and his overall brilliance as a choreographer, Leonard Harper never got the call from Hollywood that might have made him a film-directing star on the scale of a Busby Berkeley. He would remain a revue maker largely trapped in nightclubs throughout his life, which would come to a tragic and premature end in February 1943.

In many ways, the most legendary and certainly the most mysterious member of the Connie's Inn creative team that gathered at the basement nightclub daily throughout the latter weeks of February 1929 was an altogether anonymous songwriter named Harry Brooks. A Pennsylvania-born keyboardist who'd held down the piano chair in violinist Leroy Smith's "Green Dragon Orchestra"—the house band at Connie's Inn—since the ensemble's New York debut in 1921, Brooks possessed only fleeting songwriting experience. His most notable credit was the music that he had contributed to *Snapshots of 1921*, "a travesty revue in two acts and eighteen scenes," produced by Lew Fields and the Selwyn brothers, with Nora Bayes starring, at the Selwyn Theatre on 42nd Street in June 1921.

The provocative mystery surrounding Harry Brooks centers to this day around one inexplicable fact. Though the score Razaf and Waller created for their Connie's Inn debut proved to include many of their most distinguished and, in many ways, signature song compositions, Harry Brooks, for reasons that have eluded history, received full credit alongside the Razaf/Waller team as co-melodist for the entire score.

Many chroniclers of Waller's life and music over the years have speculated fiercely about Brooks's actual contribution to these songs. According to Emerson Harper, reedman in the Leroy Smith band, Brooks "collaborated with Fats by generally writing the verse of the songs while Fats wrote the choruses." A rather simple scenario does vaguely suggest itself here. Assuming that Waller was, in fact, paroled from prison in early February 1929, and that the Immermans were indeed forced to go into production for their new spring revue without him, it does seem possible that Harry Brooks was tapped to begin composing tunes for the show in order to lighten Waller's songwriting burden and impossibly tight deadline, generally writing the verses for certain songs that Waller later completed with often memorable choruses. Once he was finally sprung, Waller, in typically open-fisted fashion, then proceeded to hand over joint credit to Brooks for the entire revue score.

A surviving typed fragment among Razaf's private papers does confirm some sort of extramural crediting arrangement among the show's creators. "Agreement," the fragment reads, "made between Messrs. Thomas Waller, Harry Brooks, Andy Razaf, and Leonard Harper;

> That they shall share, equally, all royalties and advances accrued from the musical score written for the new show at Connie's Inn.
>
> Mssrs. Waller, Brooks, and Razaf, writers of said score, and Mr. Harper, producer of the show, further agree that no negotiations in connection with said score shall be carried on without the knowledge, approval, and presence of all four parties concerned.

Though the existence of this hastily typed scrap "Agreement," signed by all four men, does at first seem to resolve any doubts regarding Brooks's legitimacy, the document's very existence of course preserves the taint of suspicion. Why the need for such a contract? If Harry Brooks co-wrote the music for the 1929 Connie's Inn Spring revue, then his name on all song copyrights should have been sufficient guarantee of credit. Obviously there was something highly provisional about the creative relationships on this particular show.

Interestingly, though Leonard Harper's vital, no doubt rehearsal-centered contributions to the musical evolution of the Razaf/Waller score are clearly confirmed by his inclusion in the Agreement, he is not credited on the many song copyrights that this revue ultimately generated. Perhaps Harper eventually waived his rights pursuant to the Agreement, or, as seems more likely, was bought out. What one is left with, nonetheless, is an unlikely Razaf/Waller/Brooks credit for the music presented at Connie's Inn during the Spring revue of 1929—all of which would stand as a mere, mysterious footnote to any Razaf/Waller history had the music from this revue and the revue itself, expired anonymously. They did not, however.

There are many who still insist that the 1929 Spring revue at Connie's Inn—a revue officially titled *Hot Feet*—was the finest floor show to emerge from a Harlem nightclub during the Twenties. The production was memorably performed by a superb cast of twenty-five or so "beautiful tanskins"—singers, dancers, and comedians, including Minto Cato, a gorgeous young singer with an astonishing three-octave range, veteran comedians Louise Williams and Billy Maxey, adagio ballroom dance team Paul and Thelma Meeres, shimmying vocalist Baby Cox, a line of notoriously stunning chorines, some of whom were transvestites—a Connie's Inn specialty—and the legendary dancer Earl "Snake Hips" Tucker, "doubling" from his downtown appearance in Lew Leslie's *Blackbirds* production. In their more liberated uptown incarnation, Tucker's sinuous, brutally suggestive, masterfully executed hip-gyrating routines staggered the Inn's white visitors.

Hot Feet opened at Connie's Inn on the evening of February 28, 1929. Its "bits"—the scripted dialogue that linked *Hot Feet*'s set specialty numbers—as well as the lyric half of the show's score were credited to Andy Razaf; it was ostensibly the first time Razaf composed a full revue script. The show also constituted a milestone in the mordant history of Harlem nightclub entertainment. As the *Pittsburgh Courier* pointed out some weeks later, "This is the first floor show of New York's exclusive night clubs to be entirely the work of men of color. . . . The Immerman brothers deserve great credit for having faith and vision enough to have given colored writers a chance to prove themselves capable of equaling and even excelling the previous work of their white contemporaries." *Variety*'s opinion of the proceedings was far less enlightened but characteristically to the point. "Leonard Harper's new show is a pip," *Variety* editor Abel Green announced in his *Hot Feet* review on March 13. "Harper (colored) is a past master at this kind of floor show entertainment and Connie Immerman of the Immerman Brothers, the impresarios, are giving their customers a generous two bucks' worth for the couvert charge. 'Hot Feet' is . . . just the type show a black and tan should have."

In the month immediately following *Hot Feet*'s debut, Andrea Razaf obtained copyrights on four new tunes written with four different collaborators: "Get Up Off Your Knees," an existing Clarence Williams song whose lyric Razaf touched up and this time—perhaps due to his new professional clout—actually received credit for from Clarence Williams; "Kitchen Man," a delectable bawdy blues, written with Alex Belledna, which Bessie Smith would record in May; "My Baby Sure Knows How to Love," another of Razaf and

J. C. Johnson's refined bawdy blues, which Ethel Waters already had recorded the previous August for Columbia; and "S'posin'," an exceptionally appealing new foxtrot, written with Paul Denniker, that finally confirmed the Razaf/Denniker partnership along Tin Pan Alley as a song team of significance.

While Razaf over the previous year had established himself in the rarified realm of theatrical songwriters—on Broadway and in Harlem nightclubs—his position in the Tin Pan Alley hierarchy remained that of a talented and productive, though narrowly stereotyped, "colored"-genre songwriter who possessed moderate earning power. "S'posin'" changed all that. The song, with its alluringly pallid, short and sweetly sentimental lyric—"S'posin' I should fall in love with you?/Do you think that you could love me too?/S'posin' I should hold you and caress you,/Would it impress you/Or distress you?"—received a huge promotional boost from Joe Davis, who plugged "S'posin'" heavily over the radio nationally to white audiences, as well as in the sheet music marketplace, after Davis's Triangle Music Publishing Company released "S'posin'" on April 29. *Metronome* magazine soon praised Davis for having "done the unbelievable in putting 'Sposin'' into the hit class in less than two months." Razaf's aggressive music publisher mustered all of his song marketing weapons behind "S'posin'," in the process elevating Andy Razaf, if only for the moment, into a racially neutral Tin Pan Alley success.

The details and criminal dimension of Davis's machinations on behalf of "S'posin'"—as they became known to Razaf—were terrifically disturbing, though, particularly those involving Davis's old friend Rudy Vallee, whose relationship with Davis went back to 1921, and an early nonpublishing Davis partnership with bandleader–songwriter Rudy Wiedoeft, manufacturing custom-made saxophone mouthpieces. One of Davis and Wiedoeft's first customers had been the 20-year-old Yale student saxophonist Hubert Vallee, who ultimately became so friendly with the two music industry entrepreneurs that he, in time, even adopted Wiedoeft's first name as his own, for professional purposes. Vallee, in 1929, was gaining substantial popular recognition across the country, leading his dance orchestra, "the Connecticut Yankees," in vaudeville and on record for Victor, when Joe Davis approached him about "S'posin'." Recognizing the song's potential and determined to capitalize on it in any way possible, Davis offered Vallee a percentage of "S'posin'"'s earnings in exchange for Vallee's commitment to help break the song publicly. Vallee accepted Davis's offer and, in May, recorded "S'posin'" for Victor, while also featuring the song that month as the finale in his stage show at the Paramount Theatre.

According to Andy Razaf's widow, Joe Davis also recouped his losses on this not-at-all-uncommon payola transaction with Vallee by calling in at this time certain loans and advances that Davis over the years had paid out to Razaf, demanding that Razaf repay him, not with cash—which the lyricist hardly possessed anyway—but with song rights to a group of Triangle-owned tunes, specifically including "S'posin'." Though Razaf initially balked at selling "S'posin'" outright to Davis in this fashion, the wily music publisher would not relent—knowing, as Razaf later discovered, that Rudy Vallee's assured commitment to the song very likely guaranteed "S'posin'"'s future success.

It is, in fact, a chilling measure of Razaf's enforced practicality regarding such music industry chicanery that the lyricist, along with his partner Denniker, still signed a two-year exclusive contract with Joe Davis and the Triangle Music Publishing Company in September 1929, *after* the full extent of Davis's role in bilking him out of his deserved "S'posin'" royalties had been revealed to Razaf.

This capitulation to the exigencies of Tin Pan Alley business practices and to Joe Davis's rank dishonesty reflected how much Razaf could delude himself when confronted by his own enormous ambition. Had Joe Davis's crime against him perhaps been motivated more by racism than by shabby ethics, Razaf might conceivably have been more emphatic in condemning Davis and separating himself from the publisher professionally. Davis, though, never did seem to be motivated by anything more virulent than greed somehow, and Razaf, deeply hurt as he certainly was by Davis's betrayal, nevertheless found within himself something that could rationalize Davis's greed and even accept it on behalf of "S'posin'"'s success. As *Metronome* gushingly observed in its August 1929 profile of Davis (a profile quite possibly planted by Joe Davis), "Music publishing history is dotted here and there with instances of small firms gradually expanding to leadership; with ambitious individuals capitalizing on their ability . . . A romantic story has been unfolded before you in the above chapters, [of a man] who by dint of his own efforts, initiative, and concentration has made of himself a power in the world of music—Joe Davis, himself! . . . one of the music industry's best-liked and most favorably known individuals." Even as he swallowed his own rage, Razaf was forced to admit that most of what *Metronome* said on the subject of Joe Davis was true.

*

In 1929 the status of black musical theater on Broadway was decadently poised between eminence and decline. Since *Runnin' Wild*'s influential and successful run in 1923, twelve black Broadway musicals of wildly varying quality had opened and closed downtown throughout the Twenties, from Noble Sissle and Eubie Blake's sumptuously outfitted but failed *Shuffle Along* followup, *Chocolate Dandies*, in 1924, and Lew Leslie's unabashed *Dixie To Broadway* homage to Florence Mills, also in 1924, on through *Lucky Sambo*, a flop that folded nine performances into its 1925 run when its orchestra refused to play another week without pay, *My Magnolia*, a disaster of similar magnitude the following year, *Bottomland*, a vanity production created by and starring Clarence Williams that lasted twenty-one performances in 1927, *Africana*, the self-produced vehicle that helped make Ethel Waters a Broadway star in 1927, and Miller and Lyles's aborted success, *Rang Tang*, also in 1927.

Lew Leslie's *Blackbirds of 1928* had conversely represented what many still regard as the pinnacle of black musical achievement on Broadway in the Twenties, a production originally conceived as a showcase for Florence Mills, whose untimely death turned the Leslie spotlight over to several widely experienced and talented, but largely unknown (downtown), black entertainers, including vocalists Aida Ward and Adelaide Hall, and dancers Earl "Snake Hips" Tucker and the incomparable Bill Robinson. Each realized substantial acclaim and even stardom from his/her opportunity, particularly Robinson, a 50-year-old vaudeville veteran in 1928 who, as a late addition to Leslie's company, forgot the words to his big number on opening night only to win over the audience with his extraordinary tap dancing virtuosity.

Blackbirds represented a culmination, however, for an insidious stereotyping of the black musical on Broadway, a hardening of perceptions, even a segregating of the form by white critics into a circumscribed theatrical ghetto narrowly defined by a few largely racist formulas derived primarily from *Shuffle Along* and *Shuffle Along*'s minstrel precursors.

"Ambition" was the word that these critics dismissively wielded against any show that attempted to break free from these preconceptions, as neatly itemized by a reviewer for *Variety* in his negative assessment of *Chocolate Dandies'* efforts as early as 1924: "The absence of spirited stepping." Any "deliberate" attempts "to make the piece high-toned," such as a "leading woman" behaving "in action and manner" like a "prima donna," or a leading man utilizing "all the posing tricks of a soulful tenor in a Winter Garden musical comedy.—All of these pretensions toward white musical comedy . . . achieved at the expense of a genuine Negro spirit," leading to an evening of "white folks material, of which there is plenty . . . and not good darky entertainment, of which there is little enough for the best."

Of course, in the wake of such brutal criticism, black musical creators soon steered clear of anything that might suggest white pretension in their Broadway work, continuing to rely on hoary, minstrel-evocative stereotypes, solidly grounded in Dixie, for their situations, while jettisoning all sense of structured libretto in favor of the revue format that was the favored provenance of black entertainment uptown in Harlem.

Lew Leslie had established another, even more sinister precedent behind the scenes for black Broadway musical theater with his *Dixie to Broadway* production in 1924 by exclusively employing white backstage creative personnel for his "colored" musical comedy— from set and costume designers to musical composers. "[White men] understand the colored man better than he does himself," Leslie had insisted at the time, with astonishing insolence. "Colored composers excel at spirituals, but their other songs are just [white] songs with Negro words."

In this respect, Leslie's *Blackbirds* production team in 1928 was quintessential, both in its racial exclusivity and in its superior quality, particularly with regard to Leslie's chosen composers for the project: Cotton Club and Tin Pan Alley veteran Jimmy McHugh for the music, and young Dorothy Fields for the lyrics. Daughter to vaudeville comedian and impresario Lew Fields, the 22-year-old Fields already was terrifically accomplished as a lyricist after a season writing the words to McHugh's music for two Cotton Club revues. The team produced a memorable score for Leslie's *Blackbirds*, a score that instantly came to be regarded as a paradigm of the Negro genre, including "I Must Have That Man," "Doin' the New Low Down" and "Diga Diga Do." The revue's greatest hit, however, one of the great song hits of the decade, "I Can't Give You Anything but Love," proved, from the outset, to be of somewhat questionable parentage, casting substantial doubt over Leslie's theories regarding the superiority of white song composers for black music through the unprovable suspicions and rumors regarding its true black antecedents, suspicions that dogged the song then and continue to haunt it today.

The melody for "I Can't Give You Anything but Love" first had surfaced as a McHugh novelty number, with an interpolated Charles Lindbergh–focused lyric, entitled "I Can't Give You Anything but Love, Lindy" in *Harry Delmar's Revels*, a Broadway-bound revue mounted toward the end of 1927. This version of the song had been cut, however, just prior to the opening of *Delmar's Revels* on November 28, 1927, only to be resurrected by McHugh during the tryout run for *Blackbirds* at Lew Leslie's Le Parroquet nightclub on West 57th Street early in 1928, its title shorn of any Lindbergh reference and instead wedded to another Fields and McHugh song that was being cut from the *Blackbirds* score, a tune titled simply "Baby."

In fact, after opening at the Liberty Theatre on 42nd Street the evening of May 9, 1928, *Blackbirds* generated only marginally adequate business for the first five weeks of its run before "I Can't Give You Anything but Love (Baby)" finally began to catch on as a popular tune around town and, in Lew Leslie's stated opinion, rescued the show.

The success of "I Can't Give You Anything but Love (Baby)" established Fields and McHugh as a major song team. It also brought whispers along Tin Pan Alley that "I Can't Give You Anything but Love" had in fact been written by the "colored" song team of Andy Razaf and Fats Waller and sold to Jimmy McHugh at the offices of Mills Music sometime during the early to mid-Twenties.

The rumor was backed, if nothing else, by a circumstantial plausibility—the song sounded like a Razaf/Waller creation. Waller, ironically, more or less reclaimed the tune more than ten years later when he recorded his own deeply personalized rendition of "I Can't Give You Anything but Love" with Una Mae Carlisle in November 1939 for Victor.

Adding further circumstantial fuel to this talk, however, was the matter of Jimmy McHugh's position on Tin Pan Alley. Since April 1921, McHugh had functioned as professional manager for the Mills Music Publishing company, first at 152–154 West 45th Street, then at 148–150 West 46th. "The building might have been five stories and we had maybe three floors," Myles Norman, a cousin to Fletcher

Henderson, who worked at Mills for more than fifty years, recalled of the latter premises. "The first floor was the main offices—the professional department and Jack and Irving's offices—Jack was the president and Irving Mills was the vice-president. The others were stock rooms: sheet music, books. Each one had a piano in his office, and there were five or six piano rooms for entertainers to come in. All the famous people came to rehearse songs . . . everyone was there at one time or another, every one of them—Fred Astaire, Chevalier. . . .

"It's true, the white guys often got offices while the black guys would just come and sell their songs. . . .

"Jimmy McHugh was the Professional Manager then. He was a very handsome guy and young, in his early thirties, I guess. He played for different acts that came in especially to see him, like Fannie Brice, I remember.

"Andy came in with Fats," Norman added, unable, however, to bear witness specifically to any sale by the two of "I Can't Give You Anything but Love" to McHugh. "They'd work out a song themselves and then they'd come down to play it for Mills. McHugh would be there and sometimes the general manager, too."

Two weeks before the opening of his new musical *Hot Chocolates* on Broadway in 1929, Fats Waller was the subject of a lengthy profile in the *New York Post*, in which the discursive Waller expounded quite willingly on the peculiar underpinnings of his own Tin Pan Alley career. "He discovered that it was easy to sell tunes to white songwriters who would vary them slightly and resell them as their own," the *Post* article quoted Waller. "The average rate for such a song, he says, was $250. Among the songs thus disposed of was one [that] knocked about for three seasons until it was finally inserted in a musical comedy. Featured in that show, it became the best seller of its season and netted $17,500 to its 'composer,' who paid 'Fatts' [*sic*] $500 for it."

Was "I Can't Give You Anything but Love" Waller's "knocked-about" "best seller"? Was Jimmy McHugh in fact Waller's "composer," and if he was, did McHugh purchase only the young pianist's melody that day as Waller passed through the Mills Music offices, or did McHugh also buy a lyric from Andy Razaf as well—disgarding this lyric initially only to restore it during tryouts for *Blackbirds* in 1928?

It is impossible to say. Razaf himself addressed the song directly only once, when asked by Don Redman's widow, Gladys Redman, as she visited Razaf in the hospital in the early 1970s to "Sing me your favorite song, Andy." To Gladys Redman's surprise—though not at all to her amazement, as she later admitted—the terminally ill Razaf responded from his hospital bed with a whispered version of "I Can't Give You Anything but Love."

Connie and George Immerman apparently decided to move *Hot Feet* from Connie's Inn to Broadway sometime in May 1929. Lew Leslie's *Blackbirds* still was running strongly at the Liberty Theatre on 42nd Street. The Immermans stubbornly chose to ignore the three black musicals that had subsequently opened on Broadway since *Blackbirds*, all nearly immediate failures. *Deep Harlem* had lasted but a week in January despite an ambitious book by the vastly experienced black vaudevillians Homer Tutt and Salem Whitney, and a score by legendary ragtime pianist Joe Jordan, with lyrics by Tutt and Henry Creamer, including three interpolated numbers by J. C. Johnson and Andy Razaf. *Messin' Around* was another failed attempt by James P. Johnson and Perry Bradford to score one more Broadway hit for the Joy Club. It had lasted one month, from late April to late May—a run that sandwiched the benighted *Pansy*, a horrific black collegiate musical that managed to flop ignominiously despite a better-than-average score by Maceo Pinkard and a second act mini concert by Bessie Smith in her Broadway debut.

The Immermans acted on their plan to ship *Hot Feet* downtown in two ways. Under Connie Immerman's direct supervision, Leonard Harper began to recast and reprogram the revue, to punch it up for Broadway, and under George Immerman's auspices, an investor was brought in with the cash necessary for *Hot Feet*'s transfer—the man who had long since muscled into Connie's Inn as the Immerman's liquor supplier, gangster Dutch Schultz.

A new title was also devised for the Immermans' now Broadway-bound musical revue, something suitably condescending, obvious, and self-serving: *Connie's Hot Chocolates*. Waller and Razaf were directed to compose at least two or three additional songs for the revamped production. Waller, in later years, often delighted in referring to one of these songs as "The Alimony Jail Song," insisting that when he had been in alimony jail (of course never specifying precisely when), owing $250, "which he didn't have and couldn't get," he'd sent his lawyer to a nightclub for what Waller called "a miniature piano." In two days, on that piano, according to Waller, he'd then written "Ain't Misbehavin'," which his lawyer immediately had taken to a publisher who'd bought the song for $250. With this windfall, concluded Waller, he'd paid off his back alimony and was freed.

According to Andrea Razaf, "Ain't Misbehavin'" was conceived in Waller's 133rd Street apartment, where Razaf called on his partner one morning during *Hot Chocolates'* pre-Broadway rehearsal period, about 11 A.M. As Razaf remembered it, Waller, in pajamas, had gone to the piano and played "a marvelous strain, which was complicated in the middle. I straightened it out with the 'no one to talk with, all by myself' phrase," Razaf recalled, "which led to the phrase 'ain't misbehavin',' which I knew was the title. The whole thing took about forty-five minutes. Fats dressed and we proceeded to Jack Mills's office, where we demonstrated and sold the song. From there we went to the theater, where Harry Brooks arranged it."

Razaf also couldn't help but remember that as he and Waller marched down Broadway toward the Hudson Theatre on West 44th Street, where *Hot Chocolates* was rehearsing, with the manuscript literally in his hand, a pigeon had landed a direct hit on the music sheet. "That's good luck! That's good luck!" Razaf remembered Waller crying. "But I'm sure glad elephants ain't flyin'."

"Ain't Misbehavin'" was, in a sense, Andy Razaf's lyric retort to all the endless bawdy blues variations he'd been forced to compose since the onset of the Twenties. The song was ingenuous to a fault, modestly affirming home, hearth, and devotion to one love, while set against the undercutting drollery of Waller's melody. Razaf's words were the sincere words of a reformed man, but matched with Waller's music they reverberated with delicious double-edged whimsy. The singer of "Ain't Misbehavin'" clearly had been around —"Though it's a fickle age/With flirting all the rage." He also clearly was ready at last to settle down . . . maybe—"Here is one bird with self-control,/Happy inside my cage." The song was a double entendre that didn't even try to be naughty.

> *I know who I love best,*
> *Thumbs down on all the rest,*
> *My love is given heart and soul*
> *So it can stand the test.*
>
> *No one to talk with,*
> *All by myself,*
> *No one to walk with*

But I'm happy on the shelf,
Ain't misbehavin'
I'm savin' my love for you.
I know for certain
The one I love,
I'm through with flirtin'
It's just you I'm thinkin' of
Ain't misbehavin'
I'm savin' my love for you.

"Ain't Misbehavin'" was the quintessential expression of Andy Razaf and Fats Waller's collaboration. The lyric captured Razaf at his most steadfast and reliable—"Like Jack Horner/In the corner,/ Don't go nowhere,/What do I care?/Your kisses are worth waiting for"—while the melody was imbued with Waller at his most endearingly doubtable, despite Razaf's insistence that, "I don't stay out late,/Don't care to go,/I'm home about eight,/Just me and my radio/Ain't misbehavin'/I'm savin' my love for you."

The irresistible combination, of course, would pay off handsomely.

Ten weeks into the run of *Hot Feet* at Connie's Inn, on the evening of June 3, 1929, *Hot Chocolates* received its first public tryout, in the Bronx, at the Windsor Theatre on the corner of Fordham and Knightsbridge Roads. Many members of the cast continued to work a midnight *Hot Feet* show in Harlem after the curtain rang down on *Hot Chocolates*, and many revisions were forced upon the production by performers' complaints that "doubling to the floor show is too arduous." The beefed-up Broadway company now numbered eighty-five "artists," including Russell Wooding's Jubilee Singers, a female chorus of sixteen Chocolate Drops, a male chorus of eight Bon Bon Buddies, and a team of acrobatic dancers, the Six Crackerjacks. The lovely Minto Cato was gone, replaced by Edith Wilson. Gone too was "Snake Hips" Tucker, bound for Europe with the touring *Blackbirds of 1928* company. His absence allowed for the addition to the cast of "Jazzlips" Richardson, a rubber-limbed comedic carnival circuit veteran whose combination of blackface comedy and eccentric acrobatic dancing was a revelation for delighted *Hot Chocolates* audiences.

The final piece in the Immermans' recasting puzzle for *Hot Chocolates* proved to be by far the most fortuitous. In early March, at the instigation of his new manager, the recording director for OKeh

Records, Tommy Rockwell, Louis Armstrong had returned to New York from Chicago for a brief engagement at the Savoy Ballroom, fronting a band led by Luis Russell. The cabaret business was drying up in Chicago, the victim of reformers, and Armstrong was just a bit more disposed to pursue stardom in New York City than he had been on his first go-round with Fletcher Henderson some five years earlier. On the occasion of this return, Armstrong had reasserted his enormous local Harlem popularity at the Savoy and had even recorded with a select all-star ensemble of white jazz musicians in a session for OKeh. (Among the four songs covered was "I Can't Give You Anything but Love.") He then had returned to Chicago, working there as a feature at the Regal Theatre backed by violinist Carroll Dickerson's orchestra, and playing a number of one-nighters around the Midwest, before being summoned back to New York by his manager in May 1929. Fervently convinced that he could break Armstrong successfully with white audiences, Rockwell had managed to book his client into the pit for a new Vincent Youmans musical tentatively titled *Louisiana Lou*, soon to be retitled *Great Day*. His agreement with Youmans even held out the possibility that Armstrong might be afforded an opportunity in the show to sing, as well as play in the pit in tandem with the Fletcher Henderson Orchestra.

Still wary of the East, Armstrong spontaneously had opted to bring the entire ten-piece Carroll Dickerson band with him for company on the trip to New York, creaking across the country in a ratty three-car convoy of desperately broken-down jalopies before crawling into the city, broke and exhausted, in late May or early June. Pausing to work a hastily arranged substitute gig for the Duke Ellington band at the Audubon Theatre in the Bronx for a little quick cash, Armstrong then had continued on to Philadelphia, where he at last hooked up with a touring *Great Day* company that was in turmoil.

Apparently, a number of white orchestra players had been hired at the last minute to supplement the Henderson bandsmen in the *Great Day* pit—violinists, mostly. Now a white conductor—brought in to cover Henderson himself, who had never before handled a Broadway pit band—was capriciously firing the Henderson men in twos and threes, avowedly for reasons of artistic misdirection on the part of the production staff and inexperience on the part of the Henderson band, but most likely also because of racism on the part of the newly hired players and conductor as well. Within the week, Armstrong, too, was gone—either at the hand of management, or on his own, in disgust; the final circumstances are unclear.

Back in New York, the unemployed trumpeter with his unemployed band heatedly was shopped around by an increasingly desperate Tommy Rockwell. Fortunately for all concerned, including the Immermans, a stand-in was needed for Leroy Smith's aggregation at Connie's Inn while the Green Dragon Orchestra worked the Hudson Theatre orchestra pit with *Hot Chocolates*. An arrangement was hastily hammered out. Armstrong would augment the Leroy Smith group on Broadway. His Carroll Dickerson mates would fill in uptown at the Inn. Following the curtain downtown, Armstrong would race uptown and add his trumpet weight to the Dickerson band for the Inn's late shows. In this fashion, prospects for *Hot Chocolates'* downtown success, as well as for Louis Armstrong's professional fortune in New York City, surged mightily during the show's final preparatory week.

Razaf himself, in later years, recalled an afternoon during *Hot Chocolates'* pre-Broadway trial when he was accosted at Connie's Inn by the show's menacing financial angel, Dutch Schultz. Razaf hardly knew Schultz personally, but he certainly knew of him, the "Dutchman"'s reputation as a short-tempered, murderous mobster was legendary. Born Arthur Flegenheimer in the Bronx, Schultz was one of a generation of Jewish gangsters spawned in immigrant New York during the most recent wave of immigration. Parlaying a hard head for business with an even harsher appetite for brutality, Schultz had come a long way in a very short time within the New York underworld, earning hundreds of thousands of dollars by the age of 30 from his bootlegging operation, while expanding his influence into the Harlem "policy" rackets, along with a goodly amount of labor racketeering among city unions that represented waiters and window washers.

Schultz, this particular afternoon, complimented Razaf on his work with the show thus far, but added his pointed opinion that *Hot Chocolates* still lacked something, and Schultz knew what it was. A funny number, he informed Razaf, something with a little "colored girl" singing how tough it is being "colored." Razaf grinningly pointed out that he couldn't possibly write a song like that. Schultz responded in characteristic raging fashion by pinning Razaf to the nearest wall with a gun. You'll write it, he more or less rasped, or you'll never write anything again.

This afternoon encounter with Schultz surely left Razaf shaken. It also left him determined to write Schultz's song *his* way. Razaf first explained the situation to his partner Waller, though it is not at all clear whether Razaf actually outlined for Waller the threat that he was laboring under and the full dimension of his intended lyric response to Schultz's "request." The full song did come very quickly, though, Schultz's instructions having been quite explicit. Waller's opinion of Razaf's lyric may be measured in the perfection of the music that he supplied to frame Razaf's rather audacious words—a hauntingly mournful blues-derived melody fleshed out to thirty-two bars in a manner similar to "Squeeze Me." The number was hurriedly staged "straight" by Leonard Harper as a solo for Edith Wilson. Everything would be as Schultz had specified.

Andy Razaf and Fats Waller's "Black and Blue"—full title "(What Did I Do to Be So) Black and Blue?"—was slipped into a *Hot Chocolates* tryout just before the show's June 20 Broadway opening, spotted in the second act after "In a Telegraph Office," a Jimmie Baskette–Eddie Green comedy routine. As Razaf later remembered it, he actually had the misfortune to find himself at the back of the house with Dutch Schultz as the curtain rose for the first time on the Dutchman's number to reveal a stage awash in white—white walls, draperies, and carpet, and, at stage center, an enormous bed made up in white satin. Swathed in a white negligee, swaddled deep in white bedclothes, the jet-black Edith Wilson nestled on that bed and began to sing Andy Razaf's newly "commissioned" lyric, the first lines of which drew a "titter" from the audience, as Razaf later recalled: "Out in the street,/Shufflin' feet,/Couples passin' two by two./While here am I,/Left high and dry,/Black, and 'cause I'm black I'm blue."

Razaf had decided to evade the basic intent of Dutch Schultz's premise by presenting the song, at least outwardly, as a piece about intraracial prejudice between lighter- and darker-skinned blacks, a fact of African–American life that Razaf despised in any event and was no doubt glad to skewer in passing. Thus the ensuing lines: "Browns and yellers/All have fellers,/Gentlemen prefer them light./Wish I could fade,/Can't make the grade,/Nothin' but dark days in sight," drew more laughter from the audience, according to Razaf, who also distinctly recollected a smiling Dutch Schultz looking over to catch his eye at this point as Edith Wilson embarked on the song's chorus with the refrain: "Cold empty bed,/Springs hard as lead,/Pains in my head,/Feel like old Ned,/What did I do to be so black and blue?/No joys for me,/No company,/Even the mouse/Ran from my house/All my life through, I've been so black and blue."

Even these lines, Razaf later recalled, induced loud laughter in the audience, with Dutch Schultz really looking very pleased as Edith Wilson, on stage, plaintively reached the song's bridge with a bold, blunt announcement of stunning frankness: "I'm white inside, it don't help my case./'Cause I can't hide what is on my face."

With these words, Andy Razaf's "Black and Blue" lyric resolutely fractured the repressed traditions of black entertainment expression in this country forever. The audience certainly seems to have sensed it, suddenly, awkwardly, growing silent, as Razaf later recalled, while the Dutchman, Razaf also noted—forcing himself to glance over toward Schultz—the Dutchman no longer was smiling.

Wilson really "sold" the song's final chorus-and-a-half, according to Razaf's almost grateful later recollection, overpowering the mounting tension in the theater with a wailing, forthright delivery of the lyricist's most emphatically discomfiting lines: "I'm so forlorn,/Life's just a thorn,/My heart is torn,/Why was I born?/What did I do to be so black and blue?/Just 'cause you're black, folks think you lack,/They laugh at you and scorn you too,/What did I do to be so black and blue?" Wilson then pounded out the song's final chorus mercilessly:

> When you are near,
> They laugh and sneer,
> Set you aside
> And you're denied,
> What did I do to be so black and blue?
>
> How sad I am, each day I feel worse,
> My mark of Ham seems to be a curse.
>
> How will it end?
> Aint' got a friend.
> My only sin is in my skin.
> What did I do to be so black and blue?

In old age, Andy Razaf always insisted that on the night "Black and Blue" first was sung by Edith Wilson in the presence of Dutch Schultz, the lyricist's fate rested with the audience alone. Their reaction, Razaf maintained, ultimately constituted a life or death verdict, because Dutch Schultz never would have murdered him for writing a hit song—a function, Razaf was convinced, of Schultz's peculiar gangster code.

In the tomblike hush that momentarily greeted Edith Wilson's debut rendition of "Black and Blue," Razaf always later claimed he confronted his own demise, wondering if Schultz would actually finish him off that night, on the spot. It took a moment, Razaf later remarked, to absorb the fact that the audience suddenly was standing and applauding Edith Wilson, calling her back to reprise the strange number she'd just sung so forcefully. Schultz, however, was apparently quicker in acknowledging the ovation. Razaf recalled sensing the Dutchman behind him for an instant. There was a hard slap on the lyricist's back. And Dutch Schultz was gone.

Over the years, many have cited "Black and Blue" as America's first "racial protest song." Certainly Razaf's lyric stripped bare essences of racial discontent that had very rarely if ever been addressed by any African American musically until Razaf wrote them down in 1929.

There have always been those also who have dismissed "Black and Blue" for somehow being apologetic, even self-loathing in spirit. The charge is unfair for many reasons, but particularly in that it completely ignores the prevailing, dehumanizing racial environment in this nation in 1929, and especially within the mainstream New York entertainment community. Certainly Razaf's intention for "Black and Blue" could not have been clearer—despite those few who narrowly cite its opening verse to insist that the song is solely a plaint for dark-skinned blacks. Nor could Razaf's execution have been more deft, as he craftily littered the opening verse with humorous, minstrel-like images early in the first chorus—"feel like old Ned," "even the mouse ran from my house"—drawing his listeners in before landing his most telling lines. The courage, moreover, that it took to express those intentions on the stage of a Broadway-bound "colored" musical revue in 1929, particularly under the jaundiced eye of Dutch Schultz, simply cannot be overstated.

"Black and Blue" is a magnificent achievement of consummate lyric-writing craft, of cunning, of cleverness, of musical empathy on Thomas Waller's part, and of profound, adamant pride and conviction on the part of Andy Razaf. That the song also wound up something of a hit in its own time owes a great deal to the riveting interpretation given "Black and Blue" by Louis Armstrong when he courageously recorded it on July 22 for OKeh's "White" label rather than its "Race" label series, as well as Edith Wilson's highly theatrical rendition, both onstage and on her own November 1929 recording for Brunswick. The combination of these four talents—Razaf, Waller, Armstrong, and Wilson—on one pioneering popular song to this day remains inspirational.

"At first I was afraid," wrote Ralph Ellison some twenty years after, in his novel *Invisible Man*, recalling nights spent listening to Louis Armstrong's recording of "Black and Blue." "This familiar music had demanded action, the kind of which I was incapable . . . I sat on the chair's edge in a soaking sweat . . . It was exhausting—as though I had held my breath continuously for an hour under the terrifying serenity that comes from days of intense hunger . . . I had discovered unrecognized compulsions of my being—even though I could not answer 'yes' to their promptings.

"Please," concluded Ellison, "a definition: 'A hibernation is a covert preparation for a more overt action.'"

Connie's Hot Chocolates, "A New Tanskin Revel,"opened at the Hudson Theatre on a warm Thursday evening, June 20, 1929. Broadway's critical establishment was only moderately impressed. While the *Herald Tribune* headlined *Hot Chocolates* the following morning as the "Best Negro Revue Since *Blackbirds*," other reviewers carped about the humor ("childish prattle"), the score ("Woefully lacking in tunes"), and even the volume levels ("the music is just noise arranged for voice and instrument and played and sung noisily"). "If the rest of *Hot Chocolates* lived up to its dancing," opined the *Evening Telgram*, "it would be the show of shows. [But] some of it is plain ordinary torso-tossing from the downtown burlesque shows." "The show can boast of the liveliest ensemble to be seen on Broadway," added Stephen Rathbun of the *Sun*, concluding however with perhaps the key to *Hot Chocolates* appeal, that it "was presented with the ease, informality, and lack of artificiality of a first-class night club entertainment."

"Ain't Misbehavin'" was singled out by a majority of critics as *Hot Chocolates'* one potential hit tune, but only an unbylined *New York Times* writer seemed to have caught the song in its entr'acte incarnation. "A synthetic but entirely pleasant jazz ballad called 'Ain't Misbehavin'' stands out," he wrote, "and its rendition be-

LAND RENT FREE

Until 14th March, 1896.

TWENTY YEARS LEASES,

Twice Renewable

AT TENANT'S OPTION.

(And with right of contract with the Malagasy Government at expiry of last renewal.)

Rents,

1st and 2nd Years, namely 15th March 1894 to 14th March 1896, Rent Free.

3rd	Year,	25	Cents per Acre	
4th	,, ,	37½	,,	,, ,,
5th	,, ,	50	,,	,, ,,
6th	,, ,	84	,,	,, ,,
7th	,, ,	84	,,	,, ,,
8th	,, ,	One Dollar	,,	,,
9th	,, ,	,,	,,	,,
10th	,, ,	$1.25	,,	,,

11th Year, to expiry of term of Twenty Years, and also of renewals—if availed of, One Dollar 50 Cents per Acre, Per Annum.

The Honble. John L. Waller, ex-United States Consul in Madagascar, having been granted by the Malagasy Government a large area of land situated in the District of Fort Dauphin, South-East Madagascar, has authorized us to lease it in blocks of large or small acreage on the above terms to persons possessed of sufficient capital to enter upon its agricultural development.

The Land is advantageously situated near the Port of Fort Dauphin, at which the English Mail Steamers (Castle Mail Packets Company, Limited), between Mauritius and South Africa, are willing to call should sufficient inducement offer, and thus is particularly desirable—being practically in touch with the Mauritian, South African, and other Markets; Mauritius and Natal being, — distant but some five days steam — Fort Dauphin.

Small Farmers will reap especial advantage from this direct steam communication; Mauritius being a ready market for Poultry, Sheep, Pigs, Cattle, Eggs, and also the vegetable and fruit products which are the main-stay of small holdings.

Tamatave, also, will be a certain market for such products. And a trade in same could probably be opened up with Natal, if not with Cape Town and other South African Ports.

To Immediate Applicants for Farms, limited Timber rights for farm purposes will be granted.

Immediate Applicants for Farms, no matter how small the holding desired, will have the right to selection in priority of application in their class of holding, should their application be entertained.

Timber And Rubber of great commercial value are plentiful upon the land-grant.

John Louis Waller in the uniform of his Kansas Voluntary Infantry company prior to its tour of duty in Cuba, c. 1898. *Courtesy Razaf Estate.*

John Waller's wife, Susan Boyd Bray Waller. *Courtesy Razaf Estate.*

Mother and son: Jennie Waller Razafkeriefo and Andrea Razafkeriefo, age 10. *Courtesy Schomburg Center for Research in Black Culture.*

The aspiring Tin Pan
Alley swell. *Courtesy Razaf
Estate.*

James P. Johnson and Andy
Razaf. *Courtesy Razaf Estate.*

"Razaf—The Melody Man," c. 1924. *Courtesy Schomburg Center for Research in Black Culture.*

Joe Davis, the original "Melody Man." *Courtesy Frank Driggs.*

Paul Denniker. *Courtesy Razaf Estate.*

Jennie Waller Razaf. *Courtesy Razaf Estate.*

The dean of Harlem stride piano, James P.
Johnson, in front of his home, c. 1929.
Courtesy Frank Driggs.

J. C. Johnson. *Courtesy
Frank Driggs.*

Seventh Avenue between 131st and 132nd Streets, the locus of Harlem entertainment life, c. 1927. At left, toward 132nd Street, the Lafayette Theatre; at right, Connie's Inn. Midway between them, the "Tree of Hope," surrounded by the dapper faithful who made it their home base. *Courtesy Frank Driggs.*

Connie's Inn. *Courtesy Schomburg Center for Research in Black Culture.*

The chorus—Connie's Inn. *Courtesy Schomburg Center for Research in Black Culture.*

Connie Immerman at Connie's Inn.
*Courtesy Schomburg Center for
Research in Black Culture.*

George Immerman at Connie's Inn.
*Courtesy Schomburg Center for
Research in Black Culture.*

Edith Wilson.
Courtesy Frank Driggs.

Blackbirds of 1930.
Ethel Waters sings
"You're Lucky to Me"
accompanied by Eubie
Blake. *Courtesy Frank
Driggs.*

A sultry Minto Cato in
August 1931. *Courtesy
Razaf Estate.*

Rumpled and weary-looking, an uncharacteristically mustachioed Andy Razaf at the southeast corner of 131st Street off Seventh Avenue, within sight of the striped Connie's Inn awning just visible up the block. *Courtesy Frank Driggs.*

Louis Armstrong on Seventh Avenue exiting Connie's Inn in the 1930s. *Courtesy Frank Driggs.*

Thomas Waller in his best dress whites, c. 1935. *Courtesy Razaf Estate*.

Thomas Waller and agent Phil Ponce, c. 1936. *Courtesy Frank Driggs*.

Willie "the Lion" Smith and Thomas "Fats" Waller in Harlem, May 1936. *Photographer: Charles Peterson. Courtesy Frank Driggs.*

Andy Razaf in the late 1930s. The piano, from his mother's home, is the one on which he and Waller wrote "Honeysuckle Rose," among other songs. *Courtesy Schomburg Center for Research in Black Culture.*

The hat is off, the coat is off, the bottle is on the floor. Fats Waller at work in the 1930s. *Courtesy Frank Driggs.*

Andy Razaf and Eubie Blake on the beach in Belmar, New Jersey, August 1940, during work on *Tan Manhattan. Courtesy Schomburg Center for Research in Black Culture.*

Jean Blackwell
Razaf. *Courtesy Jean
Hutson.*

The full cast of *Tan Manhattan*. Eubie Blake is kneeling, seventh from right. Unfortunately, Andy Razaf is absent from this picture. *Courtesy Razaf Estate.*

Andy Razaf and Alicia Wilson Razaf on their wedding day, February 14, 1963, with Razaf's uncle, John Waller, Jr. *Courtesy Razaf Estate.*

tween the acts by an unnamed member of the orchestra was a highlight of the premiere." Only one critic as well, writing for *Variety*, took note in his review of the song "Black and Blue." "Miss Wilson scored with 'Black and Blue,'" this critic noted simply, then added perhaps the critical understatement of the season: ". . . quite a lyric."

With or without critical unanimity, *Hot Chocolates* was a hit. Though the white appetite downtown for "Negro" entertainment had now been greatly diminished by excess, audiences still filled the Hudson Theatre in plentiful numbers to see what would prove to be Broadway's final great Negro revue of the Nineteen Twenties. Incredibly, throughout the show's run, most of the *Hot Chocolates* company continued to race uptown after the curtain fell at the Hudson Theatre to perform once more at Connie's Inn. ("If they always pour as much energy into their work in the theater as they did last night," wrote one critic amazedly, "I cannot for the life of me see how they can do anything more uptown but stagger across the floor. But it seems they do.") This commute was interrupted toward the end of July when the Immermans instituted a "midnight matinee" downtown at the Hudson Theatre for the primary benefit of Broadway's working theatricals. In the ongoing tradition of black revues on Broadway, *Hot Chocolates* also appears to have remained in a general state of flux throughout its 219 performances downtown. Exhausted performers apparently were frequent no-shows at curtain time and had to be covered for, while the production running order seems regularly to have been rearranged, with "Black and Blue," for example, moved during the second week of July from Scene 3 in Act 2 to Scene 10 in Act 1, a choice slot just before the Act 1 finale. Louis Armstrong's participation in the proceedings also was rapidly enhanced after audiences responded to his Intermission cameo. According to Andy Razaf, Armstrong, at Razaf's suggestion, soon was designated another "Ain't Misbehavin'" reprise, playing a chorus of the song from the pit during the show's first act, immediately after Paul Bass and Margaret Simms had sung it as a love duet. Armstrong also participated in a short-lived all-star speciality number that took over "Black and Blue"'s original second act slot for a period lasting roughly from July 8–July 28, a trio billed as "The Three Thousand Pounds of Harmony"—the hefty Edith Wilson, the rotund Thomas "Fats" Waller, and the hardly svelte Louis Armstrong—performing a Razaf/Waller/Brooks tune entitled "My Man Is Good for Nothing but Love." During the show's final Broadway weeks, toward the end of November, a young Cab Calloway also joined the company as a replacement for vocalist Paul Bass, the juvenile lead whose singing duties in the show included all of *Hot Chocolates'* many hit numbers excluding "Black and Blue"—"Sweet Savannah Sue," "Goddess of Rain," "Rhythm Man," and "Ain't Misbehavin'." "Paul Bass had done a pretty good job with those numbers," Calloway later insisted, "but I really pulled the music out of them."

An incredible coda to the *Hot Chocolates* legend came days after the show's opening, as recalled by Razaf. The episode began with a phone call from Dutch Schultz one late afternoon, instructing Razaf to be ready for a car that Schultz was sending for him *now*.

They drove to Polly Adler's brothel on West 54th Street, where Schultz, as Razaf knew, was an honored regular. A jovial Dutchman ushered the black lyric writer inside personally, leading him to a back room door behind which three ladies lounged, waiting. "Take all night," Razaf later recollected the Dutchman barking as he packed Razaf inside. "It's on me. A little bonus."

Razaf, however, already was acquainted with Adler's operation. He knew most of the girls in the place, and he knew especially that one of the women presented to him in this room was Dutch Schultz's girl, a girl Schultz did not share with anyone. Razaf suddenly could not shake the feeling that if he was to have Schultz's girl, he probably would have to pay Schultz's price—yet another function of Schultz's peculiar code. Razaf never had been entirely convinced of Schultz's sincerity in forgiving him for circumventing orders with "Black and Blue." The Dutchman did not tolerate disobedience. He had, however, refrained from killing him simply because the song had worked. Well, here was the payback. Dutch Schultz was fixing it so that he had a reason for rubbing out Andy Razaf.

Whether or not this was mere paranoia on Razaf's part, whether or not Dutch Schultz ever truly comprehended "Black and Blue" sufficiently to be offended by it, will never be known. That night, Razaf recalled, he grimly found a chair in the corner of Polly Adler's crowded room and kept to it, clung to it, for dear life. One way or another, when morning came, he was in the clear.

The unprecedented quantity and exceptional quality of Razaf's song output for Tin Pan Alley and Broadway in 1929, now that both venues were anxious to use him, encompassed more than thirty tunes beside "S'posin'," "Black and Blue," "Ain't Misbehavin'," and the balance of his and Waller's *Hot Chocolates* score. He wrote six more songs, for example, with Paul Denniker, all of them published by Joe Davis, songs that reflected particularly the access that the white Denniker provided Razaf into the white music mainstream. All six (seven, including "S'posin'") were love songs. Black songwriters in 1929, even Broadway talents, rarely were afforded the chance to write love songs. Or as Maurice Dancer, a black theatrical gossip columnist, wrote in his *Stage Facts* column around this time: "Andy Razaf is one of the first colored boys on Broadway writing lyrics for the popular love songs."

Writing behind Denniker, Razaf could submerge himself in the fashionable love burblings of the moment and capitalize on them. Each of these 1929 numbers was a perfect formulaic achievement pointedly addressed to the "flapper" market: "Hawaiian Love-Bird," part of a Twenties vogue for Hawaiian guitar yodeling; "You'll Always Be Welcome" and "That Was Yesterday," two misty, wistful ballads; and "Language of Love," which coyly winked at that Twenties icon, the crooning collegian—"What if you've never been to college,/You're up in knowledge if you're in love,/Your need of English, French or Spanish/Will quickly vanish if you're in love./Go here, go there, go anywhere,/There's only one language of love."

The balance of these ballads with Denniker were composed for the crown crooning collegian of the Twenties, Rudy Vallee, who recorded all three songs to great success. Razaf's work here was exemplary, displacing bawdy "colored" lyrics with words of soppy sentiment so Vallee-esque that the singer himself might have set them to paper, songs so utterly colorless that even their smarmy one-word titles importuned but softly: "Perhaps," "Won'tcha," and, of course, "S'posin'."

Razaf also collaborated with Fletcher Henderson's former reedman–arranger Don Redman, perhaps the most technically respected black bandleader/arranger in the business in 1929 as musical director of the Detroit-based McKinney's Cotton Pickers, one of the country's finest regional bands. Redman stopped off in New York early in November 1929 for a quick Victor recording session under the McKinney's Cotton Pickers name, though the personnel on these recordings actually constituted something of a who's who of local Harlem jazz talent, including Thomas Waller on piano and celeste, backing Redman on seven titles. Prior to these studio appearances, though, on November 5, 6, and 7, Redman had sought out Andy Razaf, an old acquaintance from his Club Alabam days with Henderson, to perfect some of the rudimentary lyrics that

Redman had scribbled for tunes he'd brought for these recording sessions. Razaf polished two songs with Redman—"The Way I Feel Today," a tune co-written by Redman with Howard Quicksell, an old, Detroit-based associate of Bix Beiderbecke's, and "Ain't I Good to You?", a straight blues—two songs whose lyric starkness were at times breathtaking.

When I think of him,
How much I love him,
I get a desperate notion,
That's the way I feel today.
My heart is breakin'
Because he's makin'
A plaything of my devotion,
That's the way I feel today.

Without any reason
Or a word to say,
My man turned his keys in,
Packed and went away;
What good is livin',
I'll soon be givin'
My body up to the ocean—
That's the way I feel today.

* * *

It's love makes me treat you
The way that I do,
Gee baby, ain't I good to you?
There's nothin' too good
For a girl that's so true,
Gee, baby, ain't I good to you?
Bought you a fur coat for Christmas,
A diamond ring,
Cadillac car
And everything,
Love makes me treat you the way that I do,
Gee baby, ain't I good to you?

"Ain't I Good to You?"'s lyric question—"Gee baby, ain't I good to you?"—was in many ways a perfect blues phrase: bittersweet, wry, and plaintive all at once, a question that readily absorbed

whatever emotional experience a singer might bring to it—
insistence, recalcitrance, determination, despair—the range of possible inflection was limitless. Through the pristine craftsmanship of
Razaf's lyric line here with Redman, each line stood soulfully
complete in a fashion that almost diagramed the bar-by-bar architecture of a legitimate blues tune. To speak these lines was to sing them;
their inner rhythms were unmistakable.

Though Redman initially sold "Ain't I Good to You?" to Joe Davis
in 1929, formal publication did not come until 1944, with the title
now appended to fully reflect the lyric, as "Gee Baby, Ain't I Good
to You?" The song would stand throughout the ensuing decades as an
evocative blues paradigm, recorded by countless jazz and pop
luminaries, to the present day.

In the late summer of 1929, the Immermans approached their
new in-house songwriters, Razaf and Waller, about a new revue for
Connie's Inn. In actuality, the continued success of *Hot Chocolates*
downtown had dissuaded the Immermans from varying the existing
uptown *Hot Feet* revue very much throughout the summer months.
On August 13, though, they at last commissioned Razaf and Waller
to compose at least three new tunes for a new Connie's Inn
revue—an "up tune" (or rhythm song), a ballad, and a "soft
shoe"—with Razaf also hired to write new material for the revue,
under contract for a $125 advance and $25 a week for the run of the
show. The name of this new production would be *Load of Coal*, titled
after Bert Williams's first and only solo Broadway vehicle without
George Walker, just prior to Williams's 1910 *Ziegfeld Follies* defection, *Mr. Load of Coal*, in 1909. While an entirely new company was
pieced together for *Load of Coal*, including Jean Starr and Maude
Russell (both former *Keep Shufflin'* cast members), dancers "Red"
Simmons and "Chink" Collins, and vaudevillians Dudley Dickerson
and Dewey Brown, the music that this cast would perform, still
backed by Louis Armstrong and his Carroll Dickerson orchestra, was
almost entirely constituted of music composed for *Hot Chocolates*,
with the exception of Razaf and Waller's three newly commissioned
compositions.

Concerned more than ever with Waller's ability to concentrate on
work in the wake of *Hot Chocolates'* success and the intensified
socializing that it was breeding, Razaf initially urged his partner that
they sequester themselves for this hurried song work, as they had on
other occasions, with his mother, Jennie Razaf Coles, at her home in

Asbury Park (Razaf's mother had long since remarried), about a two-hour drive down the New Jersey coast. Seclusion, of course, was hardly Waller's working ideal, but Razaf tossed in a clincher. He reminded Waller how much he loved Jennie's home cooking; "mother Coles" always served Waller all his favorite foods, and even baked him special cookies, anything to keep the wayward pianist around and working.

Upon their arrival at the Jersey shore town, after a sumptuous breakfast consisting of five veal chops, a loaf of bread, potatoes, and a substantial draught of gin, Waller joined Razaf at the household's upright piano. Two hours later, according to Razaf, they had completed two songs: the requisite rhythm song, which Razaf for no apparent reason titled "Zonky," and a first-rate ballad, inspired, Razaf later claimed, by a run-in that he and Waller had just escaped hours before with a traffic cop in Belmar, New Jersey, as the two songwriters were racing their car down toward Asbury Park. According to Razaf, it was Waller's coy plea to the cop—"Please officer, our fate is in your hands"—that had rescued them from a speeding ticket. Now that line was transformed into a song title, with the conversation itself transmuted by Razaf into a charmingly romantic lyric.

> *Wanting you is my offence,*
> *You have all the evidence,*
> *Now I wait for you to sentence me.*
> *Must I go or must I stay,*
> *Will my skies be blue or gray,*
> *Is my dream to be or not to be?*
>
> *There's no use pretending,*
> *Love needs no defending,*
> *What is the verdict?*
> *My fate is in your hands.*
> *You're my judge and jury,*
> *What do you assure me?*
> *What is the verdict?*
> *My fate is in your hands . . .*
>
> *If the charge is loving you*
> *Then I'm guilty, dear,*
> *Tell me that you love me too*
> *And I'll have no fear.*

It is you I'm needing,
For your love I'm pleading,
What is the verdict?
My fate is in your hands.

Set simply and cleverly on a legal pretext, Razaf's lyric for "My Fate Is in Your Hands" sang with a pleasing urgency, impelled by a sweet Waller melody line that climbed with importunate daintiness. "Zonky," on the other hand, received a straightforward, slangy, dance-fixated lyric—"Got such, well, you know, what I want to say/Hot? Much? That tempo sure is tight that way!"—a rollicking treatment that did complement just as cleverly Waller's particularly irrepressible melody.

Razaf next pushed his partner for the soft shoe number. Their accomplishment in some two hours of work had been phenomenal. Razaf was now hoping they'd pull off the impossible: meeting a deadline. Waller produced no more than half a chorus for the third song, though, when he suddenly announced to Razaf, "I gotta go." And did.

Abandoned, Razaf continued to work on this final song fragment, adamantly refusing to leave it unfinished. It was then that he got, as he later put it, "the sudden thought: Why not rewrite that unpublished oldie of mine, 'Honeysuckle Rose.' Its title was much too good to be wasted."

Working from the skeletal remains of two songs—the half-chorus his partner had left him and the old version of "Honeysuckle Rose" that Razaf still vaguely remembered from the Club Alabam through the mist of five years—the lyricist soon finished up Waller's chorus, "added a verse," and phoned Waller at Connie's Inn to confirm with him what they had. The bartender, at first, at Waller's direction, apparently, denied the pianist's presence in the club, but Razaf made the man understand who was looking for Waller and why.

Their ensuing phone conversation has long since entered the realm of anecdotal jazz legend. Waller had quickly and easily forgotten this, his most recent melody. Over the nightclub din, Razaf sang it to him. By now both men had forgotten the tune's eight-bar bridge. Waller devised a new one on the spot. After untold minutes of desperate humming and shouting, Razaf left the phone for a moment to try what they had on the piano. By the time he returned, Waller had hung up.

*

Intended as mere rhythm backing for an innocuous tap number, "Honeysuckle Rose" did not make much of an initial impression on either of its two composers. "We thought very little of [it] at the time," Razaf later pointed out. "To us it was just another show number. How could such a 'quickie' be otherwise?—was how we reasoned."

The opening verse was arresting, though—teasing, knowing. "Have no use for any sweets of any kind,/Since the day you came around." Again Razaf was operating in the negative, denying mode of "Ain't Misbehavin'" and "Mama Stayed Out the Whole Night Long." An exhilarating, affirming quality consumed the song, though, a dizzy tone of sheer delight. "From the start I instantly made up my mind,/Sweeter sweetness can't be found;/You're so sweet,/Can't be beat,/Nothing sweeter ever stood on feet."

> *Every honeybee*
> *Fills with jealousy*
> *When they see you out with me,*
> *I don't blame them, goodness knows,*
> *Honeysuckle Rose.*
> *When you're passing by,*
> *Flowers droop and sign,*
> *And I know the reason why,*
> *You're much sweeter, goodness knows,*
> *Honeysuckle Rose. . . .*

For Razaf, at his writing table in Asbury Park, there was much to this lyric that was quite new. He never had utilized the affectation of interior rhyme much; the sophistication that interior rhyming imputed was altogether out of place in a "colored" song. "Honeysuckle Rose, though, was a sophisticated lark, bubbling with whimsy and smart satisfaction, and in it, interior rhymes were rampant: "Every hon*eybee* fills with jealou*sy* when they *see* you out with *me*." The self-assurance was contagious. The images also were quite bawdy—filthy, in fact: "Don't buy sugar,/You just have to touch my cup,/You're my sugar,/It's sweet when you stir it up." But the sheer exuberance of Razaf's lines rendered the imagery tasty, if not exactly tasteful: "When I'm taking sips/From your tasty lips,/Seems the honey fairly drips,/You're confection, goodness knows,/Honeysuckle Rose."

More than sixty years after its creation, "Honeysuckle Rose" remains a frolic, infinitely fresh, genuinely fun. While Waller's melody contributes enormously to this freshness, standing to this day as one of popular music's most perfect riffs, an ideal departure point for jazz improvisation, it is Razaf's lyric that gives "Honeysuckle Rose" its timeless identity. The melody is inextricable from the lyric, for the lyric gives the melody life. And yet what Razaf, in effect, managed to capture above all else in his "Honeysuckle Rose" lyric was the personality of Thomas "Fats" Waller. Vulgar, frolicsome, bawdy, self-assured, and sophisticated all at once, this was Thomas Waller definitively. The words, the music, and the man were one.

That "Honeysuckle Rose" would not command popular attention for another five years at least—not until "Swing Era" bands began to revive the tune triumphantly in the Thirties—while both "Zonky" and "My Fate Is in Your Hands" quickly rose up from *Load of Coal* to remunerative lives on recordings and the radio, purely seems to have been a function of "Honeysuckle Rose"'s placement and presentation in *Load of Coal* as a faceless tap number. "Honeysuckle Rose" was in fact sold to a music publisher, Santly Brothers, in September, 1929, along with "Zonky" and "My Fate." According to Waller's manager in later years, Ed Kirkeby, the song also got plugged with the others, though it actually was published more than a month after them, on November 20, 1929. "Honeysuckle Rose," according to Kirkeby, finally made its national debut on Paul Whiteman's "Old Gold" radio show in the early Thirties. Whiteman's broadcast competed with bandleader B. A. Rolfe's "Lucky Strike" program, where fast, brassy arrangements of popular tunes were the feature, as opposed to Whiteman's practice of playing songs at slower tempos, more or less as they originally had been written. According to Kirkeby, Waller and Whiteman vocalist Mildred Bailey came to audition "Honeysuckle Rose" for the bandleader and "rocked" him with their slow, insinuating, lilting rendition of the song, which Whiteman quickly asked his band arranger to notate and preserve. Before the song could be performed on the air, however, the "Old Gold Show" format was revamped and remodeled after its "Lucky Strike" rival. "Honeysuckle Rose"'s shuffling rhythm was at this point double-timed, horribly mutilating the song and setting its ultimate discovery back years, in the opinion of Waller's representative at Santley Brothers, Harry Link, though "Honeysuckle Rose" was recorded as early as November 1929 by an anonymous Bert Stock and His Orchestra. It would, in fact, continue to be recorded throughout the early Thirties by distinguished players like saxophonists Frank Trumbauer and Don Redman himself with McKinney's Cotton Pickers.

"I remember an ad posted all over Harlem," Annabelle Razaf's niece Edna Brown Hunter recalled. "It was for this hair pomade, and they used Andy's face to promote it—with his royal background as the hook. This ad with Andy's face was all over Harlem at one time."

Certainly Andy Razaf was now something of a star in 1929, at least uptown, where he was quite the celebrity, an absolutely, uniquely *literary* Harlem entertainment celebrity. Downtown, Razaf had his celebrity cachet too, segregated but successful. Still, there was something tenuous about it all. For all Razaf's genuine talent and accomplishment, appreciation for his work in the white entertainment industry really was intensely insecure, resting on an uneasy perception of Negro music as a fad, something fleeting and incidental. Despite the monumental attainments of Razaf's 1929 songwriting season, the year, in real dollars, had fallen far short of true value. On July 30, Razaf had in fact been forced to sell his one-percent royalty interest in the box office receipts of *Connie's Hot Chocolates*, all present and future editions, in order to pay his expenses. The fall of the stock market in October 1929 hardly reassured Razaf about his financial future either, though its specific impact on him, admittedly, was at first negligible.

Razaf's private life at this time reflected his success: Andrea Razaf now lived comfortably, if not lavishly, on West 129th Street with Minto Cato, the very beautiful, young nightclub chanteuse he'd met at Connie's Inn. "He was gonna marry her," Eubie Blake later insisted. "Some things about Andy Razaf—I don't see how he could have been that way. Minto Cato just wasn't a girl . . . a woman that I would take to marry like that. She was a nice girl to go around with, but he had a couple of others like her."

"I thought they were married," Alberta Hunter later remarked. "Minto Cato. She was his wife."

Annabelle Razaf had developed a rather severe ulcer. She'd moved up to the Bronx and was living with her sister, Lula, who wrote Razaf constantly for money. He sent a little.

"Dear Andy," Annabelle Razaf herself wrote at this time. "Just a line hoping they [*sic*] find you well and happy. I am not feeling so as I have an awful cold and then again am worried about money matters. . . .

"Well I won't say anymore as I am sick, tired and disgusted with the whole d——world and feel like h——.

"With love and fond wishes—a xxxxxxxx"

Two days later she wrote again.

> I received the telegram, many thanks for the twenty dollars, it's a great help to meet my expenses, I don't know how I could have managed without its help . . .
>
> I do wish it were possible for you to have a few spare moments to pay me a visit once in a while. It's more than lonesome up here at times. When will the sun shine for me? This home seems dark and dreary, there is something lacking to make it complete but I don't know exactly where the fault lies.
>
> I had a very pleasant dream of you a while ago. I hope it's a good omen.
>
> Well dear, come and see me soon and take good care of yourself.
>
> As ever, your own little,
> Ann

"He simply was the only man she ever loved," Annabelle's sister, Lula Wesson, finally observed. "Annabelle loved simply. When Andy left her she mourned him just as she mourned the dog Brabant when he died, and even mourned that rosewood piano when it finally got termites and we had to throw it out. They hadn't been together for years but that didn't change the way she felt about him. I believe he last came to see her in 1932 when she was living with me on Lexington Avenue and 104th Street. He brought her a new suit. Never saw him again after that."

Courtesy Razaf Estate.

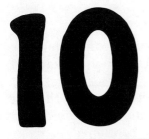

What Harlem
Is to Me

It's a symphony of many moods and shades,
It's a tapestry of all designs and grades,
It's a hand behind the bars,
Ever reaching for the stars . . .

It's a grownup running wild,
It's a helpless little child."

> — "*What Harlem Is to Me*"
> by Andy Razaf, Russell Wooding, and Paul Denniker

Musical arranger Ken Macomber once described a typical Tin Pan Alley outing with Andy Razaf and Fats Waller during the mid-Twenties. They met one particular afternoon on the corner of Broadway and 45th Street, with Waller crooning his latest melody for Razaf, who titled the tune on the spot. The trio then strolled toward 46th Street and the publishing offices of Mills Music, with Razaf trying rhymes and lines aloud rapid-fire before arriving at Mills, where Razaf and Waller actually completed their song while demonstrating it to Mills's Professional staff, selling the number for cash. From Mills, the two songmen proceeded one block up Broadway to Shapiro, Bernstein, a rival music house, at the 47th Street corner, exchanging the verse and refrain of their new tune en route. At Shapiro, Bernstein, according to Ken Macomber, Razaf and Waller then sold their new song again.

In the music publishing industry it was unwritten law that the first music firm to publish a song owned it. Long after they were found out, Andy Razaf and Fats Waller apparently continued to make multiple sales with the tacit consent of publishers who recognized that, even if their companies weren't the first to buy a song, they still could be the first to introduce it. In fact, once Razaf and Waller achieved Broadway success, Tin Pan Alley publishers apparently outdid themselves scrambling to dig up tunes they'd once bought casually, knowing then that Razaf and Waller probably were selling the song all over town. "You never knew when they were going to come up with another big hit," explained publisher Jack Mills in retrospect, "so you had to buy them, even though you knew they probably had sold it elsewhere down the street, or even across the hall." Ultimately, one suspects, publishers allowed Razaf and Waller and most of their peers—black and white but especially black—to take gross reselling liberties with new songs in order to nurture the illusion that songwriters *could* somehow one-up the industry. Any way the songwriters played it, the music publishers reaped most of the benefits, since they had purchased the songs cheaply. The trick for both parties, ironically, was to keep things as fluid as possible.

For this reason there is something inescapably dismaying about the glorious war stories, the oversized song-selling yarns spun around Razaf and Waller's early Tin Pan Alley years; the songs, according to Waller biographer Duncan Schiedt, "that went to this and that publisher for the price of a good time in Harlem that night, and tales of Fats and Andy rolling up to the publishers' offices from uptown in a taxi, with nothing in their pockets but holes and a new song, and calling up to a window far above the street, 'C'mon down an' bail us out—we've got a great tune here!!'" Within these terrifically colorful anecdotes of giddy Tin Pan Alley adventure one can trace the malevolent seed of inevitable financial ruin.

Waller was by far the worse culprit, selling off tunes for a quick drink, for dinner, or for cabfare home to Harlem. The music flowed so effortlessly from him that he clearly had a difficult time valuing his own creativity, but there seems also to have been something pathological about his willingness to abdicate all right to his musical talent. One can speculate on the source of this abnegation, rooted in

Waller's chronic emotional immaturity, compounded by Tin Pan Alley's degrading system of institutionalized racial exploitation. Better to sell the songs cheap and fast and thereby avoid the pain—that does seem to have been Waller's way out.

Razaf, on the other hand, confronted Tin Pan Alley's race-centered professional inequities more concretely than he confronted anything else in his life. Even as he played the black songwriter's puny selling game with Tin Pan Alley publishers early on in his career, he was gaining a reputation as a militant businessman who abhored the evasions and outright surrender of songwriters like Waller in Tin Pan Alley matters. From his earliest music days, Razaf lived for the moment when he could exercise some modicum of negotiating power on his own behalf. The story has been told of one revealing instance, late in the Twenties, after Razaf and Waller had established themselves to a degree on Tin Pan Alley, when the two men were demonstrating a song for a publisher who offered them $50 for the tune on the spot. Razaf countered the publisher's offer with a firm demand for $500 in advance, plus royalties— flabbergasting his partner, who would have taken the fifty without a thought. When the publisher balked, it is said, Razaf tore up the manuscript and stormed out of the office.

Perhaps the most significant moment for Razaf in terms of certification and empowerment as a Tin Pan Alley songwriter of standing was his election into ASCAP, the association founded in 1914 by composer Victor Herbert and seven of his contemporaries to preserve the rights, under U.S. copyright law, of all songwriter and music publisher members, and to collect on their behalf an established royalty from "proprietors of public amusement enterprises throughout the United States—theatres, dance halls, cabarets, restaurants," and the like, for their use of music composed and published by ASCAP members. Accepted initially, pursuant to ASCAP by-laws, as a "Nonparticipating Member," on September 27, 1928, Razaf was upgraded in December 1929 to active membership, a source of particular pride to the lyricist, enhanced by the fact that his new 1929 ASCAP membership certificate arrived signed by Society Secretary Charles K. Harris, the composer/publisher to whom Razaf had first sent his earliest lyric efforts in 1909, and whose advice to "go into some other field" was now, for Razaf, triumphantly ironic.

Though Thomas Waller would not attain ASCAP membership

until 1931, the most significant, self-defining event of Waller's Tin Pan Alley career also transpired in 1929—the tragic outright July 7 sale by Waller of twenty song compositions, including his complete *Hot Chocolates* score, to Mills Music for the appalling sum of $500. Though it has never been clear whether this figure actually represented the final consummating payment out of a larger total buyout or was simply, sadly, a flat one-time fee, the transaction still remains the most infamous of Waller's many business missteps. Panicked by the shadowing omnipresence of his alimony debts, unused to banking songwriting money on the scale that these songs were earning, Waller simply threw over his future again in the name of short-term need and expedient satisfaction. His songwriting partner was, of course, appalled, but powerless to prevent Waller from committing what had long since become his own ritual commercial suicide.

Razaf did induce Waller to join him in a perverse professional alternative to their shared freelancing duel with Tin Pan Alley when late in 1929 Waller, Razaf, and Paul Denniker all signed exclusive contracts with Joe Davis, guaranteeing Davis first refusal on anything the three men composed, along with a one-third percentage on all their song earnings, in exchange for Davis's commitment to publish and promote the trio to the best of his considerable abilities. In addition, Waller signed on as Joe Davis's in-house song plugger, working a straight week, ten to five daily, at the Triangle Music offices on 51st Street, demonstrating Davis-owned tunes to all comers for a weekly salary plus a morning bottle of gin to start the day and a five o'clock jug of Old Grand-Dad bourbon before closing.

Though these agreements favored Davis quite unfairly, it must also be understood that insider access on Tin Pan Alley was everything for a songwriter in the Twenties. To work "on staff" for a successful publisher was a guarantee that one's songs would be published and promoted, performed on radio, and recorded. Moreover, no agreement ever really was "exclusive." If Razaf and Waller or Denniker desired some extra cash or simply wanted to exercise their independence, slipping away to a rival music house was a small matter—to sell off a song or two outright, in true bootleg fashion. It was hardly the stuff of artistic or even commercial freedom, but a window out, to be sure.

Razaf and Waller had concluded 1929 with one significant final song collaboration, "Blue Turning Grey Over You," a charming ballad, published by Joe Davis, with a heartfelt Razaf lyric that included lines one might almost imagine emanating from Annabelle Razaf's heart and mind at this time:

What will I do at sundown?
What will I do at dawn?
What will I do at noontime?
Now that I've found you gone.
What will I do for sunshine?
With nothin' but the rain?
How can I smile, find life worthwhile,
With a heart that's filled with pain?
My how I miss,
Your tender kiss
And the wonderful things you would do;
I run my hands
Through silvery strands
Cause I'm blue turning gray over you.
You used to be
So good to me,
That's when I was a novelty;
Now you have new thrills in view,
Found someone new, left me blue
Turning grey over you."

Though "Blue Turning Grey Over You" proved enormously successful, Waller almost immediately again became unavailable to Razaf for further song work, embarking on a two-month tour as Louis Armstrong's replacement in a road company *Hot Chocolates* production, following the end of the show's New York run in January 1930. Razaf, in any event, was now already turning his attention to the demands of a new revue for Ed Smalls' Paradise Club in collaboration with James P. Johnson.

An affable if aggressive entrepreneur, Smalls was one uptown club owner who generally enjoyed the goodwill of Harlem's black community. In Prohibition's early years his Sugar Cane Club on Fifth Avenue had been an extremely popular neighborhood spot, and when Smalls, in 1925, shifted venues to Seventh Avenue, his new Smalls' Paradise had retained much of its black clientele while quickly gaining a sizable white patronage that found the club more genuine than its sleeker competitors. Smalls's floorshows, though not without considerable energetic appeal, generally had rated well below the revues staged at Connie's Inn and the Cotton Club throughout the Twenties. Now Smalls took steps to remedy these deficiencies in 1930 by hiring Andy Razaf and James P. Johnson, nominally the best black lyricist and composer in the business, to supply his nightclub with a floor show of distinction.

Granted substantial creative control over a revue for the first time by a club owner who, moreover, was black, Razaf proceeded to take extraordinary liberties constructing Smalls's new revue. His concept for the show was quite radical: the evening would be a knowing celebration of everyday Negroes at work and at play but mostly at work, in a musical salute to America's favorite racial stereotypes—*A Kitchen Mechanic's Revue*, according to Andy Razaf:

> *That kitchen mechanics' parade*
> *Puts all the rest in the shade,*
> *Porters, butlers, cooks, and maids;*
> *There'll be no work done today,*
> *Bosses have nothing to say,*
> *Step back, give them plenty of room,*
> *Heroes of the mop and broom . . .*

Certainly Razaf's audacity was something to savor. Rather than condescend to the fantasies of Smalls's white patrons as they motored uptown for a taste of rarified Harlem nightlife, the lyricist presented these slummers with a chorus line of "colored" menials right out of their kitchens at home, a troupe of truly unalloyed Harlemites drolly toasting their menial skills and chores.

> *We're the chefs of the Paradise,*
> *We're here at a fancy price,*
> *To cook you a musical stew for this revue.*
> *Soon you'll learn when you take a look,*
> *What we cook isn't in the book,*
> *Our recipes are melodies—*
> *We serve them as we please,*
> *We know our bass and treble clefs,*
> *For we're the musical chefs,*
> *We're the musical chefs.*

Of course, it was only Razaf's implication that was in any way revolutionary. Though the conceit behind *Kitchen Mechanic's Revue* definitely was insidious, Razaf's execution was no more than deftly amusing. No blood was let; the lyricist's pen did not drip bile. Above all else, *Kitchen Mechanic's Revue* was firstly entertaining, for as Razaf reminded (himself as much as anyone) in the revue number "Go Harlem,"

> *Harlem, you are the playground*
> *For people downtown,*
> *Harlem, they can't resist your spell.*
> *Harlem, the world is after*
> *Your magic laughter,*
> *One trip to that happy land*
> *And you will understand.*
> *So, like Van Vechten,*
> *Start inspectin',*
> *Go Harlem, go Harlem, go.*

With quite evident relish, Razaf crammed *Kitchen Mechanic's Revue* full of lyric wit in service to his black worker theme. The obligatory "shake" number, for example, was played by a shimmying Mae Brown in a scanty maid's uniform, warbling, "When the dust is inches thick, no use feelin' blue,/If you want to learn a simple trick, work the way I do:/Shake your duster up and down,/Straight across or all aroun'/Don't be afraid to bend your back,/Dust out eve'ry corner, nook, and crack,/Shake, oh shake your duster."

Of course there were conventional bawdy blues, both solos and duets, again in service to theme.

> She: Elevator Papa, Elevator Papa,
> Seems you always want to go down.
> He: Switchboard Mama, Switchboard Mama,
> You're the worst connection in town.

Razaf also detonated a nice volley at the expense of disgraceful race stereotypes like minstrelsy's hoary "Sambo" figure, in "Sambo's Syncopated Russian Dance," a neat satirical song inspired, no doubt, by an increasing infatuation among African Americans with Soviet communism.

> *Both Lenin and Trotsky*
> *They do the Kazotsky*

> *To Sambo's syncopated Russian dance.*
> *This hamsky from Bamsky*
> *Is now the man what-amsky,*
> *All through his syncopated Russian dance.*
> *Once they were about to shoot him*
> *Where the Volga flows,*
> *Now the Soviets salute him,*
> *Ev'rywhere he goes;*
> *They say this tarsky,*
> *Will soon be the Czarsky,*
> *All through his syncopated Russian dance.*

Indisputably, though, the most memorable lyric in Andy Razaf's *Kitchen Mechanic's Revue* was a lilting bit of whimsy cleverly fashioned by Razaf as a tongue-in-cheek suggestion, à la Cole Porter, of the emotional life of those who served, rather than those pampered few (like Porter) who got served: "A Porter's Love Song to a Chamber Maid."

> *Tho' my position is of low degree,*
> *And all the others may look down on me,*
> *I'll go smiling thru,*
> *That's if I have you;*
> *I am the happiest of troubadours,*
> *Thinking of you, while I'm massaging floors,*
> *At my leisure time, I made up this rhyme:*
>
> *I will be the oil mop,*
> *If you'll be the oil,*
> *Then we both could mingle*
> *Ev'ry time we toil.*
> *I will be the washboard,*
> *If you'll be the tub,*
> *Think of all the Mondays*
> *We can rub-a-dub.*
> *I will be your shoebrush*
> *If you'll be my shoe,*
> *Then I'd keep you bright, dear,*
> *Feeling good as new.*
> *If you'll be my razor,*
> *I will be your blade,*

That's a porter's love song,
To a chambermaid.

I will be your dustpan,
If you will be my broom,
We could work together
All around the room.
I will be your clothespin,
Be my pulley line,
We'll hang out together,
Wouldn't that be fine?

I will be your dishpan,
If you'll be my dish,
We'll meet after meals, dear,
What more could you wish?
I will be your window,
Be my window shade,
That's a porter's love song
To a chambermaid.

Kitchen Mechanic's Revue certainly was one of the more original cabaret achievements of the Twenties in Harlem and conceivably could have been transferred to Broadway after its March 17 opening at Smalls' Paradise, notwithstanding the nightclub specificity of its theme. The speed with which the depressed downtown theatrical economy rapidly was deteriorating, though, in the wake of Wall Street's collapse, decisively legislated against such a move. Razaf briefly threw himself in with the woefully misbegotten *Shuffle Along of 1930*, a threadbare effort with unrealizable Broadway aspirations that disastrously combined song highlights from the Razaf/Waller/ Johnson score for *Keep Shufflin'*, a pair of tunes from Razaf and Johnson's *Kitchen Mechanic's Revue*, including "Porter's Love Song," and a pair of masquerading comedians named "Mr. Miller" and "Mr. Lyles," misrepresented by the production's management as Miller and Lyles themselves (in a ludicrous stunt that was quickly detected and exposed by the press), to produce a painful evening of mayhem that disappeared soon after its Brooklyn debut in late April 1930. Razaf then turned his full attention to a Broadway commission tendered to him earlier in the year by the "Black Ziegfeld" himself, Lew Leslie.

*

Even in the eccentric universe of Broadway theaterdom Lew Leslie was an excessive character, an impresario composed of seemingly co-equal parts bluster, talent, wiliness, and lunacy. Everyone in the show business generally knew, for example, where they could find Leslie if they cared to. Day in, day out, sooner or later, throughout the Twenties and Thirties, Lew Leslie always made an appearance outside of Lindy's on Broadway, off 49th Street, with his cigar and his spats, ostentatiously displaying a fat bankroll. Cast members from Leslie productions also knew that their boss, perched hard by Lindy's with his roll of bills, was an easy touch anytime there were people around for Leslie to play to. Lew Leslie, it was understood, never lent money without an audience.

Born Lewis (Lev) Lessinsky in Orangeburg, New York, in 1886, Leslie had begun his theatrical career billed rather speciously as an impressionist, pointedly specializing in entertainment figures of the day whom his audiences, for the most part, could not ever have seen. After briefly teaming in vaudeville with vocalist Belle Baker and (Leslie always claimed) Walter Winchell, Leslie at some point began to refocus his energies away from mimicking talent toward discovering it, later insisting that a general boredom with performing had led to this pragmatic professional reorientation. Ben Bernie, Frank Fay, Phil Baker, and Bee Palmer were a few of the entertainment personalities whom Leslie, in time, took credit for having unearthed. It is certain that he brought Palmer and Baker with him to the Folies Bergère nightclub atop the Winter Garden Theatre around 1920 to star in his new cabaret revue there. It is also clear that Leslie, as early as anyone downtown, recognized Florence Mills's riveting appeal in her *Shuffle Along* performances and acted decisively upon this assessment, reconceiving the Folies Bergère as the Plantation Cafe in 1922 for the specific purpose of featuring her.

Florence Mills proved to be Leslie's star-crossed theatrical ticket to the big time. After introducing her in the *Plantation Revue* and moving the show to Broadway for a brief run, Leslie cleverly had devised *From Dover to Dixie* as an international vehicle for Mills— with an all-white first act of British and American talent and an all-black second act led by Mills—touring the show to London and Paris with smashing results. He would return to Europe with Mills twice more before her death, in a second *Plantation Revue* in 1925 and in an inaugural edition of *Blackbirds* in 1926, after presenting *From Dover to Dixie* in New York as *Dixie to Broadway*—minus the revue's all-white "Dover" section—in 1924, with commensurate success.

Leslie's stature as an impresario was founded entirely upon his facility for discovering and exploiting black talent. The producer combed the "Negro ranks" of vaudeville and Harlem cabaret revues, spotting and developing his own stars for each new Leslie production. His name in the Twenties soon grew so closely associated with black entertainment that it frequently came as a surprise to unsuspecting Broadway professionals and audiences alike that Lew Leslie was not himself black. What Lew Leslie was, consummately, was a man of the theater, a manic and in many ways intemperate perfectionist, who began planning his shows at least six to eight months prior to rehearsals, virtually closeting himself with his creative teams, working out every element of a show in advance. Like his successor at the Cotton Club, Dan Healy, Leslie prized pace in his productions, electrifying production speed, pursuing this quicksilver commodity through impossibly rigorous and protracted rehearsals. He also successfully translated to Broadway the Cotton Club's pioneering combination of racist, stereotypical Dixieana with sumptuous state-of-the-art production values, utilizing many of Broadway's finest white scenic, lighting, and costume artists to realize this blend seamlessly.

For the new, 1930 edition of his *Blackbirds* revue series, however, the erratic producer inexplicably broke with established Leslie racial form in hiring his creative staff, engaging Flournoy Miller to write the new *Blackbirds* book and Andy Razaf to contribute lyrics for a stellar company that included Buck and Bubbles (Buck Washington and John Bubbles, vaudeville's greatest black song and dance team), the outstanding comedian Mantan Moreland, Flournoy Miller, and, topping the bill, Ethel Waters. "Leslie, who had never wanted me before, asked Goldie and Gumm [Waters's theatrical lawyers] if they could get me," Waters later recalled. "Leslie had split up with Bill Bojangles [Robinson], his box-office ace-in-the-hole. Adelaide Hall, Leslie's other star, was in Europe . . . Leslie wanted me as his big name."

For his composer on the project, Leslie pursued Eubie Blake, still the musical kingpin of black Broadway, despite Blake's decided lack of success downtown since the pioneering appearance of *Shuffle Along* in 1921. Having recently separated from his lyric writing partner of fifteen years, Noble Sissle, Blake was available. He later recalled Leslie arriving at his home on West 138th Street to broach the subject of *Blackbirds*. Blake, even then the voice of experience, had but one question for Leslie: "Who's your publisher?" "Shapiro, Bernstein," Leslie replied, satisfying the veteran songwriter, who knew that a publisher's preproduction commitment to a show was a surety of funds for the composer. A $3,000 advance from Leslie sealed the commission for twenty-eight songs.

In many ways, Andy Razaf would find his most kindred songwriting spirit in Eubie Blake. One of the greatest of all early ragtime pianist–composers, Blake, born February 7, 1883, was a child of the Baltimore streets, raised by parents who were former slaves. An utterly inimitable figure who blended the robust bawdiness of formative years spent playing piano in East Coast saloons and sporting houses with a cultivation and refinement bred in his long association with James Europe's prewar "society" and Clef Club Orchestras, Razaf's newest collaborator was a vivacious, mischievous, sparkling companion, balding, small and slightly built, known to his friends as "Mouse," with a lustrous, profoundly theatrical melodic sense and a compositional facility on the order of Thomas Waller's.

Blake presented Razaf a particularly fresh musical perspective, more accomplished and far more versatile than anything or anyone he had yet worked with, perhaps excepting Waller. Blake also freed Razaf from the constraint of Waller's over sized performing personality. As Razaf later explained, "There [was] no way to write for Waller without being aware all of the time that he's the one who's going to perform what you write. When . . . writing to Eubie's music you never [had to] know. . . . Eubie's melodies [also] lent themselves so perfectly to sophisticated lyrics. . . . They were a challenge."

For Blake, on the other hand, Razaf was the quickest lyric study and the fastest lyric writer the composer had ever encountered. "He could write lyrics in the theater while everything else is goin' on," Blake later observed with no little wonderment, evidently unacquainted with the Waller/Razaf approach to spontaneous song composition. "You play a melody and he makes a whole new thing out of it. . . . He [also] never had to change anything. His meter was always *perfect* and he could write nearly as fast as I could whistle the tune. God, he was smart!"

Egged on by Blake, Razaf produced lyric writing which now seemed to take on a new dimension, though the initial songs of the collaboration, the novelty number "Tan Town Divorce," composed as early as February 1930, and "That Lindy Hop," with its throbbing, Gershwinesque melody line, only hinted at the riches to come. Late in June, working at Jennie Razaf Cole's 119 Atkins Avenue Asbury Park home, the team turned out one tune that was a gem, "You're Lucky to Me," an elegant ballad. It featured some of Razaf's most refined lyric work to date; with subtly fractured line scans, poised elegantly against the meter, that perfectly mirrored Blake's adventurous melody: "Never since a child, was I reconciled/By the folks who laughed at bugaboos/Hoodoos haunted me, trailed me constantly/Till the day you came my way with good news;/Whenever you're near all my fears disappear/Dear, it's plain as can be, you're lucky to me,/My only luck charms are your two loving arms,/Anybody can see, you're lucky to me." "Some of the intervals in 'Lucky To Me' were really innovative at the time," Razaf always delighted pointing out. "Ethel Waters enjoyed that song. She said: 'I've never sung changes like that before.' I told her: 'Neither has anyone else.'"

Razaf's beautiful live-in paramour, Minto Cato, was to be featured in *Blackbirds of 1930*, and Razaf pressed his partner to compose a new song specifically for her. Blake obliged with an extraordinary melody tailored to display Cato's extraordinary three-octave vocal range. If the Blake intervals for "You're Lucky to Me" were innovative, these for Cato's song were positively breathtaking— Blake's melody soared with unearthly aplomb while Razaf's lyric captured this sense of wistful flight with straightforward, unerring poignancy.

> *Why can't I forget like I should?*
> *Heaven knows I would if I could,*
> *But I just can't keep you off my mind.*
> *Tho' you've gone and love was in vain,*
> *All around me you still remain,*
> *Wonder why fate should be so unkind—*
>
> *Waking skies at sunrise,*
> *Every sunset too,*
> *Seems to be bringing me*
> *Memories of you.*
> *Here and there, ev'rywhere,*
> *Scenes that we once knew,*

And they all just recall
Memories of you.

How I wish I could forget
Those happy yesteryears
That have left a rosary
Of tears.
Your face beams in my dreams
'Spite of all I do,
Ev'rything seems to bring
Memories of you.

For Andy Razaf and Eubie Blake, too, "Memories of You" was a landmark composition, the most perfect ballad that either had yet written. The tune became a great hit, a staple of the American popular-song canon and an annuity for the two songwriters, their families, and their music publisher. "Memories of You" also helped propel Minto Cato to stardom, no doubt contributing immeasurably to Razaf's domestic contentment as well.

Lew Leslie's *Blackbirds of 1930* commenced its out-of-town tryout with a week at the Majestic Theatre in Brooklyn on September 1, 1930, the beginning of a grueling ordeal for Andy Razaf and the entire company at the hands of their impresario. Leslie had habitually imposed a tyrannical reign of chaos upon his productions during their pre-Broadway trials, hiring and firing performers at will, pinching pennies as no producing penny-pincher before him, reconfiguring production running orders before, after, and often during opening nights. On more than one occasion Leslie actually had leapt into orchestra pits in mid-performance to replace musicians and even conductors whose work did not meet his frenzied standards. From its inception, though, this *Blackbirds* preview period seems to have attained levels of hellishness unique even for a Leslie extravaganza. The opening night Playbill in Brooklyn gave a hint of what was to come, with a queer printed disclaimer that would appear in *Blackbirds* preview programs throughout the protracted out-of-town tour: "*Program subject to change owing to magnitude of production.*" "That show started off by almost being stranded in rehearsal," Ethel Waters later observed. "Leslie was splitting up quarters each day among the cast."

If Leslie's financial stability was in serious doubt from *Blackbirds'* very first day, matters appear to have been artistically promising, at least initially. Early Brooklyn reviews were favorable, though one critic from the *Brooklyn Eagle* did feel compelled to offer his condolences to those who had not seen the show in Brooklyn on opening night, "for it is certain," insisted the critic, "that Lew Leslie now will begin to mess with it." "Sure enough," remembered Eubie Blake, "when that asbestos curtain came down, [Leslie] called a rehearsal at one in the morning. Threw this out, changed that—tore the whole show apart."

Frustrated by Leslie's increasingly demented behavior and frightened by his own increasingly depressed financial situation (he was now sole support of both his former wife and his mother), Razaf began to keep a private journal on the entire *Blackbirds* experience shortly after the show's Brooklyn debut, recording in it all of his business and creative dealings with Lew Leslie. First he kept a strict record of his "Account with Blackbirds" in the journal, leaving behind the unmistakable picture of a production in desperate financial difficulty. On September 6, for example, Razaf apparently was paid the box office percentage owed to him for the week in Brooklyn, "2/3 of $62.50," according to his ledger, with the other third presumably going to Joe Davis. On September 8, *Blackbirds* opened a six-week run at the Shubert Lyric Theatre in Boston. On September 13, and again on September 20, Razaf was again paid his due—"2/3 of $88.30" and "2/3 of $100.00." Moneys for the week of the 27th, however—again "2/3 of $100.00"—apparently were not paid out until October 4, when Razaf recorded in his ledger a single $100.00 payment. For the final three weeks Razaf was not paid at all. His financial woes were further exacerbated by his managerial bondage to Joe Davis. In a telegram sent as far back as June by Elliot Shapiro of Shapiro, Bernstein to Razaf, at his mother's home in Asbury Park, Shapiro, apparently responding to a Razaf request for funds on advance, made clear his regrets "that inasmuch as you are writing to us through our arrangement with Joe Davis [we] must refer you to Davis for all money matters whatever that are paid you."

It is perhaps typical of Lew Leslie that even as he kept his company and production staff writhing in creative and financial turmoil, the Boston critics raved about the wonders he was working onstage. "Is it as good a show as the first edition?" asked the *Boston*

Post. "The answer is no; it is a better one. In fact it is one of the best all-colored revues that the stage has produced to date. Last night, number after number stopped the show.

"Eubie Blake wrote most of the music," the reviewer continued, unthinkingly slighting Blake's lyricist in his enthusiasm for *Blackbirds'* admittedly commanding orchestra director and composer. "Eubie Blake played one of the two grand pianos in the pit, with his own orchestra augmented to the number 30 by white players drawn from the local union forces. And it fell to Eubie Blake, performing from the piano, to sweep the house into a frenzy of applause when he and Miss Waters did the reprise 'Lucky to Me.' . . . Not since the memorable days of that famous first entrance of the chorus of 'Shuffle Along' has a number in a colored show made as great a hit . . .

"It was by no means the only feature of exceptional merit. The show abounds in them. The opening chorus of singers in 'Roll Jordan' and 'Cabin Door,' in that phrase dear to the heart of the trouper the world over, 'brought down the house.' The dancing of the colored chorus did it again and again as the evening proceeded. Buck and Bubbles stopped the show with their dancing. . . . So did the first entrance of Flournoy Miller. . . . So did Ethel Waters, with her first song hit. It became a habit.

"From the standpoint of last night's performance at the Lyric," concluded the *Post*, "it looks very much as though Mr. Leslie has accomplished that rare achievement in the theatre of repeating a former success; possibly even bettering it."

While Andy Razaf's lyric contribution to *Blackbirds* largely was overlooked by Boston's critical establishment, many of Razaf's lyrics for the show stand today among his very best. Alongside the perfection of "Memories of You" and "You're Lucky to Me," his most delightful work perhaps came in an uproarious specialty for Ethel Waters that generally left audiences limp after Waters trucked the song out in *Blackbirds'* second act "My Handy Man Ain't Handy No More." Fashioning the number as a devitalized follow-up to "My Handy Man," his unforgettable bawdy blues creation for Waters in 1928, Razaf again teased the boisterous, traditional stereotype by composing his lyric from the demurring point of view that had served him so well in previous song successes, injecting, however, a note of nastiness to the general naughty tone that in its spent powerlessness, no doubt reflected nothing so well as the torturous impotence under which Razaf obsessed, as he labored on Lew Leslie's *Blackbirds of 1930* in Boston.

Once I used to brag about my Handy Man
But I ain't braggin' no more.
Somethin' strange has happened to my Handy Man,
He's not the man he was before.
Wish somebody could explain to me
About this dual personality:

He don't perform his duties like he used to do,
He never hauls his ashes 'less I tell him to,
Before he hardly gets to work he says he's through,
My Handy Man ain't handy no more.
The way he used to handle things was "too bad, Jim,"
That man was so efficient, full of pep and vim,
Altho' he looks the same, I know it just ain't him,
My Handy Man ain't handy no more.
He's forgotten his domestic science
And he's lost his self-reliance;
He won't make a single move unless he's told.
He says he isn't lazy, claims he isn't old
But still he sits round and lets my stove get cold,
My Handy Man ain't handy no more.

Time after time, if I'm not right there at his heels,
He lets that poor horse in my stable miss his meals,
There's got to be some changes 'cause each day reveals
My Handy Man ain't handy no more.
He used to turn in early and get up at dawn,
All full of new ambitions, he would trim the lawn;
Now when he isn't sleeping all he does is yawn,
My Handy Man ain't handy no more.

Once he used to have so much endurance,
Now it looks like he needs life insurance;
I used to brag about my Handy Man's technique,
Around the house he was a perfect indoor sheik
But now 'The spirit's willing but the flesh is weak':
My Handy Man ain't handy no more.

*

"Never has any writer been forced to write under such handicaps and still [be] expected to deliver first class material," Razaf wrote in an undated journal entry while still in Boston—his header for these particular jottings reading simply, "Experiences with Blackbirds— Notes."

> My trip to Boston, at my own expense, has been a most humiliating and heartbreaking experience. With the burden of my mother's financial troubles plus those of my own, surrounded by debts, penniless, and with no consideration from Joe Davis or Mr. Leslie, I have struggled along, often hungry, and at all times obliged to ask my landlady to wait. Imagine, the writer of a show and a total stranger in Boston, worse off than any chorus girl of the show; under these humiliating circumstances, still called upon to do creative work. In the midst of all this, I cheerfully remained at the theatre twice within the week until six and seven A.M. to write additional numbers and deliver my part in full.
>
> Tho everyone on the show was paid for the week of Sept. 27th, I alone wasn't given a cent, tho the management was aware of my condition. I am awaiting this week's payday, wondering if the outcome will be the same. If such is the case, I shall be forced to return to New York, and for this I shall of course be called a 'bad fellow.' And still men speak of justice.

While the substance of this heartfelt diatribe confirms the fundamental hardships of a Lew Leslie pre–Broadway tryout tour, the entry reveals far more about Andy Razaf himself. Most forceful is the sense of Razaf's towering pride. Humiliation, again and again, is the subject of Razaf's wailing "experiences." Also impossible to ignore is the lyricist's hugely self-dramatizing, near paranoic sense of himself as an isolated, solitary victim. It is hard to imagine why Razaf alone would have been singled out by Lew Leslie to be slighted financially; probably either Razaf by this point was himself in debt to the producer on advances drawn, or more members of the company than Razaf knew or was *willing* to know about also were not being paid. Above all else, it seems clear that, having endured innumerable instances of humiliation and bitter victimization throughout his years on Tin Pan Alley and Broadway, Razaf now had begun to perceive of himself, proudly but just a bit shamelessly, as something of a martyr.

It nevertheless remains tragic that Razaf felt so desperately trapped and alone with *Blackbirds* in Boston, though similarly pointless to wonder why he did not simply resign from the production and save himself further pain. There was no place for Andy Razaf to go from *Blackbirds*, nothing to resign *for*. Already Broadway was reeling from the Depression, and Broadway continued to be Andy Razaf's greatest aspiration. To abandon a Lew Leslie production would have been the ultimate humiliation.

Lew Leslie's *Blackbirds of 1930*, "Glorifying the American Negro," opened in New York City on October 22, 1930, at the Royale Theatre on West 45th Street, in the veritable heart of a Broadway theater district that already was slipping from its former glory. "We opened right next to the flea circus," Ethel Waters later wrote, "and the fleas outdrew us at every performance. [Then] the Depression came in and made our business worse. But it didn't dent the flea circus."

Despite its first-rate ensemble, despite "Memories of You," "You're Lucky to Me," and "My Handy Man Ain't Handy No More," despite costumes designed by the very young Vincente Minnelli, vocal arrangements by J. Rosamond Johnson, Eubie Blake in the pit and Lew Leslie in the wings, *Blackbirds of 1930* closed on Broadway after sixty-two performances. The show then limped down to Philadelphia. Razaf's back salary was approaching $750 at this point, unpaid since the third week in Boston.

From Philadelphia, Lew Leslie led his *Blackbirds* company to Newark, New Jersey, where he stranded the show. "The back of my car almost broke down under the weight of all the entertainers I drove back to Harlem with me," recalled Ethel Waters, who seems to have behaved throughout this ordeal with impressive, nearly maternal solicitude, having recently even driven Razaf's last $15 to his mother in Asbury Park, "leaving me penniless," as Razaf mournfully noted in his *Blackbirds* journal, "up to my neck in debt."

By the end of January 1931, details of *Blackbirds'* final sad hours had made the newspapers. "Within the next few days," reported the *Amsterdam News*, "all Harlem will be told the story of the fall from grace of Lew Leslie, producer of the famous *Blackbirds*, which, along with a number of other shows this season, met with reverses which made it utterly impossible for the production to continue. Heroic attempts were made after Leslie pulled up stakes from Broadway and landed in Philadelphia in time to put in a glorious week," insisted the *News*—clearly loath to disparage a producer who had done much, in the view of many uptown, to display "the

Negro" in the very best possible light downtown before white audiences—"but this only prolonged the agony, if the stories being told by the actors formerly with the show can be believed."

The *News* proceeded to unfold an unseemly story of indefensible seediness, describing how "Leslie had not only the cast but all the world believing that the offering would go into Washington after the Newark engagement which closed last Saturday night after what is said to have been a disastrous week, at the end of which, people learned for the first time, that as near as Washington as they would get this trip would be Washington Street on the way to Harlem.

"The first real indication of what would be came some weeks ago," the *News* maintained, "when Flournoy Miller slapped an attachment on the box office in Philadelphia from royalties due him, which, it is said, was followed by a warrant being issued for Mr. Leslie, who was arrested and admitted to bail by a Philadelphia judge." It is interesting and quite characteristic that Razaf, despite his own woeful complains against Leslie, never seems to have sought legal action against the producer in this fashion. Impassively trusting to the end, Razaf, along with the balance of *Blackbirds'* large company, apparently, according to the *Amsterdam News*, "upon their arrival in Newark . . . expected to make the trip to the nation's capital, albeit many did wonder about the roundabout bookings, when it had previously been announced that the show was also to play the Maryland Theatre at Baltimore, advertisements to that effect having been inserted in Negro papers."

It is sobering to perceive the delicacy with which the *Amsterdam News* here felt compelled to present a story that was, in essence, irredeemably tawdry, however sad. Leslie's final, fatal machinations surrounding *Blackbirds* had been quite ruthless. "It is said that representatives of Leslie, before informing the company at the last minute of the closing of the production, saw to it that the costumes were safely packed and the scenery out of the way before breaking the news to the people," the *News* reported. "Looking at the matter with a calm eye," the paper nevertheless concluded, "it is possible to state that Leslie simply found himself in that position of many white men backing colored shows before, and turning everywhere in a frenzy to extricate himself from the depths to which he was carried by the failure of the 1930s edition of his show, he is said to have made promises which he could not live up to. . . ."

The Twenties were at an end. The wave that had swept Andy Razaf to moderate prominence downtown, the wave of the "Black Vogue" on Broadway, also had reached its ending—though neither the *Amsterdam News* nor Andy Razaf himself could yet bring themselves to admit it. The evasions, the justifications, the rationalizing by blacks in Harlem for the rudeness with which they had been embraced downtown by the white powers of Broadway, no longer had much purpose. Broadway no longer perceived profit in their presence and blacks uptown, like Razaf, sensed that the dawning economic disaster was about to bury all semblance of their recent inroads downtown, as well as some of the social, political, and cultural advances that African Americans so gradually had seized for themselves over the course of the Twenties. Looking grimly into the ashes of Lew Leslie's *Blackbirds*, all that many black Harlemites could do, as the *Amsterdam News* quietly concluded, was "to regret that another batch of performers have been thrown out of work at a time when they need it most." The truth of this narrow, simple statement pointed to a tragedy of infinitely greater dimensions that now could be made out on a not so distant horizon.

Courtesy Razaf Estate.

How Can You Face Me?

Love em', leave em', and deceive 'em,
Seems to be your game,
My romance was just your new affair;
I was happy, oh, so happy,
Till the waking came,
Now I know I was a fool to care:
How can you face me?
After what I've gone thru,
All on account of you,
Tearing my heart in two.

> — *"How Can You Face Me?"*
> by Andy Razaf and Thomas Waller

"Tin Pan Alley—Say, don't let them fool you with colorful yarns about this place," wrote entertainment columnist Sidney Skolsky in his *Daily News* column on May 24, 1933. "Those writers are telling you of yesterday's Alley. You might as well know the truth.

"A person can't come to Broadway and make a fortune for a song. Nobody is buying songs anymore, the radio has ruined that industry. There's no real money to be made in songwriting. You've got to have a good job and make songwriting your sideline. . . . The great wonder is that there are any songwriters still writing songs. What money there is in songwriting now is earned by writing a score for a picture or show.

"Poor little popular song," concluded Skolsky. "It doesn't stand a chance even if it's a hit; publishers today are almost frightened when one of their writers comes in with a new melody or lyric. There's no money in hit songs, they're afraid they won't get back the cost of publishing. A song has to pay for itself and great songs don't mean a thing anymore. They're just an echo in the Alley now."

The Depression had hit Tin Pan Alley full force by 1933, where it was said more songwriters were reminiscing full time on curbs in the vicinity of Longacre Square than doing anything else. No music sold, just memories traded idly in the late afternoon along Seventh Avenue, memories of pre-Depression days and fat royalty checks, memories of Irving Berlin earning more than $80,000 for one song, "Always," and more than $60,000 for "All by Myself," which had sold for seventy-five weeks back in 1926 and 1927; a million copies of sheet music, a million phonograph records, 150,000 piano rolls. Irving Berlin as solace for the idled on Tin Pan Alley in 1933, "America's Greatest Writer of Popular Songs." One more yardstick by which to measure collapse.

For Andy Razaf in 1933 there was very little Depression-generated nostalgia. He could never have afforded the indulgence. Success and collapse had long been such relative states for a black songwriter, conditions to be calculated primarily in units of relative frustration. Since 1928, few Tin Pan Alley lyricists had sold more songs than Andy Razaf (some 200-plus), yet into 1933, he still had never stopped struggling, selling his songs scattershot, pitching at any publisher who gave him ten minutes in an office downtown or saved them both the trouble by riding uptown some late night to buy a few numbers over drinks at the Rhythm Club, up the block from Connie's Inn. With Tin Pan Alley in disarray and Broadway restoring a de facto exclusionary rule over the black creators who so recently had graced its musical comedy stages, he took what he could get.

The most galling song market issue of the Depression for Razaf and his fellow black songwriters was not, in any event, centered around Tin Pan Alley, but rather directed toward Hollywood. Beginning in the late Twenties, with the successful introduction of "talking pictures," the film colony's influence over Tin Pan Alley had grown to virtual dominance. M. Witmark & Sons had been the first publishing house to be purchased by a West Coast film studio when Warner Brothers acquired it late in 1928. Since then, mergers and acquisitions had proliferated as the song business slowly was transmuted from sheet music purveyor for the nation to song product supplier for the movies.

The release of the first all-talking feature film, *Lights of New York*, by Warner Brothers' Vitaphone division on July 6, 1928, had combined with the stock market crash in October 1929 to precipitate an unprecedented exodus of songwriting talent from New York City to Hollywood. With sheet music sales in retreat and Broadway lapsing into moribund inactivity, the film industry's increasingly insatiable appetite for original music to ornament its newly expressive medium had rescued a substantial percentage of Tin Pan Alley's best songwriters from financial oblivion.

Unfortunately for black songwriters like Razaf, this percentage proved to be exclusively white. As early as 1929, in the wake of *Hot Chocolates'* Broadway success, Joe Davis had endeavored to subvert this trend with a series of advertisments in the entertainment trades. "MOTION PICTURE PRODUCERS!!" these ads had announced:

> We have now at your disposal the most prolific songwriters
> of the day:
> ANDY RAZAF and PAUL DENNIKER
> These writers are under contract to write exclusively
> for us and are prepared to write songs to fit any situation.
> They are composers of our current hits . . . "SPOSIN'" and
> "PERHAPS."
>
> ANDY RAZAF is the Writer of the Successful Musical Comedy
> Show Now Playing New York, "HOT CHOCOLATES," with the
> song hits
> "Ain't Misbehavin'"—"Rhythm Man" and others.
> He also wrote "Dusky Stevedore."
> If interested in securing the services of the above writers
> Wire—Write—Phone or See
> Joe Davis CIrcle-9124 1024 or 3141
>
> Triangle Music Pub. Co., Inc.   1658 B'wy. N.Y.C.

In 1932, the Harlem-based *Inspiration* magazine, in its "Theatrical Notes" column, had reported that "Andy Razaf is writing the music for Mae West's next picture, in collaboration with James P. Johnson," offering no further details on the project. West, as the white theatrical embodiment of sexuality and general naughtiness on Broadway, had been a frequenter of black Gaiety Building publishing offices throughout the Twenties in search of fresh bawdy song material for her repertoire. Despite West's acknowledged professional acquaintance with Perry Bradford, James P. Johnson, and other black songwriters, this purported Razaf–Johnson film score never seems to have materialized though. Nor did Joe Davis's promotional effort produce any noticeable results. The entrenched racism of an otherwise extremely open-handed song-hiring hierarchy in Hollywood kept Andy Razaf scrabbling for song work in New York City.

Of course, Razaf was by now an exceedingly seasoned and accomplished scrabbler. His song hits during the early Thirties came at a rate of at least one per year, all in collaboration with Thomas Waller and all of an exceptionally high quality, beginning with "Concentratin' on You," a surrealistic, freely associative lyric romp for Razaf through the delirium of infatuation:

> *Seems that I'm goin' cuckoo,*
> *Dizzy as I can be,*
> *Since the day we met,*
> *I've been all upset,*
> *Something's happened to me,*
> *All I've got, I find,*
> *Is a one-track mind:*
> *At times I'm out of my head,*
> *I act indiscreet,*
> *Forgetful the whole day through,*
> *I can't think of*
> *Nothin' but love,*
> *Concentratin' on you.*
> *At home I have my own bed,*
> *But sleep on the seat,*
> *I can't figure two and two,*
> *Oh, how I rave,*
> *Nearin' my grave,*
> *Concentratin' on you.*
>
> *I had a perfect memory*
> *Until you came to town,*
> *Now since your spell is over me,*
> *Boy, I'm bughouse-bound.*

I put my shoe on my head,
My hat on my feet,
Forgetful the whole day through,
I can't think of
Nothin' but love,
Concentratin' on you.
I put my clothes on the bed,
Sleep on the street,
I can't figure two and two,
Got crazy ways,
I'm in a daze,
Concentratin' on you.

I had a perfect memory
Until you came along,
Now since your spell is over me,
My brain seems all wrong.
Sometimes I stand in my flat,
Don't know where I'm at,
I pay bills before they're due,
I got you to thank,
My mind's a blank,
Concentratin' on you.

"Keepin' out of Mischief Now," from 1932, was perhaps Razaf's most disarming lyric concoction, a lyric again written from the characteristic Razafian stance of a roué retiring avowedly for love:

Don't even go to a movie show,
If you're not by my side,
I just stay home by my radio
But I'm satisfied;
All my flirting days are gone,
On the level from now on.

Keepin' out of mischief now,
Really am in love and how.
I'm through playing with fire,
It's you whom I desire.
All the world can plainly see,
You're the only one for me;
I have told them in advance,

They can't break up our romance,
Livin' up to every vow,
Keepin' out of mischief now.

Don't go for any excitement now,
Books are my best company,
All my opinions have changed somehow,
Old fashioned as can e.
When you really learn to care,
There's a thrill in solitaire.

Keepin' out of mischief now,
Really am in love and how.
I have told them in advance,
They can't break up our romance,
Livin' up to every vow,
I'm keepin' out of mischief now.

Finally, in 1933, Razaf and Waller had composed "Ain't-Cha' Glad?"—a blissful evocation of romantic contentment in perfectly concise stanzas:

Ain't-cha' glad,
We were mated for each other?
Ain't-cha' glad
That we waited for each other?
We agree
Constantly,
Life is just a symphony
Of perfect harmony,
Ain't-cha' glad
How we get along together?
Ain't-cha' glad
We can laugh at "stormy weather"?
Folks declare
"What a pair!"
They can see we're happy,
Ain't-cha' glad?

Just like two lovers
On picture covers,
In spite of sun or rain,
We find romance,

Ev'ry street we meet
Is lover's lane.
Ain't-cha' glad
That our kisses keep their flavor?
Ain't-cha' glad
Ev'rything is in our favor?
Ev'ry day
We can say,
Ev'rything is rosy,
Ain't-cha' glad?

In the diminished economic terms of the Depression, Razaf's initial Thirties success on Tin Pan Alley had been sizable, so much so that in late September of 1932, Razaf had petitioned ASCAP's Classification Board for an upgrading of his status within the organization. "I have no desire to exaggerate my ability as a writer." Razaf wrote, "but as my work has continued to be consistent and outstanding (and never through proxy or cut-ins), I sincerely believe that I merit a promotion. This year my 'Keepin' out of Mischief Now,' 'If It Ain't Love,' and others have received more than their share of radio honors. Since Tin Pan Alley seems more concerned about radio plugs than sheet music or records, I mention this."

On October 4, the ASCAP board affirmed Razaf's upgrading to their "CC Class," hardly the top of the organization's earnings pyramid, but a highly respectable position, to be sure.

It was Razaf's work with Waller, of course, throughout the years 1930 to 1933, that held out the greatest promise for the lyricist's continued professional advancement despite economic hard times. Their work together during this period generated over twenty songs including the three major hits, as well as lesser jewels like "How Can You Face Me?," "If It Ain't Love" (with Don Redman), and "Strange as It Seems." Waller, however, had been moving in a very different direction since the closing of *Hot Chocolates* on the road in early 1930, a direction that relegated songwriting to a secondary activity for Razaf's ebullient collaborator, nearly dwarfed as it was by his mounting success as pianist and vocalist.

For years, the subject of Waller's vocalizing had been much discussed among his intimate friends, including George Maines and especially Razaf. It had long been Razaf's opinion, supported by many others, that Waller's insouciant, modestly developed, irresistibly appealing crooning style possessed far more value than Waller was willing to acknowledge. Inherently shy and insecure, the young pianist had chosen to stick resolutely with the piano throughout the Twenties, despite Razaf's insistence that Waller should, at the very least, handle the singing chores when the team was demonstrating new songs to a publisher. Gradually, Waller did begin to give in to his partner's blandishments, accompanying Razaf vocally on occasion in publishing demonstrations and eventually surrendering himself with increasing frequency to solo vocal performances that clearly delighted the publishing staffers for whom he deigned to sing. This delight was made concrete for both Razaf and Waller with larger advances and easier sales whenever Waller agreed to act as song demonstrator. The powerful allure of this oversized, pudgy man—child with the impossibly active eyebrows and hilariously expressive face, casually crooning his own songs with offhand bemusement while accompanying himself brilliantly and effortlessly on the piano, was increasingly plain to the publishers of Tin Pan Alley, as well as to Razaf and Waller themselves.

Inevitably, Joe Davis began to parlay this allure into a paying gig. Early in December 1930, Waller had appeared on a CBS radio series, *Paramount on Parade,* at the invitation of an executive who'd appreciated Waller's work the previous year at the Paramount Theatre on Broadway, when Waller had filled in for the Paramount's regular organist, Jessie Crawford. Waller had begun to sing spontaneously on these *Paramount on Parade* programs, for reasons known only to himself and perhaps Joe Davis. The moderately approving response that greeted his vocalizing over the course of the show's thirteen-week run had then given Davis a platform for pushing his client to recording companies not solely as a pianist but as a vocalist, too. Though Victor, Waller's regular record company, was not interested in "a singing Fats Waller," Davis eventually had prevailed upon his old friend Frank Walker at Columbia to bring Waller in for a session. Walker had, in turn, somehow persuaded popular clarinetist/showman Ted Lewis that this young black musician not only should be his pianist on the upcoming Lewis record date with Columbia but that the young player should be allowed to sing as well. The session on March 5 had produced two sides, one—"I'm Draggin' My Heart Around"—with a Ted Lewis vocal, the other—"I'm Crazy 'bout My Baby"— featuring Waller's first vocal on record, backed by a stellar Ted Lewis band, including cornetist Mugsy Spanier, saxophonist Bud Freeman, trombonist George

Brunies, and Benny Goodman on clarinet. Both songs, predictably enough, were Joe Davis publishing properties.

In the wake of this debut, Davis had secured further radio work for Waller on another CBS program, *Radio Roundup*, marketing his client strongly now as a piano/vocalist and general all-around entertainer. Waller meanwhile was casually honing his entertaining skills working in a Greenwich Village nightspot known as the Hotfeet Club, a basement dive at 142 West Houston Street, where he filled out a band led by former Duke Ellington reedman Otto Hardwick and soloed on piano while performing his own miniature cabaret act full of lampooning chat and broad, raunchy patter, highlighted by his rendition of partner Razaf's "My Handy Man."

In July of 1931, Spencer Williams, who had been back in New York working primarily with Andy Razaf for the previous two years, returned to Paris and, with little difficulty, persuaded Waller to join him. Waller, in Paris proved to be as much in his element as Waller in Harlem; the nights were endless, piano driven, and gin soaked. Hugues Panassié, a French jazz enthusiast, soon to be one of the first serious music critics of the medium, recorded his recollections of Waller at this time.

> He was there [at the 'La Rumba' club] from half-an-hour after midnight. I had nothing to complain of: he played a great deal . . .
>
> I found almost as much pleasure in watching him as in listening to him. His appearance when he played was a complete reflection of his style. The body leaned slightly backwards, a half-smile on the lips which seemed to say, "I'm really enjoying myself; wait a bit, now listen to that, not bad, eh?" He rested his hands on the piano and hardly moved them at all, his fingers alone seeking out the necessary notes.
>
> He only raised his hands a very little from the keyboard. Thus the incredible power of his playing proceeds not so much from the rapidity of his attack as from its heaviness. Its force is . . . muscular. Instead of bringing his impetus from a height to strike the keys brutally, rather does Fats attack them very closely, and seems to want to bury them in the piano. This is surely why his playing, in spite of its terrific force, appears so much more placid than that of other pianists.
>
> It is well-known that Fats is not only a magnificent improvisator but also one of the best and most famous composers of jazz.

Some of his pieces have been great successes, played by all the orchestras. I was not backward in asking him to interpret some of them, especially "Ain't Misbehavin'" and "Handful of Keys." When I asked him to play "Sweet Savannah Sue," however, I was most surprised to see that he could not remember it at all.

Back in the States in the fall of 1931, and in need of a steady job, Waller had returned to Joe Davis's Broadway publishing office, renewing his employment agreement with Davis, who also found Waller a manager, one Marty Bloom. By 1932, the inexperienced Bloom had given way to the vastly experienced veteran theatrical agent Philip Ponce, who soon embarked on a shrewdly conceived marketing strategy for breaking Thomas "Fats" Waller beyond New York City through the medium of radio. Commencing with a one-shot solo appearance on Cincinnati radio station WLW, a station whose powerful signal blanketed the Midwest and could be received in cities across the nation, Ponce soon had negotiated a two-year contract with WLW for his client, setting Waller up with his own program, *Fats Waller's Rhythm Club,* as well as a half-hour, late-night (anonymously performed) set of uninterrupted romantic organ music billed as the *Moon River* program. It was while working on what quickly became a rather raucous Rhythm Club that Waller truly had begun to exercise the verbal dexterity, devastating wit, and outrageous lyric deconstructions that soon became a central part of his performing personality, distracting himself and amusing his unseen radio audience by satirizing the often inane popular song lyrics he was forced to sing on the show. Waller quickly became so confident and comfortable in his new singing, tongue-wagging radio persona that the end of one Rhythm Club broadcast found him launching into a protracted peroration on the malignancy of music publishers who were stealing the earnings of their creative artists, his uncharacteristically pointed harangue ending only with program announcer Paul Stewart's tide-stemming sign-off: "Now it's time to say goodbye to Fats Waller and his music, and even if it weren't time, it would be a good idea."

Throughout 1932, while Waller had commuted to New York City from his "little white house near the Cincinnati airport," Razaf had remained in Harlem writing floor shows for Connie's Inn, with and without his partner: the 1932 Spring Revue *Hot Harlem,* with Waller (and Spencer Williams), the 1932 Fall Revue *Harlem Hotcha* with James P. Johnson.

Hot Chocolates had put Connie's Inn on the national entertainment map. The Immerman brothers soon capitalized on this new-found recognition by repackaging *Hot Chocolates* yearly for export beyond New York City, frequently first trying out these "tab" productions at the Lafayette Theatre up the avenue from their nightclub, and at other neighborhood Harlem theaters, for a flat $2,500 per booking. The Immermans had counted on their resident celebrity bandleader, Louis Armstrong, to headline these new *Hot Chocolates* editions. Thus when Armstrong concluded his post–*Hot Chocolates* stint at Connie's Inn in early 1930 to lead the Luis Russell band on an extended tour of the United States (and ultimately Europe), the Immermans had been miffed, delaying Armstrong's June 1931 opening at the Suburban Gardens in New Orleans with their claim that the trumpeter had jumped his contract with them. Armstrong, in turn, had then sued the Immermans and his former manager Tommy Rockwell to "restrain them from interfering with his bookings, alleging threats against his life if he left their management."

After Armstrong's exit from Connie's Inn, violinist/conductor Allie Ross had come in to lead the band for the spring season of 1930, with Waller appearing irregularly at this time as well, generally performing on a small, white, piano-shaped Esty organ that the Immermans had installed in February for his exclusive use in an effort to encourage their professionally hyperactive former delivery boy to continue hanging around. That fall, the Immermans also had pulled off a huge booking coup, signing Fletcher Henderson and his orchestra away from Roseland with a one-year contract that kept Henderson at the Inn roughly from November 30, 1930, through September 1931. It had been during this stint that Henderson's star trombonist, Jimmy Harrison, then dying of cancer, apparently was fired by Henderson on Connie Immerman's orders after Harrison publicly protested a new Immerman dictum forbidding band musicians from speaking to chorus girls in the floor show. "This is a helluva place," Harrison was widely quoted as having announced, "when one can't speak to his own kind."

Henderson's replacement at the Inn in October 1931 had been Fats Waller himself, leading, at the age of 27, his first full-scale dance orchestra. Waller's sojourn was brief; the gig largely had been conceived as a break-in period for the band prior to embarking on a formal Waller tour. The Immermans then briefly had reemployed Leroy Smith and his band as a replacement for Waller during the latter half of November, before bringing in an entirely new aggregation in December, anchored by a handful of former McKinney's Cotton Pickers led by Don Redman. It was this group that had performed nightly in the new Razaf/Waller/Spencer Williams revue *Hot Harlem*, as choreographed and produced by Leonard Harper in the early months of 1932. Featuring The Four Mills Brothers, "Snake Hips" Tucker, Cora Green, and a number of *Hot Chocolates* alumni, including Baby Cox and Louise Cook, the revue—performed twice nightly in two distinct programs—had offered a number of fairly memorable new songs, including Waller, Williams, and Razaf's delightful "Do Me a Favor Lend Me a Kiss," Waller, Redman, and Razaf's "If It Ain't Love," and Waller and Razaf's "Stealin' Apples."

With Waller in Cincinnati by the latter months of 1932, Razaf next had tackled the Inn's Fall Revue score together with James P. Johnson, composing fourteen songs for a production that *Variety*'s Abel Green marvelously summed up in deathless *Variety* prose, following the revue's September opening under the title *Harlem Hotcha*:

> It packs a flock of talent, with the crack Don Redman Orchestra as the attraction for customers on the hoof, and per usual will get more than its share of the black and tan trade.
>
> "Red and Struggle" are a new pair of eccentric comedians with a new style of exaggerated panto-Negroid comedy. They'll be heard from along legit comedy lines in time. Both men are in eccentric get-up. Red, as his name indicates, being a hi-yaller with an auburn tint to his thatch. The other is under cork . . .
>
> There's the hotcha Louise Cook, of the tossing torso, who's been a panic at Connie's for several seasons now with her torrid terping . . . Cora Green, as ever, does snappy double-entendre lyrics, subtly captioned "Madame T.N.T.," the saga of a girl who isn't modest in lyrically interpreting her romantic exploits, and "Can't Take It Papa," which speaks for itself . . .
>
> Paul and Barbara Meeres are the s.a. of the show in legit ballroomology. She's a handsome Creole who . . . could be built up by the least ingenuous p.a. for swell copy. Paul Meeres rates as the Gable of Harlem. For the ofay fem customers he's always been a topic of conversation.
>
> Snakehips Tucker seconded the cute Bessie Dudley with the fastest hip and roll motions this side of the old Barbary Coast . . . She's a personable trick with a hoydenish crop of hair and both

know how to sell their stuff without bothering the spaggety-spagades too much.

Jazzlips Richardson is a familiar in vaude and elsewhere. Louise Cook in "Drums," a barbaric African conception, was very tom-tom, with Willie Jackson doing the black captive stuff . . .

Lucky Seven Trio, if they haven't been in vaude, should be . . . The Four Dancing Fools are. They do wow hoofing on heel, toe, and broken arches.

The exotic Cookie, who came into Broadway cognizance generally aside from the Harlem night loafers, is the pash of the show and an eyeful considering the epidermic expose.

Don Redman, southpaw maestro, knows his rhythmpation—and how. Like all the premier dusky batonists he has a natural sense of pace and knows how to mix up those tunes and tempos which is what pitches the Castles into demi-delirium about a band being sizzling. Besides which they have the basic merit to back it up.

Through it all Connie himself is prominent as the director–stage manager, cueing everybody and everything from encores to recalcitrant couvert charges.

It had been during the 1932 summer run of *Hot Harlem* at Connie's Inn that Vincent "Mad Dog" Coll thought to kidnap Connie Immerman. Coll, Dutch Schultz's great "bad guy" rival in New York City, knew there was substantial ransom money to be realized with an Immerman "snatch," beyond the fundamental pleasure Coll would derive from terrifying Connie Immerman and infuriating the Dutchman. Where Coll's caper eventually had gone wrong was in the timing: Connie Immerman, it turned out, was not on the premises the night that Coll's thugs came for him at the Inn; Coll's boys had been obliged to grab brother George instead. They held him for three days before the Immermans' mother finally made contact with the gangsters and got a ransom sum named for her son's release. With arrangements for the transfer finally in place, George Immerman had been delivered to Connie's Inn as planned. Trigger-happy policemen, however, had opened fire prematurely, missing the kidnappers (who apparently escaped, lootless) but nearly nailing brother George.

George Immerman's heart condition had been rather serious

before his run-in with Mad Dog Coll. Now he and a mortified Connie Immerman quickly concluded that the time for their healthful withdrawal from Harlem nightlife had come.

Of course the arrival of Prohibition's "Repeal" in January 1933 helped speed a great number of New York nightlife professionals into early retirement. Owney Madden had bowed out of his Cotton Club in May to take up residence in Sing Sing voluntarily on a minor parole violation, painlessly cleansing his record for a new, ostensibly straight life, post–Prohibition. Connie's Inn also closed in May 1933, an era's end for Harlem nightlife and, particularly, for Andy Razaf and Fats Waller, who had together attained their creative peak in the basement confines of Connie and George Immerman's "black and tan" establishment. Razaf's conflicted sense of the occasion was perhaps best summed up by a poem that he had published in the *Amsterdam News* some months prior to the Inn's formal demise, an elegy entitled simply *The Tree of Hope*, after the Harlem entertainment talisman and congregating landmark that still stood in front of Connie's Inn, off the uptown lane of Seventh Avenue.

> Under the weary Tree of Hope
>   A sad performer stands.
> His ribs (from months of "miss-meal cramps")
>   Stand out like iron bands,
> His brow is wet with gin-mill sweat,
>   Reefer stains are on his hands.
>
> And there he talks from sun to sun
>   Of the shows that he has stopped,
> But never once will he admit
>   The times that he has flopped;
> He brags about the dough he's earned
>   And the dough that he has dropped.
>
> He says show business has been ruined
>   By the chiselers in the game;
> That they treat performers worse than dogs
>   And their salaries are a shame,
> But it has never occurred to him
>   That he has himself to blame.
>
> He never stands up like a man
>   For his profession's sake,
> But plays the role of Uncle Tom

When his own job is at stake;
He'll play a dozen shows a day—
    Any cut he'll gladly take.

Week in, week out, from year to year,
    This same performer goes;
Nothing attempted, nothing done
    But installment cars and clothes;
Just a "big-timer," never looking
    Further than his nose.

Thanks, thanks to thee, my stupid friend
    For the lessons thou hast taught:
The chances and the coin you've had
    Mean absolutely naught.
What would you have, the money now
    Or the gin that you have bought?

Despite the brutal blow to his career that the closing of Connie's Inn constituted, Razaf persevered throughout the latter months of 1933. On July 27, he and Waller performed their song hits together on a Thursday night "Showboat Cruise" up the Hudson, alongside a host of outstanding popular songwriters, including "Stardust" lyricist Mitchell Parish. On August 20, he and Waller again performed publicly together, this time on Sterling Furniture's *Hour of Cheer* WMCA radio program. Then, in the fall of 1933, Razaf realized an incomparable nightclub coup with the interpolation of one of his own songs, "That's What I Like 'Bout the South"—words and music by Razaf—into the twenty-third edition of Dan Healy's Cotton Club Parade. Though the club's rigid whites-only admission policy over the previous few years had been marginally relaxed to enable relatives and friends of performers, as well as a select handful of black celebrities, to take seats inside the Cotton Club's segregated premises, frequently at back tables close to the kitchen, the exclusion of black creative talent (beyond former in-house bandleader Duke Ellington) had remained just about ironclad at Owney Madden's "Aristocrat of Harlem." Now, in a Cotton Club revue whose score, anomalously, was not the work of one white songwriting team—like McHugh and Fields or Harold Arlen and Ted Koehler— but a conglomeration of white writers including McHugh, and Arlen's younger brother Jerry, Razaf's song presence was quite extraordinary. His song contribution itself, a rapid-paced, tongue-twisting novelty number performed during the show's lengthy opening by Cotton Club bandleader Cab Calloway, accompanied by Dusty Fletcher, Gallie Gaston, and a chorus line of Cotton Club girls (including the teenaged Lena Horne), was picked up, in time, as something of a signature tune by entertainer Phil Harris. Until Razaf threatened him with a lawsuit, Harris also chose to credit himself with having penned the song.

*

Since opening in December 1928 alongside the Hotel Trenier, Chicago's finest "colored" hostelry, a striking edifice of red brick and white terra cotta at the corner of Oakwood Boulevard and South Parkway on the city's South Side, the mob-owned Grand Terrace Cafe had dominated Chicago nightlife with lavish, Cotton Club–scale revues and black talent. While the premises, the furnishings, the talent, and the profit at the Grand Terrace were all the property of Al Capone, the house band nominally belonged to Louis Armstrong's former piano cohort in Chicago, Earl "Fatha" Hines. One of the great pianists of his generation, Hines broadcasted live from the Terrace over a CBS network radio wire on a weekly basis, an arrangement that benefited both bandleader and nightclub in much the same way that remote broadcasts had secured nationwide celebrity for Duke Ellington and Owney Madden's Cotton Club in the late Twenties.

Ed Fox, manager of the Grand Terrace, hired the very best for his floor shows backing Hines. On *Rhythm for Sale*, as the new 1933 winter revue was called, Andy Razaf was brought in to collaborate with his regular Connie's Inn stage director Leonard Harper and his frequent composing parter Paul Denniker, suggesting that the Grand Terrace assignment most likely came through the efforts of Razaf and Denniker's manager, Joe Davis.

On a frigid autumn day in late 1933, Razaf stepped off the train in Chicago. "It is one thing to meet a stranger and welcome him into our World's Fair City," one black Chicago columnist soon wrote, tying Razaf's arrival to the World's Fair Century of Progress Exposition then in town. "It is quite another incident, and a very pleasant one, to welcome a rank stranger who has accomplished a great deal in his line of endeavor and stands foremost among those of his profession today.

Well, that was what happened to me Wednesday afternoon when I strode into the Trenier Hotel and happened to learn that

Andrea Razaf, noted songwriter from New York, who by the way is one of the two colored men who make their living solely by writing lyrics, was in town on a short visit.

There was absolutely no formality to confront me when I knocked on the door of his suite . . . The accoutrements generally hanging on to formal introductions were entirely left off. It was not more than five minutes before we were in the midst of a lively discussion about the roses and thorns existing in the path trod by colored artists and who puts these thorns and the few roses there . . .

I suppose your curiosity has been aroused quite a bit. It will further be aroused when I say you know him. Haven't you ever heard of "Ain't Misbehavin'," "Memories of You," "Keepin' out of Mischief Now"? You certainly know how these lyrics swing. You certainly know that in them are symbols truly characteristic of the Bronze American. Well, the best I can say after meeting Mr. Razaf, a daily worker in Tin Pan Alley for the past fifteen years . . . is that these pieces along with many others truly describe him better than any written description.

In speaking of Chicago, Mr. Razaf said that in his opinion Chicagoans appeared to be getting something done, whereas the people in New York were just talking . . .

"Yes," he said, "I like Chicago very much, though I had to ride on a freight elevator in the Drake Hotel the other night when I went there to see and hear the . . . broadcast over station WGN." We apologized for the city and promised to take the matter up with the local branch of the N.A.A.C.P . . .

Work on *Rhythm for Sale* did not proceed smoothly. There were numerous cast chages early on, and the Hines band — out on one of their frequent tours as of the new year — had to be substituted for. With Razaf and Harper in charge, *Rhythm for Sale* soon featured a large number of alumni from vintage Razaf/Harper Harlem floorshows, including vocalists Pearl Baines and Vivian Brown, the dancing Berry Brothers, and, as Hines's replacement, Carroll Dickerson and his orchestra. The show's featured performer would be Avon Long, a marvelous song-and-dance man who had broken through to stardom in New York City the previous season at the Cotton Club.

Razaf and Harper's professional activity in the Midwest, which ranged well beyond Chicago at this time, also interfered with

Rhythm for Sale's opening. Throughout December and into January 1934, the two men commuted to Cleveland on weekends, juggling the makings of a new revue for that city's "Cotton Club," with the Grand Terrace production, as a result, dragging on in preparation far longer than it should have. Its debut, though, on the last night of January 1934 banished any grumbling about delays. "In less than two weeks," enthused the *Chicago Defender*, "Leonard Harper and Andy Razaf, the celebrated lyricist, have given Chicago one of the finest cafe revues in the country. *Rhythm for Sale* is fast, peppy, and highly sophisticated."

Interestingly, in the effusion of praise for the black floorshow talent on display in *Rhythm for Sale*, Englishman Paul Denniker was entirely overlooked by the Chicago critics. "Andy Razaf wrote eight brand new songs for the Grand Terrace production," insisted one reviewer, "writing both lyrics and music." The neglect Denniker enjoyed working in the shadow of his black collaborator was something that both men savored sardonically. Had Denniker aligned himself with a white lyric writer, Razaf liked to suggest, he'd have long since been rich and famous. Denniker himself never seems to have fretted over the possibility.

To the final version of *Rhythm for Sale*, the Razaf/Denniker team contributed no songs that are recalled today with particular vividness. The critics did single out "No More Thrills"—"a daring song that may become a sensation"—together with Alma Smith's rendition of "If You Can't Get Five Take Two." Ultimately, however, *Rhythm for Sale* passed into Chicago nightclub history, from a musical standpoint, rather quietly in 1934. Razaf by now could compose these floorshow tune packages practically in his sleep, as could Harper from a staging point of view. There were numerous formulas that the two men had helped to invent in Harlem nightclubs throughout the Twenties—song species, staging conceits—most of which still wore rather well, particularly outside New York City. If *Rhythm for Sale* lacked the timelessness of earlier Razaf/ Harper revues, the show still was first class, possessing an abundance of style, humor, and, of course, rhythm. It would run on at the Terrace as a solid hit for more than seven months.

For Razaf, though, the whole revue-manufacturing business had grown quite stale and rather stifling. He longed for a fresh opportunity, a less rigidly formulaic setting for his song work, or at least some new format with new, untried formulas: a stage musical with book, a Hollywood film score. His return to New York in March 1934, however, revived only the familiar rounds of financially depressed music publishers. One number from the *Rhythm for Sale* score, "If You Can't Get Five Take Two," was sold to Mayfair Music, publication contracts materializing within weeks of Razaf's arrival. An additional name, however—the name Joe Davis—found its way to the song's title page in the transfer from Chicago nightclub to Tin Pan Alley. Perhaps this was Davis's price for arranging the Grand Terrace job in the first place.

During the course of Razaf's Chicago sojourn, his partner Waller had returned to New York, after concluding his WLW term in Cincinnati. Over the ensuing six months, Waller occupied himself performing sporadically around Harlem, primarily at Pod's and Jerry's on 133rd Street and, later, in the President Hotel, on West 44th Street at Adrian's Tap Room a bar run by baritone saxophonist Adrian Rollini, where the downtown (white) jazz elite hung out and frequently jammed with the irrepressible pianist. Waller also picked up some extra dollars working society parties, a sideline he and his various Harlem piano peers had long indulged in. "Fats and I made a lot of those parties together," Willie "the Lion" Smith later remembered. "We used to get bugged by some of the people we'd wind up playing for, but they always kept the juices flowing. . . . The parties were all shapes and sizes. Many of them turned into brawls. You sometimes wondered how the hell some of them were able to acquire and hold big money with their bird brains. Actually, a lot of them didn't—they got the money as a gift when they were born. . . .

"We played for . . . Mrs. Felix Warburg, whose husband was a big-time banker on Wall Street; Mrs. Harrison Williams, who always invited all the songwriters and publishers; Ella Logan, the singer—her apartment was quite a hangout for artists; Sherman Fairchild . . .

"At Mrs. Harrison Williams's parties we felt more like teachers. Show business celebrities would study our work and try to get our music-arranging ideas. I saw people like Harold Arlen, Gershwin, Vernon Duke, Roy Bargy [Paul Whiteman's featured pianist] at those affairs in Mrs. Williams' shack on Park.

"Sometimes the artists who tried to pick up on some of our stuff had a hard time of it. They couldn't get much out of James P. because he wasn't a talker at all. . . . They always thought they could get a lot out of Fats if they kept the jug handy, but when Fats was swinging he would sing and play for hours without saying anything sensible."

One of the biggest breaks of Waller's career transpired at a society function in 1934. The occasion was a joint birthday celebration hosted by Sherman Fairchild for George Gershwin and Paul Whiteman at Fairchild's plush Park Avenue home. The party had begun around 8:30, with Waller at the keyboard, entertaining Fairchild's guests. At ten o'clock or so, William Paley, founder and director of the Columbia Broadcasting System, arrived at the Fairchild apartment with his wife and daughter. Apparently it was Paley's young daughter who first took notice of the fat and effusive piano player. Riveted by his mugging and singing, she directed her father's attention to him. Paley was also intrigued. He inquired for details from George Gershwin.

"Gershwin told Paley to get hold of me," Waller later told the *New York Times* in a 1943 interview. "So Paley comes over to me at the piano and says, 'Drop over to the office and see me.' Man, I'm stiff, but stiff, and I don't know what he's talking about. But the next day I realized what happened. Bull Am! I didn't waste no time."

In March, Paley placed Waller as a feature on the *Saturday Revue,* over WABC radio—still a CBS affiliate in 1934. In April, he booked him as a guest several times on Morton Downey's *House Party* and on the *Columbia Revue* program, followed by a May broadcast appearance on a show called *Harlem Serenade.* Paley was, in fact, pursuing a holding pattern with Waller. His plans for the pianist included a Fats Waller *network* radio show on CBS as soon as a suitable format could be developed.

Sensing a breakthrough, Waller's manager, Phil Ponce, pressed Victor Records' new boss Eli Oberstein for a recording contract with Waller as a featured piano/vocalist, though Waller hadn't recorded for Victor under his own name since 1930. A new Waller small band was hand picked comprising trumpet, reeds, bass, guitar, and drums, with the group billed as "Fats Waller and His Rhythm." Ponce then handed Waller his new Victor contract guaranteeing the 30-year-old keyboardist an advance of $100 per selection recorded plus a 3% royalty on records sold, not a bad deal for an artist considered to be solely a "jazz musician." Shortly thereafter, Waller and his new band entered a Victor studio on May 16, 1934 to record their first four tunes, beginning with Razaf and James P. Johnson's "Porter's Love Song."

Razaf, meanwhile, in May worked briefly on a revue featuring Eubie Blake's former-lyricist/partner Noble Sissle and Sissle's International Orchestra at the Lafayette Theatre, seizing this opportunity to showcase his new protégée, a voluptuous young vocalist with a big, raw voice—Lula Mae, "The Unsophisticated Lady of Song," as she billed herself. "A scintillating singer," exclaimed one overstimulated critic in the *New York Age* after witnessing Lula Mae's debut. "Lula Mae surprised all those who heard her."

With the onset of summer, though, Razaf put behind him "The Unsophisticated Lady of Song," the naysaying publishers of Tin Pan Alley, Joe Davis, and Razaf's own wildly busy song partner, Thomas Waller, whose network radio program *The Rhythm Club* formally had debuted in June. Together with Leonard Harper and Paul Denniker, Razaf again made his way out to Chicago. Earl Hines was back. *Rhythm for Sale* was still packing the Grand Terrace Cafe despite scorching summer heat. A new revue would now be needed to celebrate Hines's return; fifteen or so new tunes, new routines, some reworking of the ageless bits. Hines was to be set off impeccably.

One afternoon early in Razaf's second Chicago stint, A'Lelia Walker Robinson, heiress to the empire of Harlem's legendary "self-made" beauty culture queen, her mother, Madame C. J. Walker—swept into the Trenier Hotel dining room for a lunchtime rendezvous with an old friend and spotted Andy Razaf at a table with Leonard Harper. A'Lelia Robinson greeted the two men and joined them.

When her friend arrived, Walker introduced the woman to Harper and Razaf—Miss Mable Dixon from Tacoma, Washington. Miss Dixon, in turn, introduced the two shy, white teenaged girls with her: the Wilson sisters, Alice and Inga, also from Tacoma, she explained, in Chicago on their summer holiday to see the World's Fair Exposition.

"He later came back to my aunt's house, my Aunt Betty, who we were staying with in Chicago," Alice Wilson (Alicia Razaf-Georgiade) later remembered, recalling her first encounter as a 14-year-old with the man she would one day marry. "He had spoken to Mabel, very properly, in the dining room that day, he'd asked her if he might call the woman we were staying with, if Mabel thought that our aunt might allow him to show us Chicago.

"He was very dapper. He wore spats and an ascot and he carried a cane, I remember. When I found that he was the man who'd written 'Honeysuckle Rose' I just couldn't believe it. It was like meeting the King of England.

"The first night he took us both out—Inga and me—to a prize fight, ringside at the Savoy Ballroom. I was horrified by the whole thing, it was just horrible. He got terribly disgusted with me. There we were, he was pointing out all the famous people around us— Congressmen, some members of the Claude Hopkins band—and I just cried. Finally he took us home.

"A few days later he called again. This was the night we went to the Grand Terrace. They put the spotlight on Andy and I was just sitting there in seventh heaven. I wasn't so much sold on him, not yet, anyway. I just couldn't believe that here I was, I mean, back home we listened to the broadcasts and here I was sitting at the Grand Terrace with Andy Razaf and Earl Hines!

"I'd bought the most beautiful gown—white crepe cut on a bias, haltered, clinging, heavy white crepe and a jacket with great fox cuffs, and I had my hair kind of in a wave— it all made me look much older and I kept thinking, if so-and-so could just see me now.

"The show ended. 'I don't think Mrs. Edwards [our Aunt Betty] would mind if you got home a little late,' Andy said, and Inga screamed 'Oh no, of course not!' Earl Hines, Billy Mitchell—a comedian in the show—and Leonard Harper all left with us. We got into this big long car. I remember Earl Hines with this silly grin on his face, and this girl running out of the club, she was one of the stars of the show and she was somebody's girlfriend, maybe Hines. 'Wait for me!' she was shouting. A hand reached out from the car and went like that and back she fell on the sidewalk. The door slammed. No one said anything. And we drove off.

"The first club we went to, I think, was Blitch's Garden; it had little spotlights in the floor. Then Johnny Woolley's Midnite Club, where Jimmy Noone, the New Orleans clarinetist, led the orchestra.

"When we walked in the show was on and this beautiful woman was singing—Mae Johnson, she was billed as 'The Queen of Chicago's Nightclubs.' She was obviously one of Andy's girls. That's what I thought, I remember, because when we walked in she was in the middle of a song, she was singing: 'Don't save your kisses, just pass them around,'—you know, the song 'A Hundred Years from Today'—Oh God, I'll never forget it—and when she got to the line 'There'll always be one to make you feel . . .'—really wailing—she saw Andy and she stopped dead. A split second—looking right at him. Then the next song she did was 'Honeysuckle Rose.' Oh, she was a handsome lady: tall, stately—yellow in color, with rather Chinese eyes. They put the spotlight on us there, too.

"From the Midnite we went to the Black Spider Club. I remembered that club for years after; I could just see it. *'The Place to Go*

Afterwards,' that was what the cards said. You walked down—it was in a basement. Very small room. The whole club, I don't think, was as big as a living room. Square. You came in and there were tables and a huge, gorgeous carved oak piano, a concert grand. There was a big black spider in a web—that was the dance floor—very tight, very small. It was an after-hours club. Show people would come in to eat after their show, take girls upstairs or whatever.

"We were at this long table. Andy wrote out a little piece of paper—oh, really small, and he wrote: *A–Alluring, L–Lovable, I–Interesting, C–Cultured, I–Intriguing, A–Amorous.* 'That's what your name should be,' he said. 'Not Alice, you're not an Alice. Your name should be Alicia.'

"Well, from then on that was my name. When I got home to Seattle I announced it to everybody, my mom and dad, the kids at school. I wouldn't answer to anything else but Alicia. 'Andy Razaf gave me that name,' I'd say.

"Andy got up to sing at the Black Spider Club that night; he sang 'S'posin'. And then Hines went over to play and I found that I wanted to sing. I got up and said, 'I want to sing,' and Hines asked me, 'What do you sing?' and I said, 'I Got a Right to Sing the Blues.'" So he played a chorus. He played another chorus. And I kept waiting for him to play, 'I Got a Right to Sing the Blues.' I'd never sung with a jazz pianist before, you see, someone who improvised. 'When are you gonna start?' I finally asked him.

"Everybody ordered food, and I remember the walls seemed to be closing at me, you know?—and everybody seemed to be staring. Andy let us drink, he shouldn't have done that. And I don't know where he had to go but suddenly he said, 'I'll be back, watch the ladies,' he said to Billy Mitchell, and then the next thing I remember is Andy sitting on this bed looking at me and I didn't have a stitch on. How long he'd been sitting there looking at me, I don't know.

"He'd come back apparently and the party was gone, and Mama Washington, who ran the Black Spider like it was her private home, Andy had said, who loved Andy like a mother, told him that the girl—that *I*—had passed out, told him that somebody had given me a 'Mickey Finn,' a knockout drop, and Mother Washington had seen what was what and had just barely stopped things from going too far. My sister was gone with Billy Mitchell, she said. I was locked in a room upstairs.

"When I woke up it was morning, seven or eight o'clock. Andy's sitting there. 'How old are you?' he asked me. 'I'll be fifteen' I said.

'Have you ever been with anyone?' he asked me. 'No,' I said. 'Who got you here?' he asked me. 'I don't know,' I said, 'I don't remember anything.'

"He was furious. 'Get dressed,' he said. 'I'll take you to my hotel and we'll find Inga and Billy. I'll call the lady you're staying with. . . .'

"First we called Mabel—he told Mabel what had happened. From the Black Spider Club we went to a place where all the entertainers came after they had worked and they served them breakfast and everybody would try to outshow everybody else. And there was Billy Mitchell out on the floor with my sister doing an act and Inga was dancing.

"He never made a pass at me. He could have taken advantage of me but he didn't. He always treated me like I was a little girl, which I was.

"Once, before we went home, Andy phoned me where I was staying and talked to me about his house in New York and his mother. 'If I brought you to New York, my friends would be jealous,' he said, 'but you're too young.' He was just talking but I sent my father a wire: 'Dear Daddy, I met Andy Razaf, the man who wrote "Honeysuckle Rose" and he wants to know if we can stay a little longer in Chicago because he wants to take me to New York to meet his mother.' And this one-word wire came back: 'No!'

"He was supposed to come by and see me to say goodbye but he never got over. I waited and waited. But when he got to New York, he eventually called to say he was sorry. He had me say hello to his mother. And he said he hoped we would meet again someday."

Courtesy Razaf Estate.

Courtesy Razaf Estate.

12

Swing Low

Swing low sweet rhythm,
Rhythms of every kind,
When I'm sad and weary,
Rhythms ease my mind;
Way back, when I was in chains,
Rhythm carried me
Over into Jordan, an'
Seemed to set me free.

Swing low sweet rhythm,
When I get bad news,
I'll shape you into work songs,
Spirituals and blues.

Swing low sweet rhythm,
Lift my weary feet,
Drown my despair and fury
With a jungle beat,
With ragtime, Dixieland and jazz,
I'm gonna make 'em swing,
My magic will be music,
I'll be rhythm king.

> — *"Swing Low Sweet Rhythm"*
> by Andy Razaf

In the constricting view of formal jazz history, the Swing Era officially began on an August night in 1935. The place was the Palomar Ballroom in Los Angeles, the protagonists were clarinetist Benny Goodman and his new big band at the end of a disastrous inaugural cross-country tour, bombing at the Palomar just as they had bombed with audiences across America since embarking from New York City in mid-July. On this night in Los Angeles, however—August 21, 1935—midway through another poorly received set of music that was performed, admittedly, with rather timid retrogressive sweetness, Goodman, in frustration, apparently directed his musicians to unpack a few Fletcher Henderson arrangements that the band often had played on their national broadcasts over the *Let's Dance* radio program Saturday nights from New York City—Goodman's first breakthrough radio appearances as a bandleader—but which Goodman, until that moment, had hesitated to play live. This swinging Fletcher Henderson infusion proved to be a revelation. With it, the Benny Goodman band at the Palomar Ballroom suddenly began to "swing" and, miraculously, to Goodman's astonishment, the Palomar patrons seem to have swung back—deliriously. There, upon the ashes of America's first great jazz-influenced African–American big band, the Fletcher Henderson Orchestra (Henderson, by 1939, would be working *for* Benny Goodman almost exclusively as an arranger, having been forced to disband his own ensemble), America's most lucrative commercial jazz age, the Swing Era, figuratively was born.

This white beginning was also very much a black ending, a transfer of the power of black music in America to white musicians who were fundamentally schooled now and ready to play black music, more or less, for an international white audience that was quite ready to listen. In this way, within the African-American musical community, what the Depression had begun in terms of economic destruction the Swing Era soon completed. It effectively completed the professional disenfranchisement of just about every established black jazz dance band, with a handful of exceptions. It rapidly completed the idling of sizable numbers of black jazz musicians, many of whom would become expatriates over the remaining years of the Thirties, playing their music in Europe for audiences still receptive to nonwhite "swing" music. And it altogether completed the evisceration of the careers of most of Tin Pan Alley's greatest black songwriters, whose decimation may be perfectly, poignantly traced through Andy Razaf.

Even as brutal riots in Harlem grimly punctuated the death throes of uptown nightlife induced by Repeal and the Depression—riots sparked specifically by the manhandling of a young black shoplifter in a 125th Street department store by white floor managers on an afternoon in March 1935, and fueled, according to an ensuing Commission of Inquiry, by "the nervous strain of years of unemployment and insecurity . . . among the colored people,"—Andy Razaf's nightclub-mired career did carry on into 1935. With Eubie Blake and other songwriters, Razaf maintained a presence on the dimming Harlem nightclub circuit, writing a series of floorshows for the Ubangi Club, a new tenant down in Connie's original basement off 131st Street and Seventh Avenue. With Paul Denniker, he also scored downtown nightclub revues for a newly revived downtown incarnation of Connie's Inn on the site of Paul Whiteman's old Palais Royal supper club, at 47th Street between Broadway and Seventh Avenue.

Each production had its points, though all were painfully familiar in form and even substance. Razaf and Denniker's score for the Immermans' downtown debut in April 1935—touted predictably as *Connie's Hot Chocolates of 1935*, with a stellar company topped by vocalist Alberta Hunter—included one stunning number, almost a tone poem, that surely reflected Razaf's wistful affection for an uptown world that before his eyes was consuming itself in a furious conflagration—"What Harlem Is to Me":

> *It's a symphony of many moods and shades,*
> *It's a tapestry of all designs and grades,*
> *It's a hand behind the bars*
> *Ever reaching for the stars,*
> *That's what Harlem is to me.*
> *It's a barricade holding back the sea,*
> *It's a big parade on a jubilee,*
> *It's a grown-up running wild,*
> *It's a helpless little child,*
> *That's what Harlem is to me.*
>
> *There is no place you will ever see*
> *Like this dusky town within a town;*
> *It's a showcase full of novelty,*
> *Sophistication done up brown.*

It's the lighter side of a heavy load,
It's the brighter side of a dismal road,
It's a day of moanin' low
And a night of Hi-de-Ho,
That's what Harlem is to me.

Razaf originally had been approached by Eubie Blake to compose a score for Harlem's new Ubangi Club back in August of 1934. "Have secured job for Ubangi chorus show, they want you to write the lyrics with me," Blake initially had telegraphed Razaf in Chicago at the Hotel Trenier. "Wire me how soon you will be here." Razaf could not extricate himself instantly, however, from the grip of his Grand Terrace agreement with the Capone organization. Not until July of 1935 was he at last able to accept the Ubangi Club's commission, by which time Blake apparently was engaged elsewhere. For his first revue work in the former Connie's Inn nightclub space—the Ubangi Club's fifth edition since reopening there—Razaf composed both words and music for a Leonard Harper floorshow that featured numerous uptown entertainment stalwarts, including Velma Middleton, Billie Daniels, and Gladys Bentley. Subsequent editions would present Razaf with a host of notable song collaborators, including Paul Denniker, bandleader Alex Hill, Thomas Waller on occasion, and finally Blake. The most noteworthy aspect of Razaf's Ubangi Club stint, which ultimately extended into the early Forties, may however have been the painfully belated desegregation of his former Twenties nightclub home in these waning years of Harlem's entertainment prime. As Billy Rowe, a columnist for the *Amsterdam News*, remarked in covering Razaf's inaugural Ubangi Club revue, "Throughout the evening, many colored parties could be noticed around the ringside, in boxes, and, in fact, all over the club. Their presence added that desired Harlem Atmosphere which for many moons has been so hard to find in a vicinity . . . famous for that same thing."

In September 1935, Razaf and Denniker signed contracts with Alphonse Delmonico, owner of Delmonico's Restaurant on 51st Street between Broadway and Seventh Avenue, to write three ensemble numbers for the restaurant's scheduled October 3 welcome-home reception for former New York City mayor Jimmy Walker (on the occasion of Walker's return from extended European exile following his forced 1932 resignation on corruption charges). The terms—$75 for all three songs plus a 33 1/3 percent share for

Delmonico in all publishing royalties accruing from the songs—sharply delineates the straitened and often sinister terms under which Razaf commonly composed nightclub floor show scores during this period. The Delmonico contract matched in diminished form the terms of Razaf and Denniker's agreement with the Immerman brothers for *Connie's Hot Chocolates of 1935*—$400 for an entire evening's worth of songs, plus an "undivided" one-half interest for the Immermans "in . . . said score and in . . . the income, issues, and profits thereof, including . . . any and all renewals and extensions of such copyright in the United States of America and in every other country in the world."

Razaf, with increasing frequency throughout the Thirties, bravely gave public voice to his rage over such professional mistreatment. One stunningly blunt example was the verse entitled "Flim-Flam Alley" that the incensed lyricist published at this time in the *Amsterdam News*.

> A prayer for the Alley, so
>   lacking in soul,
> Where "cut-ins" and "angels"
>   and "plugs" are the goal;
> Where visions and ideals and
>   ethics are rare
> And friendship is yours, if
>   you're "big on the air!"
> Where something original
>   frightens the ear,
> Just dull similarities, year
>   after year;
> Where men, uncreative,
>   control and dictate,
> And tell the creative how
>   they should create.
> Where men are like sheep, and
>   the blind lead the blind,
> Where envy and selfishness
>   saddle the mind;
> Where meeting are places
>   for beautiful speech
> But few ever practice the
>   things that they preach.

> *May God help the Alley, that*
> *street of deceit.*
> *Where writers go hungry,*
> *while other men eat.*

Despite these justifiably outraged cries of protest, however, Andy Razaf was still very "big on the air" as he entered 1936, "topping all songwriters" in the number of times his compositions were played or sung over the radio during the previous year—20,836 times, according to a *Variety* news story on January 11. Razaf nevertheless seems to have been possessed by an increasing fear for the future of a career he had fearlessly struggled to establish and perpetuate, a fear fixated on an onrushing white swing band vogue that already was threatening to stamp black presence out of American popular music. The intersection of Razaf's fortunes at this time with the doomed Fletcher Henderson Orchestra's therefore seems, in retrospect, quite symbolic.

Despite the undisputed excellence of Fletcher Henderson's musicians and the unmistakable brilliance of Henderson's all-around abilities as a musical director and arranger, the history of the Henderson band since Razaf first had encountered it at the Club Alabam in 1924 was a history of habitually missed professional opportunities and racially stymied advancement abetted by the gross if benign mismanagement of Fletcher Henderson himself. Henderson's decidedly aloof, impenetrably superior nature seems almost to have dictated the passivity that was his tragic flaw as a businessman and bandleader. Throughout a career that now numbered more than ten seasons as a topflight band director, he had remained paralyzingly incapable of positively disciplining his superb musicians and assertively pursuing with them major commercial success. As a result, his marvelous bands, throughout many incarnations, continually had disintegrated over the years through Henderson's enigmatic, lackadaisically impotent leadership. Now, in 1936, despite a notable new headline engagement at the relocated Grand Terrace Cafe on the site of one of Chicago's original Twenties "hot spots," the Sunset Cafe at 35th Street and Calumet Avenue, Henderson was entering into the final backslide of his torpid bandleading career. His exceptional musical aggregation, however, still had at least one great trend-setting musical salvo in its arsenal.

Through live broadcasts from the Grand Terrace in 1936, a new Henderson band theme, reportedly based on a bawdy song known as

"Cristoforo Columbo" and structured by Henderson's exceptionally talented brother, Horace, around a riff played by Henderson's latest tenor saxophone star, Leon "Chu" Berry, recently had caught the fancy of radio listeners across the country. Significant among these was music publisher Joe Davis, who soon purchased the tune from Henderson. After assigning Andy Razaf the job of cobbling a lyric together for the song, Davis finally published the number in March 1936 under the title "Christopher Columbus," crediting Chu Berry and Andy Razaf, to Horace Henderson's everlasting dismay, as sole authors. Within a matter of weeks, through Henderson's nightly broadcasts, a late-March Henderson band recording of the song, and subsequent cover versions by a host of emerging Swing Era big bands, including Henderson's greatest co-opting admirer, Benny Goodman, "Christopher Columbus" was a nationwide hit.

Mr. Christopher Columbus
Sailed the sea without a compass,
When the men began a rumpus,
Up spoke Christopher Columbus:
There is land somewhere,
But 'til we get there,
We will not go wrong
If we sing, swing a song;
Since the world is round,
We'll be safe and sound,
'Til our goal is found,
We'll just keep rhythm bound.

Soon the crew was makin' merry,
Then came a yell,
Let's drink to Isabel—
Bring on the rum!
No more mutiny,
What a time at sea
What diplomacy,
Cristy made history.
Mister Christopher Columbus,
He used rhythm as a compass,
Music ended all the rumpus,
Wise old Christopher Columbus.

Wonderfully irreverent, thumpingly rhythmic—the tune was sub-titled "A Rhythm Cocktail"—"Christopher Columbus" enjoyed a success which instantly rendered Razaf the lyricist of preference for swing band novelty numbers requiring lyrics prior to publication. Razaf, at Joe Davis's behest, added lyrics to three "Christopher Columbus" followups in 1936: "Big Chief de Sota," (also known as "Grand Terrace Swing") by Henderson band trombonist Fernando Arbello, "Nero," by Paul Denniker, and "William Tell," again by Chu Berry, with an acknowledged musical debt to Rossini's famous overture. Yet another big band "riff" tune worked up into a hugely popular song hit that year was "Stompin' at the Savoy" by a former classmate of Thomas Waller's, reedman/arranger Edgar Sampson and his boss Chick Webb, the diminutive drummer whose hard-swinging ensemble served as the Savoy Ballroom house band in 1936. Like "Christopher Columbus," "Stompin' at the Savoy" had enjoyed a healthy life on its own—initially as Webb's band theme since the year of its composition in 1934 and then again as a Benny Goodman recording in 1936—before Andy Razaf finally was hired to furnish the tune with a lyric.

The words that Razaf set to "Savoy" beautifully illustrate why he was in such demand at this time for swing band lyric chores. Razaf understood rhythm from a band musician's perspective. He fath-omed a song's inner pulse and understood how to inject that pulse with words that complemented and enhanced rhythmic momentum —the essence of swing. In this way, Razaf seized upon the call-and-response core that was "Stompin' at the Savoys"'s musical essence and embellished it with words borrowed, in spirit, from the Savoy Ballroom marquee, the words that read "*Savoy—The Home of Happy Feet*," to produce:

> *Savoy–the home of sweet romance,*
> *Savoy–it wins you at a glance,*
> *Savoy–gives happy feet a chance*
> *To dance.*
> *Your form–just like a clinging vine,*
> *Your lips–so warm and sweet as wine,*
> *Your cheek–so soft and close to mine,*
> *Divine.*
> *How my heart is singin'*
> *While the band is swingin',*
> *Never tired of rompin'*

And stompin' with you
At the Savoy;
What joy—a perfect holiday.
Savoy—where we can glide away,
Savoy—there let me stomp away
With you.

The last years of the Thirties proved to be grueling ones for Andy Razaf. His career at last was fatally stalled—not solely by the death of Harlem nightlife, nor even by the ascendance of a white Big Band Era, but by the unwavering racism of America's entertainment industry establishment, both in New York and Hollywood. Razaf handled his mounting disappointment by continuing to shop new songs along Tin Pan Alley, resolutely ignoring the writing on the wall. After Harlem's decisive nightclub fatality, for example—the closing of the Cotton Club's doors on February 16, 1936—Razaf fleetingly worked at a new, downtown Cotton Club that reopened in September 1936 on the 47th Street premises of the hastily terminated downtown Connie's Inn. He contributed songs—this time *with* credit, in collaboration with British West Indian composer Reginald Foresythe—to the second downtown *Cotton Club Parade* in early 1937, a lavish revue packaged with an array of Harlem entertainment luminaries, including Duke Ellington and His Orchestra, and vocalists Ivy Anderson, Ethel Waters, and the Nicholas Brothers. The Cotton Club's downtown life was a brief one, however. By June of 1940, the room would be a memory.

Most cruel, though, was the increasing professional estrangement of Razaf from his beloved partner Thomas Waller, orchestrated over the course of the last years of the Thirties by Waller's white professional managers. After his recording career had broken through nationally in 1935 with a droll hit rendition of "I'm Gonna Sit Right Down and Write Myself a Letter" (by white songmen Fred Ahlert and Joe Young), Waller had been saddled by agent Phil Ponce with an elaborately expanded big band and touring show that kept him on the road, removed from his family, the uptown music scene, and Andy Razaf for increasing stretches of time. Waller truly hated the touring life—timetables, band arrangements, and accommodations far away from Harlem did not agree with him at all and the pianist was a sporadic no-show all across the country as a result, leading to numerous breach-of-contract lawsuits. The tours, however, went forward and Waller's popularity grew in spite of his seeming indifference. The touring life also stimulated Waller's alcoholism, as the congenitally unreliable young bandleader used liquor to fortify himself against the increasing responsibilities of stardom—a development that at first did not really displease his professional handlers, since it made Waller a more malleable performer. As Waller's saxophonist Gene Sedric later pointed out, "Fats didn't think of himself as a singer . . . but with a bottle on the floor next to him, he'd sing and accompany himself at the piano. The people preferred this—and so did the managers."

The combination of impressive Victor record sales and a growing reputation as an exceptional live attraction had brought Waller a film offer early in 1935 from RKO to make a cameo appearance in the Ann Sothern–Gene Raymond picture *Hooray for Love!*, with dancer Bill Robinson. Robinson and Waller were well acquainted from the Harlem nightclub circuit and nights in the late Twenties spent working society parties together on Park Avenue and out along the North Shore of Long Island. Waller's work on the film was brief, as promised, a single day of shooting in which he'd performed Jimmy McHugh and Dorothy Fields's "Living in a Great Big Way," but it did generate a second screen job later that same year, a slightly more substantial role in the Twentieth Century Fox film *King of Burlesque* as an elevator operator who puts on a show with some other entertainer/menials to help save a friendly, financially troubled tenant in the elevatorman's building. It was during this film stint that Waller also asserted himself in rather surprising Razafian fashion, insisting that certain stereotyping dialogue lines be changed, including one that had him replying "Yassuh" rather than "Yes sir." Undoubtedly it was a measure of the pianist's evolving significance as an entertainment commodity that the demand was unhesitatingly acceded to.

With Waller incessantly on the road, band-touring and Hollywood-commuting, the years 1934 to 1935 had proved the first in a decade in which he and Razaf did not produce music together. With mounting desperation, Razaf monitored his partner's professional ascendance, longing for what he continued to believe was their inevitable songwriting reunion. Finally, unable to contain himself any longer, Razaf swallowed his pride and appealed directly to Waller's manager Phil Ponce in a letter dated April 26, 1936. "Dear friend Phil," he wrote. "Just a few passing thoughts concerning Waller and myself which I hope will bear fruit, and trust you understand the friendly spirit and sincerity of same.

"Since Thomas has been under contract to you, I feel you have overlooked the possibility of our continuing as a writing team and inasmuch as we were unmistakably one of the most prolific and outstanding combinations of this generation, this is indeed unfortunate.

"I think it would be to the advantage of all parties concerned if we were permitted to build up a Razaf and Waller catalog to be handled and marketed by you. Can't you see the possibilities?

"Furthermore, I feel the time is not far distant when some enterprising moving picture firm could be made to bid for our services. If interested, I would appreciate an interview to discuss the matter further. With every good wish, I remain, very sincerely yours, Andy Razaf."

The delicacy, wisdom, and open-hearted directness of Razaf's letter were cruelly dispatched by the impersonal dismissiveness and covert evasiveness of Ponce's terse reply.

Dear Andy:

Pardon my delay in answering your note regarding writing lyrics with "Fats" Waller. He is so active at the present time in other lines that I do not want to burden him with too many things because everything he does from now on, even to writing a song, must be "tops," to hold the top rung of the ladder which he has reached. However, I will discuss it with him the first time I see him.

With best wishes,

Sincerely,
Philip L. Ponce

Ponce's unjust imputation that, for his client Waller, writing with Andy Razaf now constituted a step down from "the top rung of the ladder" may simply have been Ponce's roundabout rationale for keeping Waller on the road and away from songwriting altogether. Or it may have been an encoded expression of Ponce's latent racism. Assuming that Ponce did in fact want Waller to continue writing songs, would Ponce have deigned to separate Fats Waller from Andy Razaf had Razaf and Waller been white? Only the fear that Waller's continued professional association with Razaf might somehow undermine Ponce's ability to sell Fats Waller to the white entertainment mainstream could have blinded the wily and highly experienced agent to the commercial value, if nothing else, of Waller and Razaf's continued activity as a songwriting team.

Within the month, Razaf turned to an old friend, music publisher Jack Robbins, now ensconced in Hollywood, for help in securing a songwriting position at one of the West Coast film studios. Robbins reply began with a rather cryptic comment: "I am sorry that Joe Trent," another talented and accomplished black lyric writer of the period, "has made it impossible for a negro lyricist or tune writer to have a permanent position at a studio for a long time to come." The nature of Trent's malfeasance remains unclear. Robbins immediately proceeded, however, without elaboration, to the main point of his letter.

> Andy, I do think you should get together with Fats Waller. I heard a tune of his that will be another HONEYSUCKLE ROSE. Also I think you should get on the road with him and keep writing all the time, so Fats can keep recording a group of numbers you and he write.
>
> When Fats comes out here from time to time you can come and do jobs with him.
>
> I will be very glad to hear from you with any suggestions you may have from time to time.

It was not until the first week of October 1937 that Razaf at last was afforded an opportunity to pursue Jack Robbins's painfully obvious suggestion and join his partner on the road for songwriting purposes, surmounting the scheduling thicket thrown up around Waller by his management consortium of Phil Ponce, the Victor Recording Company (along with its corporate parent, RCA), and William Paley's CBS radio network. Waller was booked into a Boston theater for a week, then due back in New York for a recording session. Razaf and J. C. Johnson accompanied Waller on the train up to Boston and, along the way, in Boston itself, and finally on the return trip home, the three men together wrote six songs—"Jealous of Me" and "A Hopeless Love Affair" (Waller and Razaf), "How Can I, with You in My Heart," "What Will I Do in the Morning?" and "How 'Ya Baby?" (Waller and Johnson), and one jointly composed group tune that giddily sought to evoke the spirit of a Harlem rent party. At the recording session the following week, Waller recorded this new number, with Razaf, Johnson, the studio staff, and a few lady friends supplying an outrageously realistic background cacophony that today still means only one thing:

The joint is jumpin',
It's really jumpin',
Come in cats and checks your hats,
I mean this joint is jumpin';
The piano's thumpin',
The dancers are bumpin',
This here spot is more than hot,
In fact, the joint is jumpin'.
Check your weapons at the door, be sure to
    pay your quarter,
Burn your leather on the floor, grab
    anybody's daughter,
The roof is rockin',
The neighbors are knockin',
We're all bums when the wagon come,
I mean this joint is jumpin'.

They have a new expression
Along old Harlem way,
That tells you when a party
Is ten times more than gay,
To say that things are "jumpin'"
Leaves not a single doubt
That everything is in full swing
When you hear somebody shout:

The joint is jumpin'
It's really jumpin',
Ev'ry Mose is on his toes,
I mean, this joint is jumpin';
No time for talkin',
This place is walkin',
Hit the jug and cut a rug,
I've said, the joint is jumpin'.
Get your pig feet, beer and gin, there's plenty
    in the kitchen,
What is that who just came in? Just see the
    way he's switchin',
Don't mind the hour,
'Cause I'm in power,
I've got bail if we go to jail,
So keep this joint-a-jumpin'.

The stunning record sales racked up by *Fats Waller and his Rhythm* over the course of the latter Thirties truly seem to have caught Waller's management team by surprise. Waller recordings did not merely dominate the competition in the "race" record market. Waller's Victor recordings were among the best-selling records in America. Victor executives seem to have been perplexed by the unanticipated degree of Waller's crossover popularity, uncertain as to how they should now perpetuate Waller's exhibited appeal in terms of repertoire. Simplistically fixated on the tone of childlike delight that permeated all of Waller's recorded work while increasingly dismissing the foundation of exuberant musicianship and extraordinary taste and charm that underlay Waller's clowning, Victor now began to force uniformly puerile and mawkish material on their new recording star—songs like "I'm on a Seesaw" and "Us on a Bus"—that in fact insulted the sensitive and highly intelligent performer, who responded to these songs by demolishing them both lyrically and structurally in his recordings.

Predictably, it was material written by Andy Razaf that best captured the qualities record buyers were responding to in Waller without condescending to them. Waller clearly understood this. His first four Victor *Fats Waller and His Rhythm* recording sessions throughout 1934 each had included at least one Andy Razaf tune. After a pronounced, and no doubt record company–induced, interlude of nine sessions without Razaf representation throughout 1935, Waller thereafter had featured at least one Razaf tune (often more) in every session but one out of ten ensuing *Fats Waller and His Rhythm* dates from April 1936 through the October 7, 1937, session at which "The Joint Is Jumpin' " was recorded. Waller seems to have recognized that he was often portrayed and displayed to best effect lyrically in Razaf songs, with "The Joint is Jumpin' " in many ways constituting the culmination of collaborative Waller depiction by Razaf and J. C. Johnson, a joyous portrait of Waller in his raucous element, both childlike and knowing, gloriously unaffected yet still deliciously low-down.

In a reversal of his initially stated position regarding Razaf and Waller's song partnering, Phil Ponce, on January 4, 1938, signed up all six Razaf/Waller/J. C. Johnson songs produced over the week-long Boston junket, wringing from Razaf and Johnson (Waller was already under contract to Ponce) a 15% commission on "all monies received . . . in connection with these songs" in exchange for "placing . . . these numbers for publication with a publisher." The arrangement strikes one today as rather suspicious—surely by now Ponce's influence was not required to place any Razaf/Waller/ (Johnson) tunes with a music publisher, particularly songs as marketable as "The Joint Is Jumpin'." What seems more likely is that Ponce was being politely "tipped" a 15% commission on these songs in order to allow his client, Waller, to release them to a publisher. This remains, however, only conjecture.

Despite Razaf's numerous song achievements during the last few years of the Thirties, the period clearly was one of increasing financial instability for the lyricist, due no doubt to general Depression-era economic concerns and his own financial responsibilities, as well as the commercial inequities imposed upon him by the music industry. Between February 1933 and May 1938, Razaf resided at no fewer than seven different addresses, from West 117th Street to West 154th Street, including a brief layover at his Uncle John Waller's home in Mount Vernon, New York. Over the same period, Razaf took out (and ultimately repaid) at least four different bank loans. In February 1936, Razaf also applied for and began to receive advances from ASCAP against future royalties. In June 1936, however, his request for an upgrading of his classification within the organization was denied.

Razaf even briefly considered abandoning not just New York City but the United States altogether, to join his many expatriate musician friends overseas. "I not only plan to visit your dear England in the near future," he wrote in January 1936 to music journalist Leonard Feather in London, "but hope to make it my home. I have many reasons for admiring your country; its truer and finer conception of democratic principles, its greater justice and appreciation of the artist, regardless of color, race or creed, and its superior culture have long appealed to me."

Ultimately, though, New York City and the music industry maintained their grip on Razaf despite his increasing disaffection from both, leaving the lyricist to grapple with a wildly conflicted rage that seems to have been most desperately expressed in a letter addressed to Joe Davis on August 31, 1938, that turned up posthumously among Razaf's papers. The letter is not a carbon, and it is not a copy. It simply appears to have never been mailed.

Dear Joe—

I am truly sorry for you. In all your smug financial security and with what you term business success, you are actually a poor man. Scan the ledger book of your life for your truly selfish deeds, fair and generous debts, loyalty to those who had served and stood by you, and at last, count your true friends, and what is the total?

For years I gave you loyalty and service, took the least in exchange for the most, often against my better judgment, because of my blind faith in your friendship, always "leaving everything up to you and your sense of fairness."

The result is, I am poorer in the pocket but richer in wisdom.

As the years passed, my value to you went down, not up. Twenty dollars for three songs out-right and without credit even tops the deal of years ago when adversity forced me to sell you a group of songs for less than a hundred dollars, with "Sposin'" thrown in, in order to put through the deal.

Before you deny this, look in your books.

Well, after all, I don't blame anyone but myself; I am of age and was aware of what I was doing.

No one shall ever hear of this nor any other deal between us for tho I am poor, I have a sense of honor—thank God!

Of course this letter will bring down your wrath and you will brand me as an ingrate as you once did before, but you must at least say, I told you what was *Really* in my mind and did not *grin in your face* and *stab you behind your back*.

Yes, you will laugh this off and ignore it like you did my other letter. Remember the story of the lion and the mouse? It was meant for wise men to read and ponder over. Tomorrow is yet to come, who knows that those we passed on the way up, we will meet again on the way down?

With no bitterness and all good wishes for you and yours I am still—

Your friend
Andy Razaf

This letter raises two obvious questions. The first—which three songs Razaf is referring to as sold for $20 "out-right and without credit"—is unanswerable. The songs and the secret, like so much of Razaf's life, will forever belong to Joe Davis. The second question— why Andy Razaf continued to associated with Joe Davis throughout the years preceding and even following this letter if Davis did brazenly abuse Razaf's trust—while similarly unanswerable, can at least be approached speculatively. The full scope of an answer may even be gleaned from the language of Razaf's letter. At first, it would seem, Andy Razaf trusted Joe Davis, "leaving everything up to you and your sense of fairness." "As the years passed," however, and

suspicions began to mount, Razaf apparently challenged Davis—
"before you deny this, look in your books." Joe Davis, though, was a
charming man whom Razaf very much wished to trust and the music
publisher apparently assuaged Razaf's suspicions and denied his
accusations charmingly. By the time it became irrefutable to Razaf
that Joe Davis was, and had been, systematically cheating him for
some time, Razaf's "sense of honor," his sense of shame for having
allowed himself to be misled, along with an unsettling sense of
martyrdom that again appears like a grim subtext beneath Razaf's
anger—"I don't blame anyone but myself"—all seem to have
conspired with Razaf's genuine affection for, and loyalty to his music
publisher. This sense of martyrdom in particular must not be
underemphasized or dismissed. It was a perception that plagued
many black music men, a sense of victimization that was justifiable
yet tragically self-destructive. In Andy Razaf, its whispering presence was grossly uncharacteristic, eminently understandable, and,
sadly, uncondonable.

Throughout the Twenties, the "fruitful years," the years of
achievement and triumph, Razaf had gloried in women, womanizing
to a degree that seemed a kind of reward in itself. Now, with the
onset of the late Thirties, the "lean years," Razaf, at 43, decided to
settle down. He was, after all, a practical man, and the woman he
chose to become his second wife was a far more practical choice than
Annabelle Miller had been.

Born in Florida, raised in Baltimore, Maryland, 23-year-old Jean
Blackwell was a very bright, exceedingly attractive Barnard College
graduate—small and rather delicate, with an unexpectedly robust
gentility that could be quite alluring. Forced by her mother to
transfer to Barnard from the University of Michigan after she had
involved herself, in her own words, "to an alarming degree" in
"radical activities" at Michigan, Blackwell, once in New York, had
made her way very quickly, both socially and politically, after
graduating from the Columbia Library School. She began work at
the 135th Street branch of the New York Public Library, one of the
focal points of Harlem's literary Renaissance, in the autumn of 1936.
In the summer of 1937 she visited the Soviet Union, and that autumn
she moved from Riverside Drive into a house at 43 West 66th Street
owned by the Africa Free Society. Living there at the time were a
number of rather distinguished radical black men and women,
including the notorious political activist Angelo Herndon, journalists

Fred Morrow and Henry Moon, and Moon's wife, social worker Mollie Moon—all of them Communists or Communist sympathizers. "I was a fellow traveler," Jean Blackwell[-Hutson] later admitted frankly and with some bemusement, "that's really what I was, though I somehow never actually secured my party card."

Blackwell was seeing, among others, novelist Richard Wright. "We didn't just date," she insisted in retrospect. "We shared his misery. He was a very bitter fellow. I remember I would sort of psych myself up when I went out with him because he was very, very demanding. I got to see a lot of wonderful theater with him—*Tobacco Road, Of Mice and Men*—I remember going to these shows particularly because Richard would just beat his chest, literally, with . . . with such . . . in such joyous pain; he loved the feeling of pain. I was never under any illusion that he was in love with me but he was very protective of me."

"The circulation desk at the 135th Street Branch Library was right inside the door," Blackwell remembered. "I was the Reserve Librarian, and Andy tried to bribe me to put his name up on the Reserve List—to list him first waiting for some book. I was very indignant. 'You know, we don't do things like that,' I said. He used to be around the library all the time, I think he got interested in me because I stood up to him. He tried to ask me out and I said no. I had no idea he was so important."

Ernestine Rose, the longtime Chief Librarian at the 135th Street branch, introduced Razaf to Blackwell. "Apparently Andy had gone to Ernestine about me and she was so fond of him because he was such a serious reader, so proud of his education that he'd given himself at her library. Still, he asked me to lunch and I turned him down, though he won me over eventually and we began seeing each other quite a bit.

"He was a little wary of me and my fellow traveling friends at first, very dubious of my having been to the Soviet Union, my marching in May Day Parades—and that house on 66th Street! I wasn't serious about him at first at all. He was almost twenty years older than me."

They dated for about a year, often visiting nightclubs where Razaf's reception was quite impressive. It was at least a year before Blackwell discovered that her new beau was still married, though Razaf no longer was living with Minto Cato.

"It was a very embarrassing and painful discovery," Blackwell later conceded. "I moved back to Baltimore. To escape him. But Andy was very persistent. Finally he convinced me he was going to get a divorce and he went out to Chicago for some reason to arrange it. . . . When he returned, he wanted to get married in Philadelphia and we drove there but they wouldn't marry us—the divorce wasn't final yet, they said, so we drove to Elkton, Maryland, and were married there on July 31, 1939, by a Justice of the Peace."

Jean Blackwell was Andy Razaf's first significant relationship outside the theatrical profession since his first wife, Annabelle. Where Annabelle Miller had been simple and unschooled, Jean Blackwell was sophisticated and highly educated. "Part of his feeling for me, I think, was his pride in the good education I had," Blackwell later reflected. "I guess there was envy too somewhat, but that wasn't apparent until later."

The night before the wedding, the couple drove down to Asbury Park to get Razaf's mother's blessing. "Jennie wavered in her opinion of me," Blackwell recalled. "She didn't approve of Annabelle and she really didn't approve of me. She had a wife all picked out for Andy, in fact, a friend of hers named Dorothy Carpenter who was already married, but Jennie didn't care, she kept on fostering this relationship. Dorothy was always around as Jennie's 'daughter'— that's what Jennie called her."

For Razaf, remarriage at this point in his life was an opportunity to retreat from the peripatetic theatrical existence he now had been pursuing in Harlem for nearly twenty years. He even was agreeable to his new wife's desire for a house in the suburbs.

"Immediately after the wedding, Andy and I moved into the Dunbar Apartments on Seventh Avenue but I had grown up in a house and I wanted to live in a house," Jean Blackwell remembered. "That's how we came to find this place out in Englewood, New Jersey. I believe we moved out to Englewood the following spring."

Two months after taking marriage vows for the second time in his life, Razaf realized a certain negative apotheosis in his career-within-a-career as contributor to big band novelty numbers when he was brought in as last-minute lyricist on a tune that bandleader Glenn Miller was about to record to great success, a tune called "In the Mood."

"In the Mood" was already in 1939 a big band favorite with an endlessly convoluted history. The basic riff theme from which the tune had been derived was familiar to many jazz musicians going back to the late Twenties. New Orleans trumpeter Wingy Manone had recorded the riff as "Tar Paper Stomp" in August 1930. Fletcher Henderson had used the same theme some seven months later in a tune recorded as "Hot and Anxious." Veteran black reedman/ arranger Joe Garland had composed his own variation on the theme for Mills Blue Rhythm Band in 1935, under the title "There's Rhythm in Harlem." Three years later, in June 1938, Garland had copyrighted a new version of this tune as "In the Mood," after the piece had been recorded in February 1938 by a big band co-musical directed by Garland with Edgar Hayes. Now, with a recording session scheduled for August 1, 1939, trombonist Glenn Miller was preparing to lead his own increasingly popular big band through a streamlined Miller arrangement of Garland's tune. The resulting record proved to be one of the most explosively successful recordings of the Big Band Era; in many ways, the definitive one.

But Miller first wanted a lyric for the song. According to Razaf, Miller went through a number of white lyricists before turning finally to him. Predictably, it was Joe Davis who actually called Razaf for the job. With Miller's band in rehearsal, running down "In the Mood" preparatory to recording it, Razaf strode into their studio, listened, and soon wrote out a lyric based on one of his and Waller's unpublished songs, "Whatcha Got On for Tonight?" Razaf also later claimed that in this lyric he inserted the "fills" that are to this day one of "In the Mood"'s more distinguishing musical features. He felt, Razaf later explained, that these fills helped to sustain the forward motion of the song rhythmically.

For his work on "In the Mood," Razaf was paid $200 in cash on the spot, in the studio, by the publisher, Shapiro, Bernstein. Razaf later stated that he considered the money an advance—he had never done anything "for hire" with Shapiro, Bernstein, publisher of his *Blackbirds* score and a number of other songs; "never for hire, always under contract," insisted Razaf. He soon learned, though, that this "In the Mood" lyric was, in fact, a "for hire" job as far as Shapiro, Bernstein were concerned. Razaf never received any further payment. Clearly, Joe Davis's arrangement with the publisher had been to bring Razaf in on a "for hire" basis. Davis had neglected to inform Razaf of the terms for his employment and, once again, Razaf had asked no questions in advance. It is unclear what Joe Davis himself finally netted on the song.

"Andy Razaf has made his mark," announced an unbylined news feature in the *Norfolk* [Virginia] *Journal* on February 3, 1940. "He can afford to be haughty and imperious like some performers and musicians who have had a taste of success. Instead he remains modest and democratic—a scholar and a gentleman in whom the fires of race love burn fiercely. His head shakes sadly as he indicts the musicians of his race—Cab Calloway, Duke Ellington, Erskine Hawkins, and the rest—for their lack of racial vision. 'These men,' he thunders, 'have it in their power to create hundreds of jobs in the music field for Negro men and women. All they have to do is insist on playing one or two numbers by Negro composers when they are on the air, and the radio audiences would take care of the rest.'"

Razaf's public statements were growing increasingly desperate as he entered the Forties, focused on his own growing professional unemployment. Yet the truth of the music business still remained Razaf's greatest obsession. Sinking beneath the weight of Tin Pan Alley's painful disinterest in his work, Razaf nevertheless still felt compelled to speak out. His target was not solely Tin Pan Alley; rather, he also turned his anger and frustration against the few remaining black bandleaders who still were struggling to survive on the pallid Big Band scene.

"Negro publishers like W. C. Handy and Clarence Williams have several potential hits in their safes but can't get the cooperation of Negro bands to put them over," Razaf insisted in the *Norfolk Journal* article, which was nationally syndicated in black newspapers. "And the same is true of scores of unemployed but competent songwriters. The colored bandleaders plead that they have to play what their white managers tell them to play, but I have found none who could admit that they had ever pleaded for a chance for the Negro composer. They don't believe in glorifying the other Negroes, and mainly because of that we all pull our separate ways and the white man snickers and holds the lash over our backs. We just haven't got vision and good common sense."

Razaf could not resist indulging in some pointed reminiscing about the song industry, a valuable history lesson for many younger readers not yet acquainted with the former prominence of black music men on the American entertainment scene. "I remember the time when Negro songwriters were welcomed downtown with open arms," Razaf maintained. "Chris Smith, one of the greatest, was a staff writer with the Havilland Music Publishing Co. Maceo Pinkard was on the staff of two companies, Remick and Shapiro, Bernstein. Today where are they? The white boys absorbed what they knew and now they don't want us anymore. Every so-called new music form that the whites create, like 'swing' and 'jazz,' is a steal from Negro syncopation or is based on Negro dances and Negro mannerisms.

"We are too blind to see until it is too late," Razaf concluded with cold anger and not a little resignation. "Openings for Negroes narrow down every day on Tin Pan Alley to just a very few and our only salvation, as I see it, lies with our bands that are in power and have access to the air. But colored bandleaders positively refuse to give Negro composers a break."

Perhaps the final indignity of Razaf's diminishing professional career transpired with the November 22, 1940, opening in New York City of a film entitled *Tin Pan Alley*. Some months earlier, Razaf and Waller had been paid a nominal fee by the picture's producer, Twentieth Century-Fox, for the studio's right to insert their song "Honeysuckle Rose" into *Tin Pan Alley*, a movie that had as its theme "the doings of the song profession." Now, with the film's release, Razaf and Waller discovered that Fox had in fact framed "Honeysuckle Rose" as a prison scene, with *Tin Pan Alley*'s white stars, Jack Oakie and John Payne, depicted composing the song while serving time, a presentation that probably tickled Waller but outraged Razaf, who could not resist voicing his objections loudly in a letter addressed to Fox's attorneys. "I have just seen 'Tin Pan Alley' in which 'Honeysuckle Rose' was used," he wrote, "and as a co-writer of this song I was indeed shocked at the way it was spotted in the picture. The script writer handled every other song with extreme care and tact but suddenly threw caution and good taste to the winds when he got to 'Honeysuckle Rose.'

"How do you think Irving Berlin, Cole Porter, or any other white writer would feel to see a colored man pictured composing one of their songs in a prison cell?" demanded Razaf indignantly. "Furthermore, to display a copy of 'Honeysuckle Rose' with the names of the fictitious writers on the title page was adding insult to injury.

"It is quite true," conceded Razaf, "that Waller and I received what I could call an appeasement check, but in spite of this gesture we would have been happier to have seen 'Honeysuckle Rose' in a dignified setting and to have received the proper credits as did the other writers in this film. . . . Considering that a writer's prestige is like a trademark which must be built up carefully and jealously guarded," concluded Razaf, "you will realize the extent of injury 'Tin Pan Alley' has done us."

Twentieth Century-Fox legal staffers seem to have been rather amused by Razaf's letter. With peculiar relish, they chose to take the disagreement to the entertainment community at large, turning both

Razaf's letter and Fox's reply over to *Variety*, which published the correspondence on February 5, 1941, under the headline *"Colored Songwriter Objects to 20th's 'Tin Pan' Film Treatment."*

"We used the musical number 'Honeysuckle Rose' in our picture, 'Tin Pan Alley,'" began Fox Counsel, Edwin P. Kilroe, in his indirect retort to Razaf. "We obtained permission from the composers for the use of the number in the manner it was used in the picture and also paid a sizable fee to the publisher for the recording of the music in the picture. The composers of 'Honeysuckle Rose' are Andy Razaf and Thomas 'Fats' Waller. Both composers are colored.

"I am enclosing a very interesting letter we received from Mr. Razaf who objects to the portrayal of himself in the picture as a white man. He doesn't seem to think it is in good taste," observed Mr. Kilroe. "He asks the very interesting question: 'How do you think Irving Berlin, Cole Porter or any other white writer would feel to see a colored man pictured as composing one of their songs in a prison cell?'

"I must confess I do not know the answer," replied a disingenuous Mr. Kilroe. "Perhaps Mr. Berlin or Mr. Porter would tell you the answer.

"You will note," concluded Kilroe, "that Mr. Razaf's letter is only a complaint and no action is threatened. A very interesting question of law, however, is raised, whether north of the Mason–Dixon line a Negro is libeled by being represented as a white man."

This ended Twentieth Century-Fox Film Corporation's public flaunting of black lyricist Andy Razaf's aggrieved demand for respect from Hollywood. It also may have marked the end of Andy Razaf's songwriting, for all intents and purposes, in Hollywood. Like his grandfather John Waller before him, Razaf maintained a sense of righteousness that knew nothing of diplomacy. Even during these darkening days for his songwriting career, Razaf felt compelled to speak out against what he perceived to be a wrong inflicted upon his reputation and his race. Sadly, his expectation that earnestness on his part would be met by earnestness in return was naive. Or perhaps Razaf simply did not care anymore what Hollywood thought about him. Perhaps, Razaf believed, he no longer had anything to lose.

Courtesy Razaf Estate.

13

The Outskirts
of Town

I'm gonna move way out to the outskirts of town,
I'm gonna move way out to the outskirts of town,
Where there ain't no neighbors always hangin' 'round.

    — *"I'm Gonna Move to the Outskirts of Town"*
    by Andy Razaf and William Weldon

Surely nothing in the show business climate of 1940 could have encouraged Razaf to undertake his next venture, a new Broadway-scale all-black musical comedy to be titled *Tan Manhattan*, the first and very nearly the last black musical comedy of the Forties for black creators, a theatrical species already doomed to extinction.

By the beginning of 1940, not one musical that even employed black performers was still running on Broadway, only four having been briefly mounted during the previous season: a WPA-sponsored, all-black casting of Gilbert and Sullivan operetta called *Swing Mikado*; showman Michael Todd's competing commercial production dubbed the *Hot Mikado*, starring Bill Robinson; *Swingin' the Dream*, a disastrous attempt at "jazzing" Shakespeare's *A Midsummer Night's Dream* that wasted a stellar company of featured jazz luminaries including Benny Goodman, Louis Armstrong, and vocalist Maxine Sullivan; and finally, Lew Leslie's last gasp as a revue maker, *Blackbirds of 1939*. Though none of these rather extravagant theatrical underachievers is much remembered today, all four shows at the time registered devastatingly upon the collective psyche of Tin Pan Alley's black songwriting fraternity. For while all four purported to represent black talent on Broadway in 1939, not one contained music composed by black songwriters. Each *Mikado*, of course, had come safely pre-sold with a classic operetta score that required no black song infusions (though Todd's *Mikado* did contain updated lyrics by two white lyricists). *Swingin' the Dream*'s full score had been a product of white songwriters Jimmy Van Heusen and Eddie de Lange, while Lew Leslie had again hired white composers exclusively, a mismatched array of white Tin Pan Alley regulars, to score his *Blackbirds* revue.

Yet out of this season of neglect, frustration, and even desperation for the black entertainment community in New York City, Andy Razaf, together with Eubie Blake, decided in the spring of 1940 to begin work on a black musical comedy in the classic tradition. It was a courageous decision certainly, since neither Razaf nor Blake had worked on Broadway for a decade. The two men shared, however, a stubborn faith in their ability to entertain an audience. As Blake dryly remarked some six months later, with *Tan Manhattan* approaching its first public performance: "After being in the show business thirty-nine years, a man ought to have learned something."

According to Blake, it had taken a bit of a nudge from Razaf to reunite the two songwriters for *Tan Manhattan*. "I was livin' in a rooming house on 138th Street in Harlem at that time," Blake later recalled. "Avis [Blake's wife] had died the year before and I didn't know what to do. I didn't have any reason to do anything. Who was I gonna do it for, I thought. Then I decided. I was fifty-six years old and I wasn't going to be an old man. I had plenty going for me other people didn't. I had my health and a way of making a living doing what was more important to me than anything else and better than that, I knew *how* to live.

"Least that's what Andy told me. He kinda reminded me, you know, kicked me a little. 'Let's work, Eubie,' he says to me and I thought, 'Yeah, why not.'

Razaf was living with his wife, Jean, in their new suburban New Jersey home across the George Washington Bridge. He was sick of commuting to the city for scraps of song work—sick of writing "cross-overs" for stage shows at the Apollo Theatre, sick of writing "tag lines" for big band themes, sick of waiting in the wings at movie houses for some last-minute patch-up duty, without credit, on a between-film production number. Razaf desperately wanted to develop a legitimate vehicle for his lyric writing talent. An old-style musical comedy targeted for Broadway was the most accessible, albeit unpromising, route that he could pursue.

Working at Thomas Waller's old piano in Razaf's newly furnished Englewood living room, the reconstituted song team of Razaf and Blake began to turn out tunes, the majority of them patterned rather blatantly after previous Razaf or Blake successes: "Magnolia Rose," a floral variation on the "Honeysuckle Rose" theme, with a sweet, soaring Blake melody line; "Shakin' Up the Folks Below," Razaf's 1940 take on "The Joint is Jumpin'" from the poor, suffering downstairs neighbors' point of view; "A Great Big Baby," Razaf and Blake's boisterous rephrasing of Sissle and Blake's raunchy *Shuffle Along* hit "I'm Craving for That Kind of Love," plus "The Hep Cat," *Tan Manhattan*'s attempt at unleashing a new dance craze for the Swing Era's "jumpin' jivers."

To this initial point, *Tan Manhattan*'s safe, craftsmanlike score was eminently presentable, each melody distinguished by some distinctive flourish from Blake—a sudden octave-long leap in "Magnolia Rose," a ragging break in the midst of "Hep Cat"'s period jive. Razaf's lyrics, rhythm driven and soundly rhymed, revealed sly wit, as in these lines from "A Great Big Baby."

> *Why should men approach with caution*
> *Such an extra special portion?*
> *Elephants are not contrary,*
> *Why just favor the canary?*

Razaf, though, had something avowedly more ambitious in mind for *Tan Manhattan* beyond the common "colored" musical comedy format. Continually, obsessively, he hounded Blake. This was no longer 1925. A black musical in 1940 owed itself and its audience at least some passing acknowledgment of African–American existence beyond the "stompin'" and the "partyin'" and the comically lusty cravings. Blake protested. *Tan Manhattan* was about entertainment, not enlightenment. Razaf, however, was adamant.

"He wrote a piece about the Negro for our show," Blake later recalled. "One day he passed it to me and I read this thing. Well, he'd given the white people hell.

"Now, this thing ain't no song, exactly. I think I'd written the music already and everything and then he'd written this poem, this thing that, after the song was sung, you'd talk this part out. Well this thing went right from the lynchin' of Negroes to *everything*.

" 'Andy,' I said, 'Andy, this is the greatest lyric you ever wrote in your life. But how the hell are you gonna stand there and tell . . . charge people money to open a show and have them come hear how lousy they treated us? How you gonna do that?'

"You know what he said to me? 'I am the lyricist. I am the lyricist,' he said. 'You are the melody writer.'

" 'But you're wrong,' I said. 'You're wrong. You can't do that'— have people payin' money to hear you tell them that you started from the days when you'd go someplace—this is at the beginning of black theater—you'd go someplace and hear, 'You can't go in this place, you can't do that, you can't do this'—from white folks.

" 'Andy,' I says, 'You *never* done a thing this big. But it ain't no good. You can't sell it to Sam Jones 'cause he ain't gonna buy it!' And it's true, mind you, everything he said,'cause my father was a slave, mother and father both were slaves.

"He just looked at me, though. 'You write the music,' he says, 'I write the lyrics.' He told me that eight million times.

"Irvin C. Miller," Blake continued, naming the pioneering black theatrical producer whose *Brownskin Models* revue series Razaf had written for in the Twenties, "Irvin C. Miller—great producer, great director—he's staging our show. I had seen Irvin and I had given him this thing. So he read it and he says, 'Oh, what a marvelous thing. Where did you get it?' I looked at him and said, 'Andy did it.' Now he wants the details and everything. It's the deadline day, you see, the day to have our lyrics and things finished. This is the dead day.

" 'How in the hell am I gonna charge money for you to tell them how lousy they are?' Miller says. 'Cause we just missed lynchin'. Just missed it—Razaf and Blake. Ten more years and they'd have had us. 'I can't give it to them,' Miller says. 'Change it.'

"We're in New Jersey now, at Andy's home. We're in the living room. Andy's wife, Jean, is there, layin' on the sofa.

" 'I'm not gonna change nothin',' Andy says.

" 'Wait and keep it for yourself,' Miller says. 'It ain't goin' in my show.'

" 'Did they do it?' Andy asks. 'Did they lynch us?'

" 'Yes,' Miller says.

" 'Did I exaggerate?' he asks. 'Is it true?'

" 'Yeah,' Miller says, 'it's all true. But it ain't goin' in my show.'

"I walked out the door. I stood outside.

"'I'm not gonna change a line in it,' Andy says. 'It's all true.'

"Now, I don't know a woman more brilliant than Andy's wife, Jean. She's been lyin' there all this time, silent. Suddenly she speaks up. Surprised hell out of me. 'Andy,' she suddenly says, 'change that lyric.'

"'I'm not gonna change a line,' Andy says. 'It's all true.'

"'It ain't goin' in my show,' Miller says. 'It don't go in the show.'

"'Andy,' Jean says—she's sittin' up now—'Andy, you know I never meddle with what you write. But I'm against you on this and the whole black world will be against you, the intelligent ones. 'Cause some of the guys, they want somebody to do this. But this isn't the way to do it. Andy, you can't sell it back to the people.'

"And she gets up and she gets him a pen. She isn't just tellin' him, see, she ain't tellin' him, she's *explainin'*. And he's listenin'. Irvin and me, we don't say nothin'. She gives him the pen. Damned if he don't change it."

Little of Andy Razaf's original "Recitation" for "We Are Americans Too"—the formal title of this most troubling contribution to *Tan Manhattan*—remains today to be inspected. After rewriting the piece on the spot at his wife's behest, Razaf apparently destroyed the bristling original. All that is left, printed on the sheet music endpapers of the published version, is a mildly uplifting, racially centered patriotic incantation:

> At Valley Forge, men must admit,
> With Washington we did our bit.
> When given any kind of chance
> We've made the grade and shown advance,
> In business, science, letters, art,
> We've played a most surprising part.

Who was right? Probably Blake and Irvin C. Miller and Jean Blackwell Razaf, who sadly understood that nothing could come of a crusading political production number in a peppy black musical revue in 1940, recognizing that the original "We Are Americans Too" could only sink *Tan Manhattan* before most white audiences would ever hear Razaf's lyric. In retrospect, one can certainly view Andy Razaf as a radical race spokesman well ahead of his time or simply as a frustrated Tin Pan Alley songwriter overreaching his circumscribed arena. Literally, he was the latter. Yet, one again must wonder at the great impractical scope of Razaf's expectations, willed to him by his grandfather John Waller. As with so much of Razaf's career, the inappropriateness borders on the extraordinary.

Casting *Tan Manhattan* proved a relatively simple task. So many performers of consequence in the black musical comedy world were out of work by 1940 that Razaf and Blake and Miller had their pick of great names. All three collaborators had at one time already worked with most of them. Flournoy Miller was hired to handle the comedic lead. Nina Mae McKinney, once the 19-year-old star of King Vidor's 1929 film classic *Hallelujah,* was signed, along with Sally Gooding, Evelyn Keyes, and Winnie Johnson—all former featured Harlem entertainers—for the female leads. Avon Long, the great Cotton Club star, heir to John Bubble's role of Sportin' Life in George Gershwin's *Porgy and Bess* just three years before, was offered another star spot.

The supporting creative staff was equally impressive. Addison Carey, second only to Leonard Harper as a Harlem revue producer, was chosen, together with the great tap master Henry Le Tang, to choreograph *Tan Manhattan.* An augmented orchestra to be directed by Blake was stocked with some of the finest unemployed band musicians the decade could offer—former featured players from the finest now departed black dance bands.

By the end of the year, *Tan Manhattan* was in rehearsal—a mammoth three-hour-plus production laden with numerous musical turns and comedic sketches, a hefty cast of singers, dancers, and comics, a full choir, a crowded orchestra pit, and a musical score numbering more than twenty tunes.

An out-of-town tryout week was booked at the Howard Theatre in Washington, DC. Expectation was running very high, both within the company and in the theatrically parched African–American communities down in Washington and up in Harlem where *Tan Manhattan* was slated to reach the Apollo Theatre in February.

Razaf, of course, was enormously optimistic about his show and pressed his optimism all across Tin Pan Alley. Tin Pan Alley, unsurprisingly, was little moved. "Dear Andy," wrote Abe Olman on behalf of Robbins Music in response to one of Razaf's importunate, gushing letters regarding his latest musical production. "I think it best to wait until your show opens in Washington on January 17th before we decide whether or not we are interested in acquiring the score."

Tan Manhattan opened at the Howard Theatre in Washington on January 24, 1941—one week late—premiering with the pomp of a Broadway opening. Reviews the following morning were good. "The smiles of Winnie Johnson, the tears of Nina Mae McKinney, and the dancing feet of Avon Long, aided and abetted by the tuneful score, sent *Tan Manhattan* off to a grand start Wednesday evening," reported the *Washington Afro-American*, while another Washington paper headlined the show simply: "*A Hit.*" Singled out for praise were Avon Long and Winnie Johnson's "Magnolia Rose" production number and Nina Mae McKinney's two torchy ballads, "Say Hello to the Folks Back Home" and "I'll Take a Nickel for a Dime."

"Nickel for a Dime" had entered the *Tan Manhattan* songbook late in rehearsals, turned out by Razaf and Blake to fill a need everyone sensed for another McKinney ballad in the show's second act. The song was a nostalgia piece along the lines of "Memories of You," and a fresh look at it today further confirms the reputation that this *Tan Manhattan* score has long enjoyed as a neglected minor masterwork.

As performed originally in *Tan Manhattan*, "I'll Take a Nickel for a Dime" opened with Nina Mae McKinney onstage entering a tavern, heading immediately for the jukebox, rummaging through her purse, then turning to address the audience:

> *Has anybody got change for a dime?*
> *Two nickels, if you don't mind.*
> *You only have one?*
> *Well, you're just in time.*
> *Please, if you'll be so kind.*

A bar patron stepped forward and McKinney made her change. The nickel dropped, the jukebox whirred, the music swelled.

> *I'll take your nickel for a dime,*
> *I've got to hear that record play again,*
> *Turn love's December into May again,*
> *Bring me a thrill just one more time,*
> *I'll take your nickel for a dime—*
> *I've got to hear that sweet refrain again,*
> *That carries me down mem'ry lane again,*
> *I'll take your nickel for a dime.*

> *Once two sweethearts were sweetly blended,*
> *And they sang a love duet,*
> *But today the song is ended—*

THE OUTSKIRTS OF TOWN

> *Still one heart will not forget;*
> *I'll take your nickel for a dime,*
> *So I can hear that melody again,*
> *That brings my love back to me again,*
> *I'll take your nickel for a dime.*

The song is perfectly elegant in its bittersweet simplicity. The sentiments expressed in it are moist, but the lyrics, as written, are absolutely dry-eyed, asking not for sympathy nor pity, just change for a dime. When even that is not forthcoming, the lyricist allows his singer to take a nickel because that is what she needs to get on with her business. No complaints. The lyricist's sadness, his song makes clear, is great, but the sadness does not weigh on the listener. It is born with gentle grace.

As always, Razaf's rhymes were effortless, unobtrusively propelling "Nickel for a Dime" forward despite the torchy tempos, with some smart lyric effects and the alternating repetitions of the word "again" enclosing the tune beautifully, while conveying, perhaps unintentionally, the barest suggestion of a record needle caught in its groove. Reworked and revalued by Razaf in 1953 as "I'd Give a Dollar for a Dime," the song has managed to survive despite its never having become a standard, justifying the attention bestowed upon it initially in its *Tan Manhattan* debut.

Andy Razaf and Eubie Blake were both highly encouraged by *Tan Manhattan*'s reception in Washington. Blake felt that it would take at least five days for the show's creators to determine just "how much they had"—what should be kept, what could be cut—while Razaf noted some twenty-one specific items that required further attention and, perhaps, elimination. Overall, though, the signs were positive.

One thing that clearly did not work was the comedy. Flournoy Miller's sketches were poorly received at each performance, and the book, many felt, was getting trampled to death in the avalanche of songs, which, as one reviewer put it, "literally stepped on each other's heels in such rapid succession that the audience could hardly catch the melody of one before it was frightened away by another."

Having seized for themselves this opportunity to compose for Broadway, Razaf and Blake had poured the sum of many pent-up years of songwriting creativity into *Tan Manhattan*. While it was generally agreed that *Tan Manhattan*'s problems in part resided with

this surfeit of material—much of it good but most of it indiscriminately showcased—it is a bit sobering to note how unusually
deferential, at times even apologetic, reviewers of *Tan Manhattan* in
Washington were, with the black theater critics seeming almost as
desperate as the performers and creators for the show to succeed.
"The directors," observed one, "could easily cut out at least five
numbers, strengthen the better tunes by repetition, elaborate on the
romantic angle which was lost after the first five minutes, and
reshuffle the bits so some semblance of a theme can be maintained
throughout. In its present hodgepodge form *Tan Manhattan* becomes
just another series of acts with which we are all too familiar. *Tan
Manhattan,*" he hastened to add, though, "is made of too excellent
stuff to let itself fall into this category. In fact, there was so much
worthwhile material and so many fine artists crowded into the two
hours' entertainment that to criticize at all makes me feel like a man
with a full stomach complaining because the courses were not served
in perfect order."

As the show's run was extended a second week in Washington, a
selective dampening of the enthusiasms that had first generated *Tan
Manhattan* was wrought upon the production, with excisions made in
the score and scenes trimmed and reorganized. This show, Razaf
devoutly believed, was very close.

He was mistaken. *Tan Manhattan* at the Howard Theatre in
Washington was no closer to Broadway than it would be after it
opened at the Apollo Theatre in Harlem in February 1941. It closed
shortly thereafter, dashing Andy Razaf and Eubie Blake's Broadway
aspirations one final time. Broadway producers quite simply were no
longer interested in "colored" musical comedy. What Broadway
wanted from "colored" musical comedy it had by now already
appropriated.

For Razaf, the demise of *Tan Manhattan* was an occasion for some
uncharacteristic fact-facing about his career. He was just about out of
work, willingly or not in semiretirement, exiled to New Jersey
despite one final floorshow job late in 1941 with Paul Denniker for
the "new" *downtown* Ubangi Club, recently transferred from the
increasingly dangerous precincts of Harlem to the former Moulin
Rouge restaurant on 52nd Street and Broadway.

Certainly the December declaration of war against Japan, followed by America's entry into the European conflict, did nothing for
Razaf's waning song career, though the war effort did in fact prolong
his professional song presence with Bond Drive songs. Razaf pub-

lished more than a dozen War Bond songs from 1942 to 1945 in partnership with Joe Davis, Luckey Roberts and, most surprisingly, J. Rosamond Johnson: "War Bond Man," "That's Why I Buy Bonds, and "Goin' on an Errand for Uncle Sam," among others. His professional life was dominated by yeoman bond drive duty, both as drumbeating songwriter and as singer/performer/bond salesman, the most successful of these propagandistic song novelties emerging, quite absurdly, from the failed *Tan Manhattan* score: Razaf's denatured protest song 'We Are Americans Too.' In the wake of war, "We Are Americans Too" somehow came to be perceived as black America's ultimate patriotic call to arms, a truly exasperating irony, given the lyricist's original intentions.

Razaf enthusiastically adapted to this final diminution, turning up with "We Are Americans Too" throughout the war years at any war bond affair that would have them—on radio, at banquets, in movie houses—although he eventually began to beg off from these public appearances. Time after time, though, he was called back, persuaded to sing "it" just once more for devotees like Edna Thomas, Executive Secretary of the Negro Actors Guild of America, who observed to a demurring Razaf at one point, "I hope you will pardon me when I say that it is well understood that singing is not one of your most important talents. Yet, being one of the parents of that really great number 'We Are Americans Too,' you are able to put a lot into it that even more gifted singers would fail in trying to do. I know whereof I speak because I have heard you on more than one occasion."

While Razaf, in October 1944, was cited by the U. S. Treasury Department for "patriotic cooperation rendered in behalf of the War Finances Program," and attended President Franklin Delano Roosevelt's final inauguration ceremony at the White House in January 1945 (alone, without his wife, Jean, having been offered only a single ticket), he managed to place but thirteen non–bond-related songs with Tin Pan Alley during the years 1943 to 1945. He also contributed lyrics for incidental music to a 1943 Pabst Blue Ribbon industrial show, with Eubie Blake. Except for these low points, his song career during the war years had all but come to a standstill.

It was the tragic premature death of Thomas Waller on December 16, 1943, that truly seems to have extinguished much of the lingering spark in Razaf's songwriting spirit. Waller's sudden death came in a sleeper car on a New York–bound train from Los Angeles passing through Kansas City. Influenza and bronchial pneumonia, according to a coroner's report, acted upon a 300-pound body grievously abused by alcohol, obesity, and overwork. In essence, for Razaf, this was the final blow.

Razaf and Waller had been forced very far apart by Waller's grinding, debt-financed tour schedule. Though his enormous success as a recording artist and performing attraction had brought the pianist substantial wealth—a new Morningside Drive apartment, a house out in St. Albans, Queens, a Lincoln touring car, and closets full of hand-tailored suits—as far back as 1938 Waller had come to owe his managers a fortune in unpaid commissions and cash advances while falling impossibly behind on his alimony and car payments and his taxes. He also had owed huge fines to the Musicians Union for a wealth of missed engagements, and judgments were filed against him by disgruntled dance and concert promoters whom he'd cavalierly stood up all across the nation. Waller had, in fact, so debased his reputation with promoters on this side of the Atlantic that Europe was the only market his management had been able to look to as an outlet for recouping his losses. Throughout the summer of 1938, he had toured all across the British Isles, to great acclaim, as well as throughout Scandinavia. He'd returned to Europe again in March of 1939, covering the continent this time, again on a murderous tour schedule. Again, he'd been a monumental success.

Touring seems also to have been a tangential strategy employed by Waller's new manager, Ed Kirkeby, for controlling his client's waywardness. Kirkeby, another shrewd and experienced music business professional, who had taken over from an exhausted Phil Ponce early in 1938, always claimed to have adored his adorable, uncontainable client. But Kirkeby clearly decided that the best way to keep his client out of trouble was to keep him busy to the point of exhaustion, and Waller may have paid the price for it with his health.

Still, prime responsibility for Waller's degenerating physical condition during these final years certainly resided with Waller himself, who increasingly addressed his discontent with the direction his career had long since taken by dissipation to the point of negation: eating, womanizing, and above all else, drinking with frightening intensity. Ironically, Waller had recently begun to exhibit advancing signs of maturity for the first time in his life, specifically a growing concern with professional fulfillment and a disenchantment with the clownish persona and ludicrous song material that were now expected of him. Yet, he was unsure what concrete steps he could take, and in the end had simply fled from his responsibilities.

Increasingly, Waller's behavior on the road had grown more erratic, though the vastly endearing pianist generally had managed to transmute this behavior into the stuff of entertainment legend. With unnerving frequency, for example, Waller often abandoned his own rather large-scale tours on a homesick whim, tossing his 300-pound body into his chauffeured limousine on a moment's notice, no matter where in the country he might at that moment be, with the simple cry to his driver, "Bobby, Holland Tunnel." There were also more and more nights when Waller's near mythic alcoholic capacity eluded him and he appeared drunk onstage (wrapped in a wing curtain on one occasion, and surreptitiously walked out to the piano bench by his valet and a friend). Musicians in his band later recalled that after their return from Europe in 1939, his limbs often swelled to such a degree that the pianist had difficulty walking. He developed a propensity for minor infections. His legendary strength and stamina began to wane. Toward the end, even his voracious appetite diminished. Finally, on a nightclub job in Los Angeles late in 1943 at the Cafe Zanzibar, working in the draft of a nearby air conditioner, he developed a severe bronchial condition. Death came shortly thereafter.

A letter dated August 21, 1943, from Ed Kirkeby to Waller on the road in Philadelphia, provides painful testimony to the final suicidal dimension of Waller's drinking habit, as well as the unregenerate commercial thrust of Kirkeby's concern for his client.

> Dear Tom:
>
> Last night I came away from Philadelphia with a heavy heart. I had seen you in such terrible condition from drink that your performance suffered frightfully—you announced to your audience that you were drunk.
>
> Tom, my regard for you cannot be questioned. You haven't *one* other friend like me in the thousands you know. And as that friend I'm telling you that your drinking is undermining your health, your artistry, and giving you a reputation which will interfere with your bookings and earning capacity—as sure as tomorrow will come.
>
> That is all, Tom. It's as simple as that—and as serious as that. You are getting older, and you cannot take it the way you used to. If you don't slow down, it's going to get you!
>
> But you can cut down sensibly; keep the drinking out of your

work, and still have a fuller, richer life than ever before. *Now* is the time, Tom. I pray you realize it.

Your sincere friend,
Ed Kirkeby

The tragedy of Waller's death was only intensified by the fact that by 1943, Andy Razaf's favorite collaborator truly had reached the summit of his profession. On August 9, a lengthy Fats Waller profile had appeared in *Time* magazine. (Razaf, to his delight, received prominent mention in this piece as Waller's "favorite poet next to Wordsworth.") Earlier in the year, Waller also had costarred in the movie *Stormy Weather*, Hollywood's belated tribute to the living legends of black entertainment—Ethel Waters, Bill Robinson, John Bubbles—along with younger stars like Waller and Lena Horne. Hired for a feature spot as a performer in an impending Broadway production entitled *Early to Bed*, Waller later that year had wound up, through manager Kirkeby's salesmanship, as composer of the *Early to Bed* score, collaborating not with Andy Razaf, but rather with George Marion, a white lyric writer.

This commission was galling for Razaf, who had managed between 1935 and 1943 to team with Waller on fewer than twenty songs, yet still nursed great hopes of reuniting with him on a regular basis. There even had been stirrings of preliminary work by the two songmen on an opera set in Madagascar. Waller's death represented more than a tragic suspension of these hopes. For Razaf, it was a true ending.

The funeral, a majestic affair that embraced all of Harlem, was presided over by Waller's childhood friend the Reverend Adam Clayton Powell, Jr., at Abyssinian Baptist Church. "I had an assignment from Adam at Fats's funeral," Jean Blackwell later recalled, "the assignment of seeing that only one wife turned up, but I was not able to. I tried to prevail on Anita, Fats's second wife, because I knew I couldn't do anything with the other one, but I didn't succeed. The church was so crowded anyway, in the end, it hardly mattered."

Razaf's only public comment upon learning of Waller's death had been stark and heartfelt: "He was my best friend." At the funeral, though, the lyricist amplified eloquently on the nature of his relationship with Thomas "Fats" Waller in a eulogy that the Reverend Powell read to the assembled multitude, "A Poet's Tribute to a Pal."

"To write about Thomas 'Fats' Waller as I do at this time is truly the toughest assignment of my life," Razaf began. "How can I possibly give you a complete picture of this remarkable artist in a few words when such a character as 'Fats,' as he was endearingly called by countless friends, leaves enough highlights to fill several volumes? We apply the term 'greatness' to many who never fully deserve it. In the case of 'Fats' Waller, such a word is inadequate. With all of his rare gifts, success, and world-acclaim, Waller never changed. He was too busy with his music and entertaining his beloved public to take himself seriously . . .

"I have written songs with many writers of both races, but never in my life have I found one to equal Fats Waller as an all-around composer of all types of music. It was a thrill and delight to write with him. When you laid a lyric before him he would sit at the piano, read every line carefully until he had absorbed its mood and story, then begin to weave a melody around it. The right music would come in no time. It seemed to flow from his fingertips like water from a fountain. When he considered the song finished, with every note and phrase just right, he would arch those big eyebrows that gave so much expression to his face, and then play and sing it. No lyric, whether it was just an ordinary 32-bar song or a lengthy ensemble piece, was too difficult for him to set to music. I once remarked to a reporter that Fats could set the phone book to music. . . . I meant it. . . .

"The public that marveled at this master of the piano, organ, musical composition, and stagecraft never realized that Fats had only scratched the surface of his genius. I feel that had Waller lived and finally given more time to his creative ability, he would have made greater contributions to American music . . . Nevertheless, he has left the world a rosary of melodies that will keep his memory alive . . . Some of the Broadway music publishers who encouraged and helped Fats during his career deserve mention, especially Lester Santly, Harry Link, Sol Bernstein, Joe Davis, Clarence Williams, Jack Bregman, Handy Brothers, and Jack Robbins. His closest pals and writing associates were James P. Johnson, J. C. Johnson, Spencer Williams, Bud Allen, Luckey Roberts, Ken Macomber, and myself. We will miss that big, happy-go-lucky bundle of rhythm, music, and laughter, that engaging personality. Yes, Fats Waller is gone, and for us Tin Pan Alley can never be the same."

"I only understood after I parted from him much that I didn't understand at the time," Jean Blackwell later admitted, "which was that many of the slights that he received on Tin Pan Alley, he would come home and take out on me. I was young and I didn't know how to deal with that."

The Razafs were strapped financially in Englewood during the Forties, "though it wasn't apparent to him or me in the beginning that Andy was in financial difficulty," Jean Blackwell later insisted. "If it had been, we would never have gotten involved in the Englewood property. Andy didn't save, that was a big part of the strain between us. I made very little money but I always managed to save a bit of it and he was always broke." Razaf's financial difficulties were exacerbated in 1941 by a ten-month ASCAP strike over radio royalties. Razaf, during this period, had placed some songs copyrighted under his wife's name with ASCAP's newly created rival BMI (Broadcast Music Inc., a song protectionist society founded and financed by radio broadcasting companies). He also had published a few songs at this time under the pseudonym "Andrea LaDuke." "I had to use my savings to make the mortgage payments," Blackwell later recalled. "The man practically had no identity in those years."

In 1946, Razaf wrote a number of film "synopses" for Paramount Pictures—potential film short scenarios with music. One of these was to feature Bing Crosby singing "A New Day Prayer," one of many new songs that Razaf had written with Teri Josefovits, a pianist from the Paramount Theatre orchestra. Nothing came of these submissions.

In 1946, Razaf decided to enter politics, more out of sincere social conviction and perhaps professional desperation than any real political ambition, running as an Independent for a City Council seat from Englewood's Fourth Ward. "I was drafted to run by the people of Englewood," he later pointed out, "and though I had no stomach for politics, I felt it would be a good thing for the morale of my race." Adam Clayton Powell endorsed his campaign and even came out to speak for Razaf in Englewood at a huge, gorgeously theatrical campaign rally held at the Lincoln School Auditorium on October 31. In spite of this, or perhaps because of it, Razaf was defeated by 368 votes in a bitterly contested race that split this nearly segregated northern New Jersey town sharply along racial lines. In the wake of defeat, Razaf's campaign staff produced evidence of registration record rigging and polling booth tampering committed by the victorious Republican candidate, Albert Moskin. "Registration records of a considerable number of voters suddenly became lost," acknowledged the *Englewood Press* in a post–election day article on

November 6, "and the key over Razaf's name in one of the machines was suspiciously jammed." Despite public support for these charges from many precincts and from the contest's Democratic candidate, Edwin J. Roth, who had placed third behind Razaf, Englewood's Fourth Ward election results were allowed to stand.

"That defeat distressed Andy terribly," Jean Blackwell remembered. "Not just the losing, but the manner in which the election was conducted. It enraged him. A good deal of Andy's heritage I think gave him an independent outlook; he was aware of having this royalty in him and wouldn't let people put him down. It was very hard. I guess it still would be, even now . . . to be independent and black."

For the Razafs, in Englewood there was always the added strain of being the first black couple on their block. "I know that the FBI was always checking on us because of this," Jean Blackwell maintained. "Our neighbors would tell us that the FBI had asked them whether we had any white people as houseguests."

Finally, though, the greatest strain on the Razafs' marriage emerged over a visiting African writer named Mbomu Ojike whom Jean Blackwell Razaf had met through a local African cultural society called the Paralux East and West Association. "Andy had always been the African in my consciousness," Blackwell later pointed out in accounting for the difficulty that Ojike soon posed, "the one who taught me about Africa, the link. When Ojike became very smitten with me, Andy became very jealous and made all sorts of scenes. Once, when Ojike was supposed to come to the house with a group of people, Andy forbade it and at the last minute the whole thing had to be called off."

According to Blackwell, her husband was especially suspicious because he himself was "messing around" with Dorothy Carpenter —the woman Razaf's mother continued to refer to as her daughter, and admittedly would have preferred as a wife for her son. "She was supposed to be a saleswoman of some sort," Blackwell explained, "and she would come and spend the day at the house with Andy and then pull out of the driveway just as I drove in, making sure that I saw her. There was a lot of talk in town about this, Englewood being such a little town and us being the first black family on this block. The neighbors paid special attention to our business."

At first, according to Blackwell, there were scenes between the Razafs at a couple of parties. The final blowup came at an affair at the Razaf home.

"Later that night Andy hit me. I made up my mind right then that, if I got away, I wasn't going to be there ever again. I got out the next morning and I never came back. I came to New York and stayed at a friend's house who worked at the YWCA. Finally I got a room at the YWCA.

"I'd never had that experience before. That was the first and I made sure that it was the last time. Lots of efforts were made to reconcile us after that, but that was it for me as far as I was concerned."

There were plenty of false starts for Blackwell before she could secure her divorce. One black lawyer, she recalled, took her retainer but never pursued the case because he himself admired Andy Razaf so that he firmly believed Mrs. Razaf "would never get a chance like this again." Blackwell finally was forced to find a white lawyer who wasn't nearly so impressed by her husband. "I even went down to Elkton, hoping that maybe we weren't legally married," Blackwell later recalled, "but I found that the marriage was down as legal. That's when I turned the matter over to the white lawyer. He saw it through."

The marriage had lasted less than eight years, eight of Razaf's most humbling, professionally. In the twilight of Razaf's career, Jean Blackwell might have been able to ease his painful withdrawal from his active songwriting. But it may have been impossible in the end for any woman to have stood by him during this devastating time. That Razaf did strike his wife once (though he later emphatically denied it) seems tragic, however uncondonable, confirmation of the crushing anxiety and depression that Razaf was battling.

By the beginning of 1948, Andy Razaf was divorced and living with Dorothy Carpenter in Jean Blackwell's Englewood home. On July 16, 1948, a Saturday, at 6 P.M., Dorothy Carpenter became Razaf's third wife, at the residence of friends in Washington, DC. The Reverend Emory B. Smith officiated and Razaf's Uncle John Waller gave the bride away. The third Mrs. Razaf wore a gown of white crepe with green ostrich plumes, an orchid in her hair, diamond earrings, and a diamond necklace.

On Monday morning, July 18, the couple left Washington for Madison, New Jersey, Dorothy Carpenter-Razaf's hometown. Their honeymoon plans called for a trip to the Virgin Islands at the end of August. Following that trip, the Razaf's new home would be Los Angeles, California, a beautiful Spanish-style stucco hacienda at 3429 Country Club Drive. By early autumn, they were settled there.

Courtesy Schomburg Center for Research in Black Culture.

14

Blue Turning Grey

I run my hands thru' sil'vry strands,
'Cause I'm blue turning grey over you.
— *"Blue Turning Grey over You"*
by Andy Razaf and Thomas Waller

Andy Razaf's uncle John Waller never could fathom his father's seeming acceptance of the Waller family's downfall in Madagascar at the hands of the French in 1894. Throughout the years following his father's ordeal, John Waller, Jr., was fiercely bitter, though resigned, in time, to the timeless prejudices facing him.

After enlisting, illictly, at 16 and fighting in the Spanish–American War alongside his father, John Waller, Jr., had remained a military nomad for much of his adult life, traveling the world in a self-imposed exile from the United States. His only homeward connection was the vivid, sometimes torrid correspondence he carried on with his family, specifically with his beloved father.

These letters frequently exposed the depth of his discontent, commonly expressed in a disturbing mixture of wishful thinking and blistering prognostication for the impending end of European colonial dominance worldwide and the rise of nonwhite nations like China, Japan, and India as international powers. "I suppose you know that victory for the Japanese [in the Sino-Russian War] will mean the expulsion of the white man from Asia . . ." the younger Waller had, for example, insisted to his father in a letter from the

Philippines dated July 8, 1904. "Once the force is aroused, Europe herself will not be safe from invasion and domination."

While John Waller, Jr., clearly inherited his father's forceful view of racial politics (as well as flashes of his rhetorical gift), it seems certain that Waller senior shared little of his son's apocalyptically vindictive racial yearnings. Similarly, Andy Razaf, while capable of a rage as potent as his Uncle John's, nevertheless tended, even in his years of steep decline, not to bear any overwhelming grudges. Like his grandfather, Razaf certainly recognized the racism inherent in the culture within which he lived and worked. Viewing himself, however, as a victimized figure central to that culture, rather than as any sort of disenfranchised outsider, Razaf, again like his grandfather before him, strove to change his world from within, rather than abet its destruction from without.

This difference of degree did not prevent Razaf from growing increasingly closer to his belligerent uncle John throughout their lives together. Their relationship became especially intimate during the years following World War Two, when Waller, Jr., retired to Harlem on a military pension. After his arrival in Los Angeles in 1948, Razaf immediately initiated an epistolary link with his uncle that would sustain both men for the rest of Razaf's life. Letter writing, in fact, soon constituted Razaf's lifeline to the East. His professional existence, such as it was, would be sustained in California solely by postal connection—to the music publishers of Tin Pan Alley and the overseeing offices of ASCAP, whose checks reached him through the mail; to the letters that still bound him to Joe Davis and former collaborators Eubie Blake, Paul Denniker, and James P. and J. C. Johnson; and finally, through the inumerable peripheral characters of the song business in New York who, by letter, sent Razaf word in his semiretirement of further traffic in and abuses of the name and the works of Andy Razaf.

"Dear Andy," wrote Harrison Smith, one of the black song fraternity's great gadabouts—a former songwriter, artist's manager, and press representative, as well as advertising director for the Lincoln Theatre during Fats Waller's residency there—in a letter dated April 29, 1950. "Just a line to let you know that The Bootleggers have just released your song—HONEYSUCKLE ROSE— under the TEMPLE label. With LOUISIANA and ON REVIVAL DAY this makes 3 of yours thus far to my knowledge."

Smith proceeded to enlighten Razaf regarding his efforts to advise "Mr. J. Edgar Hoover of FBI of how Copyright/Patent & U.S. Mail

Laws are being violated by these buzzards." He referred me to the NYC office," Smith added. "I await a reply."

The distribution of so-called "bootleg" recordings that featured old popular songs performed by various unidentifiable performers —many of them fairly legitimate jazzmen working under pseudonyms—had long been commonplace in the music industry. Many of the songs recorded actually were old enough to be in the public domain, thereby precluding royalty payments to their composers. The majority, however, though still under copyright, simply were treated by bootleggers as if they were public song property. Razaf hardly was a lone victim in this respect. Smith, as a self-anointed bootlegging watchdog, represented, among other old-timers, blues vocalist Victoria Spivey, jazz legend Sidney Bechet, and many of Razaf's former Gaiety Building associates, including J. C. Johnson, Perry Bradford, and Spencer Williams. As Smith pointed out to Razaf in his letter, "naturally, if purchases are made thru Bootleg sources instead of proper sources, you cannot expect royalties from above compositions." Even with the fervent support of tenacious Harrison Smith, though, there was little Razaf could do to stop the bootleggers. In fact, there was something to be said for leaving them to their business. At least the songs were being recorded.

Razaf rapidly found himself forgotten as a songwriter, as a lyricist, and even as an acknowledged contributor to the glory that had been Harlem in the Twenties after his move to Los Angeles. In December 1950, for example, he made a quick trip back to New York, in part to attend a 25th Anniversary Celebration at Smalls' Paradise. The evening proved unexpectedly painful. "To me the occasion was perfect with one exception," Razaf later pointed out in a letter to Ed Smalls. "Neither the printed program nor Jimmy Mordecai [the evening's emcee] gave a single word of credit to the ones who wrote and staged the original 'Kitchen Mechanic's Revue.'

"You are a very busy man and can be excused for such glaring injustices," Razaf conceded, with wrenching magnanimity, "but not the army of workers employed by you to take care of such details.

"Your research department should have known better. Only my long, sincere friendship for you kept me from filing a protest with ASCAP. I trust the next time your program will read: 'Kitchen Mechanic's Revue'/Original Edition Conceived by Andy Razaf, Music by James P. Johnson, Staged by Addison Carey & Charles Davis, Music played by Charlie Johnson's Orchestra.

"I laughed when Charlie Johnson took the bows for writing 'Porter's Love Song.' And had it not been for one thoughtful gentleman there," Razaf concluded, "I never would have been introduced at all."

On January 26, 1951, Andy Razaf spent the day at his home on Country Club Drive in California with a visiting friend from New York. Along with Razaf, Herbert Fauntleroy Julian had been one of Harlem's gaudiest glamour kings, a self-proclaimed "aviator" with a gloriously daffy self-promotional sense, who, having invented something that he called the "parachutta gravepreresista"—a rescuing helicopter blade device ostensibly activated by a failing parachute—had arrived in Harlem at the outset of the Twenties ostentatiously driven in a limousine directly from flight training in Canada by a white chauffeur. While concentrating the bulk of his time and energy cutting a dashing figure uptown, generally while wearing a black velvet cape, Julian in April 1923 had inaugurated his career as an aviation spectacle by selling tickets at a dollar apiece for his forthcoming parachute jump into a vacant lot at 139th Street between Seventh and Eighth Avenues. After selling viewing rights to his body in the event of disaster to the highest bidding local undertaker, Julian had made good on his promoted leap, descending in a red jumpsuit onto the roof of the post office, two blocks off course, trailing an advertising banner that announced, "Hoenig Optical Open Today." A wildly enthusiastic crowd then had carried him through the streets of Harlem to Marcus Garvey and the United Negro Improvement Association's Liberty Hall, where Julian's day had been capped with a summons for inciting a riot. Six months later, he'd jumped again, this time descending over a local music company while playing "Runnin' Wild" on a gold-plated Martin saxophone. Despite rudely flipping over the flagpole of the 123rd Street Precinct police station and finally crash-landing into the precinct house some six blocks south of his target, Julian—who termed this missed flight a failed test for his "saxophone parachutta gravepreresista"—next successfully solicited donations for a proposed hydroplane excursion to Ethiopia, finally embarking on the flight in July at the threatening behest of postal agents murmuring mail fraud. Before a huge crowd of more than 30,000, Julian—or the "Black Eagle," as he was now known—this time remained airborne only a few brief minutes before the right pontoon on his aircraft, *Ethiopia I*, dropped off, nose-diving the Black Eagle's Boeing hydroplane into Flushing Bay. "While more or less on his course," the *New York Times* acknowledged the following day, "Flushing Bay had not been a scheduled stop."

In 1930, Julian had been engaged briefly as commander of Hailse Selassie's "Imperial Ethiopian Air Force," losing the job after demolishing one of the force's three planes. Returning to Harlem in a pink shirt, riding breeches, monocle, and pith helmet, Julian had subsisted for a time by lecturing on his African adventures in florid, vaguely French-sounding speeches. Ten years later he was flying in the Russo-Finnish war. His most recent undertaking had been a challenge issued during World War II to Hermann Goering for an aerial duel at 10,000 feet over the English Channel. Goering had not accepted.

On the evening of January 26, 1951, Razaf drove Julian to the railroad station for Julian's return to New York. At the station, however, Razaf suddenly was stricken with stomach pain so severe that his friend was forced to drive the lyricist back home to Country Club Drive. Another friend, a doctor, was then summoned and gave Razaf an injection to help him sleep, assuring the patient that all would be fine in the morning. Within hours, though, despite the drug, Razaf awoke, again in horrible pain and, to his horror, unable either to walk or even get out of bed. Forcing himself forward, Razaf could only crumple to the floor. All feeling had gone from his legs.

"It wasn't just a paralysis," Dr. Maurice Haber, one of Razaf's many doctors, later explained. "It was tertiary syphilis. Andy was aware of it to a great degree, though everyone later talked all around it."

Razaf eventually admitted to Haber that he once had been diagnosed with syphilitic symptoms. It remained unclear, however, what treatment, if any, he had received. As Haber later pointed out, when syphilis first was contracted, perhaps a week to ten days after infection, a secondary stage evinced itself as a simple rash. Once this rash cleared up, there often were no further signs of the disease for years.

"Somebody might have missed the diagnosis at first," Haber readily acknowledged, "but Andy was aware that he did have syphilis, and this was tertiary syphilis, which is very, very painful: you incur lightning pains, pains that are incredibly intense—sharp, burning, and uncontrollably spasmodic. And there is nothing that can be done about it. There are two ways that tertiary syphilis can go. It can attack the brain—the patient becomes vegetative; Capone had that and apparently Columbus may have had it. Or it can become 'tabes dorsalis,' which is what happened to Andy. Tabes involves the spine and, in my opinion, it is much worse," maintained Haber, "because of the pain."

Of course, syphilis had long been the scourge of theater people practically since recorded time, though the more recent infection of entertainers with the spirochete throughout the nineteenth century in this country often had been treated as something of a joke by the nation's entertainment press. Actors themselves had also long since adopted a generally callous dismissiveness toward the disease. In the 1880s, for example, when John McCullough, a famous tragedian, insisted on remaining active in the theater despite frequent memory losses and frenzied lapses into incoherence from paresis, an advanced symptom of syphilis, contemporary variety house audiences soon rather goulishly had embraced a hurriedly introduced sketch known as "The Ravings of John McCullough." Shortly thereafter, the enormously popular musical comedy team of Harrigan and Hart was destroyed by Tony Hart's syphilitic infection, inspiring a news story in the *New York Herald* headlined: *"THAT TELLTALE LISP— Tony Hart's Trouble Begins Like That of John McCullough. All The Symptoms of Paresis. Why Ned Harrigan's Famous Partner Has Been Forced to Leave the Stage."*

The annals of black musical theater in America after the turn of the century were, to a great degree, riddled and, for a time, nearly terminated by the murderous toll that paresis exacted from the medium's very greatest figures: Ernest Hogan, Bob Cole, and George Walker. Desperately endeavoring to ignore his illness, in the summer of 1908, an infected George Walker even had danced at a benefit concert for Ernest Hogan, whose recent retirement from the stage had come at the first signs of paresis. By the following year, while performing on Broadway in *Bandana Land* with his partner Bert Williams, Walker evinced stuttering, lisping, and memory losses so painfully marked that he was soon forced into retirement himself, and died from the disease in 1911.

Bob Cole's end had come even more brutally. During the lengthy 1909 tour of *The Red Moon*, Cole and his partner Rosamond Johnson's extraordinarily successful theatrical blending of Native American music and folklore with relatively nonstereotypical black musical comedy, Cole's health had begun to deteriorate to the point that his personal physician, diagnosing a nervous breakdown, strongly recommended a rest cure for his patient, which Cole had undertaken in a Catskill boarding house. After a four-week period of uninterrupted rest, exercise, and hearty eating, the formerly lean and lanky Cole, while noticeably healthier, was exceedingly concerned to find his body growing bloated and puffy. This his doctors narrowly attributed to diet, and Cole soon returned to New York to begin an intensive vaudeville tour with Johnson. It had been while performing in New York toward the end of this tour at Keith and Proctor's Fifth Avenue Theatre that Cole suffered a flagrant nervous collapse, leading to his hospitalization at Bellevue, where doctors for the first time diagnosed his condition as a general paresis for which there was no cure. After being shifted from one private hospital to another and having his fatal prognosis again revised by specialists who now diagnosed Cole's illness as a nervous breakdown, Bob Cole had returned with his mother in the spring of 1911 to a Cole family vacation retreat in the Catskills. At this lodge Cole had seemed in fine spirits, often performing his songs for guests. One Saturday morning, though, while out strolling with some friends near a stream, Cole had excused himself to wade slowly out into the water, swimming for a few minutes only to stop abruptly. Then, in full view of his stunned and horrified friends, Bob Cole had allowed himself, without a word, to sink out of sight. His drowning death at age 43 was ultimately ascribed to syphilitic dementia.

At first it did not appear that Andy Razaf would survive his own penultimate syphilitic seizure. When he did, hope was held out that he might soon walk again as well. Two weeks after his airport attack (which the black press around the nation reported as a "mysterious stroke"), Razaf roused himself from the agony of his recuperation to dictate through a nurse a series of form letters addressed to Tin Pan Alley publishers. "Dear friend," these letters began, with the first name of each ranking publishing house executive filled in respectively:

(1) My nurse is writing this letter for me.
(2) I was stricken two weeks ago, and left paralyzed from the waist down. However, my doctors say that with good care and patience, plus my faith, of course, I will eventually walk again.
(3) With five doctors and two nurses in attendance, it is unneces-

sary for me to say that money is the prime factor in my hopes for recovery.

Razaf then added personalized messages entreating each publisher, not for charity but for heightened attention within each particular music house, to revive dormant Razaf tunes in their respective song catalogs. "Who knows but that in your files, among the idle Razaf-Waller songs, may be a sleeper," he suggested to Sol Bourne of Bourne Music, "especially one entitled 'Walkin' the Floor,' which M. [Mildred] Bailey did remarkably well some years ago. I feel that if Miss B. knew of my condition, what the cutting of such a record would mean to me, she would be only too glad to do so. Therefore, I would deeply appreciate your going over these songs, in the hopes that we might both gain from it."

"In the view of this present condition," insisted Razaf to Mark Schreck of Southern Music Publishing, "there is no better time than now to re-open the subject of my old song 'That's What I Like 'Bout the South,' of which you have my new version entitled "Why I Go South.

"This song, I have always believed to be a 'sleeper' waiting for the right artist to record it. I am positive that if . . . you . . . would talk to Joe Glazer and impress upon his mind my association and friendship with L. Armstrong, since the days of Connie's Inn and 'Hot Chocolates,' when 'Ain't Misbehavin'' and 'Black and Blue' did him a world of good; and in view of my present condition, I feel certain that Joe would have Louis record 'Why I Go South.'

"I feel doubly sure that Joe would be only too glad to do this for me, if he knew that it might mean the difference in my walking again, and since the number is made-to-order for Armstrong, I am also sure that old Satch would be glad to do his bit.

"P.S., please note, Mark, in the printed, or old version of 'Why I Go South,' it seems that someone purposely changed the word 'folks' to 'flocks,' which is absolutely ruinous to the thought of the song. I must be adamant in saying that I mean 'Folks.' Please see that the error is corrected in the new version. Thank you again."

Along Tin Pan Alley, Razaf's peers responded at first with gratifying concern to his illness. Letters and cards poured in from New York City, though nothing could nearly match the reaction of his dearest surviving collaborator, Eubie Blake. Scrawled on letterhead, scratched on postcards, in ink, in pencil, god-awfully misspelled and often grammatically beyond the pale but always displaying concern and profound affection, Blake's missives arrived almost weekly, sometimes daily:

> Dear Andy, I heard you were in the hospital. I know you will know how I must felt hearing this news.
> I really hope you're not ill, just taking a needed rest. . . .

> Dear Andy, today I rec'd your airmail card. Well I jumped for joy when I read you were so much better. Boy that made me feel good . . . Well the next nice thing you said, how much your wife was to you. You know Andy that is Ninety percent of the battle, having a good wife. Tell her I love her for being nice to you . . . Now I'll tell you again if there is anything you want me to attend to for you, Please write me and I will take care of anything you wish me to
>
> > Hurry up and get well—Your Pal, Eubie Blake

> Dear Andy, here is a melodie and title I think is good . . . I will write you more about it later.
>
> > Your pal, Eubie Blake.

In the months immediately following the onset of his illness, Razaf desperately tried to revive his dormant songwriting career, both in an effort to raise funds for his medical care and as an adamant gesture of defiance. He was outmatched, though, and those closest to him knew it—the hired nurses who now hovered over him at home, the doctors who could offer him little more than prescriptions for painkiller, his stunned wife, Dorothy.

Knowing how little there was that they could do to alleviate Razaf's suffering, his doctors freely prescribed sedatives, which the nurses administered increasingly without his active knowledge or consent. "He was almost in a state of suspended animation at times by the time I met him," Dr. Maurice Haber later observed. "Though his pain was unbearable, I do believe Andy preferred it to being so heavily anesthetized."

Through all of this, Dorothy Carpenter Razaf remained something of an enigma. A determinedly self-absorbed woman who had long pursued Andy Razaf as a sort of prize, she was devastated to find herself suddenly married to a 56-year-old invalid who would require constant attention and care for the duration of their lives together. Her immediate response was to send for her mother, who arrived from the East and moved into the house on Country Club Drive very shortly after the onset of Razaf's illness. Throughout the ensuing years, from all accounts, she ministered to her husband devotedly but at a certain remove, maintaining an aloofness from the everyday medical drudgery of his existence. ("Andy," as Maurice Haber later pointed out, "needed a tremendous amount of practical nursing.") She served her husband as a dutiful companion, managing their home meticulously, passing their days together staunchly though somewhat stoically as husband and wife. "He loved her and she loved him," insisted one of Razaf's nurses in later years. "That was the way it was."

During those periods when he could function, when the pain subsided and the barbiturate dosages were decreased sufficiently to allow him to think clearly, Razaf showed a creative energy which was extraordinary. From his wheelchair or in bed, he wrote at every opportunity—song lyrics, poems, letter after letter. "The joy of writing . . . makes me forget my condition," he explained in a note to the *Baltimore Afro–American* published on September 2, 1952. "I turn out an average of three or more songs a week."

Razaf's regular songwriting partner at this time was Johnny Finke, a young white composer with whom Razaf had dabbled before his illness. The team turned out mostly inspirational numbers with cloying titles: "Precious Rosary," "Am I My Brother's Keeper," "All the Way for Jesus." Razaf, in illness, unabashedly had discovered the Lord. He was still capable of composing an effective nonsectarian song lyric, though, like one he penned to a Johnny Finke melody for a song called "Why?"—a somber piece that uncharacteristically reflected the devastating emotional impact of his illness.

> *If my tomorrows are all like today,*
> *Every day will bring a new dawn;*
> *If every night leaves me feeling this way,*
> *There'll be no need to go on:*
> *Why is the sunshine gone from the sky?*
> *Why do the bluebirds no longer fly?*
> *Why has the night-time lost its moonbeams?*
> *Why is my pillow empty of dreams?*
> *Why does my heart ache in deepest despair?*
> *Why does each highway lead to nowhere?*
> *You are the answer, why should I lie?*
> *I'm lost without you, now you know why.*

"Dear friend Lillian," wrote Razaf to an otherwise unidentifiable acquaintance from his early radio days, in a letter dated July 3, 1952.

"What a surprise and a thrill to receive your letter! It truly was a pleasant journey into yesterday. I've often thought of those pioneer days in radio and the fun we had on station WGCP. How well do I recall Fred Hall, Helen Rogers, 'Jane' and the ever-smiling, noble-hearted Phil Elliot. By the way—there was Judge Chilton also. Do you know where any of them are now? God bless them all.

"My mother is 72 years young now and lives in Asbury Park, N.J.," Razaf continued, offering a capsulized summary of his intimate recent history. "Much to my delight she has taken a renewed interest in her writing. Her poems appear quite often in current publications.

"I know a line from you would make her happy. . . .

"Now a few words about me: I married a most wonderful girl in 1948 and came out here. We loved the town at first sight and bought the home we live in immediately. Dorothy (my wife) has been a blessing indeed, for from the day I was suddenly stricken and left paralyzed (eighteen months ago) she has stood by, thru a most trying ordeal, and nursed me back, out of the valley of the shadows.

"Six doctors, a day and a night nurse, plus every type of medicine and treatments under the sun has cost us a small fortune. Only her level-headed supervision of everything has made it possible for us to weather the storm.

"God is good. I'm up in a wheelchair now and look forward to walking again some day. In the meantime, I have my writing, reading, and other wholesome pursuits to keep me busy and make life interesting and worthwhile. To date, with the help of my partner, Johnny Finke, who is a brilliant composer-pianist-arranger, I've turned out a batch of new manuscripts (songs of all types) just waiting for some artist, publisher, or recording firm to consider.

"Of course, you know what has happened to the music business," Razaf added, revealing beneath the sunniness of his disposition a depth of contempt for contemporary musical taste commensurate with the undirected rage that he otherwise bore silently. "The writer and publisher, today, is the unimportant stooge and errand-boy of everybody from the doorman to the singer, bandleader, recordman, and disc jockey.

"Thus, the abortion of music and the overflow of synthetic, gimmick-recording stars, that has created a new low in a once respectable and truly art-conscious field. As I write this, the radio is turned in nearby and I'm hearing a good example of the hogwash in question.

"Please forgive me for going into all of this rambling," Razaf concluded almost abashedly. "Next time I'll refrain from touching on such subjects. (Smile.)

"With every good wish to you and yours, I am—Always sincerely —Andy Razaf."

In 1953, Razaf accepted an invitation from the *Los Angeles Herald-Dispatch* to contribute a weekly column on whatever subjects interested him. For more than two years thereafter, he pursued his journalistic muse, writing often about the African American's problematic place in American history, delivering lengthy paeans to "brotherhood" and fundamental Christian faith, commenting occasionally on local Los Angeles politics (he confessed to finding the pace of California politics a "bit slow"), or on the nation's nascent civil rights movement. Sometimes he wrote about music. Sometimes he simply reminisced. The column was called "Time Out for Thinking," with euphemistic reference by Razaf to his illness. Tragically and with no little irony, he had in his "time out for thinking" in fact become an embodiment of that most familiar of his songwriting poses, the mindful shut-in, staying at home, with "no one to talk with . . . no one to walk with . . . on the shelf . . . no place to go," a removal that was leading, Razaf clearly sensed, to the slow but inexorable eradication of his name from the collective memory of popular music history in this country.

"The need for more Negro historians grows more urgent and vital each day, for slowly but surely the Negro is being blacked out on the stage of achievement by omission and commission," Razaf wrote in a devastating column deploring the scant presence of black entertainers in Abel Green's book *Showbiz*, a history of *Variety*, after its publication in late 1951. (Fats Waller's name appeared in *Showbiz* only twice. Andy Razaf's did not appear at all.) "The result," insisted Razaf, "is that not only whites but Negroes themselves are shamefully ignorant of the great heritage of the Negro in America and elsewhere. . . . An all-out drive to awaken us to the greatness and rich cultural value of our achievements is long overdue."

On March 30, 1954, ASCAP marked the fortieth anniversary of its founding with a banquet at the Waldorf-Astoria on Park Avenue in New York City. In the Grand Ballroom, over 1,500 music publishers and songwriters sat through a lavish affair that saluted the society's founders, "the Victor Herberts and the John Philip Sousas who sparked the [1914] legal procedure that led to the historic U.S. Supreme Court decision for ASCAP," as the society's reigning President, Stanley Adams, stated in his keynote speech. Another speaker that evening, one of ASCAP's original founders, Irving Berlin, chose to frame his remarks as a parodied medley of Berlin hits:

> Mr. President of ASCAP,
> Fellow members, and Honored Guests:
> I don't have to say what it means to me
> To help you celebrate
> This fortieth Anniversary.

Berlin touched on ASCAP's pioneering days. He disingenuously celebrated the fact that, "as a publisher-member of ASCAP/My, how the money rolls in/To get the bit that I have to split/With just Irving Berlin." At last, he paused for a final "musical interlude":

> I'd like to express my gratitude
> To a man in my employ,
> I'm speaking of THE LITTLE COLORED BOY!

Throughout his career, Berlin, a self-acknowledged musical illiterate, informally had denied charges that Berlin the composer (as opposed to Berlin the publisher) did not at all exist but was in fact a "little colored boy" employed by Berlin to write his songs for him. For years, the consensus of speculative opinion along Tin Pan Alley, among those who held any belief at all in the rumor, was that this "little colored boy" had been Andy Razaf.

> "Sweetest Little Fella"
> And can he compose!
> No one's ever seen him
> But "He's Mighty "Lak" a Rose!"
> He wrote—"Come On and Hear, Come On and Hear" and a
> Hundred other hits.

> There are times when he doesn't show up and then
> The ink goes dry in my writin' pen,
> And things look mighty black
> Until the little boy comes back.

> A few years ago he left me flat

> Like one of those temp'ramental molls,
> It was just around that certain time
> Frank Loesser wrote "Guys and Dolls."

Of course, it was pure coincidence that Razaf had in fact left New York for California at the time that Frank Loesser was writing *Guys and Dolls*—which opened on Broadway in 1950—and it remains bizarrely coincidental that Razaf's address book from those years contains the names and telephone numbers of only two white songmen: Irving Berlin and Frank Loesser. True, Andy Razaf and Irving Berlin did share an association throughout the Twenties and Thirties via the many hours Razaf and Waller had spent in Berlin's publishing offices at 1607 Broadway, demonstrating their own songs for Berlin and diverting the great songwriter with Waller's dazzling piano improvisations on Berlin tunes. They also seem to have charmed Berlin's bullying business partner, Sol Bornestein, into serving them as an unofficial banker/business manager of sorts during this period. Whether Razaf ever worked for Berlin in any extracurricular sense, however, is impossible to document.

Irving Berlin's songful speech at the Waldorf on the night of March 30 convulsed the ASCAP crowd with its good-natured self-deprecation and the text was reprinted in newspapers around the country. On May 8, 1954, the *Amsterdam News* published Andy Razaf's formal reply to Berlin's "musical interlude," a retort that ultimately made nearly as many papers as Berlin's original remarks.

"From time to time, several readers have made inquiries about the whereabouts of Andy Razaf, regarded by many experts as one of America's most prolific songwriters and composers," the *Amsterdam News* article began. "Andy, a great friend and advisor of the Negro press, has been a resident of Los Angeles, California, and although he spends a considerable time in his wheelchair (he suffered a serious stroke a few years ago), he never forgets to pen a few encouraging lines to his friends in the journalistic fraternity.

"Recently we reproduced a parody that songwriter Irving Berlin delivered at a dinner held . . . by ASCAP on which occasion, he poked fun at himself particularly on the legend that an 'unknown colored boy wrote many of his songs.'

"Interestingly enough," acknowledged the *News*, "the name of Andy Razaf has often been mentioned in Tin Pan Alley as one who may have perhaps contributed more than his share towards the elevation of Berlin as the Nation's greatest penner of songs.

"Last week we received a communication from Mr. Razaf who speaks eloquently on this much-discussed matter. He writes:

> Please permit me to comment on the legend of the "colored boy" who was supposed to write Irving Berlin's songs.
>
> As a writer who virtually lived in Tin Pan Alley from 1913 until 1948, and who owed much of his inspiration to Irving Berlin, I for one, would like to see this ridiculous legend placed in a coffin and given a permanent burial.
>
> Berlin, as a writer, is to Tin Pan Alley what Louis is to boxing, Edison to inventions, and Einstein to science. Their kind of genius comes along once in a lifetime. Few writers can write a great tune and a great lyric. This guy does both—and how!
>
> Of all his breath-taking list of socko hits, I'd be happy to settle for just two of them—"God Bless America" and "White Christmas."
>
> Yes, if such a "colored boy" existed, many would-be writers today could really use him. To think of it, I could give him some part-time work, myself.
>
> In closing, I would like to say that any one who still insists this legend is true, that if a "colored boy" wrote Irving Berlin's songs, then a "white boy" wrote mine!

It is the juxtaposition of Andy Razaf's name alongside the names of white Tin Pan Alley legends like Irving Berlin that underscores the tragedy in this Razaf saga, for it is only in relation to their success that his relative failure may be coldly and honestly appraised. Was Andy Razaf's lyric-writing talent on a par with Irving Berlin's? It was, unmistakably; in many ways, Razaf was more like Berlin the lyricist than were any of the white lyricists who grew rich alongside Berlin on Tin Pan Alley. Certainly Cole Porter may have been droller, Ira Gershwin subtler, Lorenz Hart more lacerating and a bit more learned in his references. Razaf, though, like Berlin, was a brilliant colloquialist, very nearly as popular, in his accessible colloquial simplicity, as Berlin, the great white populist. These similarities only heighten the inequality of Razaf's long-term failure as a commercial songwriter. For while Razaf clearly was one of the most accomplished and successful lyric writers of any race during the first half of this century, the association of the Razaf name with his many successful songs and the potential value inherent in that association never was realized as powerfully nor as lucratively for Razaf as the associations promoted between the names and creative output of his foremost white peers.

Andy Razaf's place in the song business always remained confined within the boundaries of Harlem—figuratively, as a place of mind, if not literally. Harlem was the place where, white audiences and many white music professionals once believed, music and rhythm sprang as if from nature, creative consciousness and craft being the birthright solely of whites. Thus, the very notion of a black lyricist initially had been irreconcilable with the white stereotypical view of the black music world, lyric writing implying an act of written out, cogitated, idea-based creativity that was antithetical to any white conception of black music. In this way, Razaf's initial neglect—which he never really managed to overcome—was greatly magnified well beyond the point lyricists generally are neglected in comparison with their composer collaborators, magnified by Razaf's anomalous position as that never-before-considered commodity: a black lyricist.

Added to this was the degree to which Razaf *was* obscured by his charismatic primary composer partner Thomas Waller, in conjunction with Razaf's own rigid code of behavior, his seeming stodginess, which prohibited him from publicly promoting himself nearly as outrageously as Waller managed to do—though their private lives, in many ways, were not so very dissimilar. The combination of these three fundamental factors, then, certainly constituted a foundation for Razaf's long-term neglect. Obscured by his most readily identified partner, colorless in his public rectitude, and dismissed by the entertainment industry at large (though not by his songwriting peers) as a black lyricist, Razaf never was able to promote commensurate commercial value out of his vast songwriting achievements during the most productive years of his career. Though Andy Razaf always was able to sell what he wrote, he never was pursued as a "name" commodity by Tin Pan Alley, never was paid top dollar, and hence never was a truly great success as a songwriter.

Finally, though, Razaf was ultimately stymied in his already stifled songwriting career by the entertainment industry as a whole, along Tin Pan Alley, on Broadway, and out in Hollywood. Theirs was very much a passive act of indifference rather than anything conspiratorial and active. It was, however, a passive indifference derived from pervasive racism. Tin Pan Alley and Broadway and Hollywood executives never at any time concluded that Andy Razaf did not possess the talent to compose songs successfully for their various enterprises. Rather, from the onset of "talking pictures" in 1929, the Depression on Broadway after 1930, and the effective absorption by white songwriters of black songwriting style and sensibility with the

"Swing Era" in the latter 1930s, each segment of the American entertainment industry came to reject Razaf's services because, in their typecasting of him as *a black lyricist* exclusively, he no longer interested them economically. Nor were most industry executives ever truly comfortable socially working with this black lyric writer. When he at last seemed to them to have become dispensable, few executives were disposed to make any great effort to maintain relations.

There were also artistic factors in the final collapse of Andy Razaf's career. As a lyricist, he certainly had practical limitations. His ballad writing tended to be somewhat florid and bathetic. He never dared to attempt anything theatrically that remotely integrated story and character in his songs, even after the innovations of Rodgers and Hammerstein in the early Forties impelled so many songwriters to undertake some experiment along those lines— though the limitations imposed upon him by the rigid conventions of black Broadway in the Twenties could justifiably be said to have stunted his growth to some extent as a lyric writer for dramatic situations. Whether fearful, insecure, or simply demoralized and unavailing, he failed to push his songwriting gift beyond the scope of conventional Tin Pan Alley form and the theatrical revue format.

There were, however, innumerable white Tin Pan Alley lyric writers of Razaf's caliber who remained gainfully employed well into their dotage, writing freestanding popular songs that never addressed the issue of seamless plot integration; composing for Hollywood films, for the Hit Parade and even, on occasion, for Broadway, until rock and roll finally put everyone out of business in the Sixties. For the most part, during these postwar years, at this level of classic, accomplished, popular American song creativity, only Razaf and his many black songwriting peers seem to have disappeared so utterly. While his illness may have hurried the lyricist into oblivion, even as an invalid he continued to write prolifically.

Razaf never made his professional life especially easy on himself. Always combative in his dealings with the music and theatrical hierarchies in New York, he had clearly alienated many over the years and thereby contributed to the final free fall of his career. It was both ironic and an ultimate saving grace that Razaf, who had lobbied loudest of all his black peers for racial equality on Tin Pan Alley, in the end made his own unhappy peace with the constrictions that finally throttled his professional life. Like his grandfather before him, Razaf was able to accommodate sad reality. For him, it was almost sufficient that *he himself* knew what he had accomplished.

Writing finally remained his greatest consolation. "I'm writing more than ever now," he announced proudly to *Ebony* magazine in a March 1958 interview, "and I think better, too."

Razaf's pain meanwhile remained constant, jagged, and pulsating, wracking his body. He managed, nonetheless, to receive countless visitors throughout the Fifties, from W. C. Handy to Billie Holiday and Josephine Baker. He also had his intimates, who kept him sane with attention, respect, and love: songwriter L. Wolfe Gilbert, jazz critic Leonard Feather, columnist George Putnam, and especially Eubie Blake.

On rare occasions, there were small, sweet triumphs. In 1956, release of *The Benny Goodman Story*, Hollywood's sentimentalized screen biography of the swing king, returned Andy Razaf and Eubie Blake's "Memories of You" to the popular song charts briefly when the tune was used as the movie's theme. On August 30, 1956, in New York City, Leonard Feather produced the first all–Andy Razaf LP, on Period Records, with vocalist Maxine Sullivan backed by the Charlie Shavers Ensemble: former Fletcher Henderson bandsman Buster Bailey on clarinet, Jerome Richardson on reeds, Dick Hyman on piano, Milt Hinton and Wendell Marshall trading off on bass, Ossie Johnson on drums, and the marvelous Mr. Shavers on trumpet. The album was a grand musical tribute and pleased Razaf enormously; he sent a copy to his ex-wife, Jean Blackwell, at the 135th Street Library in Harlem for inclusion in the library's Schomburg Collection on black culture. Blackwell accepted the gift coolly but graciously, and Razaf thereafter began to send additional Andy Razaf memorabilia to her for the archive.

"Dear Andy," wrote Eubie Blake on February 7, 1958. "I was just sitting here thinking how you were. Well, I have lived to 75 years of age, of which I am thankful . . . today, Feb. 7th, is my birthday.

"P.S. Don't you think 'Memories of You' is a surprise after all these years."

Annabelle Miller Razaf died on March 3, 1958. Her former husband was notified of her passing with a seven-word telegram signed simply, "The Family." To the end, Razaf had entirely ignored his first wife—the first great love and, no doubt, the first great

mistake of his life. On this occasion, he sent a wreath—five
-and-a-half feet tall—with his name on an attached card.

Razaf began to collect and collate his poems (more than 1,000
pieces) for a book that he hoped to see published under the title *The
Trumpet Sounds*. Assisting him in this rather daunting task was
Charles Lampkin, an aspiring, thoroughly second-rate "pianist-
baritone-composer-lecturer-motion picture star-and-authority on
the folklore idioms and music of the Negro" (according to Lampkin's
own promotional sheet), and a friend of both Mr. and Mrs. Razaf,
who had moved into their home on Country Club Drive shortly after
his own marriage had broken up. Lampkin slept in the maid's room
at the back of the house. Dorothy Razaf had long since taken to
sleeping on a chaise longue in the dining room, away from her
husband but not too far from his bedroom door. Late one night,
about a year after Lampkin had entered the Razaf household, one of
Razaf's private nurses, a strong, domineering woman who often
borrowed money from her patient and desired one day to marry him,
awakened Razaf, lifted the lyricist into his wheelchair, and wheeled
him out to his wife's living room chaise. The chaise had not been
slept in and Charles Lampkin's bedroom door was locked.

Ensuing divorce proceedings were swift and uncontested. Razaf's
settlement was exceedingly generous. By the onset of the Sixties, the
last private humiliation of his life had been concluded and Andy
Razaf was completely alone.

"My dear Uncle John," he wrote on February 8, 1962. "The
endless agony I suffer makes it difficult for me to work out the
problems I face and I have only you to turn to for your sage advice.

"My condition grows worse with time.

"These doctors here seem to be an admiration society; one covers
up for the other, of the 26 I've had not one displays any concern over
my case, and several, after agreeing with me and putting their hand
where my agony is, tell the nurse, when they reach the front door,
that 'My pains are in my mind!'

"I, like many of my friends back East, know that the right
doctors and treatment is in New York starting with the doctors
who have worked with [paralyzed Brooklyn Dodger catcher Roy]
Campanella. . . .

"I can't even get a real therapist here, which is a vital need to a
paraplegic.

"Truly trained, intelligent and dedicated practical nurses are as scarce as hen's teeth here.

"Nurse trouble, my suffering, the mortgaged house, with no responsible person to stay here and watch it if I were able to come East, poses two vital problems. Robberies and teenage vandalism are increasing daily here.

"I'd have to bring at least one nurse with me to take care of me and teach others the very complex system used in my case.

"I have only two nurses now, one would not be satisfactory to bring. . . .

"If I had my way, I'd get whatever equity I could out of this house and sell it. Next, I'd pack (a tough job) my belongings and ship them East, to stay in storage there.

"Several friends there have begged me to come and stay with them.

"If I remain here, under conditions mentioned, I'll either go nuts or die.

"*Now,* what would you do, if you were in my place?" Razaf concluded, signing himself, "Love Andrea."

The firmly reasoned reply of Razaf's uncle John Waller to this letter contrasted beautifully with Razaf's understandably emotional outburst. "I have read your letter of Feb. 8th very carefully," Waller wrote. "I am able to understand the proposals that confront you because you have written to me about them many times. . . . You asked me what I would do in your place. I will tell you what I would do. I don't say that it would be the best thing for *you* because all people are constituted differently. . . .

"I would try first to locate a suitable hospital or nursing home in *Los Angeles* that would accept a paralytic patient," Waller began. "It would be better if you can find a suitable place because the cost of moving to New York would be tremendous as well as dangerous. . . .

"After finding a suitable hospital or nursing home, I would sell the house and get what equity I could. . . . I have always been of the opinion that you should unload that burden now that you are no longer married. Running your own private hospital at home is a tremendous expense. . . .

"I would not consider moving to New York except as a *last resort,*" continued Waller unequivocally. "The cost would be so great, and the result so uncertain, that it would not be justified unless Los Angeles has no place where you could go and I don't think that is the case.

"Now I have told you what I would do if I were in your place," Waller concluded. "Maybe you won't agree with me. But it seems to me that your main problems now are to sell the house and get into a hospital or nursing home where you can have complete mental relaxation.

"As for some of your friends in New York inviting you to live with them, don't pay any attention to that. It just wouldn't work and would surely lead to unpleasantness. You have got to be independent no matter where you are," Waller maintained, reiterating the dominant guiding principle that underlay his nephew and his own family's history. "People say things like that when they don't really mean it," he insisted, "and quite often," he added—gently but firmly reminding Razaf of the song royalties that were keeping him secure and medicated—"they are moved by mercenary motives."

Razaf's pride allowed him to pursue his uncle's recommendations only so far. Though he abandoned any further hope of moving back East, he could not bring himself to surrender the private hospital he had made of his home, however imprisoning it had grown, for the outright dependence of a nursing home. Independent and alone, he remained with his nurses at Country Club Drive.

By the mid-Sixties, Razaf's painful physical condition had deteriorated to the point that he had almost stopped writing entirely. Close friends, excepting a loyal handful, had for the most part fallen away, through age, ill health, and death. James P. Johnson, who'd never managed to transcend the advent of the Swing Era and parlay his preeminence as a pianist and composer during the Twenties into the rounded, full-scale musical career his talents merited, had succumbed as far back as 1940 to the first of eight strokes. "They were too good to the piano players with all that free booze and rich food," Johnson had scrawled in a note to Willie "the Lion" Smith during Smith's last painful visit a short time before Johnson's death in virtual obscurity on November 17, 1955. "It catches up with you."

Fletcher Henderson, too, had been felled in the Fifties by a series of strokes, the first striking him in the morning hours of December 22, 1950, and leaving him almost completely paralyzed on his left side. Two strokes had followed, one in April 1952, the second, fatal one on December 29, 1952, closing out a life and career that record producer John Hammond later characterized as "a study in frustration."

Paul Denniker, Willie "the Lion" Smith, J. C. Johnson, Eubie Blake, and Joe Davis each had managed to survive the Fifties in relatively good health, physically if not financially. Smith, having at last abandoned nightclub work, was still in modest demand as a concertizing pianist and raconteur, working on a book of memoirs that was published to great acclaim in 1964 under the title *Music on My Mind*. "Heads up," he'd written Razaf at one point. "They can't knock us out." Denniker was living modestly out in Brooklyn Heights, tending to his sick wife, teaching, and playing piano. "Financially, I'm not kicking too much," he'd insisted to Razaf, "between ASCAP . . . and . . . you know we get L.P. releases on 'S'posin'' constantly—some very good. If only we were getting full royalties!"

Joe Davis had managed to maintain a substantial music business presence for himself throughout the roller coaster Fifties as one of New York's foremost producers of black rhythm-and-blues recordings and, by association, early rock-and-roll records. His relations with Razaf had remained strained yet unbroken since Razaf's move to California, and their correspondence, aside from frequently tense exchanges about royalties, had remained compulsively cordial until Davis allowed the correspondence to lag and finally lapse in the early Sixties. "As to Joe not answering your mail, that shouldn't be too much cause for grief," J. C. Johnson had insisted to Razaf in a 1961 letter, one of many marvelously dry-eyed epistles that the ebullient, astute, and blunt songwriter addressed to his close friend over the years. "I haven't seen him either for many years and wish him all the luck in the world; and should I not see him again, I shall not cry. . . . I am not any too well lately and haven't been for quite some time, but I'll keep jumpin' 'till the butcher cuts me down. It's easy to complain, I'd rather do something more difficult. . . . Who knows what tomorrow brings. If the past has any connection with the future everything in time will work out alright. . . . Can you flex your memory chords to the tune of the past and enjoy what you hear of yesterdays? Pretty rich music, I'd say. Those days are the important pegs on which to hang the pleasures of an era that actually existed and can be neatly revived in memory—making the present moment laughable, tolerant, and easier to enjoy. *OH YEAH*, I remember. . . ."

For Razaf, the problems of these latter years were exacerbated by the absence of his ex-wife, Dorothy. In the aftermath of Dorothy Razaf's departure, Razaf's nurses took over the Country Club Drive house in an almost Hitchcockian fashion, dismissing Razaf with sedatives and casual disdain.

And then, impossibly, Alicia Wilson appeared. Surely no dramatist would have dared dream the scenario, and yet there was Alicia—nee Alice—Wilson, the smitten schoolgirl out of Andy Razaf's past in Chicago, materializing like some matured apparition almost thirty years later.

"I was out in the Valley recuperating from rheumatic fever," Alicia Wilson Razaf recalled. "I had come to L.A. to see my doctor and my mother called and said, 'Remember that man who gave you the name Alicia?' and I said, yes, and she said, 'He's in Los Angeles and he's paralyzed.' She said, 'I gave him your number. Is that alright?'

"She'd given my number to Andy's aunt at a Baha'i meeting that they'd both attended. Very soon after he called me. We talked and then he called back again and I got a little uppity, I suppose, and he never called back.

"On Christmas Eve, I got all dressed up in a beautiful lace dress, and I got into my car and started driving; I'd been thinking about him a lot, this poor man, paralyzed and all. I hadn't driven much because I'd been sick myself, and I didn't know this part of town, and suddenly I got really frightened. 'My God,' I thought, 'I can't just walk in on him on Christmas Eve!' And I turned back. So it was not until after New Year's Eve, about the middle of January, 1963, that I finally got up the nerve to go see him, and this time I drove over in the daytime.

"A nurse showed me in, he was in bed in his room. I walked in and I said, 'Hi Andy,' and he said, very softly, 'Alicia?' and I said, 'Do you remember me?' and he said, 'Alicia, you haven't changed.'

They were married on St. Valentine's Day, 1963, the thrice-divorced 67-year-old paralytic lyricist and the once-divorced 43-year-old former actress and singer, in ill health herself, whose tenderness and spontaneously childlike romanticism genuinely impelled her to now make Andy Razaf's welfare her own reason for living. "I was very scared about marrying him," Alicia Razaf later admitted. "I didn't know if I could take care of him, didn't know what he made—if he could support us both, and I was not well enough to work. Over the years I'd always thought about him, though, he was always in the back of my mind. I'd even held onto the little piece of napkin on which he'd written out my name that night in Chicago; it was never away from me, even when I was married. And all during my time as an actress and as a singer, I always knew where it was. I'd take it out every so often and look at it.

"He was so definitive. He never really proposed, just once, after we'd had this fight over nothing, really, and I threatened to leave and never come back and I asked what he was thinking and he said, in that soft, slow voice of his: 'I'm thinking about who I'm going to invite to our wedding,' and that was that—I never said no.''

Immediately after the wedding, Alicia Razaf took over the house on Country Club Drive, firing the nurses, tossing out the codeine, and teaching herself the nursing skills necessary to care for her new husband. "I was really scared," she later confessed, "but I couldn't disappoint him either because he would have died."

Alicia Razaf introduced her new husband to her longtime doctor, Maurice Haber. Together they persuaded Razaf to undergo a chordotomy, a severing of the spinal cord's pain-transmitting mechanism, in an effort to alleviate the lyricists's pain. Terrified though he was, Razaf agreed. The surgery was a success.

In this way, with his wife literally at his bedside, Razaf survived a series of medical struggles and setbacks to see the year 1972, the year in which a new organization comprising the surviving remnants of the Tin Pan Alley community, the Songwriters Hall of Fame, in the second official year of its existence, at last invited Andy Razaf to return to New York and join its ranks.

On an inaugural ballot in 1970, the Songwriters Hall of Fame had inducted all of the predictable figures—the Gershwins, Kern, Berlin, Porter, Hammerstein, Hart, Rodgers—a list of nominees that, in its familiar exclusiveness, very nearly had broken Razaf's heart. Two years later, a second honor roll of songmen was announced, an eclectic group, thirty-one names in all, including Bennie Davis (composer of "Margie"), Haven Gillespie ("Santa Claus Is Coming to Town"), Sammy Fain ("That Old Feeling"), Joseph Meyer ("California, Here I Come"), Edgar Leslie ("For Me and My Gal"), Leo Robin ("Thanks for the Memories"), Irving Caesar ("Tea for Two"), J. Fred Coots ("You Go to My Head"), Mitchell Parrish ("Stardust"), Mabel Wayne ("In a Little Spanish Town"), Pete Seeger ("If I Had a Hammer"), Paul Francis Webster ("Love Is a Many Splendored Thing"), Sammy Cahn ("Time after Time"), Carl Sigman ("Theme from *Love Story*"), Hal David and Burt Bacharach ("Walk On By"), Howard Dietz and Arthur Schwartz ("Dancing in the Dark"), Jerry Bock and Sheldon Harnick (*A Fiddler on the Roof*), Jule Styne ("The Party's Over"), Burton Lane ("Everything I Have Is Yours"), Frederick Lowe (*My Fair Lady*), Yip Harburg ("Over the Rainbow"), and Andy Razaf.

Early in May 1972, after an absence of nearly twenty-five years, Razaf returned to New York City with his wife, checking into the toweringly modern Americana Hotel, site of the forthcoming Songwriters Hall of Fame ceremony, just around the corner from Joe Davis's former Broadway Central Building offices on 51st Street, now demolished, and the transferred premises of the Roseland Ballroom on 52nd Street. Razaf's doctors had warned against this trip—he was by now an exceedingly sick man—but Razaf was adamant.

The Americana Hotel occupied an entire block on Seventh Avenue between 52nd and 53rd Streets. The Razaf's suite was on the southwest face of the hotel, the downtown 52nd Street side, off Seventh Avenue, and Razaf, from the moment he entered that suite, according to his wife, gravitated to the window overlooking Seventh Avenue and, beyond it to the west, Broadway. Directly across Seventh Avenue, one block downtown, was the Winter Garden Theatre. From where Razaf sat, he could clearly see the Winter Garden's rear stage door.

According to Alicia Razaf, her husband never slept that first night in New York. In his wheelchair, at that window, he remained until morning, staring silently across Seventh Avenue at the theater where his first professional song, "Baltimo'," had been sung in *The Passing Show of 1913*. Surrounding him were the lights of Broadway shining down into the cavern of Times Square.

"He wanted to believe in people," insisted Alicia Razaf. "'Don't tell me about it,' he would say, 'don't tell me about it! If you love me, don't tell me!' He couldn't stand to be hurt."

"My color made life interesting," maintained Andy Razaf in an interview months after his Hall of Fame induction. "With it came a sense of humor and the gift of laughter and a soul. It has given me something to strive for and shown me every advantage over thousands of white men, born with every advantage, who turned out to be nobodies."

Andy Razaf died of kidney failure on February 3, 1973 at Riverside Hospital in North Hollywood, California. He was 77 years old.

PLAYBILL®

MINSKOFF THEATRE

BLACK AND BLUE

Epilogue

A new vogue for black musical comedy, the third to sweep Broadway in this century, commenced within two years of Andy Razaf's death, penetrating Broadway's white production mainstream and lingering, like its faddish predecessors, entertainingly and quite derivatively for a time. Broadway, during the late Sixties and early Seventies, had briefly embraced a genuinely innovative new genre of black musical theater in the raw, socially relevant works of Vinnette Carroll (*Don't Bother Me, I Can't Cope*) and Melvin Van Peebles (*Don't Play Us Cheap* and *Ain't Supposed to Die a Natural Death*). These were shows that (had he been healthy enough to see them) Andy Razaf no doubt would have applauded for their outspoken sociopolitical abrasiveness even as he dismissed the crudity of their musical and lyric craftsmanship. Their moment in fashion, however, had lasted only as long as Broadway's fleeting Sixties-generated flirtation with socially relevant drama and gritty "downtown" performance style. By 1975, *Raisin* (1973), a slick, perfunctory Broadway musical treatment of Lorraine Hansberry's *Raisin in the Sun*, and *The Wiz* (1975), an uninspired African–American resetting of L. Frank Baum's *The Wizard of Oz*, had brought creative forward motion for the black musical on Broadway to an ignominious halt. Shortly thereafter a newly retrogressive (if educationally laudable) Broadway trend was inaugurated, one that reexamined in a bath of theatrical nostalgia the glories of Twenties black musical comedy, beginning in 1975 with *Me and Bessie*, an homage to Bessie Smith by vocalist Linda Hopkins, and then, decisively in 1976, with *Bubbling Brown Sugar*, an unabashed black musical revue of the old school that ambitiously attempted to dramatize the glamorous history of black musical comedy in America.

Along with Duke Ellington, Andy Razaf was a dominant presence in the pastiche score assembled for *Bubbling Brown Sugar*, with three of his lyrics represented: "Honeysuckle Rose," "What Harlem Is to Me," and "Stompin' at the Savoy." It was a presence little remarked upon, however, by critics, though Razaf's name was prominently credited in the show's program. *Bubbling Brown Sugar* generally was viewed by appreciative audiences and critics alike as the embodiment of a very distant time, place, style, and sound. The sense of that sound as the creative handiwork of individual black artists like Razaf was still difficult to apprehend.

Ain't Misbehavin' changed much of that. Conceived well off Broadway as a cabaret production at the Manhattan Theater Club on East 73rd Street in the early months of 1978, *Ain't Misbehavin'* was an intimate nightclub-scale revue that invoked with extraordinary vivacity the spirit and the music of one particular black creative genius—Thomas "Fats" Waller. It is interesting that many drama critics initially embraced *Ain't Misbehavin'* for the welcome reintroduction it provided to this now obscure black performer/songwriting master who, in the rock-and-roll–dominated years since his death, had himself fallen into neglect. Brilliantly employing a cast of five talented, marvelously disproportionate performers—one literally Walleresque fellow, two delectably corpulent "mamas," one sinuously lean gentleman, and a third positively bony young "frail"— together with an on stage piano "tickler" accompanied by a *"Rhythm"*-sized music ensemble, *Ain't Misbehavin'* managed to approximate quite brilliantly the sense and the presence of Thomas Waller.

The result was a tumultuous hit that reopened on Broadway on May 9, 1978, at the Longacre Theatre and subsequently garnered every award that a musical show could command in a Broadway season. Billed as "The New Fats Waller Musical," *Ain't Misbehavin'* effectively restored Waller to the popular American musical pantheon. In the months following the show's Broadway debut, entertainment feature writers across the country also tentatively began to note that seven of *Ain't Misbehavin'*'s signature songs (not counting "Squeeze Me" and "I Can't Give You Anything but Love") were the work, lyrically, of a writer named Andy Razaf. "Waller's most prominent lyricist, Andy Razag [*sic*] (Andrea Paul Razafkeriefo), is completely overlooked" wrote Douglas Watt in a carelessly edited *Daily News* article that otherwise sought to refute the imputation in *Ain't Misbehavin'* that some of Waller's tunes might have been sold to well-known Tin Pan Alley songwriters who'd then put their names on them. "Don't be ashamed if you haven't heard of Razaf," added another feature writer, Joe Roberts. "The name should be better treated in music history books. You know his lyrics even if you can't remember his name."

It was through *Ain't Misbehavin'* that Andy Razaf was elevated for a time to the rank of musical curiosity. Across the country, culture page features on Razaf continued to appear with some frequency, all of them offering up selected fragments of his shadowy life story, many of them full of glancing misinformation. New York's 92nd Street Y even granted Razaf an evening of his own in its prestigious *Lyrics and Lyricists* series in April 1979, enshrining Razaf yet again alongside the white luminaries of his craft whom the Y now had been celebrating in this series for nine seasons.

The intractable problem with the Razaf legend and legacy nevertheless remained that few ever had known its true scope and detail, and of those, only a handful were still alive. Paul Denniker had died in rank obscurity himself in 1967. After living to witness *Ain't Misbehavin'*'s opening, Joe Davis had passed away in September 1978. To the end, Davis still periodically sought out Razaf's former wife Jean Blackwell-Hutson as if for dispensation, repeatedly offering his side of her former husband's life story. J. C. Johnson meanwhile had grown perversely embittered with age, refusing even to discuss Andy Razaf after his former friend's death. J. C. Johnson would die in a Manhattan nursing home in 1981.

Only Eubie Blake, among all of Razaf's intimate musical associates, survived and flourished in the years following the lyricist's passing. Blake, after a series of three recording sessions conceived as a retrospective summation of his long career by the legendary Columbia Records producer John Hammond in late 1968 and early 1969, had instead seen that career magically rejuvenated when the sessions were released in 1969 on LP as *The Eighty-Six Years of Eubie Blake*. With astonishing vigor, the ageless pianist/composer immediately returned to a backbreaking schedule of active concertizing combined with increasingly regular late-night television talk show appearances that soon brought him to the attention of an infinitely greater audience than had ever previously seen or heard of either *Shuffle Along* or its ancient composer. In late 1978, Blake also added his own contribution to Broadway's most recent black theatrical vogue with *Eubie*, a lavish revue made up entirely of Eubie Blake music, much of it composed lyrically by Andy Razaf.

The curiosity that pursued Razaf following the appearance of *Ain't Misbehavin'* (and, to a lesser extent, *Bubbling Brown Sugar* and *Eubie*), waned as the Seventies gave way to the Eighties, a decade in which Blake himself finally would die at the age of 101 in 1983. Broadway's nostalgic black vogue of the latter Seventies also waned with the Eighties, producing only *Sophisticated Ladies*, a less than inspiring tribute to the music of Duke Ellington, in 1982. For the Eighties decade, in fact, black presence on Broadway ultimately came to mean white director/choreographer Michael Bennett's thinly fictionalized evocation of one riveting episode from perhaps the quintessential behind-the-scenes black music industry story of the post–Razaf age: *Dreamgirls*, the saga of Motown vocalist Diana Ross and the Supremes (with extraordinarily effective music in this instance supplied by two white composers, Henry Krieger and Tom Eyen). Indirectly, Andy Razaf even bore a shadowy connection to this latter-day chapter of black music history in America. During the Sixties, according to Razaf's widow, members of Motown's most prolific in-house songwriting trio had visited Razaf on numerous occasions to sound out the great lyricist on the subject of lyric writing and fundamental popular song composition.

For anyone in the Eighties now marginally familiar with the name Razaf, the lyricist's legend had come to embody much that was glamorous and unknowable about the vast wealth of American popular songs passed down by recordings and pop mythology from the Twenties and Thirties to the present day. The name and legend had come to represent the essence of mystery and victimization that clung to the history of African–American music. If any one figure now could be said to stand in for all the cruelly neglected and forgotten giants and mere mortals of black music in America throughout this century, surely this figure was the mysterious Razaf. And if one song could be said to embody Razaf and all that he now stood for, this song was "Black and Blue."

Nothing, not Edith Wilson's original *Hot Chocolates* introduction of "Black and Blue" nor even Louis Armstrong's subsequent recording of the song, had brought "Black and Blue" wider renown or greater attention than the performance it received as the finale to *Ain't Misbehavin'* on Broadway in 1978 and on the production's original cast album and ensuing feature-length television broadcast. With laudable sensitivity, *Ain't Misbehavin'*'s "conceiver" and director, Richard Maltby, had set the song in the show's final scene as a stunningly hushed a cappella coda to all the frivolity that had preceded it: all five *Ain't Misbehavin'* cast members perched on stools, center stage, staring out at the suddenly silenced audience, to sing with weariness, timeless dignity and stark theatricality, "What did I do to be so black and blue?" "At this [moment]," critic Jack Kroll later wrote in *Newsweek*, ". . . an immensely appealing show becomes a deeply poignant one."

If anything could bring Andy Razaf back to life for scores of theatergoers in 1978 and after, "Black and Blue" could. The song's lyric towered over the marvelous music of *Ain't Misbehavin'* endowing the music and the raucous image of Thomas Waller himself with wisdom, pathos, and heartfelt humanity.

Of course, most listeners continued to assume that all of the music in *Ain't Misbehavin'*, including "Black and Blue," was solely the work of Thomas "Fats" Waller. For this reason, as late as 1989, it still was necessary for the *New York Times* to run yet another feature on America's most elusive black lyricist. The occasion was the opening of one further paean to the black musical comedy tradition on Broadway, again packed with Andy Razaf songs: a European-based production that simply presented itself under the title *Black and Blue*—with infinitessimal acknowledgment to its lyric writing source. "The most prolific and versatile lyricist to be represented on Broadway this season remains virtually unknown," the ensuing *Times* profile pointed out, "his name buried in the fine print of . . . Playbill song credits." Two years later, in November 1991, New York's newspaper of record still hadn't mastered those most basic Razafian facts that it had itself ostensibly unearthed. "Songs of Andy Razas," announced the *Times* in a highlighted listing dated November 22, 1991, for an upcoming musical tribute to the lyricist at St. Peter's Lutheran Church on Lexington Avenue and 54th Street. "Although Andy Razas wrote the lyrics to such memorable songs as 'Ain't Misbehavin' . . . and 'In the Mood' " this *Times* piece maintained, "his name is not as well known as his nearly 1,000 songs primarily because his words were written to music by performers like Fats Waller, Eubie Blake, and James P. Johnson." Somehow, the mythology of Andy Razaf's neglect and obscurity seemed destined to outdistance not merely his vast accomplishments, but his repeated rediscovery.

During the years immediately following his own rediscovery in 1969, Eubie Blake made a number of trips to the West Coast during the early Seventies, generally for national television appearances. On at least two of these trips, Blake made it a point to visit Andy Razaf at his home on Country Club Drive. Clearly with an eye to posterity but more apparently to divert and amuse his increasingly downcast friend, Blake on one occasion decided to tape his own brief interview with Razaf. The cassette recording has survived. "You know, I tell everybody about you, Andy," Blake informs Razaf at the outset. "I *have* to talk about you. Because I wrote the biggest hit, leavin' out 'Harry'—'Memories of You' is the biggest hit that I've ever written with anybody, see. So, I'm glad to be out here, Andy."

"Well, I'm certainly glad to see you Eubie," Razaf replies softly. "You've always been very dear to me. A great friend. We got along wonderfully well as a team."

"I always talk about your mother," Blake insists. "You don't mind, do you? The best cook. The best cook in the world. Boy, that woman could cook! Down to your house in Asbury Park."

"My darling mother really was a tremendous cook," agrees Razaf. "In fact, she could cook anything. . . .

"You remember the time you fooled me into goin' in the ocean?" Blake cries out suddenly. "Down in Asbury Park. I never was in the water before."

"And I splashed around in the water up to my neck," says Razaf. Blake is laughing.

"I'd have like to drowned," Razaf admits. "Because I couldn't swim, either. I made all the girls think I could swim and when some nice lookin' girls came by I'd strut out of the water."

"And you couldn't swim a lick," howls Blake.

"I couldn't swim any more than a rock could."

Blake laughs delightedly.

"Yes, those were the days," Razaf murmurs.

Blake is suddenly insistent. "We've had good times together, haven't we, Andy?"

"Yes," says Razaf sadly. "The great days are gone."

"Yeah, they're gone," agrees Blake, without a hint of sadness.

"Yes, indeed," Razaf whispers.

"Well, we have given the world something," Blake suddenly announces.

"Yes," says Razaf, somewhat doubtfully, "that's gratifying to know."

There is a brief silence, which Razaf finally breaks.

"Well, Eubie, I guess we'd better sign off."

"All right," says Blake.

"And God bless you," adds Razaf.

"Same to you," Blake exclaims. "I always tell them about you, Andy."

There is no reply.

"I [tell] them how prolific you were—I never seen you, in my lifetime, write a line and then say, I don't like that and change it.

Then you go to the publishers and the publishers say everything is okay. . . . I tell them that I never seen you rub out a line yet and you were the most prolific writer that I ever worked with in my life."

"Well, thanks for the compliment, Eubie," says Razaf wearily.

"But it's quite true. God was with me, I never had to hesitate."

"Yeah," Blake agrees.

"I seem to be prolific, I guess," continues Razaf, almost to himself, "because I just wrote—as fast as I could think."

"Yeah," says Blake again. "Yeah."

"And that was *being* fast," adds Razaf.

"*Yeah*," Blake cries.

"I *wrote*," says Razaf emphatically.

Abbreviations in Notes

ARP—Andy Razaf Papers

DUSCT—Dispatches from U.S. Consuls in Tamatave

PRFRUS—Papers relating to the Foreign Relations of the U.S.

ARSB—Andy Razaf Scrapbook

JWJSB—John Waller, Jr., Scrapbook

NYPL/LCPA-BRTC—New York Public Library/Lincoln Center for the Performing Arts–Billy Rose Theater Collection

NYPL/SCRBC-MARBD—New York Public Library/Schomburg Center for Research in Black Culture—Manuscripts and Rare Book Division

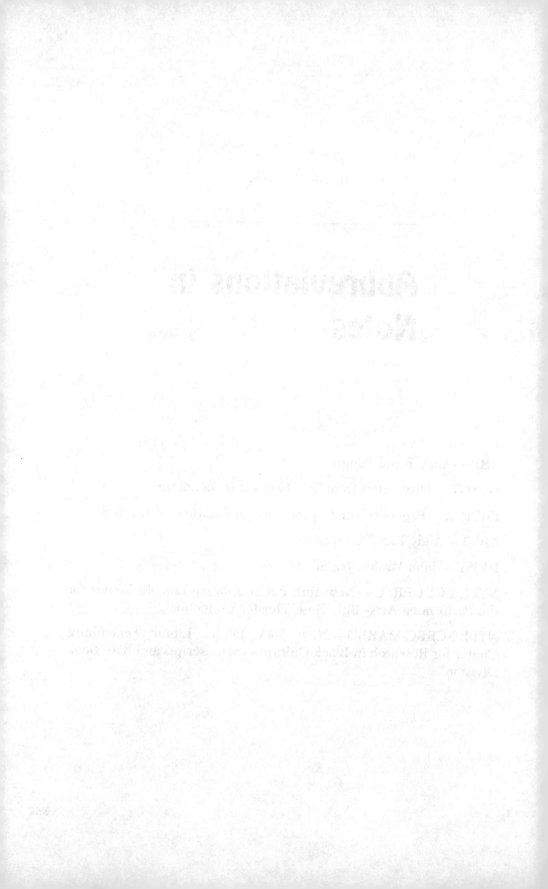

Notes

Prologue

p. vii "You can't never": Sammy Price (pianist), interview with the author, August
  28, 1981.

1 The Curtain Drawn Aside

p.   1 *"Life's Phases"* was a privately published biography 52 pages in length. It is
      unclear what relationship, if any, the author had to John Waller.

p.   2 "The Dreamer" is one of many unpublished poems among Razaf's private
      papers. Though undated, it appears to have been of a very early vintage. "The
      Dreamer" also exists in slightly different form as an unpublished manuscript
      song lyric dated 1934, credited to Razaf with Paul Denniker.

p.   4 "curtain rose": Certain opening night reviews seem to suggest that *Hot
      Chocolates* commenced performances with the curtain already up. It has not
      been possible to confirm this, however.

p.   7 "Razafkeriefo": See note p. 41.
      "Historians of American slave life": See Eugene D. Genovese, *Roll, Jordan,
      Roll* (New York: Pantheon, 1971), pp. 1–158, 325–397; and John
      Blasingame, *The Slave Community: Plantation Life in the Antebellum South*
      (New York: Oxford University Press, 1972), pp. 77–103, 154–200.
      "whipped at least twice": Randall Bennett Woods, *A Black Odyssey, John
      Lewis [sic] Waller and the Promise of American Life, 1878–1900* (Lawrence,
      KS: The Regents Press of Kansas, 1981), p. 5.
      "did not produce personal disintegration": *ibid.*

p.   8 "Apprenticing as a barber": "Barbering was considered a high-status occupa-
      tion by blacks and was one of the few professions open to them." (William

Gates, *Aristocrats of Color: The Black Elite, 1880–1920* [Bloomington & Indianapolis: Indiana University Press, 1990], p. 15.) Waller frequently returned to barbering as an income source during tough times throughout his early career.

p. 9 "Susan Boyd Bray": An Urbana, Ohio–born freewoman, Susan Waller was directly descended from the Cherokee Indian chieftain Reno, and was related as well to many well-known figures connected to the Underground Railroad. Educated and articulate, she was the widow of T. D. Bray of Urbana, and the mother of three children by this marriage: Paul, Alonzo, and Minnie Bray. Her three children with John Waller were Jennie Maria (born December 26, 1879), John, Jr. (1882), and Helen (1884).

p. 10 "He is surely one": "John Waller," *Cedar Rapids Evening Gazette*, July 31, 1895, as quoted by Randall Woods, *A Black Odyssey*, p. 16.

p. 11 "I want to say": Lyman Humphrey to President Harrison, October 17, 1890, *Waller Appointment File*, Washington, DC, National Archives, Record Group 59, Department of State.

"Waller has had reason": P. B. Plumb to Secretary of State James G. Blaine, June 18, 1890, *ibid.*

p. 13 "a ruddy complected people": "The complexion of the Hovas is a ruddy brown or tawny, with long, straight hair. Other tribes are blacker and have woolly heads." (*Washington News*, August 8, 1895, ARP.)

p. 14 "Make application": Acting Secretary of State William H. Wharton to John Waller, October 13, 1891, *Dispatches from U.S. Consuls in Tamatave, 1853–1906*, Roll 7, Volume 7.

"I desire": *ibid.* November 4, 1891.

p. 15 "coloured gentleman": *Le Madagascar*, January 18, 1894.

"the eventual supremacy": n.d., 1893, *DUSCT*, Roll 8, Volume 8.

"It is unfortunate": January 21, 1894, *ibid.*

p. 16 "Failure to enter fees": February 1, 1894, *ibid.*

"some of his assessments": February 14, 1894, *ibid.*

"a colony for American Negroes": Consul Whetter informed his State Department superiors of the Waller land grant and Waller's colonistic plans for it in a dispatch dated March 27, 1894, *ibid.*

"LAND RENT FREE": *Madagascar News*, July 21, 1894, p. 1.

p. 17 "African American political leaders": On March 30, 1894, Waller wrote to John Mercer Langston, a prominent black civil rights leader and politician, describing for Langston in tempting detail the Madagascar land grant and potential economic opportunities it now presented for American blacks. Waller ultimately named Langston and Baltimore lawyer Warner T. McGuinn his legal representatives for Wallerland, asserting a determination "to . . . keep my concession within the control of colored men." Langston and McGuinn soon inaugurated a broad promotional campaign on Waller's behalf, including a successful effort to bring the Hovas' plight in Madagascar at the hands of the French to the attention of the American press.

"colony of American Negroes": Though Waller conceived of his colony as a refuge specifically for oppressed black Americans, and as a source of investment for the African American community-at-large, he recognized that it was imperative his land grant have settlers, whatever their nationality, as soon as possible. He therefore began to recruit potential Wallerland lease-holders in May 1894 on the nearby British colony of Mauritius.

p. 18 "gross mismanagement": October 26, 1894, *DUSCT*, Roll 8, Volume 8.

"The Hovas": *DUSCT*, Roll 9, Volume 9, November 7, 1894.

"Whetter's only official response": Whetter had announced his intention to prevent John Waller from leaving Madagascar in his very first State Department dispatch as Consul (Whetter to E.H. Strobel, December 8, 1893, *DUSCT*, No. 5, RG59, DOS). Ultimately, Waller was prevented from leaving Madagascar for his U.S. recruiting and fundraising excursion both by Whetter's scheming and through the State Department's procrastination in recognizing the legitimacy of Waller's land grant under U.S. law. Clearly hoping to avoid any direct confrontation with France over Wallerland, the State Department informed Waller's legal representatives Langston and McGuinn at a very early juncture in the Affair that in the absence of any specific French infringement of John Waller's rights, the administration was "hesitant to express an opinion." (Acting Secretary of State Edwin Uhl to John Langston, October 10, 1894, *John Langston Papers*).

"Oh Sue": November 2, 1894, *Papers Relating to the Foreign Relations of the United States, Waller Case Papers.*

"We will demand": April 20, 1895, *DUSCT*, Roll 9, Volume 9.

"I immediately wrote": March 11, 1895, *ibid.* Evidence strongly suggests that Whetter's animosity toward Waller was the prime factor in the consul's supposed inability to aid his imprisoned predecessor. Though Waller did in fact appeal to Edward Whetter for assistance and support throughout his pretrial incarceration, Whetter did not even mention the Waller case to the French authorities in Madagascar until March 22, eleven days after Waller's arrest. In his reply to Whetter's note of that date, the French Commandant expressed surprise that the senior U.S. official in Madagascar would take so long involving himself in the case. "I am led to conclude," he wrote, "that it was intentionally that you kept aloof of the suit." (Captain Kiesel to Edward Whetter, *Waller Case Papers, PRFRUS*, pp. 324–325.)

p. 19 "with a view to establishing": Walter Gresham to James B. Eustis, April 10, 1895, *ibid*, p. 260.

"an avowedly Southern gentleman": Eustis, in an 1888 article (James B. Eustis, "Race Antagonism In The South," *The Forum*, September 1888–February 1889, pp. 144–154), called for an end to all Federal aid to black Americans, maintaining that blacks had made absolutely no progress since emancipation.

"Ex-Consul Waller": Unidentified newspaper, n.d., *John Waller, Jr., SB #3*, p. 11a.

"We call upon": Unidentified newspaper, n.d., *ibid.*, p. 16a.

p. 20 "Waller's color": Unidentified newspaper, n.d., *ibid.*, p. 22b.

"published reports": April 20, 1895, *DUSCT*, Roll 9, Volume 9.

p. 21 "Andreamen[en]tania Paul Razaf[in]keriefo": Though Razaf's surname appears on his birth certificate spelled Andreamentania Paul Razafkeriefo, the full Madagascarian spelling is, in fact, *Razafinkeriefo*, with the *in* silent.

Similarly, Razaf's given name, though spelled *Andreamenentania,* is pronounced with the latter *en* silent. The complete name translates to English as "Noble child of wisdom."

p. 22 "It is proper to state": Unidentified newspaper, January 7, 1896, *JWJSB #3,* p. 3b.

"an 'understanding' ": Unidentified newspaper, January 12, 1896, *JWJSB #3,* p. 7b.

"slightly humped": Unidentified newspaper, n.d., *JWJSB #4,* p. 55a.

"sold his 1 percent interest . . .": Razaf saved the original contracts relating to both of these transactions. His *Hot Chocolates* box office interest was sold to "Ernestine Lipschutz" of Cedarhurst, Long Island, who was held "harmless . . . as to the total sum charged against Andy Razaf in connection with his I.O.U.'s for the purchase of tickets and advances from George Immerman." While this contract is a typed, formally drawn legal document prepared by an attorney identified as Louis Handin, whose offices were in the Paramount Building on Broadway, Razaf's August contract with the Immerman brothers is a handwritten half-page, scrawled on Connie's Inn letterhead and signed by George Immerman and AR.

p. 23 "100,00": Charles Schwartz, *Gershwin: His Life and Music* (New York: Bobbs-Merrill, 1973), p. 197.

"$50,00": Roy Hemming, *The Melody Lingers On* (New York: Newmarket Press, 1986), p. 215.

"a two-year": Deems Taylor, *Some Enchanted Evenings* (New York: Harper Bros., 1953), pp. 132–133.

"The most money": *ibid.*

2 Li'l Brown Baby

p. 26 "details of the transaction": Waller's negotiations with the French proceeded privately through Underwood Harvey, his agent in Great Britain, and no formal State Department records therefore exist regarding this transaction. It is uncertain whether the French ever actually paid Waller the $10,000 sale price.

"Mr. Waller": "Waller's Talk," *The American Citizen,* June 26, 1896, as quoted by Randall Woods, *A Black Odyssey,* p. 181.

p. 28 "a 'refuge' ": "Refuge of the Negro," *Washington Post,* July 2, 1899, *ibid.,* p. 194.

"he was dead": John Waller died at his stepdaughter's home on October 24, 1907.

p. 29 "I was not positive": "Andy Razaf Ignores Composer's Admonition," *Los Angeles Sentinel,* June 13, 1957, *ARP.*

"hoped to confine": Romeo L. Daugherty, *Amsterdam News,* September 28, 1932, *ARP.*

p. 30 "I did not take": "Andy Razaf Ignores Composer's Admonition," *Los Angeles Sentinel,* June 13, 1957, *ARP.*

"I liked it": *ibid.*

p. 31 "about the biggest": *New York Sun,* July 25, 1913, *NYPL/LCPA-BRTC.*

"most likely Oscar Radin": Razaf recalled only that he had shown a copy of "Baltimo' " to *The Passing Show*'s "musical director." This was Oscar Radin,

NOTES for pages 31-44

Passing Show that opened in September 1913.

"one evening": "Andy Razaf, The Songwriter of 2,00 Hits—A Story in Music," *Chicago Defender*, May 28, 1949, *ARP*.

3 Swanee Fashion Plate

p. 36 "Musical journalism": Isaac Goldberg, *Tin Pan Alley* (New York: John Day, 1930), p. 99.

p. 38 "I ketch hold of Cuffee": From "Coal Black Rose," as quoted by Robert C. Toll, *Blacking Up: The Minstrel Show in Nineteenth Century America* (New York: Oxford University Press, 1974), p. 27.

p. 41 "Al Johns": b. June 4, 1878, Washington, DC; d. June 16, 1928, Paris, France.

"Shepard [N.] Edmonds": b. September 25, 1876, Memphis, TN; d. November 21, 1957, Columbus, OH.

"Irving Jones": b. 1874, unknown; d. March 11, 1932, New York, NY.

"black-faced comedians": Charles E. Ives, *Memos*, ed. John Kirkpatrick (New York: Norton, 1972), p. 56.

"the most versatile theatrical man . . . a good singer": James Weldon Johnson, *Black Manhattan* (New York: Atheneum, 1930), p. 98.

p. 42 "J. Rosamond Johnson": b. August 11, 1873, Jacksonville, FL; d. November 11, 1954, New York, NY.

"James Weldon Johnson": b. June 17, 1871, *ibid.*; d. June 26, 1938, *ibid.*

"I'm driven to desperism": As quoted by Thomas L. Riis, *Just Before Jazz* (Washington and London: Smithsonian Institution Press, 1989), p. 28.

p. 43 "Bert [Egbert Austin] Williams": b. November 12, 1874 or 1875, Antigua, West Indies; d. March 5, 1922, New York, NY.

"Will Marion Cook": b. January 27, 1869, Washington, DC; d. July 19, 1944, New York, NY.

"George Walker": b. 1873, Lawrence, KA; d. January 6, 1891, Islip, NY.

"R. C. [Richard Cecil] McPherson": b. 1883 unknown; d. August 1, 1944, New York, NY.

"Alex [Alexander Claude] Rogers": b. 1876, Nashville, TN; d. September 14, 1930, New York, NY.

"Ernest Hogan": b. 1860, Bowling Green, KY; d. March 20, 1909, New York, NY.

"the greatest of all colored showmen": As quoted by Thomas L. Riis in *Just Before Jazz*, p. 37. It is interesting to note that Hogan was a "natural-black-face comedian" who disdained cork.

"Henry Creamer": b. June 21, 1879, Richmond, VA; d. October 14, 1930, New York, NY.

"J. [John] Leubrie Hill": b. 1869, New Orleans, LA; d. August 30, 1916, New York, NY.

p. 44 "James Burris": unknown.

"Chris Smith": b. October 12, 1879, Charleston, SC; d. October 4, 1949, New York, NY.

"Shelton Brooks": b. May 4, 1886, Amesbury, Ontario; d. September 6, 1975, Los Angeles, CA.

p. 47 "palled around": Edna Brown Hunter interview with the author, September 3, 1981.

p. 48 "J. [James] Tim[othy] Brymn": b. October 5, 1881, Kinston, SC; d. October 3, 1946, New York, NY.

p. 49 "by long odds . . . preach deliverance": As quoted by Jervis Anderson in *This Was Harlem* (New York: Farrar Straus, 1981), p. 120.

"a piece of the PEACE": Undated issue of *The Crusader, ARP.*

p. 50 "Beware!": Untitled poem found among Razaf's collection of published poetry clippings (*ARP*). Appears to have originally been published in the *Amsterdam News.*

"Throw off the yoke": "Throw Off the Yoke," by A. Paul Razafkeriefo, *Amsterdam News,* n.d., *ARP.*

p. 53 "material that was insulting": *ARSB #6*, p. 11.

"My dear Mr. R:": *ibid.*

p. 56 "glorified minstrelsy": Noble Sissle, as quoted by Marshall and Jean Stearns, *Jazz Dance* (New York: Macmillan, 1968), p. 141.

"Will Vodery": b. October 8, 1855, Philadelphia, PA; d. November 18, 1951, New York, NY. Vodery was associated with Ziegfeld for 17 years, beginning in 1912. Along with Vodery, Ziegfeld employed another hugely talented and accomplished black musician as his orchestra leader for the *Midnight Frolics,* Ford T. Dabney (b. March 15, 1883, Washington, DC; d. June 22, 1958, New York, NY).

4 Boun' for a One-Horse Town

p. 59 "To 'Our Andy' ": *ARP.*

p. 61 "several interesting debates": *Cleveland Call,* undated 1921 clipping, *ARP.*

"a Class D amateur league . . . was out of the city": *ibid.*

p. 62 "in semi-pro ball": LeRoy (Satchel) Paige, *Maybe I'll Pitch Forever* (New York: Doubleday, 1962), pp. 30–31.

p. 63 "as I remember it": Willie the Lion Smith, *Music on My Mind* (New York: Doubleday, 1964), pp. 103–104. It should be noted that while Smith here seems to suggest otherwise, Perry Bradford was certainly present for this session, having arranged it entirely himself.

"raven-haired": *ibid.*

"heavy hipped": As quoted by Samuel Charters and Leonard Kunstadt, *Jazz: A History of the New York Scene* (New York: Doubleday, 1981), p. 84.

"Perry Bradford": b. February 14, 1893, Montgomery, AL; d. April 22, 1970, New York, NY.

p. 64 "white commercial songwriters": Abbe Niles, *Blues: An Anthology,* ed. W. C. Handy (New York: W. C. Handy & Edward Abbe Niles, 1949), p. 17.

"a mold": *ibid.,* p. 20.

p. 66 "finally put the new song over": W. C. Handy, *Father of the Blues* (New York: Macmillan, 1951), p. 110. Though Handy does not name the 105th Street cabaret, one possible venue suggests itself: The Campus, on 104th Street and Columbus Avenue.

p. 67 "After having": "New York Black Sox Ready," *New York News,* April 14, 1921, *ARP.*

p. 68 "To render": As quoted by Samuel B. Charters and Leonard Kunstadt, *Jazz: A History of the New York Scene*, p. 97.

"the original": James Weldon Johnson, *Saturday Review of Literature*, June 19, 1926; as quoted by William Ferris, *Blues: An Anthology* (New Introduction, May, 1990).

p. 70 "James Reese Europe": b. February 22, 1981, Mobile, AL; d. May 9, 1919, Boston, MA.

p. 72 "Jelly Roll [Ferdinand Joseph] Morton": b. New Orleans, LA, September 20, 1885; d. July 10, 1891, Los Angeles, CA.

p. 74 "The first original": Research has recently revealed that the Columbia session originally issued as the *first* ODJB recording was, in fact, from a later session than the Victor recording. Columbia's earlier, December 1917 session with the ODJB apparently never was released, due to the noisy disruptiveness of disparaging Columbia studio technicians that day, who managed effectively to ruin the ODJB's first session.

p. 75 "a noise": *New York Clipper*, April 4, 1917, as quoted by Charters and Kunstadt, *Jazz: A History of the New York Scene*, p. 55.

"*Razz*": Apparently Razaf on this occasion even altered his name to conform to the song's rustic theme.

5 Hotcha Razz-Ma-Tazz

p. 78 "5,000 speakeasies": Abel Green & Joe Laurie, Jr., *Show Biz — Variety from Vaude to Video* (New York: Henry Holt, 1951), p. 223.

"profit of $2,500": *ibid.*

p. 79 "pooled their meager resources": Robert Kimball & William Bolcom, *Reminiscing with Sissle and Blake* (New York: Viking, 1973), p. 86.

p. 80 "*Shuffle Along*": For a time the show's initial touring title was *Mayor in Jimtown*.

"It was really off-Broadway": Eubie Blake, as quoted by Allen Woll, *Black Musical Theatre* (Baton Rouge and London: Louisiana State University Press, 1989), p. 62.

"No musical": *New York World*, May 24, 1921, *NYPL/LCPA-BRTC*.

"an infection": *New York American*, May 24, 1921, *ibid.*

"a semi-darky show": *ibid.*

"Society people": Sissle and Blake, as quoted by Marshall and Jean Stearns, *Jazz Dance*, p. 137.

p. 81 "Grand Opening": *New York Age*, November 19, 1921, p. 6.

"Complaints are being heard": "Ministers and Women Join Crusade against 'Hootch'," *ibid.*, October 21, 1922, p. 2.

p. 82 "Opened in November": The Lafayette Theatre was a project of Meyer Jarmulowsky, a Lower East Side banker. V. Hugo Koehler, an established theater architect, designed the theater for Jarmulowsky in the Renaissance style and flanked it at the corner of 131st and 132nd Streets with two wing structures designed to hold stores, offices, and meeting rooms. The Shuffle Inn was installed in the basement of the 131st Street structure.

p. 83 "White people": as quoted by Jim Haskins, *The Cotton Club* (New York: Random House, 1977), p. 21.

p. 84 "Andy would bring": Albertine Glenn interview with the author, January 27, 1982.

"a former uptown showgirl": Albertine Glenn danced in the 1926 and 1927 editions of the *Cotton Club Parade*, among other credits.

"relaxed in atmosphere": Edna Brown Hunter interview with the author, September 3, 1981.

p. 85 "He would lay": *ibid.*

"He was discovering": *ibid.*

p. 86 "The Harlem house": "Shuffle Along Company in Midnight Revue," *New York Age*, October 22, 1921, p. 6.

"Jack Goldberg": Also later produced the all-black musical *How Come?* on Broadway, as well as the all-black touring revue series *The Smart Set*, out of an office in the Gaiety Building.

"There is too much effort": *Variety*, August 26, 1921, p. 17.

p. 87 "colored company": *Variety*, September 16, 1921, p. 17.

"Had the show": *Variety*, June 27, 1922, p. 16.

"ultimate fate": All financial machinations described in this paragraph are as referenced by Allan Woll in *Black Musical Theatre*, pp. 80–81.

p. 88 "It's getting very dark": *"It's Getting Dark on Old Broadway,"* by Dave Stamper and Gene Buck, 1922.

p. 89 "a plantation and levee scene . . . all-colored revue": *Variety*, February 3, 1922, p. 20.

"Florence Mills": Mills, like Razaf, was born in Washington, DC, in 1895 (January 25).

"The smartest stunt": Jimmy Durante and Jack Kofoed, *Nightclubs* (New York: Knopf, 1931), p. 175–176.

p. 90 "Hurtig and Seamon": In their early years H. & S. also produced a number of all-black musicals, including Williams and Walker's *The Policy Players* (1899), *The Sons of Ham* (1900), and *In Dahomey* (1903), the first full-length all-black musical comedy to play a major Broadway theater. That show ultimately returned a 300% profit to Hurtig and Seamon on their initial $5,000 investment.

"renamed the Apollo": Hurtig and Seamon's Burlesque Theatre at 253 West 125th Street reopened as the Apollo on January 26, 1934, under the auspices of real estate entrepreneur Sidney Cohen. Frank Schiffman and Leo Brecher took the Apollo over in May 1935 after Cohen's sudden death from a heart attack. The Schiffman family continued to operate it into the Seventies.

"Something New in Burlesque": From a handbill for *Joe Hurtig's Social Maids, ARSB #6*, p. 56.

"cleanup . . . the shimmy . . . stage business": Abel Green & Joe Laurie, Jr. *Show Biz*, p. 302.

p. 93 "determined to remove": "Harlem Cabaret Owners' Assoc. Formed," *New York Age*, May 26, 1923, p. 1.

p. 94 "Particularly [on] Lenox": "Seventh Avenue Is Rivalling Lenox as Headquarters For Delicatessen Booze Joints," *ibid.*, June 9, 1923, pp. 1–2.

p. 95 "one Connie Immerman": "Harlemites Make Protest Against Reopening of the Cabaret in Lafayette Building," *ibid.*, July 7, 1923, p. 1.

p. 95 "one of his relations": It appears that Connie Immerman may in fact have been 'Louis''s brother-in-law.

"He started telling me": Bricktop, with James Haskins, *Bricktop* (New York: Atheneum, 1983), p. 80.

"allay opposition": *New York Age*, July 7, 1923, p. 1.

p. 96 "you mention": *ibid.*, p. 12.

"The color scheme": "Broadway At Its Best Has Nothing on Connie's Inn," *Amsterdam News*, July 25, 1923, p. 7.

p. 97 "What has the appearance": "Harlem Pastors Are Called Upon to Take Position on Harlem Hootch Situation," *New York Age*, October 13, 1923, p. 5.

p. 99 "dark-skinned girls": *New York Age*, March 8, 1924, p. 1.

p. 100 "bootlegging gentry": *New York Age*, January 26, 1924, p. 1.

"Notwithstanding": *New York Age*, February 2, 1924, p. 2.

"the Gophers": According to Willie the Lion Smith (*Music on My Mind*, p. 45), Owney Madden's Gopher gang was famous for hating "Negroes."

6 Who's to Blame

p. 107 "My first impression": Duke Ellington, *Music Is My Mistress* (New York: Doubleday, 1973), p. 90.

"a light-skinned playboy": Willie the Lion Smith, *Music on My Mind*, p. 6.

p. 108 "Many of the transients": *ibid.*, p. 52.

p. 109 "All the licks": Ethel Waters, *His Eye Is on the Sparrow* (New York: Doubleday, 1951), p. 145.

"She had been around": Willie the Lion Smith, *Music on My Mind*, p. 35.

"like twins": Willie the Lion Smith, *Music on My Mind*, p. 37

p. 110 "They were popular fellows": James P. Johnson, as quoted by Tom Davin, "Conversations with James P. Johnson," *Jazz Review* (June 1959), p. 16.

"This was the Negro section": *ibid.* (July 1959), p. 11.

p. 111 "a beat-up small dance hall": Willie the Lion Smith, *Music on My Mind*, p. 65.

"I went around copping": JPJ, Tom Davin, *Jazz Review* (September 1959), p. 26.

p. 113 "The people who came": *ibid.* (July 1959), p. 12.

p. 114 "opera singers": George White, as quoted by Allen Woll, *Black Musical Theater*, pp. 90–91.

"He brought him down": Willie the Lion Smith, *The Memoirs of Willie The Lion Smith*, recorded interview on two-record LP (New York: RCA, 1968), Side III.

p. 115 "street services": In time, Waller Senior founded his own storefront church—referred to in the neighborhood as "the Subway Baptist Church" —on 134th Street, near Fifth Avenue. Eubie Blake recalled Thomas Waller playing the organ at his father's services there and often falling off the organ stool because his legs couldn't reach the pedals.

p. 117 "more than 200 pounds": Full grown, Waller ultimately weighed between 285 and 300 pounds, standing five feet eleven inches tall, with a size 15 shoe.

"the Crescent": Waller first worked Saturday afternoons at the Crescent

Theatre, a hangout for PS 89 students who came on Saturdays to watch film serials like "The Perils of Pauline." Pearl Wright, the Crescent's resident pianist (and later Ethel Waters's accompanist), had her own tune called "Perils of Pauline" which the kids loved to join in on, singing and shouting in tempo. Believing, however, that their classmate Thomas Waller could do better, they eventually talked the Crescent house manager into giving Waller a shot at the keyboard. (Kenneth Bright and Inez Cavanaugh, "That Harmful Little Armful—Fats Waller in His Formative Years," *The Crisis*, April 1944, pp. 109–110.)

p. 118 "I asked James P.": Maurice Waller and Anthony Calabrese, *Fats Waller* (New York: Schirmer, 1977), p. 26.

"I took Fats home": James P. Johnson, as quoted by Seymour Peck, "PM Visits: The Dean of Jazz Pianists," *PM* (Friday, April 27, 1945), p. 20.

p. 119 "I taught him how to groove": James P. Johnson, as quoted by Al Silverman, "The One and Only Fats Waller," *SAGA* (October 1955) V. II, No. 1, p. 88.

"Right after James P.": Lil Johnson, as quoted by Nat Shapiro and Nat Hentoff, *Hear Me Talkin' to Ya* (New York: Rinehart, 1955), p. 253.

"Even before the Depression": Willie the Lion Smith, *Music on My Mind*, pp. 153–156.

p. 120 "Every move we made": James P. Johnson, as quoted by Tom Davin, "Conversations with James P. Johnson, *Jazz Review* (August 1959), pp. 14–15.

p. 122 "Liza and her Shufflin' Six": There is a good deal of confusion surrounding these early dates in Waller's performing career. Garvin Bushell recalled touring in an act called "Liza and her Shuffling Sextet," with Fats Waller on piano, as late as 1923. (Nat Hentoff interview with Bushell, *Jazz Review*, April, 1959.) Bushell's memories of Waller on this occasion are charming: "He was still a big kid; he used to come into the theatre with an apple on a stick."

Waller's first stint at Leroy's does appear to have begun in 1921, probably before the birth of his son, with the eastern circuit burlesque tour following in late 1921 or early 1922.

"place the contest in 1921": Samuel Charters and Leonard Kunstadt in *Jazz: A History of the New York Scene* place the contest in 1919 (p. 274).

"I used to listen": Andy Razaf, as quoted by Al Silverman, "The One and Only Fats Waller," *SAGA* (October 1955), p. 88.

"During their years together": Maurice Waller and Anthony Calabrese, *Fats Waller*, p. 50.

p. 124 "Clarence Williams": b. October 6, 1893, Plaquemin, LA; d. November 6, 1965, New York, NY.

"as if he were wearing mittens": Willie the Lion Smith, *Music on My Mind*, p. 208.

p. 127 "Razaf did quietly acknowledge": In a letter to Razaf dated May 13, 1950 (*ARP*), Jack Burton, compiler of *The Blue Book of Tin Pan Alley*, acknowledged numerous corrections that Razaf had sent him regarding both his own and Fats Waller's bios in the book. Burton concluded with the promise to Razaf that "I'll give you credit for the 'Squeeze Me' lyrics"—something that Burton never, in fact, did.

p. 128 "debut song composition": Razaf apparently also sold a song composed with Thomas Waller in 1924 entitled "Please Tell Me Why" (published by Gotham Music Service) either under the pseudonym Ed Adams or to an actual person named Ed Adams. Only this name appears (with Waller's) on the sheet music for the song, which Razaf nevertheless kept in a bound volume of his song sheets, now in the *NYPL/SCRBC-MARBD*.

7 Ain't-Cha' Glad?

p. 131 "Hughie Woolford": unknown.

p. 132 "Edgar Dowell": unknown.

"He cut me": Robert Kimball & William Bolcom, *Reminiscing with Sissle and Blake*, p. 41.

p. 133 "The permanency of the purpose": "Recent Craze Bringing Another Publishing House to the Fore," *Amsterdam News*, July 11, 1923, p. 5.

p. 134 "serious entry into the 'blues' business": as quoted by Walter C. Allen, *Hendersonia* (Highland Park, NJ: Jazz Monographs No. 4, 1973), p. 63.

"Whenever business mess up": Perry Bradford, *Born with the Blues* (New York: Oak Publications, 1965), p. 131.

p. 135 "a quiet cabaret": *Variety*, April 19, 1923, p. 24.

p. 136 "it should be part": Letter from AR to journalist Dan Burley, September 15, 1951, *ARP*.

p. 137 "Black Swan records": Was initially called Willie Records and was operated out of a small office in Pace's apartment on Seventh Avenue, between 134th and 135th Streets. The firm thrived during its first year of business, grossing over $110,000 by capitalizing on the blues craze, but ultimately survived only three years. Despite Black Swan's claim that "all other colored records are by artists only passing for colored," the company often recorded white performers masquerading as black under false names.

p. 138 "Honeysuckle Rose": Interestingly, the printed credit line for a 1924 song by Razaf and Edgar Dowell entitled "You Gotta B' Natural Honey (Your Baby's Gonna Leave You Flat), published by Edgar Dowell Music Pub., reads: "writers of 'Honeysuckle Rose.'"

p. 143 "Schiffman and his partner": Leo Brecher, an Austrian immigrant who owned and operated a number of theaters around Manhattan, was the silent money man behind all Schiffman-Brecher enterprises. Frank Schiffman was a former schoolteacher, who had grown up on the Lower East Side.

'encountered Waller": Maines later pointed out that "he first heard Waller play at Baron Wilkins' club . . . and at the . . . Lincoln Theatre." (From page proof for untitled, unidentified article on Waller, *ARP*.)

p. 144 "one of the best": *Variety*, September 16, 1925, p. 45.

"absorbed Fats's teachings": Rex Stewart, *Jazz Masters of the Thirties* (New York: Macmillan, 1972), p. 21.

p. 145 "certain accounts": Maurice Waller and Anthony Calabrese, *Fats Waller*, p. 57.

"unscrupulous": Songwriter Gus Kahn called Joe Davis "one of the most charming thieves I've ever met."

p. 146 "Never sell a copyright": Bruce Bastin, *Never Sell a Copyright* (Chigwell, Essex, England: Storyville, 1990), p. 4.

"desk space": *ibid.*

p. 148 "Dear Joe": Bruce Bastin, *Never Sell a Copyright*, p. 25.

p. 150 "Maceo Pinkard": b. June 27, 1897, Bluefield, WV; d. July 21, 1962, New York, NY.

p. 151 "unidentifiable songwriting peers": Razaf addressed this subject pointedly in a poem entitled "Land of Melody—Stolen Hours," published in the *Amsterdam News* on August 10, 1927 (p. 11):

In silence he would listen
While the folks would praise his song;
His name was on the title page
Where it did not belong.
Within his heart he was the meanest
Kind of cheat.
For he had bought the number
From a fellow in the street.

"Let me tell you": Sam Wooding, interview with the author, December 22, 1981.

p. 152 "soon as we got broke": Andy Razaf, "Fats Waller," *Coda* (May 1963) V. 5, No. 10, p. 2. (As originally published in *Metronome* [January 1944].)

"take them up to Mills": Duke Ellington, in his memoir *Music on My Mind* (pp. 72–73), further illuminated the wide-open song purchasing practices employed by Mills Music. Irving Mills, Ellington recalled, "was known as the last resort for getting some money by those who had been peddling songs all day without success. I first heard of him secondhand," Ellington wrote, "and one day I joined a group of five or six songwriters . . . The procedure, they explained, was to sell . . . blues outright to Irving Mills for fifteen or twenty dollars. It was very simple—no hassle. Just give him the lead sheet, sign the outright release, pick up the money and go. This happened every day. There is no knowing just how many [blues] Irving Mills amassed."

"first song together": Razaf and Denniker's first published song appears to have been "A Bobbed-Haired Bandit Stole My Heart Away," published in 1924 by Bernard-Schweimer Music, nominally a Joe Davis subsidiary.

p. 153 "complaint": "Denniker To Publish," *New York Telegraph*, December 17, 1925, *ARP.*

"TOBA": Originally known as the Consolidated Circuit, it included theaters in all the major cities of the Midwest, the East, and the South, including Chicago, Detroit, Cleveland, Pittsburgh, Columbus, Philadelphia, Baltimore, Washington, and Norfolk, and cities in North and South Carolina, Georgia, Florida, Tennessee, Louisiana, Texas, Oklahoma, Missouri, and Indiana.

p. 154 "Spencer Williams": b. October 14, 1889, New Orleans, LA; d. September 14, 1965, New York, NY.

p. 155 "Li'l Brown Baby": Interestingly, Paul Laurence Dunbar may have influenced Razaf on this tune with his own dialect poem, "Little Brown Baby," (*The Complete Poems of Paul Laurence Dunbar* [New York: Dodd, Mead, 1913, reprinted], p. 134.)

p. 156 " 'Why Did I Go Wrong?' came": "Broadway Gets Song Thrill," *Orchestra World,* June 1926, *ARP.*

p. 157 "exemplified all the elegant splendor": From "The Savoy Story" booklet published by the Savoy Ballroom on the occasion of its 25th anniversary in 1951, as quoted by Samuel Charters and Leonard Kunstadt, *Jazz: A History of the New York Scene,* p. 186.

p. 158 "Dear Andy": *ARP.*

p. 160 "If Fats Waller," Ed Kirkeby, *Ain't Misbehavin'* (New York: Dodd, Mead, 1966), p. 100.

"That Fats": Eubie Blake, interview with the author, August 6, 1981.

p. 161 "sympathetic relationship": "I think I took it for granted that he was a womanizer," explained Anita Waller in an interview years after her husband's death (as quoted in "Spreadin' Rhythm Around," *Mississippi Rag,* August 1991, p. 7). "There were girls always hanging over them pianists. . . . But he was not an exhibitionist, you know, about his sexism. He was quite, ah, the gentleman, as I saw him."

"transformed Waller": Andy Razaf always insisted that Fats Waller loved his wife Anita and was "a good husband," pointing out, according to his own wife, Alicia (interview with the author, January 30, 1982), that "Fats never forgot his family. Even when he left the Daisy Chain, he always stopped to buy cheesecake to bring home to Anita and the boys."

p. 162 "Dear Andy": *ARP.*

"laborer": Razaf gave his occupation as "laborer" in the New York City Register of 1917–1918.

"collaborated with him": J. C. Johnson wrote "I'm Goin' Huntin' " with Fats Waller in 1923. The song was published in 1927.

8 Harlem Hotcha

p. 166 "Even the smallest": Stephen Graham, *New York Nights* (New York: George H. Doran, 1927), p. 91.

p. 167 "Broadway north": Rian James, *Dining in New York* (New York, John Day, 1930), p. 234.

p. 168 "quick-witted": Edward Jablonsky, *Harold Arlen: Happy With the Blues* (New York: Doubleday, 1961), p. 55.

"The Chief ingredient": *ibid.*

"brutes at the door": *ibid.,* p. 53.

"racial lines": Jimmy Durante and Jack Kofoed, *Nightclubs,* p. 115.

p. 169 "unspeakable": As quoted by David Levering Lewis, *When Harlem Was in Vogue* (New York: Knopf, 1981), p. 108.

p. 171 "you'll see some queeriosities": Rian James, *Dining in New York,* p. 233.

"The waffles and bacon": *ibid.,* p. 232.

"with no one caring much": *ibid.,* p. 231.

p. 172 "Between the hours": "About Things Theatrical," *Amsterdam News,* November 18, 1925, p. 5.

p. 173 "The best of Harlem's black cabarets": Rudolf Fisher, "The Caucasian Storms Harlem," *American Mercury,* (August 1927), V. 11, No. 44, p. 393.

"who 'confessed' ": "Yellow Charleston Reprieved," *Amsterdam News,*

September 9, 1925, p. 2. The story points out that "... Charleston' had requested that he be allowed to wear a tuxedo suit to his death."

p. 174 "This is the nicest": Rian James, *Dining in New York*, p. 230.

"There are those": Stephen Graham, *New York Nights*, pp. 243–245.

"a hanging out place for musicians": Willie the Lion Smith, *Music on My Mind*, p. 159.

p. 176 "two ex-vaudevillian opium smokers": *ibid.*

"the hottest gin mill: Duke Ellington, *Music Is My Mistress*, p. 92.

"phone first": Rian James, *Dining in New York*, p. 232.

"absolutely no other place left": *ibid.*, p. 234.

p. 177 "Andy had a sensitive": Ed Morrow, interview with the author, November 30, 1981.

p. 178 "the outstanding": *Opportunity*, September 10, 1927, *ARP*.

p. 179 "The unethical work": This comment appears as a notation in Razaf's hand alongside a reference to royalties for "Louisiana," *ARP*.

p. 182 "Do you remember": Letter from J. C. Johnson to AR, August 10, 1961, *ARP*.

"contributed a column": Razaf's 1927 contributions to the *Amsterdam News* appeared under a variety of column titles, including "At Home Abroad" and "Our Lighter Side—Being a Survey of Mirth, Music and Laughter On and Off the Stage." One interesting aspect of these writings was a series of reviews in rhyme that Razaf wrote assessing the many black productions that opened on Broadway that year—including shows to which he himself had contributed music.

"There's a dreadful": *Amsterdam News*, September 14, 1927, p. 8.

p. 183 "The Producer": *Amsterdam News*, July 20, 1927, p. 7.

p. 188 "I don't like": As quoted by Perry Bradford, *Born with the Blues*, p. 137.

"How 'bout some": Ed Kirkeby, *Ain't Misbehavin'*, p. 115.

p. 189 "smart satire": *ibid.*, p. 114.

"It doesn't sound": Robert Coleman, *Daily Mirror*, February 28, 1928, *NYPL/LCPA-BRTC*.

"instead of the verb": *Philadelphia Bulletin*, February 14, 1928, *ARP*.

"Keep Shufflin' is": *Philadelphia Record*, February 14, 1928, *ARP*.

p. 190 "Red hot tunes": Robert Coleman, *Daily Mirror*, February 28, 1928, *NYPL/LCPA-BRC*.

p. 193 "they'd be ossified": Garvin Bushell, *Jazz from the Beginning* (Ann Arbor: The University of Michigan Press, 1988), p. 74.

p. 194 "behind on his payroll": According to Harrison Smith (*Coda*, May 1963), Waller eventually grew so afraid of Rothstein that Smith had to go and collect his salary for him.

"raving ... over a lady": *Amsterdam News*, February 25, 1927, *Moorland-Spingarn Research Collection, Howard University*.

"Razaf impressed us": *Washington Afro–American*, n.d., *ibid.*

p. 195 "Duke Andre": *Brooklyn Daily Times*, May 27, 1928, p. 7, *ARP*.

9 A Low Down Treat

p. 199 "wistful and repentant": *Variety*, September 19, 1928.

p. 201 "overflowing the piano stool": Mary Lou Williams, "My Friends the Kings of Jazz," *Melody Maker*, April 10, 1954, p. 5.

"took great pains": "Fats Waller," *Coda* (May 1963), p. 2.

p. 202 "certain witnesses": Milton "Mezz" Mezzrow, "Memories of Fats," *Jazz Journal* (May 1953), V. 6, No. 5, p. 21: "I'll never forget my impression of the two the very first time I heard them together. I asked Fats why they didn't take part in the show as a team and Andy chimed in and said: 'Yes, Mezz, I've been telling him the same thing for a long time.' But Fats answered: 'Mezz, you know I am a musician and not an actor.'"

"a formidable producer of revues": Mezz Mezzrow, "Fats Waller," *Bulletin du Hot Club de France* (May 1952) No. 18, p. 3.

p. 203 "collaborated with Fats": Emerson "Geechie" Harper, "LeRoy Smith and His Band," March 1966, unpublished manuscript, courtesy of Frank Driggs.

p. 205 "This is the first": *Pittsburgh Courier*, March 16, 1929, *ARP*.

p. 206 "done the unbelievable": As quoted by Bruce Bastin, *Never Sell a Copyright*, p. 49.

p. 207 "Music publishing history": *ibid.*, p. 50.

p. 208 *"Africana"*: This Ethel Waters vehicle contained a second-act interpolated medley of Waters's recent song hits—billed as "Some Song Hits You Have Home on Your Records"—including Razaf and J. C. Johnson's "My Special Friend." "It is one of those ditties often found in colored shows," observed a critic for *Variety* (July 13, 1927), "the lines saying just what they mean, raw, of course. The first-nighters ate that one up."

p. 209 "The absence of spirited stepping": *Variety*, September 24, 1924, p. 12.

"[White men] understand": "Prefers to Stage All-Negro Shows. Lew Leslie Declares No White Girls Work So Hard as Do the Harlem Belles." Unidentified article in Lew Leslie file, *Theatre Collection, Philadelphia Free Library*, as quoted by Allen Woll, *Black Musical Theatre*, p. 97.

p. 210 "The building might have": Myles Norman interview with the author, September 1, 1981.

p. 211 "He discovered": *New York Post*, June 8, 1929.

"Sing me your favorite": As related by Alicia Razaf Georgiade in an interview with the author, February 22, 1982.

p. 212 "three interpolated numbers": "Couldn't I," "Brown Gal," and "Swanee Jubilee."

"A new title": According to *Variety* (June 26, 1929), *Hot Feet* "was first called *Tan Town Topics.*" It does not appear that the production ever played under this title, however. Most likely, the Immermans initially announced the retitling as *Tan Town Topics* and then settled on *Hot Chocolates.*

p. 213 "pre-Broadway rehearsal period": *Hot Chocolates* originally scheduled its Broadway opening for June 10. After the show's Bronx runthrough, though, the opening was postponed for rewrites. It was during this ten-day period that both "Ain't Misbehavin'" and "Black and Blue" were written.

"a marvelous strain": Andy Razaf, "Fats Waller," *Coda* (May 1963), p. 2.

"Harry Brooks arranged it": According to Brooks, as quoted by Richard Hadlock in *Jazz Masters of the 20's* (New York: Macmillan, 1965) p. 156: "[Ain't Misbehavin'] was an attempt to copy the successful formula Gershwin used for 'The Man I Love.' We imitated the opening phrase that began just after the first beat and the minor part of the bridge too."

"where *Hot Chocolates* was rehearsing": on June 26 *Variety* reported (p. 48) that while the "Goddess of Rain" number was being rehearsed at the Hudson Theatre, a rainstorm broke out with such force that the theater roof gave in, "drenching the company."

"That's good luck": Floyd Levin, "Andy Razaf—The Melody Man," *Jazz Journal* (October 1951), Vol. 4, No. 10, p. 2.

p. 214 "doubling to the floor show": *Variety*, June 26, 1929. *NYPL/LCPA-BRTC*.

p. 216 "Razaf himself": Razaf's detailed recollection of the events surrounding the genesis of "Black and Blue" was related to the author by Razaf's widow Alicia Georgiade in a series of interviews throughout January and February 1982.

p. 220 "At first": Ralph Ellison, *Invisible Man* (New York: Random House, 1947; Signet reprint, 1952), pp. 15–16.

"Best Negro Revue": *New York Herald Tribune*, June 21, 1929, *NYPL/LCPA-BRTC*.

"childish prattle": Robert Garland, *Evening Telegram*, June 21, 1929, *ibid.*

"Woefully lacking": Howard Barnes, *New York Herald Tribune*, June 21, 1929, *ibid.*

"the music is just noise": Arthur Pollock, *Brooklyn Daily Eagle*, June 21, 1929, *ibid.*

"If the rest": Garland, *Evening Telegram*, June 21, 1929, *ibid.*

"The show can boast": Stephen Rathburn, *New York Sun*, June 21, 1929, *ibid.*

"A synthetic": *New York Times*, June 21, 1929, *ibid.*

p. 221 "Miss Wilson": *Variety*, June 26, 1929, *ibid.*

"If they always": F. P. Dunn, Jr., *New York World*, June 21, 1929, *ibid.*

"at Razaf's suggestion": "I suggested that Louis Armstrong sing it and play a chorus from the orchestra pit." (Andy Razaf, as quoted by Charles McHarry, "On the Town," *Amsterdam News*, December 2, n.d., *ARP.*)

"from July 8": This is confirmed by *Hot Chocolates* programs from this period, in the *Theater Collection of the Museum of the City of New York.*

p. 222 "Paul Bass had": Cab Calloway and Bryant Rollins, *Of Minnie the Moocher & Me* (New York: Crowell, 1976), p. 75.

"again as recalled": As related to the author by Razaf's widow, Alicia Razaf Georgiade, February 23, 1982.

p. 223 "Andy Razaf is one": Maurice Dancer, "Stage Facts," *Pittsburgh Courier*, August 24, 1929, *ARP.*

"Don Redman": b. July 7, 1900, Piedmont, VW; d. November 30, 1964, New York, NY.

"*Load of Coal*": Appears to have opened during the last week of October 1929.

p. 226 "baked him special cookies": AR, as quoted by Leonard Feather, *Down Beat*, February 15, 1962, p. 51.

"a sumptuous breakfast": AR, as quoted by Floyd Levin, *Jazz Journal* (October 1951), p. 2.

p. 227 "I gotta go": FW, as quoted by AR, "Fats Waller," *Coda* (May 1963), p. 2.

"the sudden thought": Andy Razaf, "The Story behind a Song," October 14, 1961; written in response to a solicitation by *Variety* editor Abel Green for a

1961 *Variety* Anniversary feature: an anthology of stories by "a representative group of American songsmiths," to be titled "The Story behind the Song." Green ultimately rejected this submission by Razaf in a letter dated November 6, 1961, saying simply, "this doesn't come off." *ARP.*

p. 228 "We thought very little": *ibid.*

p. 229 "According to . . .Kirkeby": Ed Kirkeby, *Ain't Misbehavin'*, p. 124.

p. 230 "I remember an ad": Edna Brown Hunter, interview with the author, September 3, 1981.

"Minto Cato": Born in Little Rock, Arkansas, August 23, 1900, of French, Native–American and African–American descent. Cato (the name is Native American) was named after her French grandmother, La Minta. After graduating from Knoxville (TN) College, and studying voice at Howard University, she taught school for three years in Atlanta, Georgia. Cato then came to New York, appearing in the Cotton Club's debut revue in 1924 and in subsequent nightclub revues throughout Harlem. In the latter Twenties she played for a time in the original production of *Showboat* as "Queenie." After traveling internationally throughout the late Thirties, Forties, and early Fifties, she returned to the states only to find herself branded as a Communist by the House Committee on Un-American Activities. Thereafter she worked intermitently and with great difficulty in regional opera companies and nightclubs, her relations with Andy Razaf remaining cordial right up to Razaf's death. Cato died on November 26, 1979.

"He was gonna marry": Eubie Blake interview with the author, August 6, 1981.

"I thought they were married": Alberta Hunter interview with the author, July 9, 1981.

"Dear Andy": *ARP.*

p. 231 "He simply was": Lula Weston interview with the author, September 3, 1981.

10 What Harlem Is to Me

p. 233 "Macomber once described": As quoted by Ed Kirkeby, *Ain't Misbehavin'*, p. 86.

p. 234 "You never knew": *ibid.*, p. 87.

"went to this or that": Duncan Schiedt, "Fats Waller—from a Biographer's Notebook," *The Record Changer* (September 1950), Vol. 9, No. 8, p. 7.

p. 235 "The story has been told": Ed Kirkeby, *Ain't Misbehavin'*, p. 79.

p. 238 "That kitchen mechanics' parade": "Kitchen Mechanic's Parade," from original lyric book, *ARP.*

"We're the chefs": *ibid.*

p. 239 "When the dust": "Shake Your Duster," *ibid.*

"Elevator Papa": "Elevator Papa, Switchboard Mama," *ibid.*

p. 241 "of the Nineteen Twenties": Though *Kitchen Mechanic's Revue* did open in March 1930, it certainly was conceived in the spirit of Nineteen Twenties Harlem.

p. 243 "Leslie, who had never wanted": Ethel Waters, *His Eye Is on the Sparrow*, p. 215.

"Who's your publisher?": Eubie Blake interview with the author, August 6, 1981.

p. 244 "There [was] no way": Al Rose, *Eubie Blake* (New York: Schirmer Books, 1979), pp. 105–106.

"He could write lyrics": *ibid.*, p. 85.

p. 245 "Some of the intervals": *ibid.*, p. 106.

p. 246 "actually had leapt": Gene Rogers (pianist), interview with the author, August 2, 1981: "In 1931, Leslie produced a musical revue on Broadway called *Rhapsody in Black*, and in it he used Gershwin's 'Rhapsody in Blue' for a number. Well, one night the clarinetist missed the opening notes; he fudged the glissando. Leslie was up in a first balcony box. When the notes were missed he leaped from the box to the orchestra pit, ran onstage, and grabbed the clarinet—which he'd never played before—away from the guy and started blowing into it, screaming: 'Like this! Like this!' "

"That show started": Ethel Waters, *His Eye Is on the Sparrow*, p. 215.

"for it is certain": *Brooklyn Eagle*, September 3, 1930, *ARP*.

"Sure enough": Robert Kimball & William Bolcom, *Reminiscing with Sissle and Blake*, p. 214.

"a private journal": *ARP*.

p. 247 "that inasmuch": Telegram dated June 19, 1930, *ARP*.

"Is it as good a show": *Boston Post*, September 10, 1930, *ARP*.

p. 250 "We opened": Ethel Waters, *His Eye Is on the Sparrow*, p. 215.

p. 251 "The back of my car": *ibid.*, p. 216.

"Within the next few days": "Blackbirds Now Closed for Good," *Amsterdam News*, January 28, 1931, *ARP*.

11 How Can You Face Me?

p. 255 "Tin Pan Alley": Sidney Skolsky, "Behind the News," *Daily News*, May 24, 1933, *ARP*.

p. 257 "rescued": On July 3, 1929 (p. 96), *Variety* reported: "Never before in the history of Tin Pan Alley has the average songwriter enjoyed such affluence and influence, poise and peace of mind and contentment. . . . once a song is spotted in a picture . . . the writers [are] enjoying guaranteed incomes from $12,500 to $35,000 on an average, not to mention the fancy $1,000 a week paid to some."

"MOTION PICTURE PRODUCERS!!!": *Film Daily*, September 27, 1929, *ARP*.

p. 258 "noticeable results": *ARSB #6*, p. 61. Razaf aggressively pursued film work himself during the ensuing months and was apparently pursued in turn, without tangible results. On December 14, 1934, he signed off on a letter to a Mr. C. P. Hoagland, 1619 Broadway, NYC, stipulating that "In consideration of your securing for me employment, either to write music for motion pictures or to work in motion pictures, I hereby agree to pay you a commission of 20% (twenty percent) on all money secured as a result of your booking."

Shortly thereafter, Sam Fox of the Fox Movietone Corporation wrote to Razaf in Chicago on December 29, "about you and Jimmy Johnson. . . . The picture we have in mind will not go into production immediately, and I would like to have you confirm that you will work with Jimmy Johnson should we desire to make a deal." On January 18, 1935, Razaf replied: "I am perfectly willing to work with Jimmie Johnson for said picture. Our associations in the past have been both effective and agreeable." *ARP.*

p. 261 "I have no desire": AR letter to ASCAP, dated September 28, 1932, *ARSB #6*, p. 14.

p. 262 "Razaf's insistence": Razaf later claimed that the first time Waller ever sang in public was on a job they worked together on the ferry to New Jersey. Razaf said he simply walked off in the middle of a song, thereby forcing Waller to sing.

p. 263 "He was there": Hugues Panassie, *1946 PL Yearbook of Jazz,* as quoted by Ed Kirkeby, *Ain't Misbehavin',* p. 156.

p. 264 "Now it's time": Maurice Waller and Anthony Calabrese, *Fats Waller,* p. 108.

p. 265 "restrain them": Walter C. Allen, *Hendersonia,* p. 251.

"This is a helluva place": *Pittsburgh Courier,* September 19, 1931, p. 9.

p. 266 "It packs": *Variety,* September 27, 1932, *ARP.*

p. 268 "Under the weary Tree of Hope": Andy Razaf, *Amsterdam News,* June 8, 1932, *ARP.*

p. 269 "That's What I Like 'Bout the South": Cotton Club programs printed the song title with the word "About" rather than "'Bout," as Razaf specified.

p. 270 "credit himself": Harris ultimately evaded Razaf legally on this song by copyrighting his own slightly altered lyric for the tune under the title, "That's What I Like About the South." Razaf's attorneys appear to have pursued Harris about this matter for years.

"It is one thing": unidentified newspaper, *ARP.*

p. 272 "In less than": Earl J. Morris, "Harper, Razaf Show Is Peppy," *Chicago Defender,* February 8, 1934, *ARP.*

"Andy Razaf wrote": *ibid.*

"a daring song": *ibid.*

p. 273 "Fats and I made": Willie the Lion Smith, *Music on My Mind,* pp. 226–227.

p. 274 "Gershwin told Paley": *New York Times,* June 25, 1943.

p. 275 "A scintillating singer": *New York Age,* n.d. *ARP.*

"He later came back": Alicia Razaf Georgiade, interview with the author, February 3, 1982.

12 Swing Low

p. 281 "Swing Low": As many as 150 unpublished Razaf lyrics—whole lyrics and lyric fragments, titled and untitled—survive among Razaf's papers. This particular titled piece stands out decidedly. No musical collaborator is anywhere indicated.

p. 283 "the nervous strain": As quoted by Jervis Anderson, *This Was Harlem,* p. 246.

"What Harlem Is to Me": Was in fact sung in its debut at the new downtown Connie's Inn by Alberta Hunter.

p. 284 "Have secured": Telegram dated August 19, 1934, *ARP.*

"Throughout the evening": Billy Rowe, *Amsterdam News*, n.d., *ARP*.
"$75 for all three": Contract dated September 12, 1935, *ARP*.

p. 285 "$400 for an entire evening": Contract dated April 20, 1935, *ARP*.
"*Flim Flam Alley*": *Amsterdam News*, n.d., *ARP*.

p. 288 "swing band novelty numbers": The ranks of Razaf's contributions in this area are as clouded as the rest of his work. A handwritten pencil manuscript draft for the lyric to bandleader Jimmie Lunceford's 1939 band hit " 'Tain't What You Do" (officially credited to Lunceford's arranger Sy Oliver and trombonist Trummy Young) turned up, for example, among Razaf's papers, under the title "It Ain't What You Do."
"William Tell": Was performed by Paul Whiteman, conducting his orchestra combined with the Philadelphia Orchestra, in a Christmas concert at the New York Hippodrome on December 1, 1937.

p. 289 "continuing to shop": Razaf at this time wrote two songs regarded as the first original radio theme songs: "Make Believe Ballroom" and "Milkmen's Matinee" (both with melodies by Paul Denniker). Martin Block's *Make Believe Ballroom* debuted in 1935 on a then little-known independent New York radio station, WNEW. The program's revolutionary format—unheard of in those days of exclusively live music broadcasting—was the playing of phonograph records from a "make believe" sound stage, with introductions, comments, and smooth chatter from host Martin Block, as the first radio disc jockey. Razaf and Denniker's song for the show was published by Joe Davis in August 1936. Stan Shaw's *Milkman's Matinee* took Block's concept into the early morning hours. Razaf and Denniker's song for that show was sold to Joe Davis as "Milkman's Matinee" but published in November 1936 as "Milkmen's Matinee."
"Reginald Foresythe": *b. May 28, 1907*, London, England; d. unknown.

p. 290 "Fats didn't": Gene Sedric, as quoted by Alyn Shipton, *Fats Waller* (New York: Universe Books, 1988), p. 62.
"Dear friend Phil": AR letter to Phil Ponce, April 23, 1936.

p. 291 "Dear Andy": Phil Ponce letter to AR, May 7, 1936.

p. 292 "I am sorry": Jack Robbins letter to AR, May 21, 1936.

p. 294 "all monies": *ARP*.

p. 295 "I not only plan": AR letter to Leonard Feather, January 28, 1936, *ARP*.
"Dear Joe": *ARP*.

p. 297 "to an alarming degree": Jean Blackwell Hutson interview with the author, September 22, 1980.

p. 298 "I was a fellow traveler": *ibid.* All ensuing remarks are from this interview.

p. 300 "Razaf also later claimed": As related to the author by Alicia Razaf Georgiade in an interview, January 19, 1982.
"never for hire": *ibid.*

13 The Outskirts of Town

p. 306 "white composers exclusively": *Music* by Sammy Fain, Louis Haber, Vic Mizzy, Rube Bloom, and George Gershwin (Leslie abstracted Gershwin's "Rhapsody in Blue" for a number in the show). *Lyrics* by Johnny Mercer, Mitchell Parish, Dorothy Sachs, and Irving Taylor.

"After being": "Razaf and Black [*sic*] Pleased with 'TAN MANHATTAN' Show," *Call*, January 31, 1941, *ARP*.

"I was livin'": Eubie Blake, interview with the author, August 6, 1981.

p. 307 "He wrote a piece": *ibid.*

p. 309 "We Are Americans Too": The lyric, in its entirety, reads:

Shouting Hosannas,
Waving Spangled Banners!
Seems to be the order of the day.
We are not exotic,
Or less patriotic,
Now you have the reason why we say:

By the record we've made
And the part that we've played,
We are Americans too.
By the pick and the plow
And the sweat of our brow,
We are Americans too.

We have given our blood and bone,
Helped to lay the Nation's corner stone,
None have loved Old Glory more than we,
Or have shown greater loyalty.
Bunker Hill to the Rhine,
We've been right there in line,
Serving the Red, White and Blue.
All our future is here,
Ev'rything we hold dear,
We are Americans too.
Somewhere out there
In the parade,
Loudly, proudly, and undismayed,
We'll be marching along,
Singing this song:
We are Americans,
Loyal Americans,
We are Americans too.

p. 310 "Dear Andy": Abe Olman letter to AR, January 13, 1941, *ARP*.

p. 311 "The smiles": *Washington Afro-American*, January 25, 1941, *ARP*.

p. 312 "how much they had": *Call*, January 31, 1941, *ibid.*

"literally stepped": *Washington Afro-American*, January 25, 1941, *ibid.*

p. 313 "The directors": *Call*, January 31, 1941, *ibid.*

p. 314 "I hope": Edna Thomas, letter to AR, June 1, 1942, *ARP*.

"patriotic cooperation": There was a darker underside to Razaf's patriotic support for America's war effort, as expressed in poems like "Negro Volunteer":

I really don't expect much in return
For any sacrifices that I make,
But for the future generations' sake
I offer all, in hopes that they will learn
The great truth men today refuse to see:
As long as some are slaves, no man is free.
Vain are the things that we are fighting for,
And ev'ry gesture is a mockery
Which makes each war food for another war,
As long as men, steeped in hypocrisy,
Reserve the table of Democracy
For just the chosen ones, to wine and dine,
While only crumbs are left for me and mine.

p. 315 "a murderous tour schedule": An indication of Waller's attitude toward his withering international touring schedule may be gleaned from this previously unpublished letter to an unidentified correspondent, datelined May 26, 1939, Grand Hotel, Sheffield, England:

Dear Walter:
I got this swell letter you sent me. . . . It's so seldom over here, you make real contact with sincere people who enjoy and really appreciate swing. You Walter, know yourself 80% over here try to make believe they know what swing is all about; but do they? *Oh Nuts* who are not real, who don't stop and think, who don't ever relax and offer a prayer to God.
   Oh! It's nauseating to think of the tramps & *bums, accent* on the *bums!!!!!!* who try to upset your ideals that have been instilled in you from a child.
   One thing I'm glad I have someone I can pour my heart out to.
   I do hope you are enjoying the best of health, because I'll be seeing you shortly . . .
   May you be blessed always with the things God intends for you—I sign off

Your musical son,
Thomas 'Fats' Waller

P.S. I'm not drinking whiskey anymore—only wine—Some stuff.

p. 316 "Dear Tom": *Ed Kirkeby Papers*, Institute For Jazz Studies, Rutgers University, Newark, NJ.
p. 317 "I had an assignment": Jean Blackwell Hutson, interview with the author, September 22, 1980.
   "He was my best friend": "Fats Waller Taken by Death," *Amsterdam News*, December 18, 1943, p. 1.
   "To write": Reprinted in the *Amsterdam News*, December 25, 1943, p. 1.
p. 318 "I only understood": Jean Blackwell Hutson, interview with the author, November 28, 1980.

p. 319 "I was drafted": AR letter to Dan Burley, September 15, 1951, *ARP.*
"Registration records": "Razaf Runs Close Race for Council," *Englewood Press,* November 6, 1946, *ARP.*

p. 321 "a gown of white crepe": "Wedding Bells for Composer," *New Jersey Afro-American,* July 17, 1948, *ARP.*

14 Blue Turning Grey

p. 323 "I suppose": *John Waller, Jr., Scrapbook #4,* inserted.

p. 324 "epistolary link": Writing from her home in Asbury Park, New Jersey, Jennie Razaf Coles remained one of the central figures in Andy Razaf's life throughout his years in Los Angeles. Her frequent letters were full of feverish praise for "the way of the Lord," unremitting protestations of absolute love and devotion to her son, and fairly frequent requests for money and new clothing—requests that Razaf seems generally to have granted. The dynamic of their relationship remained perversely knotted to the end, with Jennie Razaf bombarding her son with poems and song lyrics of her own composition that she hoped (and occasionally did manage) to have published.

In February 1953, Jennie announced her intention to move to Los Angeles from Asbury Park. Razaf amazed his mother by attempting to dissuade her from this move. "Your letter just received and I was really astonished at its contents," she wrote on March 2. ". . . I could move out there *without one cent cost to you. . . .* I could then rent *at least two rooms,* which in time would make it so I could help out with the terrible cost of your *treatments* . . . So please *don't be upset*—I have a *right* to *try* and save *my life too.*

Jennie Coles arrived in Los Angeles on April 4, 1953. She remained, living near her son's home for six years, eventually turning against her "daughter," Razaf's wife, Dorothy, in the wake of Dorothy Razaf's infidelity. "I *begged* him *not* to take this step," she wrote of the marriage in retrospect, (May 1959) to Jean Blackwell, "and showed him *proof* of why he should not but she cast an evil spell over him . . . and he *would* not listen. It was a matter of *lust, not love,* from the *very first* . . . but oh, *how he has* paid."

Jennie Razaf Coles died in Los Angeles on August 21, 1959, of arteriosclerosis, months shy of her eightieth birthday.

p. 325 "To me": Andy Razaf letter to Edwin Smalls, December 5, 1950, *ARP.*

p. 327 "While more or less": As quoted by John Peer Nugent, *The Black Eagle* (New York: Bantam, 1972), p. 35.
"It wasn't just": Maurice Haber, interview with the author, February 13, 1982.

p. 328 *"THAT TELLTALE LISP":* As quoted by Ann Charters, *Nobody, The Story of Bert Williams* (New York: Macmillan Co., 1970), p. 96.

p. 329 "Dear Friend": All of these letters are dated February 8, 1951, *ARP.*

p. 331 "Dear Andy": Blake correspondence dated, respectively, January 28, 1951, February 19, 1951, and January 28, 1953, *ARP.*
"He was almost": Maurice Haber, interview with the author, February 13, 1982.

p. 332 "He loved her": Roxie Harper, interview with the author, February 5, 1982.
"Dear friend Lillian": *ARP.*

p. 334 "The need": "Time Out For Thinking," *Los Angeles Herald-Dispatch*, November 11, 1954, *ARP*.

"the Victor Herberts": "Berlin's 'Little Colored Boy' Steals Show," *Variety*, April 7, 1954, p. 54.

"Mr. President": *ibid.*

p. 340 "I'm writing more": "Wheel Chair Composer," *Ebony* (March 1958) p. 73.

p. 342 "Dear Andy": *ARP*.

"I have read your letter": John Waller, letter to AR, dated February 15, 1962, *ARP*.

p. 343 "They were too good": James P. Johnson, as quoted by Willie "the Lion" Smith, *Music On My Mind*, p. 257.

"a study in frustration": This was the title of Hammond's landmark, boxed LP reissue on Henderson in the Sixties.

p. 344 "Heads up": Letter from Willie "the Lion" Smith to AR, dated May 22, 1957, *ARP*.

"Financially, I'm not": Letter from Paul Denniker to AR, dated December 21, 1956, *ARP*.

"As to Joe": Letter from J. C. Johnson to AR, dated simply "May–1961," *ARP*.

p. 345 "I was out": All ensuing remarks are from Alicia Razaf Georgiade interview with the author, February 4, 1982.

p. 347 "My color": "Whatever Happened to Andy Razaf?" *Ebony* (January 1973), p. 122. Interestingly, Razaf here repeats verbatim remarks he'd made in an interview with the *Pittsburgh Courier* back on August 5, 1933, published under the title "Razaf, King of Songwriters, Has Many Hits," *ARP*.

Epilogue

p. 349 "the glories of Nineteen Twenties black musical comedy": Also including a newly rediscovered ragtime folk opera, *Treemonisha*, originally composed by Scott Joplin between the years 1905 and 1910. Presented rather inauthentically as a dance-driven, Broadwayesque entertainment, the new version of *Treemonisha* was produced on Broadway by the Houston Grand Opera in 1975.

p. 350 "Waller's most prominent lyricist": Douglas Watt, "Old Songwriters Never Just Fade Away," *Daily News*, April 23, 1978, p. L5

"Don't be ashamed": Joe Roberts, "Fats Waller: Songwriter, Piano Player and Singer," unidentified newspaper, n.d., *ARP*.

p. 352 "an immensely appealing show": Jack Kroll, *Newsweek*, May 22, 1978, *NYPL/LCPA-BRTC*.

p. 353 "The most prolific": Stephen Holden, "A Lot of Hit Songs from an Unsung Lyricist," *New York Times*, February 8, 1989, p. C19.

"Songs of Andy Razas": "Sounds around Town," *New York Times*, November 22, 1991.

Acknowledgments

This book has taken nearly twelve years to complete. It would never have been completed without the commitment of two exceptional people: Rita Rosenkranz, an extraordinary agent, and Robert Axelrod, the consumate editor. My most grateful thanks to them.

My thanks to all of those individuals—many of them now departed—who shared with me their recollections of Andy Razaf and his peers: Wilhemina Adams, A. Harlow Atwood, Jr., Walter Bishop, Sr., John Bubbles, Al Casey, Honi Coles, Leonard Feather, Albertine Glenn, Dr. Maurice Haber, John Hammond, Earl Hines, Kathryn Handy Lewis, Mr. and Mrs. Leroy McCloud, Ed Morrow, Myles Norman, Jack Palmer, Roxie Harper Patterson, Isabel Powell, Sammy Price, Dorothy Russell, Lula and Illene Wesson, Sam Wooding, and, of course, Eubie and Marie Blake. Most special thanks to Jean Blackwell Hutson.

My thanks to those who shared photographs and other ephemera from their private collections: Juanita Canegata, Frank Driggs, John McCallister, and Howard Wolverton, and to those institutions and individuals who aided me in my research: *The Billy Rose Theater Collection/New York Public Library–Lincoln Center for the Performing Arts, Moorland-Spingarn Research Collection/Howard University, The Schomburg Center for Research in Black Culture/The New York Public Library, Astor, Lenox and Tilden Foundations*, Regan Fletcher at the *Schubert Archives,* Marty Jacobs at the *Theater Collection of the Museum of the City of New York,* and Dan Morgenstern at *The Institute for Jazz Studies/Rutgers University.*

Special thanks to Stephen Holden, to George Avakian and Don Burkhiemer, to Miles Krueger for sharing so generously with me those first archival glimpses into the richness of our musical-theater tradition, to the magnificent Bobby Short, and to my friend, the equally magnificent Vince Giordano. Posthumous thanks to John Hammond for his enthusiasm, his friendship, and his taste. And a reverent note of thanks to Stephen Sondheim for our many discussions and occasional debates on the artistry of lyric writing.

Thanks to Tony and Richard Fisher for making the long delay in this book's publication so enjoyable, to Darryl and all the guys at Sadelle's mail room, and to Jim Heffernan for his legal assistance.

Loving thanks to my parents, Judith and Isadore Singer, to my brother, Mark, my sister, Elisa, and her husband, Tom Cohen, for their support and love, which I cherish.

Retailing thanks to Michael, Jenny, and Scanlynn for covering for me all these months, to all my friends for bearing with me, to Jim for waiting, and to Jenine especially.

Finally, thanks to John Moore for first pointing me in the direction of Andy Razaf. And, most significantly, to Alicia Razaf Georgiade, and her husband, Nick, for taking me into their home and sharing with me all that Andy Razaf had left behind. They made this book possible.

"My Fate Is in Your Hands," draft, in Andy Razaf's hand. *Courtesy Razaf Estate.*

"The Joint Is Jumpin'," final draft, in Andy Razaf's own hand. *Courtesy Razaf Estate.*

Songs

NOTE: It is impossible to account absolutely for every song that Andy Razaf contributed to. This list, therefore, is an incomplete, however educated, estimate comprising 822 song titles. All lyrics by AR unless otherwise noted.

Symbols and Abbreviations

( )   Indicates year song was published.

[ ]   Indicates year song was registered for copyright. Used herein for songs that either were never published or were published in years other than the year of copyright.

[nc]   Indicates no copyright found.

*   Indicates manuscript song lyric found among AR papers, often undated and lacking names of collaborators.

?   Indicates musical collaborator, if any, is unknown.

{BB}   Indicates song from the score for *Blackbirds of 1930*. Musical comedy revue presented on Broadway at the Royale Theatre by Lew Leslie/Conceived and staged by Lew Leslie/Music by Eubie Blake/Lyrics by AR/Starring Ethel Waters-Buck & Bubbles-Flournoy Miller.

{BTS}   Indicates song from the score for *Born to Swing* (1940s). Musical comedy revue premiered at the Lincoln Theatre, Philadelphia, PA/Produced by Irvin C. Miller/Music by Donald

Heywood/Lyrics by AR/Sketches by AR & Eubie Blake/Dances by Addison Carey/Starring Eddie Rector-Margaret Simms.

{CCP/33} Indicates song from the score for *Cotton Club Parade of 1933*. Musical comedy revue produced and conceived by Dan Healy/Music & Lyrics by various songwriters, including AR/Starring Cab Calloway & His Cotton Club Orchestra-Aida Ward-Avon Long.

{CCP/37} Indicates song from the score for *Cotton Club Parade of 1937*. Musical comedy revue presented at the Cotton Club (Downtown)/Conceived by Irving Mills/Staged by Clarence Robinson/Music & Lyrics by Duke Ellington, Reginald Foresythe, AR, John Redmond, Lee David, Lee Wainer, Lupin Fien/Starring Ethel Waters-The Nicholas Brothers-Duke Ellington Orchestra.

{CHC} Indicates song from the score for *Connie's Hot Chocolates* (1929). Musical comedy revue presented on Broadway at the Hudson Theatre by George and Connie Immerman/Staged by Leonard Harper/Music by Thomas "Fats" Waller & Harry Brooks/Lyrics by AR/Starring "Jazzlips" Richardson-Edith Wilson.

{CHC/35} Indicates song from the score for *Connie's Hot Chocolates of 1935*. Musical comedy revue presented at Connie's Inn (Downtown)/Staged by Teddy Blackmon/Music by Paul Denniker/Lyrics by AR/Starring Alberta Hunter-Dewey Brown.

{CR} Indicates song from the score for *Chicago (South Side) Rhythm* (1934). Musical Comedy Revue produced at the Grand Terrace Cafe, Chicago, IL, by Leonard Harper/Music by Paul Denniker/Lyrics by AR/Starring Alma Smith-Pearl Baines-Earl Hines Orchestra.

{D/27} Indicates song from the score for *Desires of 1927*. Musical comedy revue presented by Irvin C. Miller/Special Music by AR & J. C. Johnson/Starring Adelaide Hall-J. Homer Tutt.

{DH} Indicates song from the score for *Deep Harlem* (1929). Musical comedy revue presented on Broadway at the Biltmore Theatre/Staged by Henry Creamer/Music by Joe Jordan/Lyrics by Homer Tutt/Starring Homer Tutt-Salem Whitney.

{HH} Indicates song from the score for *Hot Harlem* (1932). Musical comedy revue produced at Connie's Inn by Leonard Harper/Music & Lyrics by Fats Waller, Andy Razaf, & Spencer Williams/Starring The Four Mills Brothers-Don Redman Orchestra.

{HH-A}   Indicates song from the score for *Harlem Hotcha* (1932). Musical comedy revue produced at Connie's Inn by Teddy Blackmon/Music by James P. Johnson/Lyrics by AR/Starring Earl "Snake Hips" Tucker-Cora Green-Don Redman Orchestra.

{KMR}   Indicates song from the score for *Kitchen Mechanic's Revue* (1930). Musical comedy revue presented at Smalls' Paradise/Conceived by AR/Staged by Charles Davis & Addison Carey/Music by James P. Johnson/Lyrics by AR/Starring Harriet Calloway-Myra Johnson-Charles Johnson Orchestra.

{LOC}   Indicates song from the score for *Load of Coal* (1929). Musical comedy revue produced at Connie's Inn by Leonard Harper/Music by Thomas "Fats" Waller/Lyrics by AR/Starring Louis Armstrong-Maude Russell.

{PS}   Indicates song from the score for *The Passing Show of 1913* (2nd Ed.). Musical comedy revue presented on Broadway at the Winter Garden Theatre by the Shubert Brothers/Staged by Ned Wayburn/Music by Jean Schwartz & Al W. Brown/Lyrics by Harold Atteridge/Starring Anne Dancery-May Boley-Artie Mehlinger.

{RFS}   Indicates song from the score for *Rhythm for Sale* (1934). Musical comedy revue produced at the Grand Terrace Cafe, Chicago, IL, by Leonard Harper/Music by Paul Denniker/Lyrics by AR/Starring Alma Smith-Avon Long-Carroll Dickerson Orchestra.

{TM}   Indicates song from the score for *Tan Manhattan* (1941). Musical comedy revue presented and staged by Irvin C. Miller/Dances by Addison Carey & Henry LeTang/Music by Eubie Blake/Lyrics by AR/Starring Nina Mae McKinney-Flournoy Miller-Avon Long.

{UCF/35}   Indicates song from the score for *Ubangi Club Follies* (1935). Musical comedy revue produced at the Ubangi Club (formerly Connie's Inn [Uptown]) by Leonard Harper/Music & Lyrics by AR/Starring Velma Middleton-Billie Daniels-Gladys Bentley.

{RRR}   Indicates song from the score for *Round 'n Round in Rhythm* (193?) Musical comedy revue produced at the Ubangi Club (formerly Connie's Inn [Uptown]) by Leonard Harper/Music & Lyrics by Alex Hill & AR/Additional Numbers by Fats Waller/Starring Gladys Bentley-Avon Long-Mabel Scott-Teddy Hill Orchestra.

{UCF/41}   Indicates song from the score for *Ubangi Club Follies* (1941). Musical comedy revue produced at the Ubangi Club (Downtown)/Music & Lyrics by Paul Denniker & AR/Starring Velma Middleton-Bunny Briggs-Erskine Hawkins' 'Bama State Collegians.

{UCR}   Indicates song from the scores for *Ubangi Club Revues* (Various) Miscellaneous musical comedy revues produced at the Ubangi Club (Downtown)/Music by various composers including Eubie Blake & Paul Denniker.

Titles

Absotively, Posilutely, Most Emphatic'lly, Yes! w&m by AR [1945]

Adult Delinquency m by Johnny Finke [1957]

After I've Spent My Best Years on You w&m by AR & Joe Davis (1939)

After Tonight m by James P. Johnson & Count Basie *

Ain't Misbehavin' {CHC} m by Thomas Waller and Harry Brooks (1929)

Ain't I Good to You? m by Don Redman [1929]

Ain't-Cha' Glad? m by Thomas Waller (1929)

Ain'tcha Got Music? {HH-A} m by James P. Johnson (1932)

Alexander's Back in Town w by AR & Joe Davis/m by Ada Rubin (1938)

Alabama Labor Day Parade {KS} m by Clarence Todd [nc]

All Aboard for Georgia w&m by AR & Joe Davis (1939)

All Ears m by Johnny Finke [1949]

All I Want Is a Lolli-Lollipop m by Johnny Finke [1955]

All Is Well w&m by AR & Teri Josefovits *

All My Tomorrows (For One Yesterday) m by Robert Noel *

All My Victories Are Losses w&m by AR & Paul Denniker *

All the Way for Jesus m by Johnny Finke [1952]

All the World Is Lonely (For a Little Blackbird) m by J. C. Johnson [1927]

Alligator Crawl w by AR & Joe Davis/m by Thomas Waller [1927] (1937)

Am I Awake or Am I Dreaming? m by Revella Hughes [1932]

Am I My Brother's Keeper? m by Johnny Finke [1952]

Am I On? w&m by AR & Paul Denniker (1936)

Amazing w&m by AR & Paul Denniker (1940)

The Amazons m by *

An I.O.U. {UCR} m by Eubie Blake [nc]

The Art of Self-Defense m by ? *

An Autumn Lullaby w by Jean Francis Blackwell [a.k.a. AR]/m by George Raymond [1944]

And That Is Life m by Thomas Waller [1933]

And Then Came Love m by Frank Vigneau (1942)

Anima Anceps [or] The Negro's Heart m by James P. Johnson (1944)

Any Day the Sun Don't Shine w&m by AR & Thomas Waller [1924]

Any Place Down South w by Jean Blackwell [a.k.a. AR]/m by Leonard Feather *

Anybody Here Want to Try My Cabbage m by Thomas Waller (1925)

Anything at Any Time w&m by AR [1924]

Argentina m by Harry Brooks [1929]

At Sundown m by Paul Denniker (1926)

At the Reefer Smoker's Ball {UCF/35} m by AR & Mildred Bailey [1930]

Atomic Love m by Edgar Sampson *

Aunt Jemima's Divorce (Minutes of the Case) {BB} m by Eubie Blake [1930]

Aurora m by Charles Pryme [1957]

Baby, It Upsets Me So m by Spencer Williams [1930]

Baby Mine {BB} m by Eubie Blake (1930)

Baby Please Hurry to Me w&m by AR & Frank Fields *

Back in Circulation Now m by Ray Gold [1945]

Back Where We Started m by Paul Denniker (1930)

Balboa w&m by AR & Paul Denniker [1936]

Ball and Chain Blues m by Thomas Waller [1925]

Baltimo' {PS} w&m by AR (1913)

Banjo Papa w&m by AR [1928]

Bantu Baby {KMR} m by Jimmie Johnson [1930]

Baseball Papa–Race Track Mama m by Thomas Waller *

Be Ready m by Reginald Foresythe & Ted Weems (1933)

Beautiful Legs {RRR} m by Thomas Waller [nc]

A Beautiful Girl w&m by AR & J. C. Johnson (1928)

Beautiful Land of My Dreams w&m by AR & Paul Denniker (1934)

(We're) The Berries {BB} m by Eubie Blake [1930]

Beware of Those Who Gossip w&m by AR, Paul Denniker, & Vincent Lopez (1937)

Big Boy w&m by AR [1944]

Big Chief de Sota m by Fernando Arbelo (1936)

Big-Hearted Joe m by ? *

Big-Mouth Minnie w by AR & Joe Davis/m by Cab Calloway & Walter Thomas [1938]

A Bird in the Hand (Is Worth Two in the Bush) w&m by Danny Jones, Joe Davis & AR [1940] (1941)

Black and Blue (What Did I Do to Be So Black and Blue) {CHC} m by Harry Brooks & Thomas Waller (1929)

Black Dog Blues m by J. C. Johnson [1929]

Black Man Blues m by J. C. Johnson [1929]

Black Maria w by AR & J. C. Johnson/m by Fred Rose (1940)

Blackbirds on Parade {BB} m by Eubie Blake (1930)

Blue Algerian Skies w by Joe Davis & AR/m by Jerry Sears, Bill Long & Leon Van Gelder (1939)

Blue Baby m by Johnny Finke [1953]

Blue Dream m by Erskine Butterfield (1940)

Blue Grass w by Mike Jackson & AR; m by Donald Heywood [1938]

Blue Interlude w&m by AR, John Lawrence, & Johnny Finke (1954)

Blue Monday m by Thomas Waller *

Blue Mood m by Johnny Finke & Maceo Jefferson [1955]

Blue Rendezvous m by Erskine Butterfield (1940)

Blue Turning Grey over You m by Thomas Waller [1929] (1930)

Blue Violin m by Hezekiah L. Smith [1955]

A Bobbed-Haired Bandit Stole My Heart Away m by Paul Denniker (1924)

Boogie Woogie Bunga Boo {UCR} m by Eubie Blake [nc]

Born to Swing {BTS} m by Donald Heywood [nc]

Brazilian Rose m by Johnny Finke (1955)

Breath and Breaches m by J. C. Johnson [1929]

British Subjec' Blues m by Spencer Williams [1945]

Broke but Happy m by Thomas Waller *

Broke Down Papa w&m by AR & Spencer Williams [1931]

Brotherhood m by Otis René, Jr. [1954]

Brown Gal {DH} m by J. C. Johnson [1928]

Buddie m by Thomas Waller (1932)

Bug House m by Harry Brooks [1929]

Bunker Hill w&m by Joe Davis, AR, & Paul Denniker [1940]

Burmese Babies {HH} m by ? [nc]

The Burning Bush of Israel m by Johnny Finke [1952]

Buy a Bond for Baby {BTS} m by Donald Heywood [nc]

Bye-Bye Sorrow m by ? *

Cabin Door {BB} m by Eubie Blake [nc]

Califo'nia m by Johnny Finke [1949]

Call the Plumber In w&m by AR & Thomas Waller [1924]

Can It Be True? w&m by AR & Spencer Williams (1930)

Can't Take It Papa {HH-A} m by James P. Johnson [nc]

Can't We Get Together {CHC} m by Thomas Waller & Harry Brooks (1929)

Cat 'n' Mouse m by Johnny Finke (1955)

Cellophane w&m by AR *

Charleston Waterfront m by ? *

Chee Chee Mood m by J. Russel Robinson [1950]

Cheerio, but Not Goodbye m by Johnny Finke [1953]

Children, Walk with Me w&m by AR & Alexander Hill [1931]

A Children's Day m by Johnny Finke [1950]

Chile {CCP/37} m by Reginald Foresythe

Chiropractor Blues m by Spencer Williams (1930)

Choc'late Bar {KS} m by Thomas Waller [nc]

Choo Choo m by Eugene Sedric & Thomas Waller (1939)

Christmas Comes but Once a Year w by AR & George A. Hagar/m by F. Henri Klickmann [1947]

Christmas Valley m by Johnny Finke [1949]

Christopher Columbus m by Leon Berry (1936)

Come Up and See Me Sometime m by ? *

Concentratin' on You m by Thomas Waller (1931)

Conchita m by Paul Denniker (1930)

The Conga Tap {UCR} m by Eubie Blake [nc]

Corn and Bunion Blues m by J. C. Johnson [1938]

Confusion w&m by AR [1946]

Couldn't I? {DH} m by J. C. Johnson [1928]

Cradle of Rhythm {UCR} w&m by AR & Paul Denniker (1942)

Crispus Attucks m by J. Russel Robinson (1942)

The Crumbs of Your Love m by Thomas Waller & Minto Cato (1931)

Cryin' Mood w&m by AR & Chick Webb (1937)

Daddy Treat Your Baby Right m by Harold Dellon (1923)

Daddy's Not My Daddy Anymore m by Johnny Finke [1950]

Dark Eyes w&m by AR [1942]

Dear to Me m by Johnny Finke [1950]

Death Valley, Just Half Way to My Home m by Lonnie Johnson [1930]

Deedle-Dee-Dum Teasy Easy Tune w by Nikki Mason & AR/m by Teri Josefovits [1947]

Deep Are the Pools (of My Love) m by Joe Davis *

Deep Forest m by Reginald Foresythe & Earl Hines (1933)

Deep in My Soul m by ? *

Deep Silence m by Paul Denniker *

The Dentist Song (Easy Mister, Easy) w&m by AR [1940]

Desire m by J. C. Johnson [1926]

Destination Unknown m by Irene Higginbotham (1944)

Devil Can't Hurt Me w&m by AR & Spencer Williams (1940)

Dinah {BB} m by Eubie Blake [1930]

Dip Your Brush in the Sunshine, and Keep on Painting Away m by J. C. Johnson [1928] (1931)

Disappointed in Love {CR} m by Paul Denniker [1934] (1935)

A Dismal Mood w&m by AR & Teri Josefovits [1948]

Dissatisfied Blues {BB} m by Eubie Blake [1930]

Dixie Cinderella {CHC} m by Thomas Waller & Harry Brooks (1929)

Dixieann in Afghanistan {TM} m by Eubie Blake [nc]

Do Me a Favor, Lend Me a Kiss w by AR & Spencer Williams/m by Thomas Waller [1932]

Do What You Did Last Night m by J. C. Johnson [1928]

Doin' the Mozambique {BB} m by Eubie Blake [1930]

Doin' What I Please m by Jimmy Johnson [1931] (1933)

Don't Let Your Love Come Down w&m by AR [1927]

Don't Turn Your Back on Me m by Clarence Williams [1928]

Down at That Old Cabion Door {BB} m by Eubie Blake [1930]

Down by the Railroad Track {TM} m by Eubie Blake [nc]

Dream Caravan w by Joe Davis & AR/m by Powell Edwards (1938)

The Dreamer m by ? *

Dreaming Is Fine, for Passing the Time w by Bob Carey & AR/m by Bob Carey & Maynard Gamble (1946)

Drop the Old Folks a Line m by Thomas Waller *

Dusky Stevedore m by J. C. Johnson (1928)

Dynamite Joe w&m by AR, [?] Henderson & Al Jolson *

Early Morning Blues w by Joe Davis & AR/m by Jerry Sears [1939]

Easin' Right Along w&m by Clarence Williams, Jean Wakefield, & AR [1928]

Electrician Blues w&m by AR [1931]

Elevator Papa–Switchboard Mama {KMR} m by Jimmie Johnson [1930]

Empty House Blues w&m by AR [1929]

Empty Interlude w by AR & Roger Chaney/m by Margaret Bonds (1941)

Every Show Must Have a Finale m by Johnny Finke [1953]

Evil Minded Papa Blues m by Edgar Dowell [1925]

Ev'ry Second, Ev'ry Minute, Ev'ry Hour, Ev'ry Day w&m by AR & Teri Josefovits [1948]

Ev'ry Time I Pick a Sweetie m by Allie Moore & Phil Worde [1924] (1927)

Ev'rybody Get Hot {CR} m by Paul Denniker [nc]

Ev'rybody Goes When the Wagon Comes w&m by AR [1940]

Ev'rybody's Gal w&m by AR, J. C. Johnson & Willie "the Lion" Smith *

Exclusive Love m by Thomas Waller *

Explaining m by J. C. Johnson [1928]

Fair and Square w&m by AR, Paul Denniker, & Joe Davis [1938]

Falling for You m by Paul Denniker [1925] (1926)

Farewell m by Paul Denniker (1933)

The Farm Yard Jazz w by AR & Ralph Rawson/m by AR [1920]

Father Mountain w&m by AR [1939]

The Fifteenth Infantry w&m by AR (1919)

Find Out What They Like, and How They Like It m by Thomas Waller (1929)

Finis m by W. C. Handy (1940)

Folks in New York City Ain't Like Folks down South w by AR & Margaret Johnson/m by Phil Worde [1926]

Foolin' Myself m by Thomas Waller (1955)

Footsore Blues w by AR & Andrew Robbins/m by Jimmy McHugh

For Better or Worse m by Charles Pryme [1955]

For Mary Jane m by J. Russel Robinson [1930]

Framed! m by Donald Heywood *

Friendly Light m by Lester Newell Rohde & J Russel Robinson [1950]

Friends Cause Me to Be Out in the Street m by Lonnie Johnson [1930]

Funny Little You m by J. Russell Robinson (1930)

Funnies on Parade w&m by AR [for "Joe

Davis's Folio of Children's Songs"] (1936)

Futuristic w&m by AR & J. C. Johnson (1928)

The Gal I Saw in Arkansas w by AR & Alexander Hill/m by Thomas Waller *

Gay Catin' Daddy w&m by AR [1927]

Gee Baby, Ain't I Good to You? w by Don Redman & AR/m by Don Redman (1944)

George Washington Carver m by Jean Stor [a.k.a. W. Astor Morgan] (1943)

Georgia w&m by AR, Margaret Bonds, & Joe Davis (1939)

Georgia Gal w&m by AR & Joe Davis (1940)

Georgia Gut m by Spencer Williams (1928)

Georgia May m by Paul Denniker (1934)

Georgia Trail w&m by AR & Joe Davis (1940)

Get Off {HH-A} m by James P. Johnson [1932]

Get Rhythm in Your Feet {UCF/41} m by Paul Denniker [nc]

Get Up Off Your Knees m by Clarence Williams (1929)

The Girl Who Gets Her Man {HH} m by ? [nc]

Git Away' {RRR} w&m by AR & Paul Denniker (1940)

Glory w&m by AR & Joe Davis [1931] (1932)

Glory' Glory', I'm A Sap w&m by AR & Spencer Williams

A Glutton for Love m by Alexander Hill (1930)

Go Harlem {KMR} m by Jimmie Johnson [1930] (1937)

Go Home, Little Girlie, Go Home! m by Teri Josefovits [1944]

Goddess of Rain {CHC} m by Thomas Waller & Harry Brooks [1929]

Goin' Crazy with the Blues m by J. C. Johnson (1927)

Goin' on an Errand for Uncle Sam m by Erskine Butterfield

Gone m by Harry Link & Thomas Waller [1929] (1930)

Gonna Have My Fling m by Eubie Blake *

Good for Nothin' {KMR} m by Jimmie Johnson [1930]

Good Things Come to Those Who Wait m by J. C. Johnson [1928]

Got Everything (Don't Want Anything but You) m by Jack Palmer (1927)

Got Myself Another Jockey Now {KS} m by Thomas Waller (1928)

Got to Have a Man of My Own w&m by AR [1942]

Gotta Be, Gonna Be Mine m by Thomas Waller (1932)

Grab Him m by Johnny Finke [1953]

Granny m by Johnny Finke [1953]

A Great Big Baby (Cravin' for a Little Love) {TM} m by Eubie Blake [1974]

The Great Musician m by Thomas R. Peyton [1952]

Green Pastures {BB} w by Will Morrissey & AR/m by Eubie Blake (1930)

Guess We're Gonna Get Along {CR} m by Paul Denniker & Cecilia Reeker (1934)

Guess Who's in Town? m by J. C. Johnson (1928)

Hallelujah Round-Up m by Johnny Finke [1950]

Ham and Eggs {BB} m by Eubie Blake [1930]

Hand in Hand w&m by AR & Henri Woode [1936]

Handful of Keys m by Thomas Waller [1933]

Hands Off, That's My Gal m by Paul Denniker (1926)

Handy Andy w&m by AR [1940]

Hang Up Papa, You're on a Busy Line w&m by James Cooke (a.k.a AR) [1924]

Happy in Jimtown {KS} m by Thomas Waller [nc]

Harlem {BB} m by Eubie Blake [1930]

Harlem's a Garden {UCR} m by Eubie Blake [nc]

Harlem's Easter Parade m by Hughie Walke *

Harlem Hotcha {HH-A} m by James P. Johnson [1932]

Harlem Moon m by ? *

Harlem Rhythm Dance m by Clarence Williams [1933]

Haunted m by Leonard Feather [1960]

Haunting Eyes m by Johnny Finke [1949]

Havin' a Ball w&m by AR & James P. Johnson [1936] (1937)

Havana Nights m by J. C. Johnson (1927)

Hawaiian Love-Bird m by Paul Denniker (1929)

He Does Me So Much Good m by Paul Denniker *

He Wasn't Born in Araby (But He's a Sheikin' Fool) w&m by AR & Edgar Dowell [1923] (1924)

A Heart to Let m by Paul Denniker [1926]

Heavy Sugar m by Thomas Waller [1929]

Hello New Year, Hello w by AR & George A Hagar/m by F. Henri Klickmann [1947]

The Hep Cat {TM} m by Eubie Blake [nc]

He's a Son of the South w by AR & Joe Davis/m by Reginald Foresythe [1932] (1933)

High as a Georgia Pine w&m by AR (1940)

Hit the Road (You Bumble Bee) {TM} m by Eubie Blake [1969]

Home Again m by Johnny Finke (1954)

Honey Do m by J. C. Johnson (1932)

Honey Man Blues m by Theodore Fenderson Nixon (1925)

Honeysuckle Rose {LOC} m by Thomas Waller (1929)

Home Bound w&m by AR (1939)

A Hopeless Love Affair m by Thomas Waller (1938)

A Horse and Buggy Doctor w&m by AR/m by Johnny Finke [1949]

Hot Jello {RRR} m by ? [nc]

Hot Tamale! m by Maceo Pinkard [1924]

Hotcha Razz-Ma-Tazz m by Irving Mills (1934)

Hotcho Cha Cha Hey! Hey! m by Edgar Dowell

How Can I Forget We're Not Together w&m Al Moritz & AR (1943)

How Can You Face Me? m by Thomas Waller (1932)

How Could I Be Blue? w&m by Dan Wilson & AR (1926)

How Could You Forget? m by W Hollander [1933]

How Crazy Can a Woman Be? m by ? *

How Jazz Was Born {KS} m by Thomas Waller (1928)

How to Play an Ole Banjo {BB} m by Eubie Blake (1930)

How Wonderful m by Johnny Finke (1952)

Hungry w by Joe Young & AR/m by Thomas Waller [1932]

I Ain't Your Hen, Mr. Fly Rooster w&m by AR [1928]

I Am Headed for Southland m by Lonnie Johnson [1930]

I Can't Blame the Boys for Lovin' You m by Paul Denniker (1926)

I Can't Break the Habit of You w&m by AR, Charlie Beal & Bob Causer (1937)

I Can't Forget (the Love That You Forgot) m by Willie "the Lion" Smith *

I Can't Get Away from You m by ? *

I Do I Do, I Do m by Johnny Finke [1950]

I Don't Want a Thing for Christmas m by Dick Palmer *

I Feel It m by Harry Brooks [1929]

I Got Sugar, Plenty Sugar w&m by Willie "the Lion" Smith, AR, and J. C. Johnson (1942)

I Guess We're Gonna Get Along {UCF/41} m by Paul Denniker [nc]

I Had to Do It m by Thomas Waller (1938)

I Hate Myself Ev'ry Morning m by Leroy Williams/ m by AR [1946]

I Like to Hear a Bass Singer m by Paul Denniker & Bob Emmerich *

I Never Slept a Wink Last Night m by Nat Simon (1934)

I Once Was Yours, I'm Somebody Else's Now m by J. C. Johnson (1927)

I Think You're Swell m by Jimmy Johnson (1932)

I Told You So m by ? *

I Was a Fool to Let You Go w&m by AR, Paul Denniker, & Joe Davis [1940] (1942)

I Was So Weak, Love Was So Strong {HH-A} m by James P. Johnson (1932)

I Would Rather Die (Than to Live Without You) m by Thomas Waller *

Ice Cold Papa, Mama's Gonna Melt You Down m by Thomas Waller [1924]

I'd Give a Dollar for a Dime m by Eubie Blake [1953]

I'd Rather Be Blue Than Green w&m by Clarence/Spencer Williams, AR, & Thomas Waller [1924]

I'd Rather Lose w&m by AR, J. C. Johnson & Thomas Waller *

Idle Dollars–Busy War Bonds m by Rosamond Johnson (based on an old French melody) (1945)

If m by Paul Denniker (1935)

If I Can't Sell It I'll Keep Sittin' on It w&m by AR & Alexander Hill (1935)

If I Could Have My Way m by Paul Denniker [1926]

If I Could Only Have My Way m by Jack Albin & Paul Denniker (1931)

If I Had Waited for You m by Thomas Waller [1933]

If It Ain't Love {HH} w&m by AR, Donald Redman, & Thomas Waller (1932)

It It Wasn't for Love w&m by AR *

If You Can't Be Good Be Careful w&m by AR & Thomas Waller [1953]

If You Can't Control Your Man w&m by AR [1940]

If You Can't Enlist, Buy a Victory Bond m by Joe Davis [1942]

If You Can't Get Five Take Two {RFS} w&m by Joe Davis, AR & Paul Denniker [nc]

If You Haven't Got the Things it Takes to Hold Your Man m by Harold A Dellon (1924)

If You Really Love Your Baby m by J. C. Johnson [1929]

I'll Be a Good Soldier Too m by J. Russell Robinson (1941)

I'll Be Back m by Joe Davis [1942]

I'll Keep It Turned Toward the Wall w&m by AR [1940]

I'll Tell the World That's News w&m by Ted White, Irving Mills, & AR [1935]

I'm a Stationary Woman, Lookin' for a Permanent Man m by AR & Spencer Williams [1930] (1932)

I'm Gonna Move to the Outskirts of Town w&m by William Weldon/ Special Lyrics by AR (1942)

I'm Gonna Take Something for You w&m by AR and J C. Johnson [1960]

I'm Just Wild about You m by Thomas Waller [1929]

I'm Now Prepared to Tell the World It's You m by Thomas Waller (1932)

I'm Percy Pinchill of Harlem {UCR} m by Eubie Blake [nc]

I'm Tellin' You in Front, So You Won't Feel Hurt Behind m by W. C. Handy & Russell Wooding

I'm Toein' the Line {TM} m by Eubie Blake [nc]

I'm Writing Love Letters to Myself m by ? *

Imagine w&m by Will Osborne, AR, & Paul Denniker (1930)

In a Darktown Cabaret w&m by AR [1927]

In a Very Special Way m by Johnny Finke [1953]

In Rockabye Baby Land w&m by AR [for "Joe Davis' Folio of Children's Songs"] (1936)

In Slumberland {BB} m by Eubie Blake [nc]

In the Mood m by Joseph Garland [1938] (1939)

In Time m by ? *

In Your Arms but Not in Your Heart m by ? *

Inconvenience w&m by AR & Joe Davis (1940)

India m by Leon Rosebrook (1929)

Isle of Zanzibar {BTS} m by Donald Heywood [nc]

Isn't She Beautiful m by Bailey & Barnum [1926]

It Ain't Whatcha Do m by ? *

It's A Great World After All w by AR & Don Redman/m by J C. Johnson

It's Rhumbatism m by ? *

It's the Jungle in Me {UCF/41} m by Paul Denniker [nc]

It's the Little Things m by Paul Denniker *

It's You Who Taught It Me w&m by John Harley, Joe Davis, & AR (1939)

I've Fallen for Love m by James P. Johnson [1933]

I've Got to Make a Living m by ? *

I've Lost My Head over You w&m by W. Asher, M. Deas, & AR [1924] (1925)

Japan m by AR & Chappie Willet [1944]

Japanese m by Harry Brooks [1929]

Jealous of Me m by Thomas Waller [1938]

The Jitterbug Tree m (from Fred Rose's "Black Maria") revised by Thomas Waller/ w by J. C. Johnson & AR [1938] (1939)

John Henry, That Superman m by Thomas Waller [1933]

The Joint Is Jumpin' w by AR & J. C. Johnson/m by Thomas Waller (1938)

A Jug of Jive, a Loaf of Bread and Thou m by Johnny Finke & Vincent Redmond [1950]

Jungle Rhythm Roundup {UCR} m by Paul Denniker [nc]

Just a Scamp m by Johnny Finke (1955)

Just an Old Manuscript m by Don Redman [1943]

Just Another Dream m by ? *

Just Because I'm French m by Alice Simms (Simon) [1944]

Just Look at the Gal m by Alexander Hill *

Just One Girl w&m by AR & Terry Shand [1940]

Just One More Time m by Edgar Sampson

Just Over the Hill w by AR & J. C. Johnson/m by Charles L Cooke [1942]

Just Over the Mountain. m by Johnny Finke [1949]

Just Sociable w&m by AR & Harry Brooks (1930)

Just When I Needed You the Most (You Let Me Down) m by Willie "the Lion" Smith *

Ka-Choo! (The Sneezing Song) m by Teri Josefovits [1944]

Kath'rine the Great m by Teri Josefovits [1944]

Keep Shufflin' {KS} m by Thomas Waller [nc]

Keep Your Nose out of Mama's Business w&m by AR (1932)

Keepin' out of Mischief Now m by Thomas Waller (1932)

Keepin' out of Trouble m by Erskine Butterfield (1942)

The Key to My Heart {BB} m by Eubie Blake [1930]

The Kind of Man for Me m by Jack Palmer [1929]

Kitchen Man w&m by AR & Alex Belledna (1929)

Kitchen Mechanic's Parade {KMR} m by Jimmie Johnson [1930]

Knock Me a Kiss w&m by Mike Jackson, special words by AR (1942)

The Land of Make Believe m by Johnny Finke [1950]

A Language of My Own w&m by AR *

The Language of Love m by Paul Denniker (1929)

Last Night I Kissed a Dream w by Andrea La Duke [aka AR]/m by Teri Josefovits (1945)

Laughing Water {CHC} m by Thomas Waller & Harry Brooks [1929]

Leaving Me m by Thomas Waller (1955)

Let's Get Over and Get It Over w&m by AR, Paul Denniker & Ben Barton [1942]

Let's Keep It a Dream w by Larry Yoell & AR/m by Robert E. Spencer (1937)

Let's Speak Up and Shame the Devil m by ? *

Li'l Brown Baby m by Maceo Pinkard [1919] (1926)

Lie to Me m by J. C. Johnson *

Little Chickadee w&m by Gerry Sanger *

Little Pops Is Tops with Me m by Louis Armstrong & Henri Woode (1940)

Loco Over You m by Teri Josefovits [1944]

Lonesome Ghost Blues w&m by AR [1934]

Lonesome Me m by Thomas Waller & Con Conrad (1932)

Lonesome One m by Thomas Waller & Clarence Williams [1926]

Lonesome Swallow m by J. C. Johnson [1928]

Look in Any Mirror m by Bob Emmerich *

Lost Love m by Thomas Waller (1937)

Louisiana m by J. C. Johnson [1927] (w by AR & Bob Schafer/1928)

Love Has Come to Me At Last w&m by AR, Alexander Hill & Thomas Waller *

Love, I'm Calling w by AR & Bob Schafer/m by J. C. Johnson (1932)

Love Me Little, Love Me Long w by Joe Davis *

The Loveliest Thing in Life m by ? [1948] *

Lovely Liza Lee {CHC/35} m by Paul Denniker (1935)

A Lover's Lullaby m by Frankie Carle/w by Larry Wagner & AR (1940)

Love's Made a Humpty-Dumpty out of Me m by Harry Brooks [1930]

Lovie Lee w&m by AR & Thomas Waller (1928)

Lovin' Man m by Erskine Butterfield [1942]

Low Tide Down in My Heart m by Harry Brooks (1936)

Lucille w by Joe Davis & AR, music by Henri Woode (1939)

Lucky Beggar w by AR & Lester Santly/m by Nat Simon [1934]

Lucky You, Lucky Me m by Luckey Roberts *

Lumber-Jack m by Alex Hill [1930]

Machinery {CHC/35} m by Paul Denniker (1935)

Madame T.N.T. {HH-A} m by James P. Johnson [1932]

Magnolia Rose {TM} m by Eubie Blake [nc] (see: "Sweet Magnolia Rose")

Make Believe Ballroom w&m by AR & Paul Denniker (1936)

Make Believe Danceland w&m by AR, Paul Denniker & Joe Davis (1940)

Make Hay Day m by ? *

Make or Break Me m by W. C. Polla *

Make People Laugh w&m by AR *

Mama Do Good, Papa Do Bad (Is Wrong) w&m by AR *

Mama Stayed Out the Whole Night Long w&m by AR & Dan Wilson [1926]

Mama's Well Has Done Gone Dry w&m by AR [1927]

Mammy Land [KMR] m by Jimmie Johnson [1930]

A Mammy's Lullaby {BB} m by Eubie Blake [1930]

Mary Jane m by J. Russel Robinson (1931)

The Marriage Waltz m by ? [1950] *

Massachusetts m by Luckey Roberts (1942)

Matthew A. Henson m by Luckey Roberts (1944)

Me Go Where You Go, Amigo w&m by AR, Charles S Brower, & Bob Christy (1946)

Meet Mister Hines, That Piano Man m by Paul Denniker [1934]

The Meetin's Called to Order w by AR & Joe Davis/m by Ada Rubin (1936)

Memories of Southern Seas w&m by AR & Paul Denniker [1937]

Memories of You {BB} m by Eubie Blake (1930)

Mighty Fine m by Thomas Waller (1940)

The Milkmen's Matinee w&m by Paul Denniker, Joe Davis & AR (1936)

Misery m by James P. Johnson [1931]

Mississippi Basin m by Reginald Foresythe (1933)

Mister Answer Man w&m by AR & Teri Josefovits [1948]

Mister Mammy Man m by J. C. Johnson [1930]

Mr. Swing for President m by Paul Denniker [1936]

Mommy, Daddy m by Johnny Finke [1950]

Montezuma m by ? *

The More You Get It, the More You Want It w&m by AR (1924)

Most Emphatically Yes w&m by AR [1946]

Mother's Little Man w by AR & Noble Sissle/m by George Raymond (1932)

Mother Nature's Cabaret m by Johnny Finke [1956]

Mound Bayou m by Leonard Feather (1942)

My Baby w&m by AR *

My Baby Sure Knows How to Love m by J. C. Johnson [1929]

My Best Gal {BB/cut} m by Eubie Blake [nc]

My Daddy Don't Do Nothin' Bad w&m by AR [1928]

My Daddy's Growin' Old, So I'll Have to Look Aroun' m by Andrew Robbins (1924)

My Faith m by Teri Josefovits [1950]

My Fate Is in Your Hands {LOC} m by Thomas Waller (1929)

My Gift of Dreams m by Thomas Waller & Edgar Dowell [1932]

My Handy Man w&m by AR (1928)

My Handy Man Ain't Handy No More {BB} m by Eubie Blake (1930)

My Headache {HH-A} m by James P. Johnson (1932)

My Heart Is Closed for Repairs m by ? *

My Jamaica Love m by Thomas Waller [1924]

My Joe Louis of Love {RRR} m by Paul Denniker (1935)

My Linda m by Jack Palmer [1929]

My Love Will Never Grow Old m by J. C. Johnson [1931] (1933)

My Man Is Good for Nothing but Love {CHC} m by Thomas Waller & Harry Brooks (1929)

My Man o' War w&m by AR & Spencer Williams (1930)

My Man's Done Done Me Dirty w by AR & Margaret Johnson/m by Phil Worde [1926]

My Mother's Wedding Ring w&m by AR & Paul Denniker *

My Only One m by Chick Smith & Alexander Hill (1930)

My Pathway of Love m by Frank Weldon [1930]

My Reg'lar Man Is Back in Town m by J. C. Johnson [1930]

My Right Hand Man w&m by AR & Alexander Hill (1935)

My Song of Hate m by Thomas Waller [1942]

My Special Friend (Is Back in Town) m by J. C. Johnson [1926] (w by AR & Bob Schafer 1927)

My Sweet Baby Irene w by AR & Spencer Williams/m by Thomas Waller [1924]

My Texas Man m by J. C. Johnson [1924]

My Used to Was m by ? *

My Waltz Divine m by Hughie Woolford (1923)

The N.A.G m by Charles L. Cooke [1953]

Natiesha (Bright Eyes) m by Paul Denniker (1926)

A Native Son {UCR} m by Eubie Blake [nc]

Nero w&m by AR, Paul Denniker, & Joe Davis [1936] (1937)

Never Brag about Your Man w&m by AR [1940]

Never Let the Blues Go to Your Feet. {CR} m by Paul Denniker [1934] (1935)

Never Mind the Words w&m by AR & Jack Palmer *

A New Day Prayer m by Teri Josefovits (1946)

The Newspaperman's Blues m by Charles L. Cooke & W. C. Handy (1953)

Nicol in the Picilo {BTS} m by Donald Heywood [nc]

A Nickel for a Dime {TM} m by Eubie Blake [nc] (see: "I'd Give A Dollar for a Dime")

The Night, the Wind & Me m by Louis A. Ruben (1935)

Nina m by Russell Wooding & Edgar Dowell [1933]

No More Thrills {RFS} m by Paul Denniker [nc]

No One Can Toddle Like My Cousin Sue w&m by AR & Edgar Dowell [1923] (1924)

No One Ever Freezes in Chile w&m by AR & Paul Denniker *

Nobody But My Baby Is Getting My Love w&m by Clarence Williams & AR (1926)

Nobody Knows m by Johnny Finke [1949]

Nobody Shows What My Baby Shows w&m by AR (1928)

Nobody Understands Me m by ? *

North of Central Park m by ? *

Not Now m by Frank T. Grasso [1946]

Not Until Now m by Johnny Finke [1953]

Now Vote Republican m by Johnny Finke [1952]

Off-Time [CHC] m by Thomas Waller & Harry Brooks (1929)

Oh, Baby! w&m by AR, Eubie Blake, & Jeff Clarkson (1942)

Oh Malinda m by Jimmie Johnson (1927)

Oh! You Sweet Thing m by Thomas Waller (1932)

Old Jim Crow m by J. C. Johnson (1928)

Ole Fashioned Susie's Blue w&m by AR, Thomas Waller, & Clarence Williams [1924]

On Rainy Days w&m by AR & Thomas Waller (1938)

On Repentin' Day w by AR & Joe Davis (1940)

On Revival Day w&m by AR (1930)

On Robinson Crusoe Isle {RRR} w&m by AR & Paul Denniker *

On Sunday When We Gathered 'Round the Organ w by Alexander Hill & AR/m by Thomas Waller [1933]

On the Level with You {KMR} m by James P. Johnson [1930]

One More River w&m by AR & Teri Josefovits [1948]

The Only Time You're out of Luck {CHC/ 35} w&m by AR & Paul Denniker (1935)

Oriental Moonlight m by Hart Jones *

Our World m by Johnny Finke (1954)

Pa Don't 'Low No Strangers Here w&m by AR, Johnny Finke, & Merle Prince [1952]

Papa Ain't No Santa Claus, Mama Ain't No Christmas Tree m by Alexander Hill [1930]

Patty Cake, Patty Cake (Baker Man).

w&m by AR, J. C. Johnson, & Thomas Waller (1938)

Paul Laurence Dunbar m by Joe Jordan (1941)

Peach Tree Street w&m by AR, Margaret Bond, & Joe Davis (1939)

Penguins on Parade m by Johnny Finke [1950]

Perhaps m by Paul Denniker (1929)

Pillow Full of Dreams m by Gus Edwards *

Please Come Back to Me m by Thomas Waller *

Please Don't Talk about My Man m by Reginald Foresythe [1932] (1933)

Please Take My Heart {CHC/35} m by Paul Denniker (1935)

Please Tell Me Why w by Ed Adams [a.k.a. AR]/m by Thomas Waller

A Porter's Love Song to a Chamber Maid {KMR} m by James P. Johnson (1930)

Pouring Out My Heart w&m by AR & Henri Woode [1942]

Practical Pete m by Johnny Finke [1950]

A Prayer for Mother and Dad w&m by AR [for "Joe Davis' Folio of Children's Songs"] (1936)

Prisoner of Love m by Thomas Waller (1930)

Precious Rosary m by Johnny Finke [1952]

Procrastinatin' w&m by AR & Paul Denniker *

The Radio Ballroom m by AR & Margaret Bonds [1940]

Radio Papa, Broadcastin' Mama m by Thomas Waller [1929] (1932)

A Rag, a Bone and a Hank of Hair w&m by AR & Leon Rene [1953]

A Railroad Man's Goodbye Sometimes Ain't Gone m by Allie Moore [1924]

Rainbow Land m by Luckey Roberts (1942)

Rampart Street Blues w&m by AR & Paul Denniker [1936]

Rector Rhythm {BTS} m by Donald Heywood [nc]

A Red {UCR} m by Eubie Blake [nc]

A Red Man Is Blue w&m by AR & Paul Denniker *

Redskinland {CHC} m by Thomas Waller & Harry Brooks [nc]

Reefer Man m by J. Russel Robinson (1932)

Rest w&m by AR Paul Denniker & Joe Davis [1938]

Rhythm for Sale m by Edgar Dowell [1931]

A Rhythm Lullaby {CR} w&m by AR & Paul Denniker (1935)

Rhythm Man {CHC} m by Thomas Waller & Harry Brooks (1929)

Rich Old Woman, Poor Young Man m by Johnny Finke [1957]

River Boy m by ? *

Rock Me Just Like a Sweet Daddy Should m by Thomas Waller [1924]

Roll, Jordan {BB} m by Eubie Blake (1930)

Run, Run, Run, for I'm a Yankee w&m by AR [1918]

Sambo's Syncopated Russian Dance {KMR} m by Jimmy Johnson [1930]

San Anton' w&m by AR & Paul Denniker [1936] (1937)

Santa Has His Eye on You m by Johnny Finke [1950] (1953)

Savoy, Home of Happy Feet w&m by AR & Paul Denniker [1940]

Say Hello to the Folks Back Home {TM} m by Eubie Blake [nc]

Say It with Your Feet {CHC} m by Thomas Waller & Harry Brooks (1929)

Say Yes w&m by AR, J. C. Johnson & Thomas Waller (1939)

Scat Mr. Crow! m by ? [1950] *

Seeds of Brotherhood m by Otis J. Rene Jr. [1953]

Send It Out on the Air w&m by AR *

Send Me a Man {BTS} m by Donald Heywood [nc]

Seven Years Bad Luck m by Phil Worde [1926]

Shake Your Duster {KMR} m by Jimmie Johnson [1930]

Shakedown {HH} m by ? [nc]

Shakin' Up the Folks Below {TM} m by Eubie Blake [nc]

Sharp-Shootin' Soldier Man m by Johnny Finke *

She Belongs to Me w&m by Howard Johnson, AR, & Paul Denniker

Shet Yo' Mouf w&m by AR, & Thomas Waller [1924]

The Shim Sham Shimmy Dance m by Clarence Williams (1933)

The Short Trail Became a Long Trail w&m by Tom Walker [sic] & AR [1924]

Shotgun Papa {HH} w&m by AR [1940]

Shoutin' in That Amen Corner w&m by AR & Danny Smalls [1933]

Show Me Your Qualifications {RFS} m by Paul Denniker [nc]

Simple Simon w by AR & Joe Davis/m by Jerry Sears (1939)

Since Hannah from Savannah Came to Harlem {BB} m by Eubie Blake [1930]

Sittin' Up Waitin' for You m by Thomas Waller (1933)

Slippery Hips {KMR} m by Jimmie Johnson (1930)

Slow and Easy Man m by J. C. Johnson [1928]

Slow Poke m by Clarence Todd *

Slow Up Papa w&m by AR & Paul Denniker [1927]

Slower Than Molasses m by Thomas Waller [1933]

Small Papa–Big Mama {RRR} m by ? [nc]

Smooth and Soothing m by Horace Henderson *

(That) Snake Hip Dance {CHC} m by Thomas Waller & Harry Brooks (1929)

A Snake in the Grass {CR} m by Paul Denniker [nc]

The Snooty {UCR} m by Eubie Blake [nc]

So Happy! m by Russell Wooding *

So Soon m by Janice Luce [1945] (1947)

Somebody Else m by Eubie Blake [1977]

Somebody's Lyin' w by Joe Davis *

Something Tells Me w&m by M. S. Stoner [pseud.] & AR (1946)

Something to Live for m by Eubie Blake *

Somewhere Someone Is Waiting for Me m by Maceo Jefferson & Jack Palmer (1924)

Song of the Cotton Field {CHC} m by Thomas Waller & Harry Brooks [nc]

Sooner or Later Sweetheart m by ? *

Soulmate m by George B. McConnell & Paul Denniker (1934)

The Spider and the Fly w&m by AR, Thomas Waller & J. C. Johnson (1938)

Spirit of the Weed {HH-A} m by James P. Johnson [nc]

Spiritual m by ? *

S'posin' m by Paul Denniker (1929)

Squeeze Me m by Thomas Waller & Clarence Williams [1924] (1925)

Star Spangled Susan Brown {BTS} m by Irene Higginbotham *

Stay m by Elizabeth Handy (1936)

Stay Out of My Dreams w by AR & Ray Rivera/m by Maceo Jefferson & Billy Ver Planck [1957]

Stayin' at Home (Happy to Be by Myself) m by Thomas Waller (1940)

Stealin' Apples {HH} m by Thomas Waller (1936)

Stealin' My Thunder {RRR} m by AR [nc]

Sticks and Stones Will Break My Bones w by Jimmy Cavanaugh & AR/m by Jack Palmer (1937)

Stingy w by George A. Haggar & AR/m by F. Henri Klickmann (1946)

Stompin' at the Savoy m by Benny Goodman, Chick Webb, & Edgar Sampson (1936)

Stop That Dog {HH} m by James P. Johnson (1932)

Strange As It Seems m by Thomas Waller (1932)

A Straw in the Wind m by ? *

Strugglin' {RRR} m by ? [nc]

Summer Was Made for Lovers (Why Let It Go Rolling By?) {HH-A} m by James P. Johnson (1949)

Sunday Dress {BTS} m by Donald Heywood [nc]

Sunflower Sue {RRR} m by ? [nc]

Sunset m by Johnny Finke [1949] (1955)

Sunset in Bermuda m by AR *

Swanee Fashion Plate {KMR} m by Jimmie Johnson [1930]

Swanee Jubilee {DH} m by J. C. Johnson [1928]

Sweep No More My Lady {UCR} m by Eubie Blake [nc]

Sweet and Tender m by Clarence Todd (1938)

Sweet Emmalina m by Jack Palmer (1928)

Sweet Land of Liberty w by AR & Joe Davis [1939] (1940)

Sweet Magnolia Rose w&m by AR & Eubie Blake (1942)

Sweet Remembrance m by Luckey Roberts *

Sweet Savannah Sue {CHC} m by Thomas Waller & Harry Brooks (1929)

Sweet Talk w&m by AR & Irene Higginbotham (1946)

Sweet Virginia Blues {D/27} m by J. C. Johnson [1926]

Sweet–You Know Who w&m by AR & Edgar Dowell [1926]

Swing-Dilla Street w&m by AR, James P. Johnson, & Abner Silver [1940]

Swingin' at the Golden Gate m by Clarence Williams [1939]

Switch It Miss Mitchell {RRR} m by ? [nc]

Sympathetic Little Star m by Edward Matthews & Johnny Finke [1951]

Take a Trip to Harlem {BB} m by Eubie Blake [nc]

Take It Easy m by Eubie Blake [1953]

Take Your Tomorrow (and Give Me Today) m by J. C. Johnson (1928)

Tall Timber m by Thomas Waller (1933)

Tan Manhattan {TM} m by Eubie Blake [nc]

Tan Town Divorce m by Eubie Blake [1941]

The Tap Is Tops {CCP/37} m by Reginald Foresythe

Taxi Dan w&m by AR & Paul Denniker *

Teasin' Tessie Brown m by Luckey Roberts & Jimmy Lunceford (1937)

Teenage Rag m by Johnny Finke [1954]

Tell the Truth and Shame the Devil m by Thomas Waller *

Thaddeus Stevens m by Charles L. Cooke (1944)

Thank You for the Bitter Truth I'm Learning m by Teri Josefovits

That Calloway Rhythm m by Henri Woode *

That Good Old American Way m by Eubie Blake *

That Grand Terrace Trot {CR} m by Paul Denniker [nc]

That Jungle Jamboree {CHC} m by Thomas Waller & Harry Brooks (1929)

That Lindy Hop {BB} m by Eubie Blake (1930)

That Musical Tonical Dance w&m by AR [1920]

That Rhythm Man {CHC} m by Thomas Waller & Harry Brooks (1929)

That Rhythm Parade {CHC/35} w&m by AR, Paul Denniker, & Russell Wooding (1935)

That Shufflin' Tune m by Johnny Finke [1955]

That Was Yesterday m by Paul Denniker (1929)

That Zooty-Zoot m by Irene Higginbotham

That's the Kind of Man for Me m by Jack Palmer (1931)

That's the Stuff You've Got to Watch w&m by AR & Una Mae Carlisle *

That's What I Like about the North m by Johnny Finke (1957)

That's What I Like 'Bout the South {CCP/33} w&m by AR [1933] (1944)

That's What They Call Singing m by ? *

That's Why I Buy Bonds w&m by AR & J. Rosamond Johnson (1944)

There Never Was a Girl Like You, Wonderful Girl of Mine m by Babe Thompson & S. Walter Williams (1923)

There's a Little Bit of Scotch in Me m by J. C. Johnson [1941]

There's Been Some Changes Made m by J. C. Johnson [1928]

There's Nothin' Papa's Doin' That Mama Ain't Did w&m by AR [1940]

This Is It m by Johnny Finke [1949]

Those Men! Men! Men! w&m by AR & Rose Murphy *

Three Cheers for Our President m by Joe Davis (1942)

Throw It Out of Your Mind m by Una Mae Carlisle [1945]

Throw Out Your Chest, Keep Up Your Chin w&m by Joe Davis, AR & Bob Emmerich (1934)

Thumpin' and Bumpin' w&m by Harry White, AR, & James P. Johnson (1931)

Tick-Tock m by Johnny Finke [1950]

Time Out (for Love) m by Luckey Roberts *

Time Out for Thinking m by Francis Carter [1955]

Tippin' Out Tonight {RRR} m by ? [nc]

Tired of Explaining m by J. C. Johnson [1966]

To Arms (Dear One, Divine) {UCR} m by Paul Denniker [nc]

To Dance with You m by Johnny Finke (1955)

To Me, You're Wonderful m by Thomas Waller *

Tomboy Sue m by Paul Denniker (1926)

Too Bad m by ? *

Too Bad Jim m by Edgar Dowell [1925]

Toussaint L'Ouverture m by James P. Johnson & Eubie Blake (1944)

Train Whistles m by Willie "the Lion" Smith & Artie Shaw [1942]

Treat Me Like a Baby m by Jack Palmer (1931)

True Blue m by Henri Woode *

Twelfth Street Rag m by Euday L. Bowman [1914] (1942)

Twilight {CR} m by Paul Denniker [nc]

Two Shades of Rhythm m by ? [nc]

Two Strangers w&m by AR & Lee Morse (1930)

A Twosome m by ? *

Under the Cocoanut Tree w&m by AR [1943]

Under the Jungle Moon {BB} m by Eubie Blake [1930]

Unemployed Papa–Charity Workin' Mama m by Asbestos Jones [1931]

The Unholy Four m by Thomas Waller *

Unsophisticated Sue m by Nat Simon & Harold Raymond (1934)

The Valley of My Dreams w&m by AR & Paul Denniker *

The Verdict Is Life (with You) m by Len Joy (1930)

Vesuvius m by William C. Handy (1935)

Wait and See m by Thomas Waller (1936)

Waitin' for the Day m by Charles Titus Pryme [1950]

Wakin' Up the Folks Downstairs m by Eubie Blake (1930)

Walkin' the Floor m by Thomas Waller [1932] (1933)

Waltz Divine {CHC} m by Thomas Waller & Harry Brooks (1929)

Want Me w&m by AR & Fletcher Henderson (1952)

The War Bond Man w&m by AR (1944)

Washington Is Like That m by Luckey Roberts *

Wastin' Away m by J. C. Johnson [1929]

Wastin' Our Talents {RRR} m by ? [nc]

Way Down South {HH} m by James P. Johnson [nc]

The Way I Feel Today m by Donald

Redman & Howard Quicksell [1929] (1930)

We Are Americans Too {TM} w&m by AR, Eubie Blake, & Charles L. Cooke (1941)

We, the People w&m by AR & Paul Denniker (1938)

Weary {TM} m by Eubie Blake [1947]

The Wedding of the Chocolate Soldier w&m by AR [for "Joe Davis' Folio of Children's Songs"] (1936)

Weep No More My Lady m by ? *

Welcome Home Boys w&m by AR [1919]

Welcome, Love m by Teri Josefovits [1944]

We'll March to Hell and Back Again m by Luckey Roberts (1942)

We'll Stay Sweethearts w&m by AR & Gerry Sanger *

We're Dancers on Parade m by Johnny Finke [1954]

We're Out to Get the Jap w&m by AR & J. Rosamond Johnson *

We're the Berries {BB} m by Eubie Blake [nc]

What a Man w&m by AR [1940]

What Good? m by Johnny Finke & Eddie Matthews [1951]

What Harlem Is to Me {CHC/35} w&m by AR, Russell Wooding & Paul Denniker (1935)

What Have You Done to Make Me Feel This Way m by J. C. Johnson (1927)

What Kind o' Love Is That m by Phil Worde [1927]

Whatcha Gonna Do When I'm Gone w&m by Jack Palmer & AR [1926]

Whatcha Got On for Tonight m by Thomas Waller [nc]

What's Cookin' w&m by AR, Joe Davis, & Paul Denniker (1940)

What's Your Price m by J. C. Johnson [1928] (1932)

When m by J. C. Johnson [1926] (w by AR & Bob Schafer/1928)

When a Black Sheep Is Blue for Home m by Spencer Williams (1930)

When a Feller's in Love m by Henri Woode & Francis Schuman

When Gabriel Blows His Horn m by Thomas Waller (1932)

When I Can't Be with You w&m by AR & James P. Johnson (1931)

When Lulu Does the Hula-Hula Dance w&m by AR [1924]

When Malinda Sings m by ? [1932]

When That Dixie Sun Goes Down {RRR} m by ? [nc]

When the Lord Created Adam m by Eubie Blake (1931)

When the River Don Runs Dry m by Teri Josefovits [1944] (1945)

When You Press Your Lips to Mine m by Julian Woodworth (1930)

When Your Door Closed Another Door Opened w&m by AR [1925]

When You're Tired of Me Just Let Me Know m by Thomas Waller [1924]

Where Can I Find a Cherry {CR} m by Paul Denniker [nc]

Where Do I Stand with You? m by ? *

Where's My Dream m by ? *

Whistle Song m by ? *

Whistlin' Tune m by ? *

Who Made Bluebeard Blue? {CR} m by Paul Denniker [nc]

Who Said Black Birds Are Blue {BB/cut} m by Eubie Blake [1930]

Who's Afraid of the Bogey Man? w&m AR & Paul Denniker [for "Joe Davis' Folio of Children's Songs"] (1936)

Why? m by Johnny Finke [1952]

Why a Woman Loves a Heel w&m by Jeanne Burns & AR *

Why Am I Alone (With No One to Love) w&m by Spencer Williams, AR, & Thomas Waller (1929)

Why Did I Go Wrong? m by Maceo Pinkard (1926)

Why Do We Hurt the Ones We Love w by Al Jolson & AR/m by Thomas Waller [1933]

Why Do We Say "Good Morning" on a Dreary Day m by ? *

(Now You Know) Why I Go South m by ? *

Why Not? m by AR & Ford Dabney [1944]

William Tell m by Leon Berry (1936)

Willow Tree {KS} w&m by AR & Thomas Waller (1928)

With a Dream {TM} m by Eubie Blake [nc]

With a Million People All Around Me m by ? *

With Love m by Fritz Kreisler [1949]

With You or without You, I Will Get Along m by Hartwell Cook & Henry W. Santly [1932]

Without Your Love m by Thomas Waller *

A Woman in Love Ain't Got No Sense w&m by AR & Eddie Mallory (1937)

Wompum-Pompum m by Paul Denniker (1926)

Wonder m by Spencer Williams (1930)

Wondering When m by J. C. Johnson [1926]

Won't Be No Room Down There m by Johnny Finke *

Wont'cha m by Paul Denniker (1929)

Wooden Shoes m by Johnny Finke [1957]

Words Can't Express m by Don Redman & Charles Stanton [1929]

The World's Greatest Sweetheart Is You m by Paul Denniker (1929)

Wotta' Wonderful Dame w&m by AR *

Ya Gotta Be Versatile {KMR} m by Jimmie Johnson (1930)

Yancey Special m by Meade (Lux) Lewis (1938)

A Yankee Doodle Tan m by J. C. Johnson (1942)

Yankee Cocktail m by AR *

Yes-Suh m by Edgar Dowell (1932)

You Always Can Come Back to Me m by James P. Johnson [1932]

You Are Mine 'Til the End of the Waltz m by Frank Weldon (1931)

You Broke It Up (When You Said Dixie) {UCF/35} m by Duke Yellman [nc]

You Broke It Up When You Said "Georgia!" w&m by AR & Paul Denniker (1940)

You Can't Get Away from Love m by Paul L. Specht [1954]

You Can't Have It Unless I Give It to You w&m by AR [1927]

You Can't Get Away from the Lawd m by Leon Rene [1953]

You Gotta B' Natural Honey m by Edgar Dowell (1924)

You Let Me Down m by Willie "the Lion" Smith *

You Never Know m by Johnny Finke [1953]

You Out-Smarted Yourself w by AR & Joe Davis/music by Jerry Sears (1939)

You'll Always Be Welcome m by Paul Denniker (1929)

You'll Come Back to Me m by J. C. Johnson [1928]

Your Hand in Mine m by Thomas Waller *

Your Worries Ain't Like Mine w&m by AR [1928]

You're Dancing with the Devil (When You Dance That Way) w&m by AR, James Cavanaugh & Nat Simon *

You're Everything Sweet w&m by AR, Paul Denniker, & Charles Bayha (1936)

You're Killing Me m by ? *

You're Lucky to Me {BB} m by Eubie Blake (1930)

You're Such an Angel m by Erskine Butterfield [1940]

You're the One w&m by AR & Gerry Sanger *

Yours All Yours {HH-A} m by James P. Johnson (1932)

You've Got to B'Natural Honey m by Edgar Dowell (1924)

Zonky {LOC} m by Thomas Waller (1929)

Courtesy Razaf Estate.

Discography

An informal, highly selective overview of Razaf song lyrics on recordings, arranged by song title and performing artist.

Song Titles

Ain't Misbehavin'
see: Louis Armstrong
      Ella Fitzgerald
      Bobby Short
      Maxine Sullivan
      Fats Waller
      Dinah Washington
      Ain't Misbehavin' (Original Cast Album)
      Souvenirs of Hot Chocolates (Original Cast Album)
Ain't-Cha' Glad?
   This early Benny Goodman Orchestra recording features a delectable vocal by trombonist Jack Teagarden. (Originally issued: 1933/ [Columbia 2835D] Reissued on LP/ "King of the Blues Trombone: Jack Teagarden" [Epic 6044]).
see: Dinah Washington
Ain'tcha Got Music?
   This obscure Razaf/James P. Johnson tune, as performed by two Fletcher Henderson alumni—Henry "Red" Allen (trumpet) and Coleman Hawkins (saxophone) (1933/[Banner 32840])—is a highlight of the Smithsonian

compilation album: "Henry 'Red' Allen & Coleman Hawkins—1933" (LP/[Smithsonian Collection R022 P15740]).

Black and Blue
see: Louis Armstrong
       Bobby Short
       Dinah Washington
       Ethel Waters
       Ain't Misbehavin' (Original Cast Album)
       Souvenirs of Hot Chocolates (Original Cast Album)

Blue Turning Grey over You
see: Louis Armstrong
       Maxine Sullivan
       Fats Waller

Christopher Columbus
see: The Ink Spots
       Maxine Sullivan
       Fats Waller
       Dinah Washington

Concentratin' on You
see: Mildred Bailey

Recording as Blanche Calloway & Her Joy Boys (1931/[Victor 22862]), Cab Calloway's younger sister, Blanche, brilliantly delivers the daffy essence of this Razaf lyric. (Reissued on LP/"Blanche Calloway" [Harlequin HQ2057]).

Cryin' Mood
see: Ella Fitzgerald
       Fats Waller

Gee Baby, Ain't I Good to You?

Billie Holiday reveals both the poignancy and the wit in Razaf and Redman's deceptively simple lyric with this 1946 live performance recorded at one of Norman Granz's "Jazz at the Philharmonic" concerts. (LP/"Billie Holiday at Jazz at the Philharmonic" [Verve UMV 2520]).

Nat "King" Cole's impeccable taste and charm here lend this lyric a slightly different interpretive twist. (1943 [Capitol N-16260]—Reissued on CD/"Jumpin' at Capitol" [Rhino R2 71009].)

Guess Who's in Town?
see: Bobby Short
       Ethel Waters

Honeysuckle Rose
see: Louis Armstrong
       Mildred Bailey
       Ella Fitzgerald
       Bobby Short

Maxine Sullivan
Fats Waller
Dinah Washington
Ain't Misbehavin' (Original Cast Album)

I'd Give a Dollar for a Dime
see: Eubie Blake

Vocalist Joe Williams rediscovered this number from Razaf and Eubie Blake's neglected *Tan Manhattan* score in the early 1980s and has since made it something of a signature tune for himself. (CD/"Every Night—Live at Vine Street" [Verve 833-236-2].)

In the Mood

Bette Midler brought "In the Mood" to the attention of a whole new generation with this 1973 recording, displaying Razaf's lyric to stellar effect, though she doctored the lines a bit to accommodate time's passage and her own persona. (CD/"Bette Midler" [Atlantic 7270-2]).

The Joint Is Jumpin'
see: Fats Waller
Ain't Misbehavin' (Original Cast Album)

Keepin' Out of Mischief Now
see: Louis Armstrong
Maxine Sullivan
Dinah Washington
Ain't Misbehavin' (Original Cast Album)

Kitchen Man

Bessie Smith's definitive interpretation. Razaf bawdy blues songwriting at its most suggestive. ([Columbia 14435-D]—Reissued on LP/"Bessie Smith: Any Woman's Blues" [Columbia CG30126]).

Louisiana

Paul Whiteman's orchestral rendition features tantalizing glimpses of cornet legend Bix Beiderbecke and a vibrantly youthful Bing Crosby vocal. (1928 [Victor 25369]—Reissued on CD/"Bix Lives" [RCA 6845-2RB]).

Memories of You
see: Eubie Blake
Duke Ellington

Frank Sinatra's brooding 1962 rendition is a classic. (LP/"Point of No Return" [Capitol W1676]).
see: The Inkspots
Maxine Sullivan
Ethel Waters

My Handy Man

Though Alberta Hunter, one of the original blues legends of the Nineteen Twenties, often performed what may well be the definitive version of this bawdy blues classic, she never recorded the song. Hunter did, however, record the sequel, "My Handy Man Ain't Handy No More," in 1980, on her

Amtrak Blues album (LP/Columbia [JC 36430]). No one has ever done it better.
see: Ethel Waters
A Porter's Love Song to a Chambermaid
see: Mildred Bailey
         Bobby Short
         Fats Waller
S'posin'
see: Louis Armstrong
   Helen Humes blended her naughty innocence with "S'posin'"'s sweetness in a terrific 1980s small-group recording. (CD/Contemporary [OJC 608-2]).
see: Bobby Short
         Maxine Sullivan
   Rudy Vallee's original recording with his Connecticut Yankees (1929/ [Victor 21998]—Reissued on LP/"Hi Ho Everybody" [Olympic 7128]).
see: Fats Waller
Squeeze Me
see: Mildred Bailey
         Fats Waller
         Dinah Washington
         Ain't Misbehavin' (O.C.A.)
Stompin' at the Savoy
see: Ella Fitzgerld
         The Ink Spots
         Maxine Sullivan
When
   Paul Whiteman Orchestra (1928/[Victor 21338]). (See: *Louisiana)*
Willow Tree
see: Mildred Bailey
You're Lucky to Me
see: Duke Ellington
   Helen Merrill's elegantly contemporary take on this song suits both lyric and melody beautifully. (CD/"The Complete Helen Merrill" [Mercury 826-340-2]).
see: Ethel Waters

Artists

LOUIS ARMSTRONG

Commencing with his 1929 Broadway debut in *Connie's Hot Chocolates*, Armstrong became the foremost musical exponent for the songs of Andy Razaf and Fats Waller. His initial recordings from the show of "Ain't Misbehavin'" and "Black and Blue" (Originally issued: 1929/[OKeh 8714]), "Sweet Savannah Sue," and "Rhythm Man" (OKeh 8717) are definitive and are currently available on CD/"Louis In New York/Volume V" [Columbia 46148], a disc that also includes Armstrong takes of "S'posin'" and "I Can't Give You Anything But Love"). Armstrong's subsequent recordings of other Razaf/Waller songs, rerecordings of the aforementioned titles, and recordings of many other Razaf songs composed with other collaborators are too numerous to annotate here. A nice place to start is Armstrong's 1955 LP release, "Satch Plays Fats," recorded with the All Stars, including Velma Middleton sharing vocal chores. Songs: "Black and Blue," "Honeysuckle Rose," "Ain't Misbehavin'," "Blue Turning Grey over You," "Squeeze Me" and "Keepin' Out of Mischief Now." (CD/ Columbia [CJT: 44049]).

MILDRED BAILEY

Bailey was another early champion of the music of Razaf and Waller. Her delightful recordings of "Willow Tree," from the *Keep Shufflin'* score, and "Honeysuckle Rose"—a song she was instrumental in uncovering (1935 [Parlophone R2201])—along with "Squeeze Me" (Parlophone R2257), are all currently available: ("Squeeze Me"/CD [Charley Records AFS 1013]). Her equally delightful renditions of "Concentratin' on You" (1931 [Victor 22880]) and "Porter's Love Song" recorded under her husband Red Norvo's name (1936 [Brunswick 7744])—are also available: ("Harlem Lullaby" CD/[Academy Sound AJA 5065]).

EUBIE BLAKE

Though Blake, as a pianist, recorded many of his Razaf song collaborations, none of these instrumental turns offers vocals. A delightful exception is the 1977 album "Wild about Eubie," recorded by composer/pianist William Bolcom and his wife, vocalist Joan Morris, with the 94-year-old Blake as featured guest pianist on a number of familiar and obscure Razaf/Blake tunes: "Memories of You" and "My Handy Man Ain't Handy No More," from the original *Blackbirds of 1930* score, and "I'd Give a Dollar for a Dime," "Weary," and "Hit the Road," from the neglected *Tan Manhattan* score. Highly recommended. (LP/[Columbia M34504]).

DUKE ELLINGTON

Ellington, with his orchestra (vocals by Dick Robertson), recorded marvelous versions of three hit tunes from *Lew Leslie's Blackbirds of 1930* shortly after the show closed on Broadway—"You're Lucky to Me," "That Lindy Hop," and "Memories of You." (Originally issued 1930/[Victor 23017/HMV B6355/HMV B6280]—Reissued on LP/"Duke Ellington–Volume 5" [RCA 741-048]).

ELLA FITZGERALD

As a teenaged vocalist in Chick Webb's band, Fitzgerald sang any number of Razaf lyrics, including the beautiful "Cryin' Mood," written by Razaf with Webb, and recorded by the Webb band with Fitzgerald (1936/[Decca 1273]. Later Fitzgerald sessions with Louis Armstrong (LP/1957 "Ella & Louis" [Verve], reissued on CD [Verve 835-313-2]), and Count Basie

(LP/1963 "Ella & Basie—On the Sunny Side of the Street" [MGM], reissued on CD [Verve 821-5762), generated memorable renditions of "Stompin' at the Savoy" and "Gee Baby, Ain't I Good To You?" ("E&L"), and "Ain't Misbehavin'" and "Honeysuckle Rose" ("E&B").

THE INK SPOTS

This glorious vocal group's handful of Razaf recordings—"Christopher Columbus" (1936 [Decca 883]), "Memories of You" (1939 [Decca 2966] and "Stompin' at the Savoy" (1936 [Decca 1036])—offer opportunities to savor Razaf's lyric writing in pristinely uncluttered vocal settings. To date, "Stompin'" appears to have been the only title reissued: (CD/"The Ink Spots" [Academy Sound & Vision AJA 5082]).

BOBBY SHORT

In 1987, this contemporary master of the American popular song canon recorded only the second all–Andy Razaf LP ever undertaken ("Guess Who's in Town" CD/[Atlantic 81778-2]), a perfect introduction to Razaf's work, comprising 11 songs, obscure and familiar, including: "Ain't Misbehavin'" and "Honeysuckle Rose," "Black and Blue" and "Stompin' at the Savoy," "Guess Who's in Town," "S'posin'," "Porter's Love Song," and *Tan Manhattan*'s rarely heard title tune.

MAXINE SULLIVAN

One of the great pop vocalists of her age, Sullivan, in 1956, recorded, under the direction of Razaf's close friend, jazz critic Leonard Feather, the *first* all-Andy Razaf LP ("Maxine Sullivan, Volume II," [Period Records SPL1207]), a charming collection of relatively familiar Razaf song lyrics, including: "Keepin' out of Mischief Now," "S'posin'," "Ain't Misbehavin'" and "Honeysuckle Rose," "Savoy," "Blue Turning Grey," "Christopher Columbus," "Memories of You" and the far less frequently recorded "Massachusetts," "How Can You Face Me?" and a lovely Feather/Razaf collaboration, "Mound Bayou." The album has long been out of print.

FATS WALLER

A more or less complete listing of primary Waller studio recordings *with vocals,* covering songs with lyrics by Andy Razaf: "Porter's Love Song" (1934/[Victor 24648]), "Georgia May" ([Vic 24714]), "How Can You Face Me?" ([Vic 24737]), "Honeysuckle Rose" ([Vic 24826]), "Christopher Columbus" (1936/[Vic 25295]), "Stay" ([RW 1]), "Big Chief de Sota" ([Vic 25342]), "S'posin'" ([Vic 25415]), "Nero" ([Vic 25498]), "Cryin' Mood" (1937/[Vic 25551]), "San Anton'" ([Vic 255579]), "Blue Turning Grey over You" ([Vic 36206]), "The Joint Is Jumpin'" ([Vic 25689]), "We, the People" (1938/[Vic 25898]), "The Spider and the Fly" ([Bluebird B-10205]), "Patty Cake, Patty Cake" ([Bluebird B-10149]), "Squeeze Me" (1939 [Bluebird B-10405]), "It's You Who Taught It to Me" ([Bluebird B-10527]), "Swing-Dilla Street" ([Bluebird B-10858]), "Mighty Fine"

([Bluebird B-10744]), "Wait and See" ([Bluebird B-10405]), "Lonesome Me" ([Unknown]), "Ain't Misbehavin'" ([Jazz Society AA-535]), "Black Maria," (1940/[Bluebird B-10658]).

Waller reissues on CD have thus far been extremely spotty. About the only useful disc currently available appears to be: "Fats Waller—The Joint Is Jumpin'"/[RCA-6288-2-RB]), which includes the aforementioned "Squeeze Me," "S'posin'," and "The Joint Is Jumpin'" recordings, as well as a legendary all-instrumental studio jam session on "Honeysuckle Rose."

DINAH WASHINGTON

Washington's contribution to Razaf recorded song iconography was her album "Dinah Washington Sings the Fats Waller Songbook" (CD/[Emarcy 818-930-2), a bold and deliciously brassy collection that includes the standards, "Ain't Misbehavin'" and "Honeysuckle Rose," "Black and Blue," "Ain't-cha' Glad?" "Keepin' out of Mischief Now," "Squeeze Me," and a wonderfully raucous "Christopher Columbus," among others.

ETHEL WATERS

Another early champion of Razaf's work, most often in collaboration with composer J. C. Johnson, Waters made definitive recordings of "Guess Who's in Town (1928/[Columbia 14353-D])," "Lonesome Swallow [Co 14411-D]," "My Special Friend" [Co 14182-D], and "My Handy Man" ([Co 14353-D]). All were once available on the Columbia LP: "Ethel Waters' Greatest Years" [KG316571]. Her quixotic take on the song "Black and Blue" ([Columbia 2184-D]) is currently available: (CD/"1930s–The Jazz Singers" [Columbia CK 40847]), as are her recordings from *Blackbirds of 1930*, "Memories of You" and "You're Lucky to Me" (1930/[Co 2288-D]: (CD/"Ethel Waters On Stage and Screen, 1925–1940" [CDS A2792]).

Other

AIN'T MISBEHAVIN' (Original Cast Album)

A delightful theatrical reassembly of classic Waller sides, featuring at least seven Razaf lyrics—"Ain't Misbehavin'," "Black and Blue," "Honeysuckle Rose," "Squeeze Me," "Find Out What They Like," "Keepin' out of Mischief Now," "The Joint Is Jumpin'"—and a possible eighth: "I Can't Give You Anything But Love."

SOUVENIRS OF HOT CHOCOLATES (Original Cast Album)

An effective compilation of existing recordings by original members of the *Hot Chocolates of 1929* company, including Louis Armstrong's aforementioned recordings of "Ain't Misbehavin'," "Black and Blue," "Sweet Savannah Sue," and "Rhythm Man" (see: LOUIS ARMSTRONG), a Fats Waller "Ain't Misbehavin'" piano solo, and Edith Wilson's original recordings of "Black and Blue" and "My Man Is Good for Nothing But Love" ([Brunswick 4685]).

Andy Razaf

A listing of Razaf's own vocal recordings:

"Don't Forget, You'll Regret Day by Day" [3-7-25/Gennett 3082]
"He Rambled (Till the Butcher Cut Him Down)" [Gennett—rejected]
　"Razaf (The Melody Man)"
"Who Takes Care of the Caretaker's Daughter (While the Caretaker's Busy Taking Care)?" [4-4-25/Gennett 3052]
"Yes, Sir! That's My Baby" [4-4-25/Gennett 3052]
"On Rainy Days" [5-25-25/Gennett 3119]
"Someday We'll Meet Again" [5-25-25/Gennett 3119]
"Because of You (The World Is Mine)" [6-17-25/Gennett—rejected]
"Her Have Went, Her Have Gone (Her Have Left I All Alone) [6-17-25/Gennett—rejected]
　"Razaf (The Melody Man with His Banjo Uke)"
"Cecilia" [7-1-25/Gennett 3102]
"I'm Gonna Charleston Back to Charleston" [7-1-25/Gennett 3102]
"Because of You (the World Is Mine)" [8-16-25/ARC—rejected]
"When a Blonde Makes Up Her Mind to Do You Good" [9-15-25/Gennett—rejected]
"My Sweetie Turned Me Down" [9-15-25/Gennett—rejected]
"Her Have Went . . ." [9-15-25/Gennett—rejected]
　"Crooning Andy and His Ukelele"
"Falling for You" [1926/Harmony]
"Give Me Just a Little Bit [1926/Harmony]
　"Rex Stewart's Harlem Serenaders"
"Ten O'Clock Blues" [4-4-27/Vocalion—unreleased]
"Oh, Malinda" [4-4-27/Vocalion—unreleased]
　"Crooning Andy Razaf" (Accompanied by J. C. Johnson/piano, Eddie King/organ)
"Empty Arms" [11-4-27/Columbia 14265-D]
"All the World Is Lonely (for a Little Blackbird)" [11-14-27/Columbia 14265-D]
　"Fletcher Henderson's Collegians" (a.k.a. The Fletcher Henderson Orchestra) These three recordings are currently available on CD/ "Fletcher Henderson and His Orchestra" [Classics Records 572].
"Dear, On a Night Like This" [11-26-27/Regal 8441-A]
"There's a Rickety Rackety Shack" [Regal 8442-A]
"Sorry" [Regal 8455-B]
　"Johnny Thomson" [a.k.a. AR] (Accompanied by Howard Nelson/violin, David Martin/violin cello, Fats Waller/piano)
"Back in Your Own Back Yard" [1-17-28/Columbia 14285-D]
"Nobody Knows How Much I Love You" [1-17-28/Columbia 14285-D]
　Jimmy Johnson and His Orchestra

"Go Harlem" [3-25-31/Columbia 2448-D]
"Porter's Love Song" [Columbia 14668-D]
"Just a Crazy Song" [Columbia 2448-D]
"Lost Love" (LP/[1937/Ristic 22])
 (Assorted performers, including Fats Waller, Eubie Blake, James P. Johnson, Willie "the Lion" Smith.)
"Is It to Be or Not to Be"
"The Jitterbug Tree"
 (Andy Razaf/Fats Waller/J.C. Johnson [11/21/38—privately recorded at Harry Smith Recording Studio/2 West 46th Street])

Index